MAN OF TREACHEROUS CHARM

MAN OF TREACHEROUS CHARM

TERRITORIAL JUSTICE
EDMUND C. FITZHUGH

CANDACE WELLMAN

WSU
PRESS

Washington State University Press
Pullman, Washington

Washington State University Press
PO Box 645910
Pullman, Washington 99164-5910
Phone: 800-354-7360
Email: wsupress@wsu.edu
Website: wsupress.wsu.edu

Library of Congress Cataloging-in-Publication Data
Names: Wellman, Candace, author.
Title: Man of treacherous charm : territorial justice Edmund C. Fitzhugh /
    Candace Wellman.
Description: Pullman, Washington : Washington State University Press, 2023.
    | Includes bibliographical references and index.
Identifiers: LCCN 2023004275 | ISBN 9780874224221 (paperback)
Subjects: LCSH: Fitzhugh, E. C. (Edmund Clare), 1818-1883. |
    Lawyers--United States--Biography. | Lawyers--Washington
    (State)--Biography. | Washington Territory--History.
Classification: LCC KF373.F525 W45 2023 | DDC 340.092
    [B]--dc23/eng/20230406
LC record available at https://lccn.loc.gov/2023004275

The Washington State University Pullman campus is located on the homelands of the
Niimíipuu (Nez Perce) Tribe and the Palus people. We acknowledge their presence
here since time immemorial and recognize their continuing connection to the land, to
the water, and to their ancestors. WSU Press is committed to publishing works that
foster a deeper understanding of the Pacific Northwest and the contributions of its
Native peoples.

Cover design by Jeffry E. Hipp

Maps in this volume were prepared by Chelsea M. Feeney, geologist/cartographer,
www.cmcfeeney.com.

Dedication

To three generations of my family who have lived with, and supported, my writing project that produced three books. Mike, Christine, Ame and Ron, Jim and Amy, Jake, and Addy have my greatest appreciation and love.

To Rita, Sue, Judy, and Suzann, my dear Gonzaga Girlz, who always believed in me and encouraged me to keep going. It has meant more than they know.

And lastly, to Penny the Writing Supervisor who fetches me every morning and leads me into my office, then perches on the desk most of the day to make sure I'm working. Her contribution has been huge since we adopted her from the shelter six years ago.

Writing Supervisor Penny, apparently trying to absorb vocabulary from the author's thesaurus. Photo by author.

Contents

Illustrations and Maps

Preface

"History is a messy business for humans are a messy breed."
—Bill Woodward, 2003

MAN OF TREACHEROUS CHARM is the first complete biography of any Washington Territory Supreme (and District) Court justice. E. C. Fitzhugh was appointed to the second panel in 1858, while under indictment for murder. He influenced territorial history in economic, political, and legal ways, so his biography fills a void in Washington State history. It also contributes to some of the nation's bigger history as he moved between regions and national events.

I first "met" E. C. Fitzhugh while a volunteer research assistant at the Washington State Archives branch in Bellingham, Washington. I'd read short pieces about him in local histories published in 1926, 1949, and 1968, but there has been no extensive research or re-telling of his life in the years since. None of the three books contained much about his earlier or later life surrounding his time in Whatcom County. As well, those authors lived in a different time with different social attitudes, and they did not have the benefit of easy access via email or the internet to distant institutions and people to illuminate more of his story and avoid some of the inaccuracies that crept into their texts.

Much of my initial research sprang from an interest in him as a local official who married two important indigenous women in the 1850s. My concentration in *Peace Weavers* (WSU Press, 2017) and *Interwoven Lives* (WSU Press, 2019) was biographies of eight intermarried women and their contributions to new communities. One of the women was married several times, including to Fitzhugh, but his story had to be greatly abbreviated. As I researched his life for *Peace Weavers*, I became fascinated with the strange, complex life of a man locals knew mainly as the coal mine manager, and I wanted to tell his whole story. Fitzhugh's life, from his birth in 1821 in Virginia to San Francisco and his lonely death in 1883, embroiled him in many national events and societal changes. On a personal level, he married four women in ten years and profoundly affected their lives, as well as those of his six children, in ways rarely positive.

I have researched E. C. Fitzhugh for twenty-four years, updating and expanding on the basic information found in those earlier books. That included reading more than two hundred district court cases over which he presided, his Supreme Court cases, as well as two in which he was the defendant.

At least fifty people and institutions contributed to this project over the years. Many stayed on the alert to spot Fitzhugh as they pursued their own historical or genealogical research adventures. The creation of *Man of Treacherous Charm* would have taken even longer had they not doggedly assisted over the years in telling the story of this complicated, likable, heroic, disgusting man. Their names and their help are found in the Acknowledgments.

Acknowledgements

M̲ANY THANKS ARE DUE to the people who, over two decades, have assisted me in researching, writing, and publishing Edmund C. Fitzhugh's biography. Some collaborators have gone several years before they contacted me with a new "find" for me to use. If I have failed to recognize anyone, please tell me and I will tender my appreciation.

A big thank you goes to the present and past staff of Washington State University Press in Pullman, Washington. They have believed in the value of my two-decade project enough to publish three books that resulted from it: Edward Sala, Linda Bathgate, Robert Clark, Beth DeWeese, Caryn Lawton, and Kerry Darnall, as well as those people I haven't met who patiently worked with my maps and images.

Fitzhugh extended family (local and national): Julie Reid Owens, Laurie Cepa, Virginia Brumbaugh, Sherry Guzman, Charlene Oerding, Leta Fitzhugh, Sallie Lee Fitzhugh, and Patricia Fitzhugh.

Historians, genealogists, collaborators, and mentors: Lummi Chief Tsi'lixw (William) James, Dr. Wayne Suttles, Dr. Coll Thrush, Michael Vouri, Lynn Hyde, Carole Teshima, Janet Oakley, Pete McLallen, Kellen Diamante, Carol Ericson, Patricia Neal, Martha Holcomb, Robert Guard, Charles Gay, Doug Fendall, Juanita Rouleau, Kris Day-Vincent, Boyd Pratt, Jerilynn Eby MacGregor, Joseph Rizzo, Tyla Jones, Dr. William Lang, Tim Wahl, Kathie Zetterberg, and Roger Newman.

The present and past staffs of museums, historical societies, libraries and archives: Washington State Archives, Northwest Region, the Center for Pacific Northwest Studies (Western Washington University), Jeff Jewell, photo archivist at Whatcom Museum, Fredericksburg (VA) Public Library, State Library of Virginia, Virginia Museum of History and Culture, Georgetown University Lauinger Library, Oatlands Plantation, Loudoun Museum (VA), Stafford County (VA) Museum and Cultural Center, Stafford County (VA) Historical Society, Fort Dodge (IA) Public Library, Webster County (IA) Historical Society, Jefferson County (WA) Historical Society, Des Moines (IA) Public Library, Orcas Island Historical Museum, Jamestown S'Klallam Tribe Enrollment Office, Island County (WA) Historical Museum, and University of Washington Libraries, Special Collections.

As always, my deepest thanks go to my husband, children, and grandchildren who have listened endlessly to Fitzhugh's story, new information I thought exciting to share, information-turned-bad, and all the steps along the way to a finished book.

Fitzhugh Genealogy

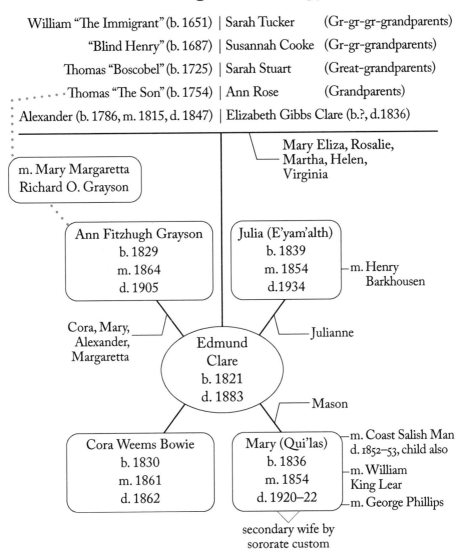

William "The Immigrant" (b. 1651) | Sarah Tucker (Gr-gr-gr-grandparents)

"Blind Henry" (b. 1687) | Susannah Cooke (Gr-gr-grandparents)

Thomas "Boscobel" (b. 1725) | Sarah Stuart (Great-grandparents)

Thomas "The Son" (b. 1754) | Ann Rose (Grandparents)

Alexander (b. 1786, m. 1815, d. 1847) | Elizabeth Gibbs Clare (b.?, d.1836)

Mary Eliza, Rosalie, Martha, Helen, Virginia

m. Mary Margaretta
Richard O. Grayson

Ann Fitzhugh Grayson
b. 1829
m. 1864
d. 1905

Julia (E'yam'alth)
b. 1839
m. 1854
d.1934

— m. Henry
Barkhousen

Cora, Mary,
Alexander,
Margaretta

Julianne

Edmund
Clare
b. 1821
d. 1883

Mason

Cora Weems Bowie
b. 1830
m. 1861
d. 1862

Mary (Qui'las)
b. 1836
m. 1854
d. 1920–22

— m. Coast Salish Man
d. 1852–53, child also

— m. William
King Lear

— m. George Phillips

secondary wife by
sororate custom

b = born | m = married | d = died

Edmund C. Fitzhugh Chronology

1821: Fitzhugh born at
Boscobel Plantation

1835–1838: Attended Georgetown College

1840–1841: Attended West Point Academy

1843: Started law practice in
Fredericksburg, Virginia

1846–1847: Served in Virginia House
of Delegates

1849–1854: Attorney, San Francisco

1853: *Washington Territory established*

1854: *Whatcom County split from
Island County—included present
Skagit and San Juan Counties*

Established Sehome Coal Mine
at Bellingham Bay

Married Julia and Mary by
tribal custom

1854–1856: Whatcom County auditor

1855–1856: Appointed Interpreter at
Bellingham Bay

Military Aide to Governor
Isaac Stevens, Treaty War

Appointed Special Indian Agent
for Bellingham Bay

1857: Elected Democratic Party
Central Committee chairman

Andrew Wilson homicide

1858: Judicial appointment

Murder indictment

1858–1861: Associate Territorial Justice,
3rd District and Supreme Court

1859: Murder trial

1860: Gambling trial

Worked on Breckinridge for
President campaign in
Washington, DC

Abducted children, wives Julia
and Mary left

1861: Married Cora Weems Bowie
in Maryland

Law practice and farmer,
Whidbey Island, Washington

1862: Cora died

1863: Captain, Confederate Army
Brigade Inspector,
Pickett's Division

1864: Assistant Adjutant General,
Eppa Hunton's Brigade,
Pickett's Division

Married Ann Fitzhugh Grayson
in Virginia

1867–1874: Lived in Fort Dodge, Iowa, with
Ann and four children

1874: Left family, visited Whatcom,
Washington

1878: Clerk, San Francisco seawall
project

1881: Attorney, San Francisco

1882: Unemployed

1883: Died in San Francisco

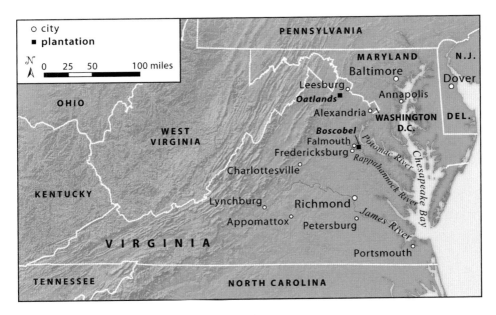

Map 1. The Virginia of Edmund C. Fitzhugh, 1830s–1865.

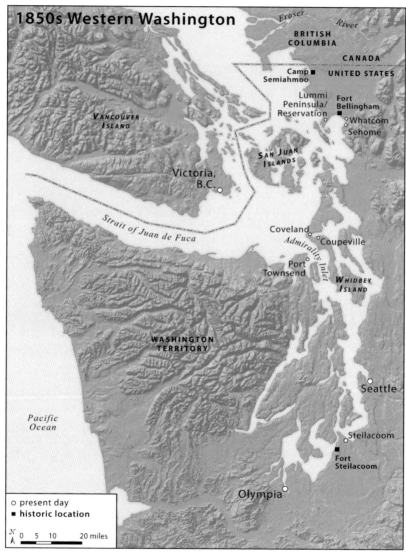

Map 2. 1850s Western Washington Territory. Seattle is shown but was very small and never mentioned as a part of Edmund C. Fitzhugh's life.

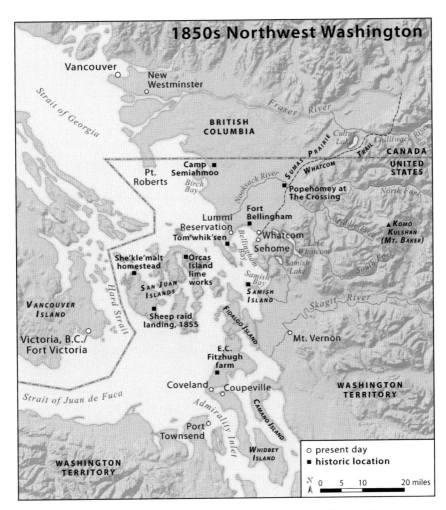

Map 3. 1850s Northwest Washington Territory. Ownership of the San Juan Islands—site of the sheep raid and "Pig War"—was still in dispute at the time of Edmund C. Fitzhugh's departure to fight in the Civil War in early 1863.

Introduction

LOTTIE ROEDER ROTH, daughter of the first non-native colonizer at Bellingham Bay, wrote of her parents' friend in her 1926 Whatcom County history: "[E. C.] Fitzhugh was typical of the adventurous, high-strung Virginia gentlemen in the days before the Civil War. A born fighter, quick to take offense, absolutely without fear, something of a roisterer, imperious and self-willed, following his code of honor without thought of consequences, but withal a man of superior intellect and many kindly impulses. Generous, hospitable, impulsive, self-indulgent, honest, and brave."[1]

From the moment Edmund Clare Fitzhugh's tall leather boots struck the mud flats in front of the Roeder-Peabody Mill in 1854, the effects of the charismatic man on the infant community and Washington Territory were wide and, for some people, destructive.

Territorial Justice Fitzhugh was put on the federal bench while under indictment for a murder at his coal mine. He made measured judicial decisions, helped organize the early Democratic Party machine in California and Washington, helped run a national presidential campaign, and fought heroically in the Civil War. And yet...

He died alone in a rusty iron bed in a dingy San Francisco hotel next to a liquor store.

None of his four wives was there.

None of his six children.

None of his famous Virginia family.

None of his important California friends.

None of his coal mine syndicate associates.

None of the Washington Territory politicians whose elections he had secured.

None of his old Whatcom County friends.

None of his legal colleagues.

None of his Civil War companions.

Just, no one.

This complicated, puzzling, and charismatic Virginia blueblood's persona was deeply influenced and formed by the family history, privileged education, and ethical system within which he grew to manhood. What he did with that background was another matter. How did it all go so wrong?

ര汉න

For most Americans, it might seem irrelevant to look backward several generations to examine how they were shaped as individuals. This is not so for the "First Families of Virginia," the "FFVs." At least in E. C. Fitzhugh's time, much that a member of the Fitzhugh family became could be traced back generations and centuries to those who in colonial times were wealthy and prominent, both socially and politically. The FFVs still know "who" they are, and they know "who" they were. They know the role models whose examples and traditions other FFVs expect to see. And they know how they are connected to other FFV families by blood and in-law relationships, even if it was many generations past. By the Civil War, the Fitzhugh family included such a dazzling array of collateral cousin families that any of them could quickly establish links to George Washington, the Lees, Randolphs, Monroes, and other famous Virginia patriots of earlier times. This was a handy treasure in a national culture that built power and influence on personal connections and political patronage.

And so it was for Edmund C. Fitzhugh, of the Stafford County "Boscobel" Fitzhughs. In the nineteenth century, those three descriptors implied residence, religion, education, expectations, behavioral mindset, political involvement, and allowable male careers. To be an FFV also implied how non-whites, women, and children were to be treated. The subculture dictated what a man's personal honor meant and how it was to be defended, even for those who migrated elsewhere.

Traceable sources of E. C. Fitzhugh's personality and conduct throughout his entire life, in every location, can be found even in William "The Immigrant" Fitzhugh, his English great-great-great grandfather who sailed in 1670 for Virginia Colony. Twenty-year-old William's own forbears had enriched themselves in business, law, and the purchase of confiscated Catholic monastery lands. English Fitzhughs served as mayors and Bedfordshire burgesses. They set the pattern of committed political, business, and law professions for the American Fitzhughs.

William left for Virginia because he was the son of a Royalist father who had been forced into exile after the beheading of King Charles I, possibly accompanied by his entire family. After the Restoration, King Charles II awarded land in the colonies to men loyal to the crown through the civil war. Primogeniture laws meant that only the eldest son would inherit the wealth, so younger sons left England to manage the colonial lands. They became most of the FFVs, some having married women imported for that purpose, even sold.

It is often assumed that all Virginia's "King Charles Cavaliers" were enriched in that way, but William Fitzhugh multiplied his landholdings on his own. Historians and family agree that shortly after arrival he married eleven-year-old heiress Sarah Tucker, signing a property agreement with her mother that also sent her to England for education. That document gave him the dowry money to buy 54,000 acres of tobacco land in Virginia's Northern Neck. He had at least some legal training in England and is said to have been a land agent for Lord Fairfax, owner of most of that area. William also served in the colony militia and the Jamestown assembly. He and Sarah had five sons who then founded the five branches of the Fitzhugh family in America on land given to each. Branch descendants identified with the great house and plantation that each of those five sons established on his land.[2]

The Stafford County area was first settled about 1649, years after Captain John Smith's 1608 trading expedition visited. In a historic event that curiously echoed centuries later in Edmund Fitzhugh's own marriages, the first permanent British settler Giles Brent married an elite indigenous woman. Brent could not have settled among his wife's people without their permission, and his marriage secured that, a pattern seen even on Bellingham Bay in Washington Territory two centuries later. Over the next decades Catholic Giles Brent honored religious freedom by welcoming Anglican Cavaliers and Protestant French Huguenots. Many of the former city-dwellers would have starved without help from the indigenous people whose territory they invaded at Brent's invitation. One of those welcomed was new landowner William "The Immigrant" Fitzhugh. Stafford County quickly became a tobacco-growing region where labor came from indentured servants and enslaved Africans.[3]

During an interview with the author in 2000, when Stafford County's family elder Miss Sally Fitzhugh heard how E. C. Fitzhugh had conducted his life, she described another tradition William "The

Immigrant" established: "Fitzhugh men always married for money and power." And Edmund would do exactly that, four times.[4]

William "The Immigrant's" five sons built the initial Fitzhugh web of personal connections that benefited centuries of descendants, including Edmund. One of those was "Blind Henry" of "Bedford," his great-great grandfather. After Oxford University in England, he married Susanna Cooke. Exemplifying the spreading FFV web, Susanna's father was also the ancestor of Confederate General George Pickett, E. C. Fitzhugh's Bellingham Bay friend and later Civil War commander. In the FFV world, they were close cousins. "Blind Henry" used his 6000-acre power base to serve his county as high sheriff, militia colonel like his father, and in the House of Burgesses. Like his mother Sarah Tucker Fitzhugh, Henry suffered night blindness that deteriorated into total blindness, a genetic disorder passed to many descendants. A second son of William "The Immigrant" Fitzhugh and Sarah married neighbor Ann Lee, becoming the ancestor of both Confederate General Robert E. Lee, and his wife. A third son married neighbor Lucy Carter from the richest and largest landholding Virginia family. The other two of William and Sarah's sons married into the Mason family of Revolution-era fame. All five sons made marriages that brought wealth and power to the Fitzhugh men. The web grew ever wider over the generations as FFV families sought to keep their land and money among themselves by marrying within their group, sometimes to first cousins.[5]

☙❧

Edmund C. Fitzhugh's hometown Falmouth began in 1727 as a tidal river port for the planters and became a Fitzhugh family seat. It was the only Stafford County community that developed between the southern boundary Rappahannock and the Potomac on the county's north boundary. Six area Fitzhughs served in the Revolutionary War, including E. C. Fitzhugh's great-grandfather, ("Blind Henry's" son) Captain Thomas Fitzhugh whose brother started Hunter Iron Works at Falmouth and made equipment for the Continental Army and anchors for the Navy, before his election to the Continental Congress. The tiny settlement on the Indian trail to the river crossing became the major north-south route through Virginia, surrounded by the vast holdings of the Fitzhugh family. Though the British government designated Falmouth an official tobacco inspection station, Falmouth's white community showed little growth because of the planter-slave labor setting.[6]

When landless settlers moved across the Appalachians' Blue Ridge into the Shenandoah Valley, Falmouth became the logical trade center with the "West" and grew to a few hundred residents. It lay beside "The Falls of the Rappahannock" where the river dropped about twenty-two feet into tidal waters. Grain, cotton, and illegal whiskey from the west, plus local tobacco, were loaded on vessels that sailed down the tidal river to Chesapeake Bay, and the ships bound for England. The tobacco trade brought in middlemen and merchants from Scotland, followed by other Scots who started major industrial mills powered by the river. Prosperous ones married into the Fitzhugh clan, tying all the wealthy people (and their children) in town together personally and professionally. However, while the Fitzhughs and allies made money from the trade, the increasing population above the falls clear-cut forests for farmland, and the resulting silt washed downriver to settle at the foot of the picturesque falls. The deposits would soon cause serious problems.

⊂∂∞

Edmund Fitzhugh's great-grandfather, Revolutionary War Captain Thomas Fitzhugh, married his first cousin, Sarah Stuart. She brought religious elite into Edmund's family branch because she was the daughter of Scottish Anglican Reverend David Stuart whose church had become an influential FFV gathering place. Sarah's sister married into George Washington's family downstream at "Ferry Farm." Not only that, but her grandfather was Governor of Barbados, another British colony that traded with Virginia in what became known as the "Triangular Trade" involving tobacco, rum, and slaves. One of Thomas and Sarah Fitzhugh's daughters married Falmouth's wealthiest Scot merchant, William Knox. In the 1800s, Edmund Fitzhugh would grow up among both his Knox and Fitzhugh cousins. Once again, a Fitzhugh marriage and progeny enhanced connections, influence, and financial health that would benefit Edmund decades later.[7]

Thomas and Sarah Fitzhugh built "Boscobel" with slave labor and named it for the hiding place of King Charles II after his defeat at the Battle of Worcester. Their descendants were labeled the "Boscobel Fitzhughs," the county-town-great house shorthand for FFV members, and it lay at the heart of Edmund C. Fitzhugh's identity. The FFV shorthand counted for Edmund (and everyone else) when he entered the law profession, when he entered politics, when he got to California, when he was in the Civil War, and with the last two women he married. Where it didn't count was in Washington Territory.

Boscobel house and plantation sat on the highest ridge between the Potomac and Rappahannock Rivers about four miles out of Falmouth. Edmund's great-grandparents built a homey frame country house with dormer windows upstairs and a long shady porch to welcome guests in the hot summer. It was unlike Thomas's brother William's nearby imposing brick mansion "Chatham," meant to impress like many others. Still, the couple's standards demanded that materials and furniture all come from England for the eleven rooms and large outside kitchen.[8]

CЗ℘О

Captain Thomas "Boscobel" Fitzhugh and Sarah Stuart had just one son, known as "Thomas the Son," and he was Edmund's grandfather. By the time "Thomas the Son" was born, the Fitzhugh men had solidified the FFV male traditions and attitudes that would influence Edmund's own relationships and activities. They included fine whiskey, cigars, horse racing, education, political office, a paternalistic attitude toward women, and slavery with all its master-slave attitudes and abuses. This Fitzhugh culture of owning other human beings as property, including the right over life and death, only ended with the Emancipation Proclamation and Civil War, though the attitude continued.

"Thomas the Son" inherited Boscobel and, with Edmund's grandmother Ann Rose, greatly improved the plantation's home and increased its surrounding gardens and buildings. She was the daughter of Revolutionary Army Colonel John Rose whose children and descendants predictably intermarried with many other FFVs.[9]

"Thomas the Son" died in 1821, the same year Edmund was born.

CHAPTER 1

The Doctor's Son

IN 1786, ONLY FIVE YEARS after the British surrender on Virginia soil, Edmund Fitzhugh's father Alexander was born to "Thomas the Son" and Ann Rose Fitzhugh at Boscobel. America's ultimate style of government was still in flux.[1]

During Alexander's childhood, his parents continued to improve Boscobel's home and plantation, as well as expand their ownership of enslaved people. By the time Edmund was born there in 1821, the unpretentious house was surrounded by lush flower, vegetable, and formal gardens, with an orchard, dairy, stone grist mill, stables, granaries, barns, and slave quarters. Two other houses sheltered the miller and farm overseer. Boscobel was by then a small agricultural powerhouse instead of just a tobacco plantation.

Five sisters and four brothers grew to adulthood with Alexander at Boscobel, probably educated by a private tutor at home. Honoring the Fitzhugh Loyalist history, Thomas and Ann named one son Charles Edward Stuart after the Restoration king. Another son was clearly disabled, mostly confined to one room with a slave caregiver and in need of lifelong financial support. Alex's sister Mary Margaretta wed one of the Loudoun County FFV Graysons, a descendant of an American Revolution icon. Her daughter, Edmund's first cousin, would become his fourth wife half a century later.[2]

CSRO

Edmund's father expected to inherit some family land and money in the future. But as a younger son, it would not be Boscobel. As he reached maturity, Alexander attended many social events with the local FFV bachelor contingent. Without doubt, they had many discussions about their futures if they were younger sons not destined to be a "Mansion Tract" owner. Apparently, he found the attraction of being a planter on his lesser acreage unattractive, especially as tobacco was increasingly depleting the soil. Alexander's first cousin, Dr. Thomas Fitzhugh Knox, practiced medicine for the county in Falmouth and was the most likely older mentor for Alex, who decided to become a doctor.[3]

At twenty-two and with a loan from his father, Alexander Fitzhugh entered the University of Pennsylvania Medical School, the nation's first, founded by Benjamin Franklin. He graduated two years later, having learned what comprised modern medicine from professors who would forever be associated with the history of American medicine: Dr. Joseph Leidy for anatomy and Dr. Benjamin Rush for medicine. His classmates included Thomas Jefferson's grandson, studying both surgery and his grandfather's great interest, natural history. The two studied with Dr. Rush, who had prepared Meriwether Lewis for his expedition to the Pacific just a few years earlier. Alexander's required graduation essay was "Typhus State of Fever," an important topic because typhoid took thousands of lives every year and its cause and prevention were poorly understood.[4]

When Alexander's portrait was painted years later, he held his textbook *Rush's Inquiries.* Also a signer of the Declaration of Independence, Rush was revered by followers like Alexander as the "Hippocrates of American Medicine." He was ahead of his time in advocating humane treatment of the mentally ill, but he also taught that African-Americans' dark skin was due to a form of leprosy, and that tobacco caused tuberculosis and insanity. He thought the yellow fever epidemics were due to noxious miasmas in the air.[5]

When Edmund's father studied under him, Rush's methods in the age of what was called "heroic" medicine were already being questioned by peers as harmful and ineffective. He taught Alexander treatment that centered on bloodletting, blistering, purging, vomiting, and sweating to produce "morbid excitement" in blood vessels and cure the illness. Rush had taken those treatments to the Continental Army as surgeon general. They probably led to some needless deaths, but his belief in a vegetable-rich diet, vaccinations, no alcohol, and clean army camps probably saved other lives. Alexander absorbed all of it.[6]

Newly-graduated Doctor Alexander Fitzhugh moved back to Falmouth, opened his county-wide practice, and purchased a house and extra lot, again with his father's help. He had only been out of medical school for two years when the War of 1812 began. He joined 824 others in Stafford County's 45th (Peyton's) Regiment, including four other Fitzhughs. The militia unit was not activated until July 1813, when the British became a threat along the Potomac River on the east side of Fitzhugh family lands. While Alexander served as surgeon's mate, his brother William H. was captain of one of the seven companies that faced down the British. Alexander earned a promotion to surgeon in 1814 during British landings along the Potomac, while Boscobel on the Rappahannock was never threatened. The regiment was discharged about five months before the war's end. Dr. Fitzhugh went home to Falmouth and resumed his practice, though he soon faced medical and financial competition when three other doctors were licensed to serve the large county.[7]

Alexander married Edmund's mother, Elizabeth (Eliza) Gibbs Clare, in 1815, and unlike most Fitzhugh wives, she was not an FFV daughter, or even from nearby. She was the daughter of John Clare and his second wife. The Clares were a prominent old Maryland Eastern Shore family who owned parts of founder Lord Baltimore's land grant. It is likely that Alex met her during his militia unit's wanderings because she seems not to have had any familial connection to Stafford County.[8]

Given Eliza's earlier life, Alexander's home on Caroline Street may have been less than impressive. It was a modest dwelling much different from either of the newlyweds' childhood homes. One advantage, however, was the second lot in back that provided plenty of space for a garden and future children's play. It was also only a block from the river and its cooling waterfalls. The single-story house was just 24 x 26 feet with a long porch and adjoining shed. The detached kitchen for the house slaves was nearly the same size as the house. The village centered around the industrial and port operations of the Fitzhughs' Knox and Gordon relatives. Storekeeper Thomas Seddon's son James would one day become the Confederate secretary of war. By the time the couple married, the small town also had its slave jail that both attracted and repelled children for decades.[9]

For his time, Dr. Alexander Fitzhugh was one of the nation's most highly trained physicians. He and Eliza raised their children in a professional's home in town rather than on a tobacco plantation. Mary Eliza, the first baby to live, was born three years after the marriage. Edmund Clare Fitzhugh followed in 1821, named for his mother's brother and uncle. No other male child lived, but sisters Virginia, Rosalie, Martha, and Helen were born before Edmund was a teenager. When he was seven, his physician father was unable to save four-year-old Martha, who died thirty hours after becoming ill. In hindsight, using Rush's methods could have worsened the unnamed non-contagious illness. Because Edmund's father had by then been elected county magistrate, Virginia's influential *Political Arena* newspaper gave Martha's sudden death a brief obituary.[10]

Shortly before Edmund's birth in 1821, his grandfather Thomas "The Son" Fitzhugh died. His complex will was a tangle of disbursements, annuities, and obligations, even a threat if the eldest son (William) disputed it. Some of the will deeply affected Edmund's parental finances and what they could do for their children. It required Alexander to help support the disabled son and Charles (still a minor) with annuities to come from profits on land Alexander inherited. If he did not pay up, his executor brother could sell a piece of the land to get the annuity owed. In the patriarchal tradition, Thomas also decreed that his five daughters could live at Boscobel and be supported until they married. However, they did not get their full inheritance until it became their dowry, another example of how marriage enriched planter-class husbands.[11]

If Thomas had saddled his son Alexander (and Eliza) with continuing contributions to two brothers' support despite already having one child and Edmund on the way, the direct bequest to him was encumbered by more demands that hint at Alexander's finances, or shaky money management skills. He inherited 1100 acres to the north, but there was a catch. Alexander could only take possession if he repaid, within two years, the sizable loans for his medical school education and purchase of the house with extra lot in Falmouth. Alexander had not yet re-paid his father nine years after graduation. In effect, Thomas said that he'd waited long enough and if Alexander did not meet the deadline, some of his inherited land would be sold to pay off the loans. The will gave his executor (elder brother William) the option of deducting the entire amount from Alexander's share of the personal estate residue.

Edmund's father inherited enslaved people as well as land and money. Their numbers, possibly added to slaves Eliza brought into the marriage, presented a problem to a family with their own "house slaves" already in place. The solution for them, as it was for others in a similar situation, was not to sell or free the people, but to rent them out. They were only sold when Edmund took over his father's finances and estate two decades later.

⊗⊗⊗

Falmouth was a young boy's heaven. The river ran beside town, full of flat rocks, swimming holes, and fish. Lush greenery linked river shallows and the village of tightly knit people. A French visitor noted that the river was "a bit savage, noisy, rocky, with waves and little islands of greenery romantically placed in the middle of the riverbed." A small creek ran down to the river from a hillside spring behind the Temperance Tavern. Because Falmouth covered less than a dozen short streets, Edmund could easily find his cousins and friends, while other family members were at Boscobel four miles out the river road. The large red brick Union Church welcomed a rotating service by four different denominations, and included slaves and freed people relegated to a separate entrance, staircase, and balcony. The church received much of Eliza's devotion and service in what spare time she had, later lauded in her obituary. On days Edmund crossed the downriver wooden toll bridge to Fredericksburg with his family, he may well have joined one of the marble games played in the middle of streets that local males had made a town tradition.[12]

For most of his childhood, as the doctor's son rather than as one in a commercial family, Edmund may have been somewhat oblivious to the permanent changes happening to his town. The deforestation by upriver settlers in the Shenandoah Valley, and dozens of small gold mines along the tributaries, sent silt down the Rappahannock and over the waterfalls near his house to settle below. Tidal sands from Chesapeake Bay dropped from suspension in front of the rocks, joining the silt. The irreversible build-up was a problem that all the Fitzhugh strategic marriages and investments couldn't solve. Eventually, the dual action blocked Falmouth's stone wharf, and vessels that sailed upriver to load commodities for the coastal ports began to dock a mile downstream at small Fredericksburg. Fredericksburg kept growing after the local ferries were replaced by a wooden bridge that blocked any but small boats from going to Falmouth. Once the little brick customs house in Falmouth was no longer needed to process cargo, it became the magistrate's courthouse, soon to be a second hub of Edmund's father's life. As the county's tobacco fields wore out, people left the area for the Ohio region and the long-time planters sold pieces of their holdings to replace crop income. When hogs, drunk after eating home-distillery mash, came to freely roam the dirt streets of a quieter Falmouth, outsiders gave the town the moniker "Hogtown," which stuck for more than a century. The village of 500 in Edmund's time stagnated for two hundred years as a real life "backwater" with gently decaying original buildings and nearly the same population.[13]

Figure 2, Falmouth, Virginia, with Fredericksburg visible across the Rappahannock River. Sketch made at the time of the Civil War shows Falmouth appearing nearly the same as it had during E. C. Fitzhugh's youth. Alfred Waud, artist. *Library of Congress, Morgan Collection of Civil War drawings, #2004660892.*

There was another side to the rather idyllic setting for young boys blissfully unaware of Falmouth's serious economic problem. Since the early 1700s, Stafford County and Falmouth were completely supported by the labor of enslaved people. By the brink of the Civil War in 1860, Stafford County's population was 42 percent black, including a few freedmen and women. The percentage was probably much higher in the preceding decades of heavy tobacco cultivation.[14]

The "King's Highway" passing through Falmouth along the riverbank became the link between Boston in the north and Charleston, South Carolina. It was not just the major north-south route for all sorts of travel and trade, it was also the main route for the slave trade. The road that took two months to traverse end-to-end had all been built by slave labor, people counted as property along with horses and cattle in tax records. While Edmund and his friends happily splashed in the river, enslaved women carried buckets and tubs of water on their heads, down the hill from the spring to his house and others. The town trustees earlier had created an enforcer to keep order and run the slave jail. He could even whip slaves found in town on Sunday without a pass. The slaves and free men and women attended the Fitzhugh's Union Church because Virginia blacks were not allowed to have their own pastor and church. Remembering the famous 1804 slave revolt at the Fitzhugh "Chatham" plantation, whites feared they might plan an uprising at an independent church.[15]

When Edmund's father was elected magistrate, it became his responsibility to enforce the laws and regulations that governed his own slaves and those of others in the town that was nearly half slave, as well as in the surrounding plantations. The man who preceded Alexander had just recently tried four elderly slave women for murder. Holding the office for decades, Alexander could order people lashed or executed for transgressions alleged by white owners. They took the slaves they wanted punished to the crude stone slave jail in the center of town. There, the town constable flogged them, or worse. One man remembered that "the respectable family heads of Falmouth were always particularly strict and careful in forbidding their children any play or loitering in the neighborhood of [the slave jail]." He recalled that the jailer never smiled or talked as he walked to-and-fro in front of his house attached to the stone jail.[16]

Figure 3, Magistrate's office in Falmouth, Virginia. E. C. Fitzhugh's father, Dr. Alexander Fitzhugh, handled minor local legal matters there for many years. Photographed by F. B. Johnston in the 1930s. Carnegie Survey of the Architecture of the South. *Library of Congress, Prints and Photographs Division, #LC-J7-VA-2798.*

The situation in Edmund's hometown was abhorrent to seemingly only one resident, Moncure Daniel Conway, the former magistrate's son, but also the son of a Methodist mother who taught a home Sunday School to children of both races. Conway became one of the nation's leading abolitionists before he collected escaped and former slaves in the Washington, DC, area (probably some he knew from home) and led them to establish a free colony in Yellow Springs, Ohio. He captured Falmouth's atmosphere during Edmund's early years when he said, "I was exiled from the spot where I was born, simply for an honest conviction that Freedom was better than Slavery."[17]

The small-town Virginia milieu of Edmund C. Fitzhugh's first decades was built on family, class, politics, and slavery. When added to his Fitzhugh family traditions, his ambitions, his sense of self, and his attitude toward non-white people grew.

CHAPTER 2

Loss and Latin Lessons

OLD-SCHOOL PHYSICIANS WHO adhered strictly to the teachings of Dr. Benjamin Rush found the 1830s unkind. They fought increasing competition from medical school graduates using new medicines and surgical methods to treat disease. New doctors used alcoholic tonics, opiates, and digitalis, rather than the "bleed, blister, and purge" methodology. Homeopaths built upon herbalism and folk medicine and attracted many of the wealthy. The rural upcountry patients usually stuck to folk medicine and did not trust physicians of any kind. Dr. Fitzhugh's medical income was now subject to the fracturing of American medicine, as well as Stafford County's economic woes. He was fortunate to have supplementary income from his agricultural acres, slave rental, and magistrate fees.[1]

⚭

Edmund Fitzhugh's early schooling is unclear. Virginia had no public schools and most of the population was illiterate. Elite families isolated on plantations hired live-in tutors. In Falmouth, one prominent family's children were described as walking to a school, evidence that families with means gathered their children together. Perhaps their teachers held classes at the old former "Master Hobby's School" building, or they gathered at one of the big houses. The Fitzhughs and allied families expected their sons to enter professions, i.e. medicine, law, or the ministry, if they weren't managing a plantation or a large business. All of those paths required an early education that qualified them to enter a preparatory academy or university. Planter-class Southerners established thousands of such academies for their children.[2]

When Edmund reached age fourteen, his parents sent him to Washington, DC, to attend one such preparatory academy. Georgetown College overlooked the Potomac River in Washington, DC, far upstream from Stafford County. Founded by the Jesuits in 1791, the traditional liberal arts academy was elevated by the 1815 Congress to also award university degrees. While it might seem unusual for the Anglican Fitzhughs to send their only son to a Catholic school, it offered a location in the center of national government and politics. The Capitol was a short walk away, allowing student spectators to attend Congressional debates and Supreme Court cases, an advantage that students in other cities did not have. Georgetown also offered the rigorous academics for which the Jesuits had been known for centuries. Edmund needed to complete seven years of difficult mandatory classes in a regimented order to finish the Bachelor of Arts. Alexander and Eliza's hopes for their only son were high.

Unlike the sprawling university campus Georgetown College became, when Edmund entered in 1835 everything was concentrated within a low wall surrounding the college's quadrangle, sending a symbolic message of the school's pride in paying the "strictest attention" to student morals. All students had to attend Mass, which the Jesuits believed help keep order. Walks to the Capitol or anywhere else had to be supervised. Edmund could not leave on his own for the day unless his parents were in town, and the school forbade any long absences from campus other than once a year for the "Great Vacation." The prospectus explained: "Experience has proved that mere complimentary visits have given occasion to disorders."[3]

Figure 4, Georgetown College campus, 1851. The only structure different from E. C. Fitzhugh's time there as a prep student is the observatory in the background. Artist unknown. *University Archives Photographic Collection, Georgetown University Archives.*

The descriptions of the school in the 1835 prospectus the Fitzhughs consulted did not paint an attractive picture to a fourteen-year-old used to having the run of town and countryside with his numerous cousins. Georgetown supplied a list of clothing he was to bring, categorized into winter dress suit, warm-weather dress suit, and two daily-wear suits, plus a cloak or coat for rain and cold. It even specified the number of shirts, socks, hankies, shoes, and one hat. He was to bring nothing else. Dr. Fitzhugh's attention probably focused on the listed costs of his son's education. Tuition had risen to $200/year, equal to well over $5000 in the twenty-first century, but it included materials, board, and laundry. An additional $3.00/year was charged for medical care, and if Edmund wanted to take a modern language, music, art, or fencing, then fees were added. If Dr. Fitzhugh didn't pay the tuition semi-annually, the school would send Edmund home after a two-month grace period. Georgetown also required Edmund to bring as little spending money as possible and directed it to be deposited in the hands of the college president who would dole it out if he thought the reason was good enough. Edmund's father was to supply his boy with no more than fifty cents a month. In all of this, Georgetown's requirements, price, and schedule were very much like other academies for elite Southern students, but it had a prestige factor for its academic excellence and location.[4]

The journey young Edmund took from Falmouth to Georgetown was long and cold in December 1835, twenty miles to Aquia Landing and then forty up the Potomac River to enter school on the day after Christmas. He brought his own bedding as required and was assigned a dorm room. His father certainly accompanied him, leaving a pregnant Eliza home with the girls in Falmouth. Dr. and Mrs. Fitzhugh failed to pack the required silver spoon in their son's baggage, so it was issued (probably at his first meal) and immediately billed.

On December 26, 1835, Edmund entered a culture as different from his own as he could imagine, though it still was a school of Southern students in a de facto Southern city. The school even owned nearly three hundred slaves on a Maryland plantation to generate income for the college.[5]

The prefect of studies first quizzed Edmund to determine his academic level for placement in appropriate classes. Not only did his parents seek the academic atmosphere of the Jesuit institution, but a non-academic goal was to promote an international atmosphere. Some of the Jesuit teachers were Europeans, and students were Catholic, Protestant, and Jewish. Diplomatic corps students from nearby foreign embassies brought Edmund into daily contact with boys whose experiences were more cosmopolitan than his own.[6]

Among the many ways Georgetown culture contradicted Edmund's experience as an adolescent was the expectation of personal and moral discipline, without any underlying tolerance for rebellion against rules. Though parents in the Fitzhughs' patriarchal slave society claimed to raise their sons to be sober, courageous, and hardworking scions of the family name, white privilege allowed young men to flaunt the lip service ethics. Boys were expected to be strong-willed, rambunctious, and resistant to rules. They suffered few consequences for bad behavior related to women or race, which led to lack of empathy. Edmund's adolescent mind absorbed this complexity, and the attitudes followed him into adulthood wherever he lived. Jesuit teachings of self-discipline did not.[7]

Edmund entered in the midst of the first semester. Most students already knew each other, but he was smart and personable so it may not have taken him long to blend in once classes resumed. Georgetown called the first-year course of study the "Class of Rudiments." It included Latin and English grammar, reading, spelling, geography, and history of the Old Testament. Students read Cicero's letters in Latin, wrote "easy" compositions in English and Latin, and started beginning Greek grammar. Edmund took ninety minutes of math a day, assigned to a level anywhere from arithmetic to calculus. His father had paid for him to study French one hour a day. He was only in classes for two months when the midterm exams began, but those in July preceding commencement would be more important.[8]

Edmund had been at Georgetown only four months when his mother died giving birth to a baby boy, who also died a few days later. According to an obituary, her health had been "feeble and declining" for several years, and she was said to have other babies who did not live, who came either before Edmund's birth or in the four years since Helen arrived. Two obituaries paint a picture of Eliza as a deeply religious woman whose "duties of a wife, mother, and [slave] mistress were tenderly, affectionately, and faithfully discharged." She was said to have been a friend to the "distressed and afflicted" and her demeanor was "calculated to cherish peace, harmony and love in society."[9]

The published description of Edmund's mother falls in line with the Southern ideal of womanhood and slave mistress. A "lady" had servants and class, with no bad behavior or bad manners as "women" might. Eliza was apparently deeply charitable, but her visits and helpful acts did not imply equality with women she saw as common. According to historian Elizabeth Fox-Genovese, charity was inseparable from condescension for the planter-class "lady" because it supported her privileged identity that allowed her to maintain position in her own society. Edmund absorbed this part of his mother's persona, and years later he would undertake charitable behavior in Washington Territory, though his behavior toward indigenous women and men, as well as hungry gold miners, never implied equality.[10]

After two months of summer vacation at home with his grieving father and sisters, Edmund started the new term in September 1836. The same focus on math and French was supplemented by North American geography and the beginning course in humanities. He read more classic letters and professors assigned compositions in Greek, Latin, and English. However, two months after the term started, Georgetown dismissed him on November 11. Dr. Fitzhugh had failed to remit the half-yearly payment due in September and the two-month grace period ran out. Edmund returned to the school as soon as his father paid up. Most likely there was a problem with reduced income, or financial mismanagement led to the late payment, rather than forgetfulness.[11]

After the 1837 summer vacation, Edmund advanced to even more demanding classes. He studied Caesar and Ovid, wrote prose in three languages, studied ancient history, and the geography of South America and Europe. English studies were given particular attention, as well as the continuing ninety minutes a day of math. He still spent an hour a day learning French, the language of medicine, diplomacy, and the military.

Edmund left Georgetown permanently on March 12, 1838, after mid-year exams. The result was still the same: a solid, if incomplete, intellectual foundation. Nothing in his record indicates academic failure, or if his father ran out of money for the semi-annual tuition bill, or if he rebelled against the regimentation. However, from the first of the semester, his father had been working on another educational plan for Edmund.[12]

∞

Maybe Edmund had expressed an interest in the United States Military Academy, though few elite Southern young men aspired to attend. Or perhaps his father decided that Edmund should pursue a superior engineering education within an equal amount of discipline and structure, instead of the classical education offered by Georgetown. Better, he would not have to pay any tuition or fees with everything, including uniforms, provided. First, Dr. Fitzhugh enlisted help from a local FFV connection, Congressman John Taliaferro, a Fredericksburg lawyer, and obtained a short reference letter from R. N. Johnson, a West Point alumnus. On January 29, 1838, the congressman wrote to Secretary of War Joel Poinsett about the seventeen-year-old he personally knew and called of "fine manly form" with "ample" education. Dr. Fitzhugh took Edmund to meet Revolution icon Patrick Henry's grandson, Senator William Harrison Roane, who had represented Virginia in the House of Representatives and Senate on and off since 1817. Roane then wrote to Poinsett at Fitzhugh's "earnest request." Adding the political connection, he said he knew Dr. Fitzhugh as a staunch "republican of high character" and would be happy if his request was "gratified." Senator Roane told Poinsett that Dr. Fitzhugh would also be calling upon him to discuss Edmund's application.[13]

Edmund did not make the cut despite the reference letters and a possible visit to the secretary of war. Taliaferro immediately wrote to the admissions office on February 26, 1838, that since Edmund had been rejected, he would like him to be appointed to the first vacancy that occurred. He said he was urgently asking for the admission "from a conviction of his superior merit and that he will do honor to the Institution." Edmund left Georgetown only weeks later. Nothing indicates that he expected admission sooner rather than later, but it is possible if not probable.[14]

Eliza's death in April 1836 had triggered a new direction for Alexander. Dr. Fitzhugh was already the respected county magistrate hearing local cases in his tiny courtroom, but he became more involved in state politics for his Democratic Republican party. "Court Day" attracted men from all over the county to watch or be in the proceedings. The Stafford County party met on Court Day because it was the one day when many, if not most, voters were present. In 1836, fifteen men vetted the interested candidates for representative to the Virginia House of Delegates, one of them being Alexander. Two years later he won election to the House, not long after Edmund returned from Georgetown.[15]

If Edmund and his father anticipated he would soon get an open seat at West Point, they were disappointed. Nothing happened for the next two years. There are no records of what Edmund might have done during that time in Falmouth. Besides having fun with other young men, he may have assisted his physician father and gained some medical knowledge by observation or assisted his father in the courtroom. Later evidence suggests that Edmund canvassed for votes during his father's three successful campaigns for the House of Delegates. He might have also assisted his delegate father at the Capitol in Richmond. If he did, the period between schools heralded the start of his own involvement in politics for the next twenty-two years.[16]

On March 16, 1840, Congressman Taliaferro wrote for the third time to Poinsett and requested that his political colleague's son be admitted to West Point. This time he specified the Virginia seat vacated by (future Confederate general) Richard Ewell's graduation and asked Poinsett to review Edmund's previous reference letters. Curiously, he requested the admission decision to be sent via himself for the Fitzhughs. Two weeks later on April 1, Edmund wrote to Poinsett, the final document in his application file. He "hasten(ed) to communicate to you my acceptance" of the West Point appointment.

In the antebellum years, West Point's admission system sought to balance the nation's sectionalism and uneven educational opportunities by bringing in 250 hopefully smart boys from all walks of life and all states. Cadet selection was wholly a result of political patronage without any military input. Each year, a congressional district got one cadet, each state got two at-large cadets, and the president also got some choices. The goal was to equally offer a superior education, at a school widely known as the best in the country, to students from parts of the nation with inferior educational opportunities. Some cadets arrived in dire need of remedial work, resulting in a high failure and dropout rate.

Although West Point provided one of the best educations in the world, the FFVs and other regional elites did not often send their sons because the system threw together so many kinds of young men.

According to historian James L. Morrison Jr., "Throughout its existence, the corps of cadets has mirrored with fair accuracy the socioeconomic composition, the tensions, and the prejudices of the American middle class." Edmund would be exposed to a very different student body than the one he lived and studied with at Georgetown.[17]

CHAPTER 3

West Point Reptile

A T AGE NINETEEN Cadet Edmund Clare Fitzhugh stepped off the Hudson River steamer from New York City at the West Point landing on July 1, 1840, with only his trunk and without money if he followed the West Point rules. Summer encampment started in June, but he was not as late as some cadets with long, more difficult, journeys. Three doctors examined him on arrival before he was sent to a forbidding gray stone barracks. There he would live in a 12 x 12 room housing five cadets that was hot in the summer, cold in the winter, and lit only by whale oil lamps. The U.S. Military Academy that was to be his home for the coming years was another school as different from home as could be. The sound of drums now dictated Edmund's daily life and would hopefully lead him toward being a professional military officer and engineer, a profession becoming more respected in the South as well as the North. Once provided with his uniform and assigned an upperclassman to teach him military ways, he became a "plebe" or a "reptile," depending on who was addressing him. Hazing, generally designed to elicit personal embarrassment, commenced immediately. He joined his classmates drilling on The Plain, forty acres of pitted, uneven ground that was almost always either muddy or dusty. There his cadet group learned to march in formation and other military maneuvers, no matter the ground's condition, until classes started in September.[1]

One positive to his arrival date was that he was just in time for the Fourth of July, summer's major social event. Festivities and academy rituals went from dawn's reveille to dusk's cannon salute to every state. On August 30, the academy marked the end of summer's military training by hosting a dance with local girls before the year's studies began.

If Edmund was tired of drilling, the academic year did not bring comfort. He had only two hours a day of free time and was required to eat his meals (heavy on boiled beef and potatoes) in twenty minutes. Chapel was required, as it had been at Georgetown. The course of study

Figure 5, The Plain at West Point in an 1828 engraving from a painting by George Catlin. The campus was much the same when E.C. Fitzhugh attended. *U.S. Military Academy Library, Special Collections. Public Domain, accessed at Wikimedia Commons.*

never deviated from math, science, and engineering since the faculty did not teach military tactics or strategy until the final year. For Edmund's first two years, math "in all of its heinous incarnations" would comprise seventy percent of the curriculum, and require a daily recitation in front of the class to earn his homework grade. Surviving the math curriculum those first years was critical to eventual graduation and a commission in the U.S. Army. As he had at Georgetown, Edmund studied French but now it was to read Napoleon's thoughts on war. Being a first-year cadet who had already studied French was a large advantage over Indiana farm boys with a very basic education.[2]

Plebes only had temporary appointments until they passed their first semester of work. Ninety percent of dismissals from West Point resulted from math incompetence, and half of any entering class was dismissed before graduation. June and January exams brought final recitations for all 250 cadets. The exams were called "the Inquisition and the Agony," because they dictated class standing. A professor would call each to the blackboard before the entire faculty to demonstrate what he had learned. When Edmund sank to the bottom level of math expertise, he was labeled an "immortal." Like most other "immortals," Edmund then "died of January Fever." West Point dismissed him on January 13, 1841, for "deficiency in studies," though without many demerits from breaking rules. Edmund either couldn't succeed, or he didn't want to, and flunked out after one semester.[3]

No published works that summarized Edmund Fitzhugh's life mention that he attended West Point, even though in Washington Territory he served as a military aide to West Point graduate Governor Isaac Stevens during the 1856 Treaty War. He knew a number of West Point graduates in the Northwest and two were his close friends: Stevens, who graduated the year before Fitzhugh entered, and Fort Bellingham's Captain George E. Pickett, Class of 1846 and fellow elite Virginian. It is possible that embarrassment prevented Fitzhugh from telling others he had flunked out of the Academy. If his friends knew, they discreetly kept it quiet.[4]

CನಿಲಿO

Edmund went home. His father probably endured some awkward conversations over the young man's second failure to graduate from a prestigious school. In the same way second-son status led his father into medicine, Edmund needed to find a career path quickly that would place him in an approved profession.

No records tell exactly how or where Edmund pursued his law education, but in the autumn of 1843 he advertised his solo law practice. He did not attend either of his state's major law schools: University of Virginia or College of William and Mary. Early Whatcom County historians who associated him with Georgetown assumed that Fitzhugh was a graduate of the law school there and accepted it as fact without checking dates. Georgetown did not establish their law school until 1870, thirty years after his time as a student. In the 1840s an adequate legal education before representing clients was about eighteen months, so Edmund wasted little time before turning to law studies.[5]

There are two possibilities regarding Edmund's study of law. He might have "read law" in Blackstone's *Commentaries* and other available books at the Fitzhugh & Little law firm across the river in Fredericksburg. The firm of Edmund's cousin William H. Fitzhugh and his brother-in-law was well-established, and they might have been happy to sponsor the young man William had known since childhood.

The second possibility was Fredericksburg Law School owned by John Lomax, the University of Virginia's first law professor. In 1830 he left there to become the circuit judge at Fredericksburg. Lomax supplemented his income by opening a small private law school in the basement of his home to produce practicing Virginia attorneys instead of budding politicians. He reconsidered his own lecture and Socratic-method teaching style, and changed to one with textbooks, explanations of material, and examinations. He assigned students daily homework in standard commentaries and tested them every day in class. If Fitzhugh entered in 1841 after leaving West Point, he joined a dozen others in the judge's basement that year.[6]

☙❧

After opening his law practice at age twenty-two, Edmund joined his father in Virginia politics. Alexander had been out of office since Edmund left West Point after serving for three House of Delegate sessions. Falmouth voters dominated local politics in their sparsely populated county, and the Fitzhugh clan dominated affairs both politically and economically. It was not a place of small farms and businesses that would birth a more populist vote. Edmund worked again as a canvasser, touting the Fitzhugh-approved candidates and counting expected votes from the all-male, all-white electorate. It was a job he did well, developing persuasive skills he would use for his profession, as well as his political future in the West.[7]

Dr. Alexander Fitzhugh was succeeded in office by several one-term Stafford County delegates until Edmund ran for the seat in the early months of the Mexican-American War. Elected, he served for the December 7, 1846, to March 23, 1847, term. In Richmond, he joined the Virginia General Assembly whose bicameral legislature, founded in 1619, was the oldest continuous law-making body in the Americas. Edmund joined 133 other men in the magnificent neoclassical Capitol designed by Thomas Jefferson. It faced Capitol Square and the first-ever statue of George Washington, portrayed in civilian retirement with a cane rather than as a military leader. It was certainly an inspiring sight for a newly elected delegate. House leaders assigned Edmund to the First Auditor's Office Committee, which coincidentally provided another skill and political experience he called upon later in Washington Territory.[8]

Though Richmond seemed cosmopolitan with its capital city hubbub, rich cultural life, many free Blacks, and connections to Northern businesses, it also had a seamy side which the city elite chose to ignore as much as possible. When Charles Dickens visited the year after Dr. Fitzhugh left the Assembly, he observed that "slavery sits

Figure 6, State Capitol in Richmond, Virginia, as it appeared during E. C. Fitzhugh's term in the legislature and was photographed in 1901. Although it looked imposing, it was a frame building, not stone. *Library of Congress, Prints and Photographs Division, #LC-D4-13440.*

brooding...there is an air of ruin and decay abroad which is inseparable from the system." Dilapidated slave quarter cabins sat behind the swanky mansions of prominent Virginians. Some slaves in the city had been rented out by slave masters like Edmund's father and given an allowance to find their own housing anywhere they could. Just a few blocks from the Capitol and its governmental hub on Shockoe Hill was Wall Street, with its slave jails, holding pens, and auction houses for thousands of men, women, and children soon to be traded and sold like any other property. In Richmond, the slave trade was a legitimate business that may have dated to the city's founding in Virginia Colony.[9]

If Edmund hadn't met State Senator Lafayette ("Fayette") McMullen when his father served in the Assembly, he surely met him during his own term. The former stagecoach driver and farmer from the Shenandoah Valley served ten years in the Assembly and four terms in the U.S. Congress. By the time Edmund met him, McMullen had already established a reputation for condescension, a puritanical streak, and a hot temper which sometimes led to fist fights and assaults, even while in the legislature. He and Edmund were destined to meet again a decade later and thousands of miles away.[10]

Edmund and his fellow legislators could not have perceived the monumental importance in the future of one action they took during his single term in office. The Assembly authorized Samuel F.B. Morse and partners to build telegraph lines along the growing web of railroad lines that intersected at Richmond and ran from major Northern cities to Washington, DC, and south to the Carolinas. In early 1847 only three years had passed since he sent the famous first telegram with his invention, but it had already shown its importance in the Mexican-American War.[11]

☙❧

Edmund did not serve Stafford County again in his father's former House of Delegates seat (perhaps at the same desk) after his term ended on March 23, 1847. Despite the ongoing war with Mexico, he failed at least once to appear that summer for the required monthly muster of the 45th Virginia Militia, the same regiment Dr. Fitzhugh served in during the War of 1812. Because of white fears of slave uprisings, a few years earlier the state counted 111,000 militiamen, almost fourteen times the men in the U.S. Army. Stafford County's militia was energized by the 1804 revolt of the 250 Fitzhugh "Chatham" slaves only four miles from Falmouth and the 1831 Nat Turner revolt when 55 whites died in Virginia.[12]

It is possible that Edmund's legislative career ended after only one term neither by choice nor by electoral defeat. Though Dr. Fitzhugh was only fifty-nine, he seems to have needed help (requested or not) from his lawyer son to administer his property of 295 acres and slaves, though he still continued as magistrate after leaving his medical practice.[13]

Until E. C. Fitzhugh left Virginia, he was fully immersed in slaveowner culture and the slave trade. On February 16, 1846, Edmund did the writing for his father in a letter to R. H. Dickinson, the biggest slave dealer in Richmond, though he was only a beginner in the trade. Between 1846 and 1849, Dickinson and his brother sold about two thousand people every year. They had usually acquired them from smaller traders and individuals like Edmund's father, then resold to other traders who took the enslaved people to the slave markets of New Orleans and other Deep South cities. At the time Dr. Fitzhugh sent some of his slaves to Dickinson for auction, the price for a desirable male slave reached $860, a comparable value of almost $27,000 in 2021.[14]

In his letter, Dr. Fitzhugh "beg[s]" Dickinson not to sell Lucy for less than $500 [2021 = over $16,500] and Maria for $450. He wanted them returned to him if those prices could not be met. Edmund added his own note that his father was surprised and "rather vexed" that his man Godfrey had sold for only $571, and he regretted sending him for sale at all, since he could have brought $600 in Falmouth "very readily." Perhaps an indication of his physical decline, Dr. Fitzhugh added a shakily written postscript to what Edmund had penned for him, saying that he was also angry Edmund's expenses in taking the slaves to Richmond and boarding them had been $50, possibly because Edmund had stayed in the nearby hotel Dickinson ran for the slave traders. Alexander thought the cost was excessive if Godfrey did not bring a large enough profit to be worth it.[15]

Alexander's main concern was the maximization of his profit, not what happened to Godfrey, Lucy, or Maria. Edmund left them behind in the holding pens on Lumpkin's Alley until sale day when they would be auctioned, probably to other traders who would take them to Louisiana for another auction. There was no mention of the trio being a family unit to be kept together or the loss of their familiar home.

The several slave holding jails that comprised Lumpkin's Alley were also known as "the Devil's half acre." The main building had bars, high fences, and chained gates. People passing by on the way to the Capitol three blocks ahead smelled a miasma of cooking smoke and human excrement. People often died of starvation or disease in the nearly airless jails without toilets. That was where Godfrey, Lucy, and Maria waited to be auctioned off, destination unknown.[16]

By the mid-1840s, Edmund's hometown was a shadow of its past, its decline increasingly visible. It would never have Richmond's bustle. It would never be the cultural, political, and business center that Edmund had come to appreciate in the city. It may be that in wartime 1847 Edmund began to consider a different future for himself other than as a small-town lawyer and incoming family patriarch. After his ailing father died, Edmund would be responsible for Virginia, then 19, Rosalie (age 17), and Helen (age 15), continuing the paternalistic supervision and support customary in an FFV family. His older sister, Mary Eliza, had recently married Dr. Hezekiah Magruder (from another prominent American family) and moved to Washington, DC. In 1847 the unmarried girls would never be left to live alone before marriage if they wanted to be "ladies."[17]

It was also a time of national turning points. Edmund's legislative term went on while the Mexican American War continued and young men everywhere joined the Army. Though he was twenty-five, as an Assembly representative and a professional man he did not volunteer despite his earlier West Point and militia experience. The term "Manifest Destiny," coined in 1845, was becoming part of the national lexicon and young men like Edmund at least considered the possibilities for riches and adventure—new lives that would help fulfill the country's expansionist ambition all the way to the Pacific coast. The 49th parallel had recently been affirmed as the dividing line with Canada west of the Rocky Mountains and assured new possibilities in the "Oregon Country" of the Pacific Northwest. National expansion and the proliferation of new states brought the issue of legal slavery's extension into a national dispute. In just a few months gold would be discovered at Sutter's Mill in California.

Before any nascent ambitions could emerge, Edmund faced family trouble when he returned from Richmond in March 1847 to resume a full-time legal practice. Just three months later Dr. Fitzhugh deeded everything he owned to his son in a trust, revealing that he had financially betrayed his children. When Edmund was a small child, his mother's brother James Clare died unmarried in 1824 and his will left Eliza's present and future children all proceeds from the sale of his land and slaves. Edmund's uncle had appointed their father the trust administrator, holding the proceeds for their benefit when each child came of age. For the girls, that would mean a substantial dowry; for Edmund, a start on his financial future. It's possible that the children were kept ignorant of their inheritance because Edmund and his sister Mary Eliza should have received their share some years earlier, but Alexander never transferred the funds to them. In the years since 1824 their father had looted the fund for his own benefit. This could have been to buy land, or it could have been for gambling on horse races at the Chatham track, or some other selfish desire. The 1847 trust deed to Edmund did not indicate what Alexander did with all the money, nor how much had been lost. It is even possible that he did not spend the money until after his wife died. The new Deed in Trust to Edmund stated that everything was to be sold, and the surviving five siblings were to be repaid with interest what Alexander had squandered *before* his other debts were paid.[18]

Dr. Alexander Fitzhugh died exactly three months after signing over all his property to his children. Edmund began disposing of the property to pay back himself and his sisters what they should have received, then he paid the debts, and dispersed the remainder to the five heirs. In late October 1847, Edmund (as trustee) placed an ad in the *Richmond Enquirer* for the auction of his father's property in front of the United States Hotel at Fredericksburg's main intersection. This included a 278-acre plantation known as "St. George's Place" (from its former owner's name), a house, outbuildings, and a carriage. There were also horses, cattle, sheep, and hogs, as well as equipment and crops of corn, oats, hay, and fodder. Edmund was willing to sell all these on time contracts to dispose of them quickly, but the enslaved people he was selling were a different "commodity" in his eyes.[19]

Edmund's advertisement listed the most important property first—his father's slaves. One by one they stood at auction on the 800-pound, flat-topped stone on the Fredericksburg corner where the other property would later be auctioned. For a local auction, Edmund and other slave masters kept their enslaved people, old and young, in a warehouse until their time to step up on the block, as former slave Fannie Brown later recalled. She called the warehouse a "brutish, inhuman" place where prospective white buyers milled around examining the people they were considering buying.[20]

The ad made it clear that only cash would be accepted for slave purchases, implying that Fitzhugh wanted to insure against the slave dying, and the buyer refusing to pay off the contract. He said there would be thirty to forty "likely" men, women, and children. Among the men were a "first-rate blacksmith" and an "excellent cooper." Several "valuable" house servants were among the women. He either did not sell a few, or purposely kept some to continue working at the Falmouth home, because three years later he paid property tax on three slaves over sixteen and three who were twelve to fifteen (only nine to twelve at the time of the auction, perhaps children of older women). Years later, in January of 1858 when he lived in Washington Territory, he still owned an elderly infirm woman in Falmouth, perhaps living with one of his sisters.[21]

Historian Elizabeth Fox-Genovese wrote that Southern men never abandoned brutality and force, traits that lay just under a surface disguised by heavy drinking, gambling, and dueling. The willingness to sell children away from their mothers was part of that. This attitude was fully part of Edmund, ready to emerge later at Bellingham Bay, Washington.[22]

In early August of 1848, after the Mexican-American War ended, news of California's gold strike finally made its way into the eastern newspapers. Young men everywhere started making plans to go west and become millionaires, including the gold miners who were fruitlessly working the nearly played-out Rappahannock and Rapidan River deposits.

While the first shiploads were leaving for California, the slavery issue was enflaming national politics. Senator John C. Calhoun of South Carolina wrote an address to the nation protesting Northern "acts of aggression" against the slaveholders of the South with the intent to destroy their institution. Still under military authority, California's undetermined status regarding slavery was becoming a national issue.

During the post-war year when news of the California gold strike spread, Edmund engaged in an assortment of personal transactions that benefited himself and his sisters. He moved toward severing most financial ties to Virginia and turning investments into cash. In order to leave for the West, he also needed to get his three unmarried sisters settled. Three of their aunts now owned Boscobel, and it is most likely that the sisters were able to live there. Several other Fitzhugh clan houses would also be available. Edmund freed himself from daily responsibility for the girls.[23]

In March 1850 Edmund filed a debt collection lawsuit in Fredericksburg's circuit court, which also raised cash. Real estate sale transactions in the two towns continued for several years in absentia. The twenty-nine-year-old lawyer from Falmouth was already long gone from Virginia.[24]

CHAPTER 4

A Young Lawyer's Paradise

AFTER THE CALIFORNIA GOLD STRIKE made eastern newspaper headlines in August 1848, gold fever took hold, but winter weather was closing in and trips west by any means were postponed. Edmund Fitzhugh had time to gather his funds. When the bachelor was ready to leave home in 1849, the largest migration in American history was on. He joined about six hundred other lawyers headed for California, knowing that gold miners and new businesses would need legal expertise of every kind. Statehood was coming soon and there would be elected and appointed positions in the federal, state, and city governments for lawyers.[1]

A constitutional convention in Monterey approved California statehood while Fitzhugh was en route, and it joined the union as a free state. The politically minded Democrats who favored California's becoming a slave state had to settle for expanding their power through numbers and promoting a slavery-friendly West Coast congressional bloc going forward. Fitzhugh would fit in.

Lawyer Joseph Baldwin summed up his profession's national utopia during those years: "[the] most cheering and exhilarating prospects of fussing, quarrelling, murdering, violation of contracts, and the whole catalogue of crimen falsi...What country could boast more largely of its crimes. What more splendid role of felonies! What more terrific murders! What more gorgeous bank robberies! What more magnificent operations in the land offices!"[2]

Most of the prospective gold miners were young men who, except perhaps for service in the Mexican War, had never been far from home. They were generally without gold mining experience, although many from the Rappahannock mines headed west. The prospectors, skilled workers, and the lawyers all believed in Manifest Destiny and the fortunes to be had in the West for the ambitious. Working-class men (and some women) rarely had the savings to travel the sea routes, so they started the long trek across the country on foot, by horseback, or in wagons hoping to live through the overland route's many dangers.

The Cape Horn route by sailing ship was the choice of skilled laborers and others with some money. It was also the most disease-free route. The negative was monumentally stormy seas off Cape Horn and in the open oceans that could sink a barely seaworthy vessel commandeered as a gold rush profit-maker. Passengers also endured seasickness and the tedium of five to nine months of boredom and bad food.[3]

The Panama route chosen by Edmund Fitzhugh was the fast "clean-fingernails route…the way of the wealthy, the well-educated, and the fastidious." Fitzhugh fit in with the shipload of lawyers, well-financed entrepreneurs, ambitious potential bureaucrats and candidates, some professional gamblers, and a few women of questionable character. His trust fund monies, financial transactions, and attorney's fees financed the steamer reservation and his stake in a new life. Though the steamer ticket to San Francisco would cost well over $10,000 today, Edmund Fitzhugh had the $420 it cost in 1849. He packed his baggage and law books, bade farewell to his sisters, and left Virginia for what would be eleven years. One sister would not survive to see him again.[4]

Edmund's expensive choice of routes to San Francisco cut many months and 8,000 miles off the voyage. It meant taking a steamer to the small town of Chagres on Spanish Panama's Caribbean coast. The sail-assisted side-wheelers were the latest in technology, but it still meant the first leg of his journey took about two months. California-bound "argonauts" found a place where "bilious, remittent, and congestive fever, in their most malignant forms, seem to hover…ever ready to pounce down on the stranger." For the next leg, Fitzhugh either boarded one of the small river steamers brought into Panama that year, or a bungo canoe piloted by a local boatman who poled and navigated the shallow water of the Chagres River. If Fitzhugh had to take the canoe option, he camped out at night in clouds of mosquitos and other biting insects, listening to the rain forest symphony of screeches, howls, and growls. Crocodiles inhabited the shallows and might invade the tent encampment looking for a meal themselves. The deadly fer-de-lance snake might slither beneath a man's blanket. After reaching two soggy riverside villages forty miles inland through the rain forest's hills, Fitzhugh stayed in one of the new small hotels or a home, both plagued by fleas and mosquitos. The final leg meant walking (very undesirable) or a mule train twenty miles down the Pacific drainage to the west coast. Fitzhugh saw narrow-gauge railroad tracks under construction, but the line wouldn't be finished for another six years when the train would make the forty-seven-mile trip across the isthmus in four hours, instead of a torturous week. Fitzhugh and his miserable companions anxiously awaited the first sight of Panama City's ornate cathedral in the distance above the jungle. American travelers were overwhelming the small city where sometimes a thousand men waited days or weeks for the next steamer. When it anchored offshore, the ship might have only 250 berths—most pre-paid before leaving the States. Any lucky extras who obtained a bargain ticket up the Pacific coast slept on the deck. That part of Fitzhugh's journey took another twenty days of tedium interrupted by gambling and the women of questionable character.[5]

The Panama route, like the overland one, held disease dangers the Cape Horn ocean route did not. Despite being the quickest route, tropical diseases awaited on the isthmus when '49ers had to stay over for any length of time. Hundreds died of cholera, yellow fever, and malaria before they ever embarked up the Pacific coast. Fitzhugh himself contracted what he called "Panama Fever," a malaria variant caught from tropical mosquitos that were most numerous during the months he traveled. Malaria victims suffered a cold stage of chills and shakes; then a hot stage of fever, headache, and vomiting; and finally, a sweating stage if they survived. While yellow fever conferred immunity on the survivor, malaria did not. Fitzhugh survived it all, but he suffered from recurrent malarial episodes for over a decade, if not for the rest of his life. Those who survived Panama didn't know that one-fifth of the early migrants would then die of diseases caught in California in their first six months.[6]

The Panama route also exposed the young Americans to their first experience with foreign peoples in exotic towns and cities who spoke unintelligible languages. Fitzhugh had met foreigners from the diplomatic corps while a student at Georgetown College, and perhaps some others when he was in Richmond. His French classes at Georgetown may have provided a small advantage in understanding Spanish. He soon encountered foreigners from a myriad of countries in San Francisco, and he would learn to live among a diverse population without the social buffer his Virginia privileges had provided.

⋘⋙

The entrance to San Francisco Bay was hair-raising for any type of ship, and many shoddy sailing vessels foundered and sank there. Fitzhugh's steamer entered wide San Francisco Bay through the roiling, tide-driven, narrow gap between hills. Gold rushers called it the "Golden Gate," entrance to their dreams of quick wealth. As twenty-eight-year-old Fitzhugh passed through the island-studded bay and saw San Francisco for the first time, his new home gave the word "vibrant" a whole new meaning. He saw a port city like no other.

Hundreds of vessels floated in front of, and beyond, a thrown-together business district of canvas and wood. New and old. Large and small. And built on land and ships never to sail again. Abandoned vessels became boarding houses and stores along the wharves where gaps would soon be infilled to make new streets. Sometimes ship cabins were ripped off and turned into "rooms" for the fortunate few among thousands of new arrivals. By late in the year when Fitzhugh arrived, a two-story hotel had risen from the deck of the scuttled ship *Niantic* where it was permanently jammed tight against its wharf. Nearby a store rose above the deck of another grounded ship, its masts still intact.[7]

Fitzhugh walked into the cacophony of sawing, hammering, and piles being driven into the sand to expand the waterfront with wharf after wharf. Where at first there was a dire shortage of needed (and unneeded) goods, by the time he arrived a glut of barrels and boxes was building on the waterfront and in nearby streets where spilled contents rotted. From the streets beyond, he could hear "music, music, music; the rattle of the roulette, the monte, the faro bank [that] salute you about twice in each square; jamming into restaurants, butchers' stalls, vegetable stores, and red flags before some going, going, gone auctioneer who sells a cargo in just about three shakes of a sheep's tail."[8]

In the distance around the crescent from the main townsite, Happy Valley's tents and shanties housed unskilled men, while carpenters, blacksmiths, and other skilled workers lived in Pleasant Valley. Thousands of miners pitched flea- and rat-infested tents as far as two miles inland until they began making their way up the fifty-mile-long bay toward the rivers descending from the Sierra Nevada and into the gold fields. That would not be Fitzhugh's world. His would be the few blocks centered on the dirt of Portsmouth Square. The re-named plaza in front of the old, red-roofed adobe Mexican custom house became the center for merchants, money men, and professionals. Morning fog inevitably cloaked all the infant city and hills behind.

Once a quiet outpost of the Mexican government called Yerba Buena, the now-American outpost of San Francisco had two thousand residents in April 1849 as Fitzhugh probably prepared to leave home. By the 1850 U.S. census the town had ballooned to 34,776. These argonauts were sure they would go home millionaires, either by mining or preying on miners, and the fortune-seekers just kept coming on hundreds of ships from ports American and foreign.[9]

And who were these young men who elected to stay in San Francisco? Early California historian H.H. Bancroft derisively summed them up: "Fugitives from trouble and dishonor had been lured to California, graceless scions of respectable families and never-do-wells, men of wavering virtue and frail piety, withering before temptation and sham-haters, turned to swell the army of knaves." It was a perfect milieu for Fitzhugh, professionally and personally.[10]

Fitzhugh always told people he arrived in 1849 and evidence suggests he disembarked late that year, having transited Panama in prime mosquito-transmitted disease season. If Panama had been an eye-opener, San Francisco must have seemed like a foreign country. It probably hit Fitzhugh his first day that the genteel life he knew in Virginia was gone. He was a newcomer in a whole new world.

◑◐

First, Fitzhugh needed a place to sleep. His new lodgings may have been like those of most arriving professional men in 1849: a tiny, over-priced enclosure with a bed. The *New York Evening Post* reported in November that year that there wasn't a house in the city that didn't leak. People considered the new Montgomery House a top establishment with its small carpeted sitting room separated from the dining room by a shabby cloth strip, the saloon with a box stove, and short narrow rooms that slept two. Better places with soft mattresses, clean sheets, and an upscale menu were still on the way. After a spare beginning, Fitzhugh may have lived in the law office he joined, as many did, or in one of the few private homes that took in well-heeled boarders. No matter what his living quarters were, they weren't Boscobel's big house or even his parents' small home. When even the best accommodations were crowded, and the worst were rat-infested tents where dysentery reigned, an "acquired insensitivity" to death soon infected '49ers from the city to the gold fields.[11]

The prices Fitzhugh saw in makeshift restaurants and produce stands probably shocked him. He could afford the prices that only attracted the well-heeled or someone with a desperate craving, but it was still a surprise to the newcomer. For example, a $1.00 apple would cost over $35 today, and some grocers sold them for $5 that year. Four-cent bread in New York City commanded as much as seventy-five in San Francisco. Despite that, when Delmonico's opened on Portsmouth Square in 1850, lawyer Fitzhugh could afford mock turtle soup, "boeuf a la mode," and apple pie for dessert, all accompanied by a fine bottle of "St. Julian Medoc" wine from France.[12]

During Fitzhugh's first winter, rain fell nearly every day. He walked half-liquid streets, into which Edmund could sink to his knees in his expensive boots as he began to put a new life together. Legends grew about men and horses disappearing into the deep mud—the men's bodies recovered and the horses' not. The bad winter led to some planking of the streets around Portsmouth Square, but the next dry seasons and careless burning led to the first of six fires that ravaged the city over the next few years. Historian Bancroft called the 1850 city an "eyesore" of burned buildings and hill regrades with "dumps and blotches of hills and hillocks of bleak spots of vacancy and ugly cuts and raised lines." The gold rush momentum was unstoppable, and residents quickly replaced lost wooden structures to enable business to go on as usual.[13]

Already by summer 1849, while Fitzhugh traveled west, a letter back to the *Washington National Intelligencer* said, "This is one of the strangest places in Christendom. I know many men who were models of piety, morality, and all that sort of thing, when they first arrived here, and who are now the most desperate gamblers and drunkards." That described the first vanguard of the thousands to follow and it only got worse, despite new city laws and a small influx of "respectable" women and clergy who diligently fought the moral rot they saw around them. Fitzhugh never abandoned this boisterous lifestyle that exacerbated the behavior he learned in Virginia.[14]

Loneliness, despite the crowds, miserable accommodations, possession of pokes of gold nuggets, and high wages for service providers (like Fitzhugh), led to gambling and drinking everywhere and at every hour day or night. San Francisco birthed as many as one thousand saloons catering to every professional man, blue-collar worker from Pleasant Valley, or ragged miner trying to escape tent city squalor for a few hours. The cacophony of music, shouts of the winner, and wails of the newly impoverished loser filled the air. The vast amounts of money lost amid a sea of alcohol, drunk for entertainment (and because there was no clean water), fed pervasive fighting and other violence. Within a few months of Fitzhugh's arrival, "The Empire" had a frescoed 140-foot-long gambling hall, though in September a new city law prohibited gambling on Sunday. City fathers hoped that by having one day without vice, men would do laundry and maybe reclaim some of the religion they left far behind. However, a bull ring and other Sunday amusements still offered a place to empty the pockets of those with cash.[15]

Fitzhugh's life quickly centered on the treeless old plaza that remained the center of all commercial life. The surrounding streets housed merchants, money exchange houses, speculators, and lawyers. The dirt square itself was occupied by booths hawking provisions to miners heading out, piles of building supplies, hotels, restaurants, gambling houses, and even animals on the way to slaughter. The new Jenny Lind Theater on the square offered more cultured entertainment. Fitzhugh could leave his office to read local or eastern newspapers at the Merchant's Exchange or a sizable bookstore. When a Pacific Mail steamship came in every two weeks or so, excited crowds converged on the square waiting for the post office to distribute mail from home and send theirs back. Portsmouth Square hosted all speechifying and any important large event, especially the July Fourth celebration when patriotic residents raised an American flag (gift of the citizens of

Figure 7, Portsmouth Square, San Francisco in January 1851. Telegraph Hill is in the distance. Daguerreotype by Sterling McIntyre. *Daguerreotype Collection. David D. Porter family papers #DAG1331. Library of Congress, Prints and Photographs Division.*

Portland, Oregon) atop a 111-foot flagpole. Fitzhugh was there for the October 29, 1850, celebration of the new state's admission to the Union with sunrise and sunset gun salutes and a ball in the evening.[16]

⊂ℬℛ⊃

Fitzhugh's sartorial style fit right in since the men of Portsmouth Square's neighborhood separated themselves from the miners in work boots by wearing suits every day and dressing up in order to frequent the upscale restaurants and saloons. Miners and others in their homely work clothes saw a big difference in manliness between themselves and the "dandies" in suits with clean hands, be they gamblers or professional men. The hundreds of lawyers pursuing clients often earned the workingmen's anger because they and other professionals sought to fill every possible political office in the new state. The notion of freedom and equality many '49ers were attracted to turned out to be unattainable when a professional elite built another social structure of haves and have-nots. Already by the time Fitzhugh arrived, lawyers were "reaping a tremendous harvest" with their lowest fee being $100, according to a reporter warning those still home about the gold rush economy. Equal to about $3000 today, at the same time their first law offices were in cellars and shanties for which they paid only $250 a month in rent. At those rates, Fitzhugh could expect his financial circumstances to quickly change.[17]

When Fitzhugh, in business suit and expensive boots, stepped off the Pacific Mail steamer, he had his trunk and carried Virginia connections that would ease his way. Some were Fitzhugh-related, some political, some from his profession, and some just because he was a fellow Southern gentleman. Contacts, whether in letters of reference or simply in his memory, helped Fitzhugh join two of San Francisco's most prestigious law firms.

At twenty-nine, Edmund Randolph headed Crittenden and Randolph, the most important law firm in the city. Fitzhugh joined his third cousin's firm for an indeterminate time, though not as a partner. Some people called Randolph an "impetuous Southerner," hardworking but not companionable and with few good friends. H. H. Bancroft described him as "gifted, eccentric…excitable, and proud of his standing." Close cousins by First Family of Virginia standards, their ancestors and extended families had been intertwined in politics, social circles, and marriages since colonial times. Randolph carried the name of his grandfather Edmund Jennings Randolph, the nation's first attorney general, then U.S. secretary of state and governor of Virginia. That background alone made Randolph a major player in founding California's new Southern-dominated social and political elite. He was also the grandmaster of the Virginia Masonic Lodge, an organization with which the Fitzhughs were deeply involved for generations. Joining Crittenden and Randolph gave Fitzhugh instant credibility.[18]

Randolph's partner A. P. Crittenden was serving in the first legislature, and two self-taught lawyers were members of the firm. Frank Tilford, an up-and-coming politician from Kentucky, handled criminal cases. Rufus Lockwood had once appeared before the Connecticut State Supreme Court, but he soon dumped his San Francisco firm and his family to be a sailor. Fitzhugh joined the firm, and some evidence indicates that he did the firm's business upriver in the gold fields.[19]

The Vigilance Committee of 1851 was the first test of democracy and the rule of law in San Francisco. The 700-member vigilante group formed in response to lax law enforcement in the face of an Australian gang and hung four people before disbanding.

The Crittenden and Randolph firm publicly opposed the extra-legal, self-appointed judge and jury group that threatened the rule of law and people's lives. Randolph and associates defied the Committee out of both regard for the law and personal pride, according to Bancroft. Fitzhugh's name does not appear in accounts of his firm's opposition, but all the lawyers he worked with in San Francisco were part of the opposition and his name appears nowhere on Committee membership lists. Vigilance Committee membership did include the names of several men with whom he would do business two years later: Charles Minturn and R. P. Hammond. Others he would meet again in Washington Territory, most significantly J.J.H. Van Bokkelen, an incompatible nemesis.[20]

Twenty-five-year-old Calhoun Benham affected Fitzhugh's Washington Territory future the most. They joined forces as Benham & Fitzhugh sometime in 1851, after Benham was elected U.S. District Attorney for Northern California.

From Cincinnati, Benham was the son of a former Ohio Supreme Court chief justice. Benham had his own political connection that Fitzhugh might think he could use to his advantage someday. Benham's uncle was former Vice President John C. Calhoun from

South Carolina, who had recently died while serving in the U.S. Senate. Benham carried both his uncle's name and his defense of states' rights. He was a Southern sympathizer, which made his politics acceptable to California's South-leaning Democrats. Benham's mother-in-law was another of Fitzhugh's third cousins and knew his family in Virginia. Edmund's sister, Mary Eliza, had also married into Benham's Fendall-Marbury extended family. This admittedly intricate web of marriage and social relationships was important to such men, and easily discovered and used when the two met. A conversation that began "Oh, my mother-in-law is a Fitzhugh" would quickly lead into one about the multiple family connections.[21]

⊂ॐ⊃

Bankers, newspapers, and law offices collected along Montgomery Street between the chaotic waterfront and Portsmouth Square, the site in 1851 of speeches, protests, and also Vigilance Committee hangings. Because of that concentration, the street also became the center of newly organized Whig and Democratic parties. Incoming Northerners (often Whigs) focused on commercial business, leaving the door open for the Southern Democrat minority to focus on politics. The new elite, almost all Southerners, organized the California Democratic Party in October 1849, close to when Fitzhugh arrived and a year before statehood. They were determined to influence the government into a pro-South stance despite California's entry into the union as a free state. California's first senator and "Southern gentleman," William Gwin, led the pejoratively labeled "Chivalry," the pro-slavery faction of the party, and his presence in Washington, DC, meant he influenced hundreds of federal appointments in California. David Broderick, an immigrant's son from New York City, led the working-class Democratic faction called "The Shovelry" who were only mildly anti-slavery. Virginians found their way into appointive and elective offices at every level.[22]

Fitzhugh worked once more as a Democratic Party canvasser, but this time it was with a rowdier, and often drunk, constituency. He worked the streets, saloons, offices, and anywhere else a voter could be found in the establishments that had become the city's living rooms. He counted votes and tried to convince men to show up for the Democrats' candidates, especially the ones approved by Senator Gwin. Stuffing ballot boxes and the buying of votes were common. By the time Fitzhugh canvassed in Whatcom County, Washington Territory, a few years later, he saw no problem using intimidation, threats, and ballot box irregularities to obtain votes that went the Democratic way.

Senator William Gwin was fifteen years older than Fitzhugh, both a lawyer and physician who had been President Andrew Jackson's personal secretary and knew Benham's uncle, Jackson's vice president. In that position, Gwin learned the art of patronage before he represented Mississippi in Congress. Like Benham, he spoke for Southern pro-slavery conservatism in California's politics, as well as leading the drive for a Pacific voting bloc or even republic. He had no problem with obvious corruption, open bribery, and lack of secret elections while still managing to cultivate an image of the magnanimous, wealthy, well-educated, and astute Southerner. He made himself California's most powerful national spokesman.[23]

Senator Gwin mentored Edmund Fitzhugh, a relationship that proved highly advantageous. People coveted invitations to Senator

and Mrs. Gwin's informal and formal gatherings at their home, where a thirty-year-old budding political operative in his perhaps-frilled linen shirt and frock coat could meet more people who might be useful to him later.[24]

❦

Figure 8, Senator William McKendree Gwin, E. C. Fitzhugh's friend and political mentor. Photographed by Matthew Brady's studio. *Daguerreotype Collection #DAG 197/#LC-USZ62-11003, Library of Congress, Prints and Photographs Division.*

Twenty-four-hour gambling and drinking for any size wallet continued to be the most readily available entertainment during Fitzhugh's years in San Francisco. He could bet on card games, dice, bull fights, cockfights, boxing, and even horse racing. It was inevitable that the mixture of liquor and men who were winners and losers led to arguments and fisticuffs. Elite Southern men, however, still believed it was socially acceptable to challenge a cheater to a duel. Most challenges never progressed to imminent death from a pistol shot, but some did. The lack of any consistent law enforcement in those early years led men to believe correctly that avenging personal wrongs by duel would not be punished.[25]

Fitzhugh took part in an important one in 1852. Seventy-odd years later, Lottie Roeder Roth wrote that he was a "Second" in the much-publicized fatal Broderick-Terry duel of 1859. What she did not realize was that David Broderick ("Shovelry" leader) was in two duels, not just the one that killed him. Or that Fitzhugh was in a courtroom in Port Townsend, Washington Territory, that day in 1859. Fitzhugh was, however, the second at Broderick's first duel seven years earlier.[26]

Dueling had a long history in the United States, including those fought by congressmen and two presidents as well as the famously fatal one between Vice President Aaron Burr and Secretary of the Treasury Alexander Hamilton. Duelists included a number of Fitzhughs. Laws forbidding it were on the books, but until the social consensus agreed there was more disgrace in dueling than in shrugging off an insult, the laws were often ignored. Southern men like the Fitzhughs believed that there were simply some personal offenses that could not be settled by any other means, and dueling communicated to other men that the opponents were men of honor. That led to both social and internal pressures on a man to risk his life, though frequently opponents shot past each other on purpose.[27]

Californians fought duels over personal slights like cheating at the gambling table, but also over political differences that reached the boiling point. This was how Fitzhugh became involved. Those who supported political duels thought they cemented ties between politicians when one demonstrated his commitment to principles over the value of his own life. This was thought to make him worthy of loyalty from his fellows. The custom was carried to San Francisco with Southern men from the social class most committed to duels of honor. For them, filing a lawsuit communicated weakness instead of commitment to the rule of law, though duel opponents were frequently lawyers themselves. Most politics-based challenges in California were never carried through because seconds like Fitzhugh negotiated a settlement.[28]

The dispute started at the 1851 Democratic Party convention, when "Shovelry" leader Broderick was not only denied election to delegate for the national convention, he wasn't awarded even a delegate seat at the state convention. He rightly saw it as the machinations of William Gwin's faction and got into several physical altercations at the convention. In a speech to the assemblage, Broderick insulted former Virginia governor William ("Extra Billy") Smith who was there, whereupon his son, Judge J. Caleb Smith, issued a challenge.[29]

Caleb Smith chose Fitzhugh as his second—to prepare the pistols, make sure he didn't get ambushed, and that the code was followed. Smith's father was in the Virginia Senate at the same time as Fitzhugh's father was in the House of Delegates. Their young sons could have met in the Capitol halls and become friends close enough that Smith would want Fitzhugh by his side. In addition, William Smith was governor when Edmund Fitzhugh held a seat in the House of Delegates. In 1850 then-Congressman William Smith was present in California to preside over the first Democratic Convention before he returned to Virginia. He traveled to San Francisco to see his son Caleb, now a judge, and attended the 1851 convention during which Broderick insulted him publicly. Lastly, for everyone, Fitzhugh was obviously familiar with the *code duello,* even though Virginia had outlawed duels ten years before his birth.

The code duello dictated a duel's ritual, and the steps were clearly laid out in order after the insult. There was an exchange of letters that demanded apology or explanation for why the offense was not an insult. Next came the challenge with the acceptance and appointment of seconds. The seconds made the when-and-where arrangements. Usually, the duel took place far from the local authorities at a commonly used "dueling ground," this time across the bay on the empty future site of Oakland. The ritualistic steps would give Fitzhugh and Broderick's second more time to negotiate and prevent the actual duel from taking place.[30]

Assistant Fire Chief "Dutch Charley" Duane supplied one of the pistols and a few years later gave the most accurate eyewitness account of the March 17, 1852, Broderick-Smith duel. He said the New Yorker believed that if he refused the Virginian's challenge, he would not be able to move in "good society" and would be treated with contempt as a coward.[31]

Boats ferried spectators across the bay all night long in deep fog. At the appointed time, about two hundred gathered in two crowds about a quarter mile apart. Congressman William Smith stood by to support the son risking his life to defend his father's personal honor.[32]

Fitzhugh and the other second had already negotiated the use of Navy revolvers ten paces apart, with the signal to be "1, 2, 3...fire." The men were to advance toward each other if they desired and keep firing until all six shots were used. Each man was to bring a pistol with him. Broderick had borrowed a previously defective and repaired gun from Duane. When the seconds tossed a coin for who got which pistol, Fitzhugh got the borrowed (and possibly still defective) Duane pistol for the judge to use. Caleb Smith's own pistol was the same make, but he had never fired it. That one went to Broderick. Thus, each man was to shoot with the unpredictable and potentially defective pistol brought by the other.

Broderick had a heavy, double-cased watch in his pocket and tried to give it to his second, who said to keep it and told the New Yorker "if you are shot, die like a gentleman." Fitzhugh and his opposite handed the designated pistols to the men and counted out ten paces. The duel commenced. Broderick's Smith-owned pistol showed the same defect as the repaired Duane pistol, now in the hand of Smith. When Broderick put it between his knees to cock it, Smith shot him in the stomach. Although Broderick fell to the ground, he still managed to cock the pistol. He and Smith kept firing at each other until all their bullets were gone. Fitzhugh ran to Smith, but he had not been hit. The bullet that hit Broderick had struck him in the watch case and his only wound was from fragments that cut his stomach.

Broderick wanted to reload and keep shooting. Fitzhugh and his counterpart ordered the spectators who had crowded around to move back and discussed what to do before conferring with the principals. Fitzhugh then announced to Broderick's second that Smith acknowledged that Broderick was an honorable man by answering his challenge. Broderick accepted it as sufficient before he and Smith shook hands. What might Fitzhugh and the other second have talked about that led to the end? The usual argument that led to a resolution without shooting was that there was an inequality of skill or an age difference.[33]

Five years later, after another duel challenge involving Fitzhugh, future Confederate General and Virginian Captain George Pickett would save the life of U.S. Secretary of War Jefferson Davis's nephew because he knew how much experience Fitzhugh had with duels and guns. Two years after that, David Broderick was not saved by his watch when Fitzhugh's former law partner Calhoun Benham served as second for his duel opponent.[34]

♋

Fitzhugh certainly helped fight at least six major San Francisco fires by the end of November 1852, because every adult's help was needed on the bucket brigades. Starting on Christmas Eve 1849, fire swept away the Portsmouth Square area of important offices and businesses over and over, often within just a few months. The worst were the ones of May and June 1851.

The May 4-5 fire started in a paint and upholstery shop next to the post office on the square late at night when a high wind was blowing. The plank sidewalks built to keep people out of deep mud and animal waste helped spread the fire to more buildings. By the next day the "very heart of the city, the center of trade and business, was eaten out." Eighteen blocks containing two thousand buildings burned, most of the city. One new supposedly fireproof iron building's residents died when the doors melted shut during the ten-hour inferno. Bewildered and despairing residents gathered on the open ground of Portsmouth Square.[35]

Said witness Heinrich Schliemann, an archeologist: "The roaring of the storm, the cracking of the gunpowder, the falling stonewalls, the cries of the people and the wonderful spectacle of an immense city burning in a dark all joined to make this catastrophe awful in the extreme."[36]

Each time San Francisco went up in flames, its residents built the burgeoning city again, bigger and better. And each time, as the population continued to grow, the demand for lumber and coal grew far beyond resources available close by. Events that seem unrelated would present financial and political opportunities for Fitzhugh in the Pacific Northwest, where a newly organized territory was full of timber and coal.

CHAPTER 5

One Mine, Two Marriages, and Thirty-four Stolen Rams

IT WAS 1853, AND THE LAW FIRM "Benham and Fitzhugh, Attorneys" occupied "#1 McAllister Building" on Clay Street, a mark of success for Benham (age 29) and Fitzhugh (age 32). Georgian attorney Ward McAllister and his father had already made a fortune in the West, and built the professional office center a short two-block walk to Portsmouth Square after one of the city's many fires. McAllister shortly retired and moved to New York City where he became an arbiter of society with Mrs. William Astor. Making that kind of money was just what all the lawyers wanted to do.[1]

The city had greatly changed from the ragged collection of canvas and board that Fitzhugh found when he arrived four years earlier. Transformed by gold and energy, new brick multi-story buildings were everywhere, one of them "towering" six stories high. Where once he'd scrambled for a place to eat a decent meal that wasn't out in the fog and wind, now there were over sixty restaurants and coffee houses. Nineteen banks handled the money pouring in. The consulates of twenty-seven countries served the multinational populace. Fitzhugh could take a jaunt over to the new, more fire-proof, brick three-story Merchant's Exchange where businessmen and city traders accessed a library, meeting room, and information on arriving ships. He could read from any of twelve local newspapers, plus others from around the country. Near the square, the What Cheer House (named after a gold rush ship) was an island of expensive status and propriety for men only, with no saloon, liquor, or prostitutes. At least eight thousand women lived in the city, greatly calming the atmosphere by their presence and that of thousands of children.[2]

There is no documented evidence that Fitzhugh brought a slave to California, but many Southerners did, despite's the state's anti-slavery law. Some people enslaved indigenous children, which seems to have side-stepped California being a free state.[3]

Enterprising men seeking a new way to make money took notice of the ever-present and growing demand for lumber generated by the repeated fires, even when the city finally turned to an emphasis on brick construction. Two of them were Henry Roeder and Russell Peabody, ne'er-do-well Northerners who had tried, together and separately, a gold field store, cargo transport to the mines, and supplying salmon to miners. The gold rush was not making them millionaires. In December 1852 Fitzhugh's city enacted new fire prevention and firefighting rules that led to a downtown of solid brick buildings, making fires less devastating than previous conflagrations. Another fire just weeks earlier showed the way forward when it claimed thirty downtown buildings but was halted by the newly built brick buildings. However, the growth of private homes outside the city center and in new towns from California north to Washington Territory meant that lumber demand would only grow, and there would be economic opportunities north toward Canada for enterprising men.

The same month the new fire codes were passed, Roeder and Peabody visited Puget Sound (in what was still "northern Oregon") to search out a waterfall emptying into the saltwater that could power a small lumber mill. With the help of *Xw'lemi* (commonly called Lummi) canoe pullers, they found a likely creek on Bellingham Bay. Just north of Puget Sound on the Salish Sea, the bay was relatively close to the Strait of Juan de Fuca route to the ocean and California. That route offered Port Townsend and Victoria as additional potential customers.

Figure 9, Henry Roeder, first colonizer of Bellingham Bay, owner of the Whatcom Mill, and legislator. Tintype portrait, about 1850s. *#3882, Whatcom Museum, Bellingham, Washington.*

The stepped cascade's fall, depth, and location was perfect for a small mill in a place where no Americans had established a colony among the Coast Salish residents. Around the bay near its entrance William Pattle, a former Hudson's Bay Company (HBC) employee, had recently opened a small, under-equipped coal mine he called *Ma'mo'sea* by its Coast Salish name. It had only a few miners, little commercial capacity, or quality coal. The Lummi canoe crew took Roeder and Peabody across the bay to their major village, *Tom'whik'sen*. Chow'it'sut spoke for the village instead of his brother, the wiser Tsi'lixw, who was ill in the midst of a winter epidemic. He gave permission for the Americans to use the waterfall for a mill that would employ Lummi men. It was not to interfere with the salmon run or the surrounding clam beaches where they already owned three longhouses. The whites would be the Lummi's "Boston men" to counteract the advantages had by villages near HBC forts. The British "King George Men" offered trade and jobs that profited everyone but established no invasive colonies. Little did Chow'it'sut and the other elders know that the American men had no intention of just using the waterfall cooperatively. They meant to take it, harness it, and establish a permanent settlement that would not adhere to Lummi customs and rules. Before other Americans could claim access to the falls, Roeder and Peabody marked land claims, returned to San Francisco, and brought equipment and skilled workers to the site early in the new year. They also hired Lummi men for the mill near Tsi'lixw's secondary longhouse. They named the settlement "Whatcom," anglicizing its original Coast Salish name *Xwot'com*.

A NEW COAL MINE

The U.S. government sought to establish full control of the Pacific coast. To that end, they needed sites for Army forts, as well as Navy depots and repair facilities. They also needed coal to power government steam, and steam-assisted, vessels. To generate steam in the boiler, it took ten times as much space for a wood supply, impractical for long voyages up and down the coast. Only forty years had passed since the war with Britain, and the only place to load coal was the British-owned Nanaimo mine on Vancouver Island. In August 1853 Army Corps of Engineers Lieutenant William Trowbridge, of the U.S. Coast Survey, hired a forty-foot cedar canoe with five Coast Salish pullers to take his party from Fort Steilacoom (near today's Tacoma) to Bellingham Bay to examine the coal deposits at William Pattle's mine. Once engaged, to Trowbridge's astonishment, the men were willing to pull the canoe from five a.m. to midnight on little food or sleep. Trowbridge's additional mission was to scout for a future U.S. Army fort site to stop "Northern raider" attacks on Coast Salish villages and new settlers.[4]

A settlement on Bellingham Bay would be as vulnerable as nearby villages. The raiders, called the *Laich-wil-tach* ["unkillable ones"] by the Coast Salish, lived mostly in southern *Kwakwaka'waka* ("Kwakiutal") territory, especially Quadra Island near the north coast of Vancouver Island. Some other villages from southeast Alaska, mostly Tlingit, had formed a loose raiding confederation. All were equipped with hundred-man ocean canoes bought from the Haida carvers able to travel hundreds, or thousands, of miles with the sea as their highway. They could easily outrun British or American ships. At first, the northerners roamed widely in search of sea otter pelts for the British fur trade, but later earned the Laich-wil-tach name when they traveled south to Coast Salish territory in quest of slaves, plunder, or revenge. "War was their profession," said a French anthropologist, and the Lummi took great pride in the defeat of the Laich-wil-tach by a Coast Salish alliance at the 1840 Battle of Maple Bay on Vancouver Island. By Fitzhugh's time, some northerners worked for the Hudson's Bay Company at Fort Victoria and along the Fraser River in the salmon trade. Raids had decreased in favor of seasonal work for cash or trade goods, but they did not cease, and even the workers could be dangerous when heading home. Theft of a village's cache of the year's smoked salmon could lead to serious winter hunger. Captured people were sold into slavery and never seen again by their families. Nearby American settlements now provided new targets. Unable to distinguish between different northern peoples in the ocean-going canoes, Americans called them all "Hyders."[5]

Trowbridge's team stopped on Whidbey Island to pick up merchant Captain William Howard. He was manager for the Puget Sound Coal Company that had taken a ninety-nine-year lease on William Pattle's land claim atop the coal deposit, plus on two adjacent ones owned by men who left. The party examined the coal seam, which Pattle had only discovered shortly before Roeder and Peabody arrived on the Bay looking for their waterfall nine months earlier. Team member James

Lawson called the mine a "grand failure" whose coal would barely make enough steam to turn ship wheels, and "clinker and ashes about double the volume was taken out of the furnaces that was put in."[6]

Trowbridge described the new mill, the only other settlement: "Here in a lonely bay forty or fifty miles from any other whites, a few men have put up, without oxen, pulleys, or any other assistance, an immense frame saw-mill." Trowbridge failed to credit the Lummi employees with centuries of expertise erecting large buildings without oxen or pulleys.[7]

About two weeks after Trowbridge's visit, a larger coal seam was found by accident between the sawmill at the waterfall and the Pattle Mine (PSCC) enterprise. Henry Roeder called the discoverers his "laborers," but Henry Hewitt (also from Roeder's hometown in Ohio) and Sam Brown later maintained they were also minority investors. The pair was scouting timber on the bluff above the beach when they noticed that a large, overturned tree had exposed a coal seam on unclaimed land between the mill and the PSCC-leased claims.[8]

Uninterested in coal mine ownership but seeing an opportunity to make a lot of money, Hewitt and Brown marked off a land claim, grabbed coal samples, and boarded a southbound steamer out of Port Townsend for San Francisco as soon as they could. Once there, the coal samples' quality immediately got the attention of the port customs collector, Richard P. Hammond. It didn't take long for the Bellingham Bay Coal Company (BBCC) syndicate to form, its members including Fitzhugh's law partner Calhoun Benham. Acting as the syndicate's agent, he went to Bellingham Bay in October to examine the coal seam and bought the claim from Hewitt and Brown on December 9, 1853. Benham realized that haste was necessary because the same month of his visit, the Duwamish Coal Company mine had been established on Lake Washington's shore near the future town of Renton. On Bellingham Bay, Thurston County's (Olympia) former U.S. Marshal and surveyor Alonzo Poe's land claim lay between the two coal-bearing sites, and he excitedly wrote to a crony that the price Hewitt and Brown agreed upon with the San Francisco men was "$20,000 in the hard stuff," the equivalent of nearly $700,000 in 2021. The complex and often contradictory financial dealings, loans, failures of Benham to pay, and receipts in surviving evidence show a financial mess that resulted a few years later in a civil lawsuit that went to the Territorial Supreme Court. The records are difficult, if not impossible, to truly understand. After Hewitt died, the convoluted financials became more complicated with his widow added to the mix of warring individuals, banks, and corporations.[9]

The new coal syndicate sold $40,000 in shares to San Francisco investors. That immediately repaid their own investments and raised an additional $20,000 to open the mine.

In California's early gold rush days, nearly all businesses were individual or partnership enterprises, as it was with the miners and their "pardners." By 1853 however, companies with money to build bigger mining operations than a pick and a pan were taking over the gold fields. In the same way, well-financed San Franciscans formed joint stock corporations to take on major infrastructure projects, including the Bellingham Bay Coal Company (BBCC). Fitzhugh's law partner Benham, as managing syndicate partner, would organize the coal mine project and handle the legal details, overlapping with his job as U.S. Attorney. Fitzhugh was immediately drawn into the syndicate's work.[10]

The BBCC syndicate included some of the most prominent men in San Francisco and central California. Like Benham (age 29), all were ambitious men in their prime and interested in shipping (which required coal sources for expansion), finance, and politics. Most important, they had the funds to speculate on all of it.

Jacob Rink Snyder (age 41) was from Philadelphia and a veteran of the Mexican War. Starting as a government surveyor, by 1853 he had parlayed his political activism into the post of Assistant U.S. Treasurer at San Francisco. He would shortly run the new federal San Francisco Mint handling millions of gold rush dollars, despite membership in the three-month-long extra-legal Vigilance Committee that tried and hung several criminals in 1851. Snyder was one of those men Fitzhugh's first law firm had vigorously opposed.[11]

Speaker of the California House of Representatives, Major (ret.) Richard P. Hammond (age 33) was a Marylander, West Pointer, and Mexican War veteran. He had been a lawyer and land agent in Stockton before his election to the legislature. Democratic President Franklin Pierce appointed him the U.S. Collector of Customs for the Port of San Francisco in March 1853 with all the power over harbor activities that usually went with the post. Only a few months later he spied the wealth opportunity in Brown and Hewitt's coal samples that passed through his hands at the port.[12]

The fourth syndicate member was New Yorker Charles Minturn (age 48) who ran the Contra Costa Steam Navigation Company, operator of the first ferry system across the bay. He developed the Petaluma River route to the gold fields and owned the side-wheeler *Clinton,* the first steam ferry built in California. Like Snyder, Minturn's response to the rising crime rate in a city of burgeoning population had been membership in the 1851 Vigilance Committee.[13]

There was a problem with the grand plans of the BBCC under the 1850 Oregon Donation Claim Act. A corporation could not file a land claim. It had to be an individual, but there were no strings attached to leases and sales of the land or mineral rights by the original claimant. The syndicate needed a temporary man on-site to technically hold the claim until they could get all the paperwork together for their own man to file a donation claim and then transfer mineral rights to the BBCC syndicate.

The syndicate's choice for temporary placeholder was Captain William H. Fauntleroy, a sometime pilot and captain for Charles Minturn on the Sacramento and San Joaquin Rivers. In 1853 he was employed on the U.S. Coast Survey's ship *Active* on the Pacific Coast. Like so many others in Edmund Fitzhugh's life, Fauntleroy came from one of the old Rappahannock families who owned large tracts of land near the Fitzhughs in early Virginia. The men's ancestors had once served together in the House of Burgesses, but while the Fitzhughs established a family tradition in the law, the Fauntleroys chose professional maritime careers in the U.S. Navy and Coast Survey. William Fauntleroy's appointment to represent the syndicate at Bellingham Bay, without actually taking the land claim for himself, certainly stemmed from approval by Minturn, Benham, and fellow FFV Fitzhugh.[14]

For a substantial commission, Fauntleroy agreed to stay at Bellingham Bay until the syndicate's man arrived. That permanent claimant would be lawyer Edmund Fitzhugh, whose only mining expertise was handling gold rush legal issues. Without coal mining experience, as manager he could hire those who did have it. He was an office guy who probably made sure his hands were always clean.

Benham made another trip north to check the mining situation at Bellingham Bay in January 1854. He found the Pattle Mine to be just sixteen feet deep with a forty-five-degree dip. The clay-surrounded seam lay forty feet above the high-water mark, making it safe to work if there were no leaks when the mine reached a greater depth. Benham could see that the syndicate's own coal seam would probably continue with the same dimensions. Pattle and Howard had already sent one hundred tons of their coal to San Francisco and gotten a high price for it. The syndicate's investment seemed solid and promising.[15]

Fitzhugh's reward for moving north immediately would be a land claim and BBCC stock while serving as the on-site coal mine manager and syndicate agent. This would make Fitzhugh one of the most important employers in lightly settled Washington Territory. After relinquishing the mineral rights, Fitzhugh would own 500 shares of potentially enriching BBCC stock. In July the Washington territorial legislature passed a law that claimants could sell their land prior to receiving the patent if they had lived on it for four years. That legislation was probably already in process when Benham visited in January, and Fitzhugh knew it was inevitable that, as a single man over twenty-one, he'd own 160 patented acres for his own speculation and development. What everyone ignored was that the Lummi, or others that had resource territory there, had not signed any treaty allowing Americans to permanently take the land at Bellingham Bay. In reality it was theft of their territory to enrich the BBCC and others.[16]

E. C. Fitzhugh agreed to leave city life and lucrative legal fees behind for the financial and political opportunities Washington Territory offered. Perhaps equally important to everyone, he was to involve himself politically and help build the West Coast alliance that the California Democrats envisioned. In effect, he was to spy on the new territory's Democrats and influence their actions. Fitzhugh's job and location change turned out to be far more lucrative for him both monetarily and politically than he imagined.

"The Old Settler"

[excerpted from a popular poem about Puget Sound in the 1850s by Francis Henry]

Arriving flat broke in mid-winter,
I found it enveloped in fog,
And covered all over with timber
Thick as hair on the back of a dog.

As I looked on the prospect so gloomy,

The tears trickled over my face,

For I felt that my travels had brought me

To the edge of the jumping off place.[17]

A New Life in the Northwest

On February 13, 1854, Fitzhugh arrived at Bellingham Bay during the cold mid-winter rains. New Washington Territory was still organizing, and he made it there two weeks before territorial governor Isaac Stevens addressed the first legislature. Inside the southern point he saw Pattle's crude mine the syndicate planned to surpass, and at the bay's head he could see the Roeder-Peabody mill. It was dwarfed below the high foothills and Mount Baker's crystalline immensity above a never-ending forest of giant trees the likes of which he'd never seen. On the bay's northern side smoke rose from the fires of Lummi longhouses at Tom'whik'sen village. Fitzhugh understood, from what he observed there and on his trip to the bay, that white colonizers were vastly outnumbered by their Coast Salish neighbors whose land they were taking. Only a few crude cabins, a small bunkhouse, and Lummi leader Tsi'lixw's secondary longhouse surrounded the waterfall on Xwot'com Creek. No conventional homes. No store. No saloon. No long wharf over a mudflat that stretched from the beach far into the bay at low tide. Present on the beach were the Coast Salish painted cedar canoes that supplied human and cargo transportation for a fee. Fitzhugh's closest neighbors would be at the mill a mile away in one direction, or in the other, where lived the men at Pattle's mine and Alonzo Poe, who left his posts in Olympia and moved north to file his own claim beyond the mine near the bay entrance (Poe's Point).[18]

Wisconsin native Poe had written his friend William Winlock Miller in Olympia a few soggy, windy months before Fitzhugh arrived: "I am living a lonesome disagreeable sort of a life. Nearly a week sometimes without seeing anyone." Then he offered to sell his claim to Miller so he could get out. Miller declined.[19]

For a Virginia bachelor in expensive leather boots, a business suit, and white linen shirt who was used to the stores, saloons, gambling, city bustle, and fancy women of San Francisco, it must have seemed like he'd entered a personal hell. Benham and Fauntleroy had seen where Fitzhugh's employees would excavate the mine above a Lummi longhouse and beach, but had they told him what he would really find at Bellingham Bay? Or did they minimize the negatives of his new job, political future, and speculation opportunity. Did they tell him that no vessels regularly visited the settlement, or that it took two days in a Lummi canoe to reach Port Townsend? And that it took even longer to get to Victoria with its shops and restaurants courtesy of the HBC outpost of three hundred-odd people and a major British Navy outpost in the midst of the Crimean War with Russia? Did they tell him about the Laich-wil-tach raiders who would terrorize colonizers who dared to settle on the bay? Did they tell him that no Army forces would be coming to help the indigenous villagers and settlers fight off the yearly invasions? Fitzhugh left behind no record of his thoughts when he arrived, and only his letters to authorities about the northern raiders convey some of that precarious existence.[20]

Fitzhugh's first task was to get the land claim deed from William Fauntleroy, travel by canoe to Whidbey Island, and file the deed in Island County which still included what would eventually become Whatcom, Snohomish, Skagit, and San Juan Counties. He used February 23, 1854, as his official date of settlement on the land when he registered his claim at the ad hoc Island County courthouse on Whidbey Island. The difference from his arrival date probably means only that he stayed with Roeder, Peabody, or Teresa and Edward Eldridge until mill employees built a cabin for him to show legal residency, and when he registered the claim. Fauntleroy signed over the claim on March 2 and Fitzhugh sold the mineral rights to the BBCC on May 1. Everyone hoped that the projected six hundred tons of coal a month would happen.[21]

Exactly how any major equipment got to shore, even on the deep-water side of the bay in front of the mine site, was never recorded. After arrival at the Port of Entry, Port Townsend, by sailing ship, equipment probably went to Bellingham Bay on a smaller vessel, perhaps Roeder's newly-built scow *H. C. Page* or in the large Salish cargo canoes. It is not clear when Fitzhugh brought in mules, but the mine required them to pull sleds of debris and coal when a shaft was excavated. Building a wharf and opening the mine were major priorities for the syndicate. With lumber from the Whatcom Mill available, men built an office, a bunkhouse, and mess hall, followed by skilled worker houses. Lummi and other native men could live in the longhouse down the bluff like the mill men who lived in Tsi'lxw's near the creek. Sometime in the first couple of years, Fitzhugh had a two-story house built on what was loosely called a "street." Keeping as professionally unsullied by dirt as possible, lawyer Fitzhugh was probably uninterested in the technical and grimy work that actually built a coal mine. Mining engineer McKinney Tawes, civil engineer/surveyor John Tennant, and blacksmith Tom Wynn organized the construction to operate it.

E. C. Fitzhugh became the largest employer in the territory almost immediately and for some time, though his crew was only seven or eight men to start. Fitzhugh's skilled laborers came from San Francisco and miners moved over from other settlements or the Pattle Mine if the money was good. Some came from Lummi and other villages. In January, just before Fitzhugh arrived, the Pattle Mine was still advertising for twenty miners at $60–70 a month or $1 per ton of coal dug. That Capt. "Bill" Howard was still looking for workers indicates that his offer may not have been enough to lure miners to the mine clearly vulnerable to Northern raiders.[22]

Though Benham did the first enthusiastic examination of the coal formation, the true nature of what was to become a large mine was not initially obvious until Fitzhugh got it opened. The entire coal formation was six miles wide. It dipped to the north at forty-five degrees and sometimes more, meaning it went out deep under the bay. Five coal veins, two to eight feet thick, rested in slate. At first Fitzhugh's men worked the surface, but within two years that coal was exhausted. Steam pumps and more machinery were shipped in to extract the coal from a shaft that reached 121 feet deep and out into the bay. Flooding, gas, and fires became potentially fatal factors for miners as the mine extended deeper and farther out, but employment steadily increased to sixty in 1857.[23]

The BBCC's mine supplied coal to the U.S. Navy's steam and propeller-driven *Massachusetts*, as well as the Coast Survey's *Active* and other vessels. It freed the nation from dependence on the British mine at Nanaimo, though American ships continued to buy higher quality coal there for years. Fitzhugh's coal turned out best suited for home stove use, a trend away from wood stoves that was taking over the country in the mid-1800s. The best result of the BBCC mine establishment was that it brought in much-needed cash to the territory, no matter what the coal was used for.

Fitzhugh's skilled mine workers who stayed to become part of the "Old Settlers" group found numerous ways in the early decades to contribute to their new community, both privately and in public offices.[24]

After Arkansas-born civil engineer John Tennant arrived from San Francisco, he did the surveying, was the office clerk, and studied law with Fitzhugh. Tom Wynn, the Philadelphia Quaker blacksmith, left the mill to set up the mine's forge but continued to work for everyone, including meeting home needs. Mining engineer McKinney Tawes brought his wife to the bay, where she became the midwife for mine and mill personnel wives in the coming years. When carpenter Nicholas Sheffer arrived in the fall of 1854, he saw that between the two industries, fifteen to twenty men were at work. Fitzhugh helped him build a little house near the mine where he could bring his wife from another mill in the region. Former Scottish mariner and erstwhile California gold seeker Edward Eldridge and his Irish wife Teresa were the first people to work for Roeder and Peabody, but they moved over to the mine. Eldridge worked for Fitzhugh while his wife ran the boarding house. The path along the bluff became a primitive community street. A list of personnel at the mine in its early years demonstrates that almost every permanent settler in the first two decades of Whatcom County's legal existence worked at some point for Fitzhugh. They and their wives were the people of vision who built the Whatcom County community.[25]

JULIA

It didn't take long for Fitzhugh to realize that if he were to live in his own home, eat and have clean clothes in the long term, he needed help. Many of the bay's new men decided to put down permanent roots after living for years without a "home" in the best sense, and many of them married one of the local indigenous young women, including Roeder and Peabody. Some marriages failed, and some women were abandoned when a white wife was found, as Roeder did to his wife and two children when his Ohio fiancé arrived. But Tennant, Wynn, and others formed lifelong family bonds with important native women. It is unclear how Fitzhugh viewed a marriage to one of the Coast Salish young women because his bride would be a woman of color in his eyes. He still owned the elderly female slave in Virginia. Cross-cultural marriages with indigenous women in San Francisco may have been non-existent. Whatever his attitude, Fitzhugh approached obtaining a wife in a tribal custom marriage for his home as another task to be done. Almost certainly following Fitzhugh tradition, though in a cross-cultural way, he wanted a wife who brought some kind of influence and wealth to him.

E. C. Fitzhugh was correctly viewed by native leaders as an important man, but he may not have realized at first what it meant if he was to marry a woman he saw as one of the native elite. If he wanted to marry a leader's daughter by tribal custom, her parents would have their own standards by which to judge the self-important man. In addition, tribal custom marriage demanded that parents also receive a dowry in gifts and services to compensate for the loss of their daughter to the family circle. That custom was actually familiar to Fitzhugh, as elite Southerners expected to receive a woman's dowry. First, he went out to Tom'whik'sen and asked the Lummi headmen for one of their daughters. The wealth one of their daughters would bring to him would be access to a middleman with indigenous workers, salmon, other food resources, and a labor pool of in-laws for the mine. The Lummi told him there were no eligible women available, but they knew of a leader's daughter on Samish Island, just south of Bellingham Bay. The Lummi men and their wives very likely saw Fitzhugh's arrogance and biased attitude toward them. Another influence on their decision to send Fitzhugh away could have been Lummi desire not to lose any young women when they were rebuilding population after an earlier epidemic.[26]

Fitzhugh hired two influential Lummi men to canoe him to Samish Island and the trio arrived late in the evening at the main village. According to family, leader Seya'hom would have refused Fitzhugh if the Lummi were not men he knew and respected, and if the important white man had not been persuasive. Fitzhugh met E'yam'alth (Catholic baptismal name Julia), who was about fifteen and the daughter of Seya'hom and his wife Tse'swots'olitsa (Emily). Seya'hom was originally from the northern Olympic Peninsula's leading S'Klallam family whose father Whey'ux was one of seven brothers who had linked the S'Klallam villages together. Seya'hom's family village at *Kah'tai* (Port Townsend site) lay within the lively crossroads atmosphere between peoples from the coast, southern Vancouver Island, Salish Sea, and Puget Sound. Julia's mother was an important woman of Lushootseed speaking *Nu-wha-ha* and Straits Salish-speaking *Sam'sh* (Samish) parentage from the family of the last war chief of the Nu-wha-ha, Cha-das-kadim III. Epidemics in the recent decades had taken so many Nu-wha-ha that survivors joined the Samish, with whom they had many family ties, on their island.[27]

When an epidemic disrupted the Samish leadership structure, they asked Seya'hom to leave his Kah'tai longhouse and move to Samish Island to lead his wife's people. He may have been expendable at Kah'tai because close relative Chet'ze'moka was the acknowledged leader there, leaving Seya'hom free to move his family to Tse'swots'olitsa's home village on Samish Island if he wanted.[28]

There may have already been an intermarriage within the Samish village when "Blanket Bill" Jarman, an itinerant Brit who never settled long in one spot, is said to have married Seya'hom's sister Alice. The Jarman marriage, if true, may have been successful enough to reassure Seya'hom that his daughter would have a successful marriage to a man equally important as himself. Benefiting Seya'hom's family, Fitzhugh would have cash jobs for family men at the mine, could mediate with the multiplying colonizers and their leaders, and would help protect the Samish from the Laich-wil-tach. Fitzhugh would have had to follow the protocols of tribal custom marriages since the Coast Salish did not countenance premarital sex or cohabiting without marriage. Julia's prospective bridegroom needed approval from her mother and other family elders, as well as to present acceptable gifts and services to partially atone for the loss of her help and companionship in the family circle. Approval of the marriage meant that Julia had finished her puberty seclusion and learned everything she needed to know to be a successful wife and mother. Seya'hom would pledge help to the new couple for a year if they asked for it, but he also expected Fitzhugh to help the family when needed. For Fitzhugh, in addition to the things he expected to get out of a cross-cultural marriage, Julia brought two dialects of Northern Straits Salish, plus Lushootseed, language skills that could benefit him.[29]

Julia's young age mattered little to Fitzhugh, whose ancestry included marriage to an eleven-year-old and as a witness to other marriages of girls as young as thirteen. Julia did not want to marry the man twice her age with piercing dark eyes, heavy brows, and beard. Family members said she cried and cried about the arrangements that would send her to Fitzhugh. Coast Salish custom was to marry outside one's longhouse and village, so she expected to leave home, but not to be alone in the house of this strange white man.[30]

Fitzhugh became a "stern taskmaster," as family later said, and life was hard for the young wife learning to cook and keep house his way. Southern planter-class men like Fitzhugh expected absolute obedience to their authority and often sought a much younger wife. His cousin George Fitzhugh, the famous apologist for the South's social structure, wrote "In truth, woman, like children, has but one right and that is the right to protection. The right to protection involves the obligation to obey." Fitzhugh came to exemplify that deeply authoritarian patriarchal attitude.[31]

Julia soon became pregnant, and her homesickness worsened. Seya'hom's grandmother had married a Lummi, so he could reasonably ask his cousins for permission to occupy the longhouse near the mine and the family moved there. On November 6, 1854, Julia gave birth to a baby girl her husband named Julia Anne, soon called Julianne. Nearly all white American men claimed the right to choose their children's names if they wanted. Fitzhugh could have named the baby after his mother or one of his sisters, but he did not. Given the family names he gave to his white children years later, it was a sign of how he viewed the marriage to Julia.[32]

According to family, Fitzhugh honored Seya'hom when he named the mine for him, asking permission first. It became known everywhere as the "Sehome Mine." Henry Roeder's daughter wrote that Seya'hom frequently visited Julia, and her father was a "favorite" of Fitzhugh. If true, the men got along well, but Fitzhugh would never see his important father-in-law as an equal.[33]

MARY

Only two settlers in the region are known to have had two wives at the same time. One was "Blanket Bill" Jarman, and the other was Fitzhugh. It was common practice among wealthy Coast Salish men at that time, often to assure support for a widow. By custom, a woman was a member of her husband's longhouse by virtue of her marriage, while her life-long ties remained to her birth family's house that was nearly always in another, often distant, village. A widow's remarriage to one of her late husband's brothers was the most desirable way to keep her children in the longhouse family, called by anthropologists a "sororate" marriage. In the Fitzhugh case, it happened differently.

Seya'hom's half-sister Qui'las (baptismal name Mary) was a few years older than Julia and is believed to have lost her husband and baby boy in a recent epidemic. Had Mary's son lived, a marriage within her late husband's house would probably have been arranged, but she was alone. The epidemic killed many prospective husbands for the young widow, and she did not go back to her home village of Kah'tai or any other S'Klallam family longhouse. She went to her brother's legendary 1,200-foot-long house on Samish Island, or if he and his family had already moved near the mine, she went there.[34]

At a time when many eligible men had died, and pregnant Julia was so homesick and lonely, Seya'hom's solution was to send his sister to be Fitzhugh's secondary wife several months before Julia gave birth. Mary was soon also pregnant and gave birth to their son June 7, 1855. Fitzhugh named him Charles Mason Fitzhugh, after his friend who was Territorial Secretary.[35]

Life with Fitzhugh was materially easier for Julia and Mary in his modern frame home, but his unpredictable temperament made life harder. Still owner of the enslaved elderly woman in Virginia, his attitude toward the two young indigenous mothers would never be the same as toward a white woman. Three years after Mason's birth, a visitor from the U.S. Boundary Survey overnighted with the Fitzhughs and wrote home that his host "lives very well and is one of the old Virginians whose hospitality and friendship is genuine."[36]

A New Community

The settlement growing around the mine became known as "Sehome," while that around the mill a mile away was "Whatcom." Other indigenous wives from Samish and Lummi joined the mining community in little houses on the muddy street, including Julia's older sister Sarah (married to miner Charles Pearson) and their maternal aunt Fanny whose husband George Richardson became the first teacher.

From the first, any stereotypes of indigenous people that Fitzhugh brought from California or Virginia were dashed. Lummi women supplied floor mats, household goods, and foodstuffs to the colony while the men provided his transportation. They taught the first white women how to find and cook unfamiliar seafood, fruits, and vegetables. Many plants were also medicinal in a place with no doctor. First white female settler Teresa Eldridge readily admitted that everyone would have starved without their kindness. Friendly and hard-working Lummi men were essential employees at the mill and mine, and their expertise moving timbers was invaluable. Both peoples shared the fear of northern raiders.[37]

Fitzhugh had been at his new mine only three months (and already married) when Laich-wil-tach struck the Pattle Mine. On May 24 they landed at Joel Clayton's cabin outside the entrance of Bellingham Bay, seeking revenge for losing at least one young leader in a skirmish elsewhere. Eyewitness reports said the raiders had already killed a settler on Vancouver Island, thinking they were in U.S. territory, before the British military scared them off. They headed farther south and the first settlement they found was at Bellingham Bay. Clayton knew their intent when he saw that the two ocean canoes carried no women, but over one hundred men in paint. He fled to the Pattle Mine where he and the miners hid in the woods. After darkness fell, two sentries canoed out about a quarter mile to keep watch. When their single old musket went off while being cleaned, the sound was met with a volley of gunfire from the water. The concealed men thought it might be a warning from their men in the canoe, but the number of gunshots was suspicious. When Clayton and the miners finally emerged, they found an empty blood-soaked canoe on a beach three miles away.[38]

Fitzhugh was shocked enough to head south to Fort Steilacoom and Olympia asking for help from the army and governor, since they considered the mine a critical asset and Americans expected protection. The help offered by Territorial Governor Isaac Stevens was twenty muskets and six hundred cartridges to supplement fifty muskets already offered by James Douglas, British colonial governor and Hudson's Bay Company (HBC) head at Victoria. Fitzhugh spread these among the Whatcom Mill and Sehome Mine, as well as the Pattle Mine.[39]

Witness Edward Eldridge wrote later that the two unfortunate victims were the only lives ever lost to the raiders, meaning white lives. Even though settlers were in no danger from the region's friendly villages, after the Pattle Mine raid they "lived in constant alarm" that the Laich-wil-tach would come again at night and kill people before anyone else knew it was happening. Fear led to sleeplessness for everyone at the mill and mine until they built a blockhouse where families could shelter at night if there was a threat.[40]

The following March 1855, Governor Stevens, acting as Superintendent of Indian Affairs, appointed Fitzhugh to the post of Interpreter. He wanted someone "of judgement, discretion and energy" trusted by everyone to facilitate communication with the Coast Salish of the bay area. This also provided Stevens and Territorial Indian Agent Michael Simmons with a spy on local village activities. Clearly, Fitzhugh (once a French and Latin student) had already learned enough Northern Straits Salish and Lushootseed from Julia, Mary, and their family to supplement *"Chinuk wawa"* (Chinook trading jargon) by early 1855.[41]

Figure 10, Territorial Governor Isaac Ingalls Stevens, about 1855. *Courtesy of the Washington State Historical Society at WashingtonHistory.org. #2015.0.23.*

A NEW COUNTY

On March 9, 1854, a week after Fauntleroy quit-claimed the 160-acre coal mine site land claim to Fitzhugh, the legislature officially established Whatcom County. This northernmost county included today's Skagit and San Juan Counties within its boundaries. It spanned perpetually snow-covered volcanic peaks, prairies farmed for centuries by the Coast Salish, salmon-bearing rivers, large inhabited islands, and the Bellingham Bay settlement. Henry Roeder, Russell Peabody, and new employer Fitzhugh cheered the split because until then, all Island County officials lived on distant Whidbey Island, most around Penn Cove and the meager county seat of Coveland. Because of that, the fledgling Bellingham Bay community had no local representation in the legislature, despite its cluster of economically important industries. A monetary benefit also came with the split. Everyone knew that once the county commission established local taxes and licenses, part-time officials would earn some additional cash income in a place where bartering dominated. One complication was that almost no Americans lived in the San Juan Islands and despite being added to Whatcom County, they were not officially part of the United States. The archipelago was peacefully shared with the British HBC's new sheep operation.

Legislators appointed provisional officers, including Deputy Auditor Fitzhugh, probably after discovering that he had been on the Auditor's Office oversight committee while in the Virginia legislature. Until the county held its own elections, he served under the provisional county auditor, unhappy land claimant Alonzo Poe. Temporary County Commissioner William Cullen moved over from Whidbey Island. The ad hoc courthouse was Russell Peabody's cabin beside Whatcom Creek. It served until the county built a two-room shack four years later on what was planned to be a town square. Until then, Fitzhugh and other officials kept their records at the mill and mine offices.[42]

By legislative decree, the first election of Whatcom County's officials was held on September 9, 1854. Mine voters gathered at Poe's cabin for the Ma'mo'sea precinct, and mill workers at Peabody's cabin for Whatcom precinct. The voters made Fitzhugh the official county auditor. He made all recordings in a set of slender red deed books and the speckled volume inexplicably labeled "Book of Liens H," most likely an unneeded book inherited from the Island County auditor. One of his first actions was to backdate Calhoun Benham's purchase of land from Hewitt and Brown to December 16, 1853, long before the county had split from Island. He listed himself as "County Clerk" for the change. Two weeks after the election, he also presented the newly elected commissioners with a bill of $57.50 for services already performed, an equivalent of almost $1700. He received no salary or reimbursements until a year after he left office in 1856, perhaps being generous to the new county or because the commission put repayment of the richest man in the county a low priority.[43]

The very small coterie of literate men in Whatcom County capable of organizing and keeping records were all Democrats, which handily played into Fitzhugh's political plans to fit into the territory's politics. The mostly Southern territorial Democrats wanted to ally with President

Franklin Pierce's view that abolition was a threat to national unity. An examination of who held which office during the county's early years also leads to the impression that the men met over whiskey and cigars to divvy up the offices that yielded some money in the next year or two. Political wrangling on the local level, as well as the territorial, could be rough and tumble, where friends could be rivals the next election and political enemies could be friends depending on the stakes for future appointments and elective offices. Fitzhugh thrived.

In what would much later be considered an inexcusable conflict of interest, shortly after the election Fitzhugh exerted his clout after new sheriff Ellis "Yankee" Barnes assessed the coal mine for property taxes. Acting as both county auditor and mine manager, Fitzhugh's ethics did not present a problem when he demanded the valuation be drastically reduced. Or if others raised the problem before the commission meeting, Fitzhugh convinced them to stop questioning his own revised valuation. He did not bother to appear in person at the commission meeting to argue his point but sent his deputy auditor to present the assessment he wanted. Two of Fitzhugh's arguments were that Barnes hadn't met with him at the mine office, and the tax notices posted in public places weren't the territory-required number. The commissioners, unwilling (or afraid) to argue with the new county's biggest employer and biggest potential taxpayer, agreed to lower the assessment from $24,925 to $6,425. His tax was reduced to $44.97. Doing what Fitzhugh wanted significantly cheated the county out of income to start a proposed road along the shoreline, salaries for officials, for payment to men hired on contract, and savings for a future school. In present-day terms, the initial assessment was equal to about $778,000. In effect, he got it reduced to about $200,500, leaving the mine's new property tax slightly over $1400. Fitzhugh demonstrated no loyalty to Whatcom County, his new home whose interests equaled his own and those of the coal syndicate. His avarice would be long remembered in county histories.[44]

The Great Sheep Raid of 1855

The legendary result of Fitzhugh's action to reduce the mine's property tax was "The Great Sheep Raid." This singular fiasco made such an impression that it first made its way into participant County Commission Chairman William Cullen's narrative for historian Hubert Howe

Bancroft, then into print by a small newspaper near the Canadian border in 1893, before appearing in multiple Whatcom County histories.

On May 3, 1854, after Whatcom County's birth, U.S. Collector of Customs Isaac Ebey and Henry Webber visited Charles Griffin, the Hudson's Bay Company's Bellevue Sheep Farm manager on San Juan Island. They discussed taxing authority. Three days later, Ebey arrived with a demand for Griffin's inventory of all livestock and their origin, which was refused. Ebey then installed Webber as the resident customs agent in an American flag-bedecked tent. Governor Douglas at Victoria decided that he would leave Webber there as a private person and not push a confrontation over ownership of the islands.[45]

During the county commission's first meeting after Fitzhugh's re-assessment, the members under Chairman Cullen discussed assessing and collecting taxes on the sheep operation established shortly before Whatcom County was established. Henry Webber was the one American living on the island, theoretically the U.S. Treasury Collector of Customs, but in fact tolerated by the British. However, when the territorial legislature unilaterally placed the San Juan Islands into Whatcom County, it gave the county commission (short on cash because of the Fitzhugh re-assessment) tacit permission to collect property taxes there. Fitzhugh and Cullen conferred with Governor Stevens who said to go ahead because the collection of taxes would establish the authority of the U.S. and publicly acknowledge it. Acting as the assessor, Cullen applied a value to the resident sheep and Sheriff Barnes presented Charles Griffin a bill for $80.33 on October 19, 1854. It was nearly twice as much as Fitzhugh's revised bill. Griffin refused the demand for tax payment before he and the men at his office ridiculed the authority of the U.S.[46]

At the next county commission meeting, the board ordered Sheriff Barnes to again canoe the twenty miles out and post ads for a Sheriff's Sale of enough of the HBC sheep to pay the tax. Starting from 1,300 sheep in 1853, the herd would soon rapidly increase during lambing season. Barnes posted the ads three weeks later. When no buyers appeared on December 9 after his third trip in winter wind and rain, he postponed the sale. The sheriff appeared again at Griffin's place on Christmas Eve, greeted once more by derision. Barnes and his canoe pullers spent the holiday headed back to Bellingham Bay on the rough, cold tidal waters where waves were intimidating, and drenching rain or gale-force winds the norm.[47]

"Yankee" Barnes had apparently reached the end of his patience with the new job that brought him some extra cash in a community without crime. Now, he had been put into a confrontation with the Hudson's Bay Company and by extension, the British government. He told Chairman Cullen he would not go again just to carry a communication. It was either "drop it a flat failure, or push it through by a display of power and authority," in Cullen's words. He convinced Barnes to go over one more time and post a tax sale sign for March 31, 1855, and the commission would assist. At a secret session, the commissioners decided to organize a bodyguard for the sheriff and collect the taxes.[48]

In March, Fitzhugh (as auditor) joined Cullen, Barnes, Alonzo Poe, and four others who assembled provisions and strapped on their pistols. Keeping their twenty-mile voyage theoretically secret, they took to the water. Beaching the afternoon of March 30, Fitzhugh and Cullen walked to Griffin's house and tried to convince him to pay the taxes under protest. They offered to hold the money until the boundary dispute was settled. Griffin was smart enough to know that was unlikely to happen anytime soon, and Whatcom County was starved for working capital, so he refused their offer. The party then wasted precious daylight hours searching for the sheep farm at the lower end of the island before camping in a protected spot by the shallow landing. On the sale morning, they found a corral with forty-nine rams a mile or so from Griffin's house. The valuable imported rams were Southdowns, Cheviots, Leicesters, and Merinos, some without horns, others with curled horns for butting, and some may have had more imposing horns that could spear a local wolf. Griffin had already ordered his Hawaiian shepherds to drive the purebred ewes and their new lambs into the forested interior to hide them from the "marauders" he was expecting.[49]

At nine a.m. on the 31st, the advertised hour, Barnes jumped the corral and declared a tax sale. Fitzhugh instantly bought twenty rams, and others divided the remainder. The auction did not bring enough to cover the taxes, but the men thought they could sell the rams at home and make up the tax, plus make a profit. Thus began an episode that a century later might be described as a "clown car" attempt to take home boatloads of rams, underestimating rams fully capable of facing island wolves.[50]

Men tackled each 175- to 200-pound ram before binding it, and others carried the bleating sheep downhill to the waiting vessels. It did not go well. Either responding to a shepherd's report or hearing the commotion from a mile away, Griffin and the Hawaiians arrived sporting knives and demanded that the Americans cut the loaded rams loose. Barnes ordered his party to protect their sheep "in the name of the United States." In a stand-off, the display of guns prevailed over the display of knives for the moment. Griffin retreated, pronouncing the Americans' actions an "outrage," and his own men took to canoes heading as fast as they could for Victoria twelve miles away. Tide and wind favored the messengers. Fitzhugh and friends lacked cargo capacity enough for themselves and all the squirming, struggling rams, and the party "pressed into service" several island Coast Salish village men and their canoes to help before the HBC's *Beaver* could arrive with reinforcements.[51]

One of the shepherds sent a young runner back to Griffin with a note about what was still happening at the sheep pen. While there were more rams to load, Griffin returned alone with his dog and in the ensuing scuffle the remaining rams jumped the corral and escaped. He left and returned with twenty employees demanding that the Americans surrender the rest. When Griffin's men tried to untie the rams ready to load, Fitzhugh and Cullen drew their revolvers and told Griffin that if he tried to take them it would be "at the peril of his life," because they would stand with Sheriff Barnes and his job to collect the tax. Griffin headed for Victoria in his own canoe to consult with James Douglas.[52]

When Fitzhugh and friends in their now filthy, water-soaked clothes and boots, finally got off hours later, they managed to take thirty-four of the rams after stealing an HBC boat. Left behind with the rest of the rams were twenty-four ewes and lambs Barnes had auctioned sight unseen. The sun was setting, the tides were against them, and they had seen the *Beaver* on its way to chase them down. The exhausted party rowed or paddled as hard as possible until darkness hid them, and they spent the night on a small island. Little sleep was had after the wind came up in the middle of the night and threatened to swamp the boats and canoes holding the rams. The next day brought a miserable trip across Rosario Strait and Bellingham Bay in canoes full of animal waste. The angry, hungry rams, accustomed to supplemental oats every day, had nothing at all to eat. Perhaps Fitzhugh spent some of his night on the deserted island asking how his new managerial job and elected position had involved him in such a debacle.[53]

The men's final humiliation was the realization that they had no place to put their rams until they could sell them. Cullen took his to Eliza Island across the bay where they all died due to a lack of fresh water. Fitzhugh ended up with only four or five sheep, which he took to the mouth of the Nooksack River and sold to the Lummi or a lone settler. The price did not cover his canoe rental to take them there. At least some of the rams may have contracted a skin disease developing among the HBC flock that might have discouraged prospective buyers.[54]

In the subsequent county commission meetings with notes taken by Fitzhugh, nothing was recorded of the sheep raid. The subject of collecting delinquent taxes and overdue license fees was addressed, but those from the islands were never mentioned.[55]

Whatcom County continued to assess taxes on Bellevue Sheep Farm, but they never again tried to collect before the boundary was settled many years later. Charles Griffin filed a report and tenaciously claimed reparations in the thousands, but nothing ever came of it. Governor Douglas wrote to Governor Stevens a month after the incident and told him that the dispute over ownership of the islands needed to be settled before "the most serious evil" with "dissension and bloodshed" resulted. The episode prompted Congress to finally appropriate funds for a boundary commission that, with British counterparts, would measure and affix the U.S.-Canadian border, though on which side of the islands the line would be drawn remained in dispute. "The Great Sheep Raid," and Fitzhugh's participation in it, was the first armed conflict in the dispute over islands where both British and American citizens shared undefined space. Four years later it culminated in a dead British pig and another jurisdictional argument that nearly started a shooting war between former adversaries, now edgy friends. It was called "The Pig War."[56]

Voters re-elected Fitzhugh in August 1855, twenty-one to thirteen, and he served until June 2, 1856. He presented his unpaid salary and bills, which were treated cavalierly by the county commission until they finally paid him fourteen months after he left office. They never paid his expenses in traveling to Fort Steilacoom in search of help after the Pattle Mine attack in 1854.[57]

Fitzhugh's sister Rosalie died of a "long and painful sickness" at one of the Fitzhugh family houses in Virginia shortly after his re-election, but her brother did not receive word promptly, given the six weeks it took for mail from the East Coast to arrive in Olympia, and lack of any regular mail service to Sehome. He complained about the abysmal mail service in the Olympia newspaper in late August, perhaps aware of Rosalie's failing health.[58]

DEEPER INTO TERRITORIAL POLITICS

Fitzhugh never ran for office again, but it didn't affect his climb to power in the Democratic Party as Senator Gwin and his other mentors in California had hoped. Even without an elective office, he exerted almost overwhelming political power in the county and added multiple appointive territorial positions or Democratic Party positions, while he continued to run the Sehome Mine.

Fitzhugh had involved himself in Washington Territory's political life as soon as the legislature appointed him provisional deputy auditor, followed by his election to county auditor. In addition to being the territory's largest employer, he brought to territorial politics experience from Virginia and California not everyone had. Initial Third District Territorial Justice Frank Chenoweth appointed Fitzhugh his court commissioner in April 1855, just weeks after he had clerked for a session. Fitzhugh oversaw any legal questions needing immediate attention between Third District Court terms whenever Chenoweth was unavailable. That drew him farther into the territory's political and legal life. Fitzhugh built an intricate web of overlapping political, legal, and economic positions that many believed he expected would carry him to higher office.[59]

A political and personal friendship grew between Fitzhugh and Territorial Governor Isaac Stevens, a Northern Democrat appointed by new President Franklin Pierce. When Stevens arrived in Washington Territory, he appraised the four thousand residents of a territory that stretched east across northern Idaho into western Montana, as "starry-eyed greenhorns with visions of the Garden of Eden, zealots demanding Utopia, a sprinkling of 'fast-buck' entrepreneurs, a small cadre of seasoned westerners…, political hotheads who saw nothing but evil machinations in the activities of the Hudson's Bay Company and its former employees, a contingent of mercantilers steeped in the eastern merchant-financier tradition, and a continuing influx of southern democrats—each one trying to fashion the cloak of territorial function from a different pattern." Together, the new Washingtonians Stevens met equaled a very discordant electorate whose remote location held no importance to politicians on the East Coast, though Washington Territory was three times the size of New England.[60]

Massachusetts native Isaac Ingalls Stevens was a five-foot-tall West Pointer, first in his graduating class the year before Fitzhugh entered his ill-fated semester. He was a decorated Mexican War veteran who moved into the Coast Survey regional command, and first came to the Northwest to head the Northern Pacific Railroad Survey before his appointment to territorial governor in 1853. President Pierce added the appointment as Superintendent of Indian Affairs to the governorship. Stevens arrived in Olympia in November 1853 to organize the government and hand out to Democrats the territory's federal appointments that he controlled. Only thirteen months later he started negotiating with the territory's tribes to take their land and resources, and by then Fitzhugh was in a good position to advise him about those in the northwestern counties.

While Fitzhugh was county auditor in 1855, the Democratic Club formed in Olympia. Like Fitzhugh many, if not most, of its leading members were Masons who took leading roles in the territory's establishment and first election. Their Olympia lodge continued to add members to the oldest organization of any kind in Washington Territory. Male Fitzhughs had joined Masonry since the Revolution. As the 1850s passed, Masonic ties between the territory's leading men in politics and business made them instant colleagues. Besides Governor Stevens and William Winlock Miller (who became the party head), other members were Michael T. Simmons (Territorial Indian Agent), competing newspaper editors J.W. Wiley and Edward Furste, Alonzo Poe, Justice Frank Chenoweth, plus most other lawyers and influential settlers. Surveyor General James Tilton and his wife presented the Olympia lodge with a lock of George Washington's hair once owned by his ancestor, the first U.S. Army Surgeon General. Masonic ties became another of Fitzhugh's ways to make useful connections.[61]

While Stevens officially controlled political appointments in the territory, it can be argued that the de facto man of most influence was William Winlock Miller. He once said, "Ambition has always been my God since childhood." He believed that individual effort resulted in meeting ambitious goals of money and politics, and connections developed would further both. Born in Kentucky, Miller was two years younger than Fitzhugh and the son of Virginians, which gave him and Fitzhugh an immediate connection that fueled their friendship.[62]

Figure 11, William Winlock Miller, June 1854. Holmes, photographer. University of Washington Libraries Special Collections. *Pendleton Miller Photographic Collection, PHColl 344/UW14328.*

Courtesy of Miller's family connections to their Whig congressman, in 1851 he arrived at the Port of Nisqually, "northern Oregon," as the newly appointed U.S. customs inspector. Most weary colonists stopped at the isolated Hudson's Bay Company fort there. By virtue of his singular responsibility that included facilitating shipments of settler commodities, and his trips to Olympia, Miller met virtually all the earliest territorial men focused on economic growth. After the new territory was founded, Governor Stevens found Miller's unquestioned integrity and efficiency impressive and started to consult him. With a new Democratic president in power, Miller switched allegiance from the out-of-power Whigs to the Democrats and received new appointments in customs and revenue. With proceeds from the well-paid jobs, he invested in local ventures and started loaning money to officials and entrepreneurs. He grew his business connections and political influence until territorial Democrats were completely under the sway of Miller and Stevens in two years. In what was still a cash-poor economy, Miller was always ready with money to lend, or to co-sign for a risky venture that would increase his wealth if it worked out. His personal honesty made him a well-liked and trusted asset all around Puget Sound, which only increased his political influence with Stevens, Fitzhugh, other party men, and voters.[63]

In the first years that Fitzhugh occasionally went to Olympia, the capital was still a primitive little peninsula town in the wilderness with less than three dozen houses. The legislature abandoned the upstairs room in a store where they first met for the new two-story Masonic Temple for the 1855 session. The earliest saloons and businesses spread along the block that surrounded the wood-frame building, which also housed the first school. At the forest's edge, the town's only imposing building fronted on a wide trail usually knee-deep in mud during the winter. Men, women, and children picked their way over and around fallen timbers and charred stumps that dotted the erstwhile "street."[64]

Olympia historian George Blankenship described the town's early Masonic Lodge members as more "censorious" than later, which suited a few politicians trying to impose order on the new territorial Democratic Party. Though the Masons disapproved of bad behavior as they defined it, legislators customarily kept a large bottle of "high-voltage frontier whiskey" behind each chamber door. The delegates called it "taking the pledge of allegiance" as they went into the chamber. When the legislature was in session, men of both parties gathered from near and far and talked politics over dinner and whiskey in the evenings. In a short time they became part of what historian William Lang called the "vigorous male life, with gambling, whoring, and generally opportunistic activities that fed their self-centered desires" in a town eager to supply those despite the leadership of Masons.[65]

The 1855 legislature began to tinker with the initial boilerplate marriage law. "Censorious" (but ignored) attitudes toward perceived public misbehavior contradicted with part of the new social structure. Like Fitzhugh, many legislators and their friends had married indigenous women by tribal custom, not church or justice of the peace county ceremony. The legislature first amended the marriage act by voiding and forbidding intermarriages, but at the same time another amendment required those already living together as man and wife to get a "legal" marriage by county or church officiant. They contradicted that by imposing an outrageous $500 fine on any officiant found performing such weddings, causing clergy and justices of the peace to simply fail to record the marriages. The legislature continued to revise their marriage law's contradictions for many years once members realized that by voiding and forbidding intermarriages, they were disinheriting their own children. In Whatcom County, between eighty and ninety percent of all marriages for the first twenty years were intermarriages, almost all by tribal custom ceremony. To his credit, Fitzhugh never paid any attention to the new law and its amendments.[66]

When the Democratic Party, dubbed "Club," formally organized in 1855, Fitzhugh was already an important figure after only a year in the territory. At the club's core was a web of personal friendships within a limited group with reciprocal loyalties. For many, that included patronage positions. Patronage authority and the salaries to be had was a potent weapon or gift, useful in a place far distant from the national supply chain and where bartering often replaced cash. For Stevens's own national political career, he depended on keeping good relationships with party members and the local population. Luckily for his popularity, Stevens's desire for a transcontinental railroad route that would end in Washington supported local efforts to develop the economy enough to make the territory more than an ignored hinterland of little importance to the East Coast. At the same time, he supported a local Democratic Party machine that wanted as little interference from Washington, DC, as possible. Members of the inner circle exchanged local and national information and protected the territorial capital's interests. These men became known to others as the "Olympia Clique," as much a controlling political machine as others in the nation. It was what Fitzhugh's Democratic colleagues in California hoped and believed he would foster.[67]

A month after Fitzhugh became a court commissioner as well as county auditor, the new central committee of the Democratic Party chose him as the Whatcom County member of the party's disciplinarian committee. When the committee convened the first time to choose legislative nominees and clarify their policies, he served as Whatcom's delegate and on a committee to verify voting credentials and resolve contested seats at the convention. At that time, there were no secret ballots, so parties had their vote enforcers and bribers, much like Fitzhugh's experience in California. A "slip ticket" was printed by a party with the names of its nominees, which would be distributed at the polling place. If the list was in the voter's hands, it was more likely that he would vote for everyone. Without ballot secrecy, Fitzhugh used his charm and if that didn't work, he shrewdly turned to bribery and financial or physical intimidation. It was a long time before someone called him out publicly on his methods to ensure that Governor Stevens and W.W. Miller got the winners they wanted. In 1859 Fitzhugh told his long-time mining engineer McKinney Tawes that if he wanted to keep his job, he should vote Stevens for congressional delegate, rather than the new Republican Party's candidate. Tawes immediately quit his job rather than submit to the intimidation. Fitzhugh lost both his mining engineer and Mary Bird Tawes, midwife and maker of shrouds for dead miners. Until then, few Whatcom County men defied Fitzhugh's orders of how to vote.[68]

BUILDING WEALTH

W. W. Miller's financial acumen, and the influence he developed with it, was instructive for other men. Fitzhugh had lived in San Francisco where an organized money system quickly developed in the wake of millions of gold rush dollars flowing through the city. There was no such system in Washington Territory in its first years, but W. W. Miller showed Fitzhugh and others how to be informed "hip-pocket bankers" while he forged the new Democratic Party. Fitzhugh needed this at the mine where he opened a saloon and store, had other building projects, and paid it all from his small office safe. Fitzhugh learned from Miller how to use money to make more money, as well as how to influence voters (though Miller's well-known ethics might not have encouraged Fitzhugh to use threat of job loss or asset foreclosure to influence an election).

Miller's example of wealth-building through informal banking combined easily with Fitzhugh's Virginia culture of building a web of informal money transactions. Collection was often delayed, especially for gambling advances, but when the lender wanted his money, he had no problem using litigation. Making loans at interest was probably the fastest way to build wealth in 1850s Washington, and sometimes to obtain land when it became the repayment. Belonging to the Democratic Club, or holding a salaried government position, opened many opportunities in a group effort that built Washington's economy and the men's personal wealth. For Edmund C. Fitzhugh, it was a method to build IOU obligations to and from others, political and personal loyalties, plus increase his public standing and visibility.[69]

At Bellingham Bay, major employers Henry Roeder and Fitzhugh both gave and got in this system of hip-pocket banking. They combined political offices, work, and being informal bankers for the locals who kept individual sacks of cash in their safes. As a lawyer, Fitzhugh was equipped to serve as a broker for both lender and borrower, which earned him a commission he could then invest. Both men traded loans, collateral, and leases with friends to finance community advancements. For example, in 1855 Fitzhugh loaned $55.78 at four percent a month to Roeder, who put up his two-thirds interest in his cargo scow the *H.C. Page* as security. In the opposite type of transaction, in 1859 W.W. Miller loaned Fitzhugh $1,500 to expand the Sehome Mine store. Fitzhugh offered to pay in six months if Miller would give him the lowest interest rate. He secured the loan with a majority (350 shares) of his Sehome Mine stock, assuring Miller that it would soon be worth three or four times its value. However, Miller was short on cash and could only send him $1,000, but wrote that if Fitzhugh would sign two notes, he would get him two percent interest elsewhere, as long as he would pay it back "promptly." Such a statement implicitly warned that Miller would bring suit and take Fitzhugh's stake in the mine if he had to. However, Fitzhugh "proved up" on his land claim on Christmas Eve 1855 and received his patent to 160 acres that included a small "village" and a coal mine. When he dealt with Miller for a loan that year, he may have anticipated that the settlement of Sehome might be far more valuable than his coal mine stock.[70]

An examination of Fitzhugh's financial dealings in Whatcom County led an early historian to conclude that "as to business acumen, no other local man could approach him; when they could not meet their obligations and had to mortgage their holdings, Fitzhugh was the financier and took their paper at such exorbitant rates as three percent a month." Fitzhugh had even exceeded that rate with Roeder.[71]

CHAPTER 6

Death in the Garden

Treaty War

ONE EVENT IN EARLY 1855 signaled the start of a tumultuous period that engulfed County Auditor Fitzhugh's politics, appointments, mine defense, and even family life. Occupied with his obligations, Fitzhugh did not directly participate in the event that involved and affected his in-laws. Governor Stevens (acting as the Superintendent of Indian Affairs) had begun to negotiate treaties with the territory's indigenous peoples who, in colonizing settler consensus, inconveniently occupied millions of acres of land the newcomers coveted. He negotiated sovereign nation business contracts, rather than the total surrender treaties seen after the Civil War. Stevens was driven to get treaties signed with all Washington tribes, east and west, so title to vast swaths of land would be freed for white takeover and development. His personal ambitions included securing the planned route for the northern transcontinental railroad route that Stevens had surveyed and mapped under direction of the War Department. In 1855 the Stevens party moved about the territory negotiating with leaders at large gatherings on prepared treaty grounds as fast as possible, leaving Territorial Secretary Charles Mason to govern. Reservations were laid out and approved by both sides, though the native leaders certainly did not recognize the concept of "ownership" in the way that whites did because indigenous leaders administered territories only. The treaties and negotiations passed from English to a chinuk wawa (Chinook jargon) speaker and then to the native language (or languages), and back again. The limited vocabulary of the trading jargon meant that nuances of treaty language and replies were lost in the middle translation. It is questionable just how freely the signatures were obtained, given the sizable military escort's well-armed presence. The Treaty of Medicine Creek with the Nisqually and others closest to Olympia in December 1854 was the first.

In January 1855 Stevens's party moved northward to negotiate the Treaty of Point Elliott at Mukilteo, between Seattle and Everett. He cajoled and coerced the relinquishment of millions of Coast Salish acres in northwest Washington for whites to claim. The inadequate translations left Lummi, Samish, and other leaders without a true understanding of the finality of their treaty's contents and the extent of their loss of resources and villages. The government had officially divided the Coast Salish of northwest Washington into individual "tribes" with whom they would deal in the future, based on major villages. In reality, the Coast Salish were a vast extended family web whose members lived from the Columbia River on the south and north into British Columbia's mainland and lower Vancouver Island. Stevens and witnesses from both sides, including Fitzhugh's father-in-law Seya'hom representing the Samish, signed at the end of the month. Many families stayed at the treaty grounds with the negotiators, and though one of Julia's friends said she went with her father, it is highly unlikely that Fitzhugh would have allowed his infant daughter to be taken to a rude camp during frigid January. The weather was bad enough that the Nookh'sahk (Nooksack) leaders were unable to canoe down their frozen river to attend, and they never signed a treaty.[1]

Dr. George Suckley, Fort Steilacoom's doctor (and Smithsonian Institution naturalist), grew increasingly angry about what he saw and wrote a letter to his friend, the governor of New Jersey. He saw the treaties as conducted in a "rash and hasty manner...with Stevens dictating his terms and to a certain extent bullying the Indians into his arrangements." He thought there were "pitiful considerations" for twenty to thirty thousand people. In fact, their negotiators thought they were obligated to sign the treaty before returning home to talk it over with others and reach a decision. Suckley saw Stevens's whole focus on making the treaties advantageous to the whites, thereby gaining popularity and future votes favorable to himself in Washington Territory.[2]

Before long, tribal suspicions about the treaties' real intent began to grow everywhere. Stevens had even rejected requests for prairie necessary for horses and cattle, particularly east of the Cascades where they were wealth and critical resources. He appointed Fitzhugh an official "Interpreter" about six weeks after the Point Elliott Treaty, giving himself a spy in the northern end who had already become fluent enough in the language of his wives to do the job.[3]

WAR

Tribal leaders around the Territory soon concluded that their treaties had not, in fact, treated them as equal sovereign nations, and results entirely favored the white government and permanently deprived the tribes of their traditional lives. Those east of the mountains rebelled and within months some whites were killed on both sides of the Cascades. Leaders of eastern and western tribes were often related through marriage, sometimes closely despite differences in language and culture, which led to easy alliances. For example, as the rebellion gained momentum, Snoqualmie Chief Patkanim, acting in his people's perceived future best interests and realizing who would prevail, brought his warriors to the side of the whites. His brother-in-law Leschi, war chief of the Nisqually, allied with the rebelling eastern Klickitats and Yakamas, to whom both men were related by family marriages.[4]

On October 14, 1855, though the Army was at Fort Steilacoom and on the Columbia River, the governor established a parallel civilian military organization, with himself at its head. The militia would operate separately from the Army, an untenable arrangement to confront an armed conflict. The majority of his staff knew little of standard military procedure. Stevens appointed Fitzhugh lieutenant colonel and his military aide, apparently based solely on one semester of drilling at West Point. The aide-de-camp was surveyor Isaac Smith who grew up near Fitzhugh in Fredericksburg. Stevens appointed Territorial Surveyor James Tilton his adjutant general at the rank of brigadier general. W. W. Miller became the brigadier general to handle quartermaster and commissary duties. Twenty-six-year-old Benjamin Shaw became Stevens's main field commander with a rank of lieutenant colonel and an eagerness to fight Indians. He had fought under his father's command in the late-1840s Cayuse War in southeast Washington Territory. Given to vulgar language, he had spent several years as Stevens's primary interpreter and a freewheeling special agent. Six months after organization, Lieutenant Colonel James Doty, the experienced treaty attendee, was reported to be "in an almost helpless state of intoxication" at Fort Steilacoom and now-"General" Stevens dismissed him. At that time, at least, Stevens had his limits for staff behavior.[5]

Officer corps members were already local Democratic politicians and close advisers to Stevens. Historian William Lang concluded that the Treaty War bound many staff and volunteers to each other to an even greater degree than their migration and settlement experiences. This included Fitzhugh. Everyone expected that after the war their commander would reward their loyalty and efforts with patronage positions.[6]

At the end of 1855 Gov. Stevens called for local militia companies to form and commit to six months duty for what was now an armed conflict. Sehome and Whatcom's Company "H" would join those from Port Townsend and Whidbey Island to become the Northern Battalion under an elected major. Stevens's order called for unconditional enlistment, as companies might have to be moved away from home. Under Captain Russell Peabody and First Lieutenant Charles Vail, the miners and mill workers coalesced. On February 1, 1856, General Order #3 called for the building of a blockhouse, plus fifteen men to stay and guard the Bellingham Bay communities as long as no regular steam patrol vessel was available, and for all citizens to turn out in case of attack, though Northern raiders remained the only threat. Essential mine and mill personnel became the home guard.[7]

J.J.H. Van Bokkelen from Port Townsend was elected major for the Northern Battalion. He and Fitzhugh never got along, and the estrangement may have gone all the way back to San Francisco when Van Bokkelen was part of the 1851 Vigilantes, where Fitzhugh had been allied with the opposition. Van Bokkelen had filled similar positions in Jefferson County government to those of Fitzhugh in Whatcom, plus election to the legislature. He was haughty, critical of staff officers, and a later divorce described him as an alcoholic who inflicted significant injuries on his wife and had threatened to kill his family. His temper seems to have matched that of Fitzhugh.[8]

CSSO

The day after the general order of February 1 established the defense of Whatcom and Sehome, Lieutenant Colonel Fitzhugh received another appointment from Stevens, this time acting as Superintendent of Indian Affairs. Fitzhugh became the "Special Indian Agent" for the future Bellingham Bay Agency. The agent salary was significantly larger than that of his interpreter position, and he was still salaried as county auditor and Stevens's military aide. Fitzhugh now had official influence over everyone at Bellingham Bay and nearby villages. Stevens placed many friendly tribes under the charge of special Indian agents who would keep them in their present locality, but not allow them to leave without a pass from the agent in charge. In effect, the Lummi, Samish, and others were hostages and prisoners.

One of Special Agent Fitzhugh's duties was removal of the Snoqualmie with allied Snohomish and Skykomish villagers to Holmes Harbor on Whidbey Island. Fitzhugh was to watch them for the duration of the war and supply the families with food and other supplies. The related villagers lived on the Snoqualmie, Snohomish, and Skykomish Rivers flowing from two major passes across the Cascades, today named Stevens and Snoqualmie. They were relatives of several groups on the east side of the mountains and thus their loyalties were suspect, unlike the people who became in-laws, employees, and friends with the settlers at Bellingham Bay. The alliance of Snoqualmie Chief Patkanim with the white government, based on what he felt was best in the future for the three groups who followed his leadership, complicated matters. In his dual role, Isaac Stevens promised him care for the elderly, women, and children if his men formed a fighting company. Fitzhugh told the families that if they followed his instructions, they would be considered friends and protected, but evidence reveals he did not follow through. There was a storehouse at Holmes Harbor, but Fitzhugh made no regular issues of food, and instead issued supplies in exchange for work on the camp. He expected the hostages to rely on the hunting and fishing available nearby as well as provisions they brought downriver with them. Later, the Snoqualmie people's history told of 700 people who died in the camp of poisoning. If the numbers are accurate, it was likely some kind of food poisoning directly attributable to the slipshod way Fitzhugh paid attention to the supplies. He left behind no record of the deaths at Holmes Harbor.[9]

Stevens became increasingly suspicious of intermarried Hudson's Bay Company men living at Nisqually Prairie (Pierce County), including one married to Patkanim's eldest daughter Margaret. On April 2, he declared martial law in the belief that the men were "evil-disposed" and arrested "some poor fellows for treason," as Dr. Suckley reported. Stevens usurped the sole power of the U.S. President to declare martial law in a territory and bypassed the U.S. Army. At least publicly supported by Fitzhugh and other staff officers, Stevens took to himself the legislature's power to abrogate civil rights or suspend habeas corpus under martial law. These actions placed too much power in the hands of the governor and a backlash was inevitable among independent-minded Americans. The prisoners, who kept arms to hunt and protect their families, may have, in truth, supplied some weapons to their also-threatened native in-laws. The men retained prominent lawyers and applied for a writ of habeas corpus. When Territorial Chief Justice Edward Lander (also a militia company captain), tried to hold court in the absence of the supposedly ill Justice Francis Chenoweth to pronounce the martial law declaration illegal, Stevens had both arrested and jailed in Olympia. Dr. Suckley wrote a few months later that he saw Stevens's move as an attempt to destroy the law courts as well as the principle of habeas corpus. Volunteer companies differed in their support for Stevens's martial law, and one was dismissed. Events got messier. There was a facedown between a county sheriff's posse and a militia company. The U.S. Army command was asked to intervene. A military commission held court. In late May, the U.S. District Attorney released the defendants.[10]

Once Governor/General Stevens terminated martial law on May 26, 1856, Chief Justice Lander levied a hefty fine for contempt of court, but Stevens pardoned himself. He received a strong letter of disapproval from the U.S. Secretary of State saying the President did not view his appointee "with favorable regard." The U.S. Senate demanded that Stevens lose his second job as Superintendent of Indian Affairs or lose appropriations. The long-term local effect of this controversy was that the legislature split into pro-Stevens men, opposed by anti-Stevens men who controlled the legislature that year. Suckley wrote that Stevens "recently declared in the bar rooms at Portland, Oregon that he would be d---d if he would not make any son of a b---- rue the day he attempted to thwart him in the matter of martial law....As I have said before, he has become so much debased by strong drink as to be utterly unfit for his position."[11]

A month after martial law ended, Stevens ordered Special Agent Fitzhugh to go upriver with Territorial Indian Agent "Big Mike" Simmons to the prairie above Snoqualmie Falls and meet with representatives from eastern Washington groups who were Snoqualmie relatives. The pair were to negotiate in an effort to get them to "submit unconditionally to the justice and mercy of the government." Stevens told Fitzhugh and Simmons to try and punish any murderers who had fought against the government. They could either execute someone convicted or suspend the execution if they thought it would make things worse. If they got submission from the rebels, then they could immediately send supplies upriver for them. He told Fitzhugh to secure the cooperation of Major Van Bokkelen's Northern Battalion, which had been in the Falls area since early spring. They occupied several blockhouses in Snoqualmie territory and spent most of their time fishing. Fitzhugh was to tell Van Bokkelen to ensure the safety of the tribal representatives coming west through the pass to the rendezvous.[12]

Some weeks later Fitzhugh reported that the mission was "a perfect failure." He attributed at least some of it to U.S. Army Colonel George Wright, who spent a month working with the eastside tribes, giving them presents while at the same time telling them their defeat was imminent. Wright told them he was the "big dog" and could make everything right for them if they stopped fighting. Fitzhugh said the recalcitrant Snoqualmies who allied with those groups would not come down because they were hoping Wright would offer better terms. He saw that his lengthy efforts expended a serious amount of territorial funds and had been used by the adversaries to gain time and information, but if Wright had stayed out of it, he could have gotten everyone to come in. He believed Wright and his own superiors, having left the actual fighting to the territorial volunteers, just wanted to take credit for patching up the treaty agreements and ending the war.[13]

Fitzhugh remained a stalwart Stevens man, despite the public accusations and general dislike of his friend after the martial law dispute. He could foresee that likable Stevens would regain his popularity and keep his political power. After the war came to an end in August, Stevens rewarded Fitzhugh's loyalty by leaving him on the payroll until late February of the new year. Stevens saw that he was paid for both his military aide position, and for inspecting militia units being discharged in October. And Fitzhugh was still being paid $1,000 a year as Special Indian Agent. This was more than double-dipping into federal funds. It was triple dipping.[14]

SEHOME MINE

Throughout 1855–56, while Fitzhugh was in charge of the internment camp, negotiating a possible surrender, and in Olympia with Stevens, as well as doing political and county auditor duties, he was still the Sehome Mine superintendent, though John Tennant as clerk and engineer McKinney Tawes were doing the actual job most of the time. When militia company "H" organized, only thirty local men were capable of bearing arms. The twenty-four who enrolled included some mixed-bloods from the San Juans, and ten Alaskan Haida who worked for the HBC near the Semiahmah village to the north but offered their services for the pay all militia volunteers expected to receive eventually. Whatcom County's company had very quickly been sent out to guard Snoqualmie Pass. Fitzhugh stopped by the *Pioneer-Democrat* office in Olympia and told the editor of the "almost utter impossibility of obtaining labor" for the mine and that he was only able to operate the important coal depot at a minimal level. Most of the employees had left with the militia, except for the men essential to keep the mine operating at some level and families protected. It is likely that many of those who kept the mine open were men from Seya'hom's people or the Lummi.[15]

In some ways, the year "E. C." or "Ed" (as most people called him) Fitzhugh turned thirty-six started out to be a breather for him. In 1857 he was in his prime, energetic, well-connected, and had multiple sources of income to support his family, speculate, and loan. It looked to be a year of prosperity and opportunity, with more territorial peace than before. Holmes Harbor internees had gone home, so the position as Special Indian Agent demanded little. With no more militia duty, local miners returned to work. The U.S. Army command had finally taken steps to protect the settlement and indigenous villages with Fort Bellingham, which was under construction a few miles around the bay from Whatcom. Captain George E. Pickett's company from the Ninth Regiment had arrived in August 1856 as the Treaty War was ending. The site that topographical engineer Lt. George Mendell chose provided a twenty-mile view north and south, ideal for advance attack warning should the northern raiders return. Fitzhugh's brother-in-law Dan Samish worked for Pickett as a runner, and Fitzhugh knew he would want his sister and parents warned of a Laich-wil-tach attack as quickly as possible. The soldiers brought an infusion of cash to the local economy whenever the army got around to paying them. Fitzhugh probably foresaw a year dominated by improved output at the mine, his efforts to send Stevens to Congress as the territorial delegate, and his support

Figure 12, Captain George E. Pickett, commander of Fort Bellingham. Later Confederate General, E. C. Fitzhugh's division commander. Studio portrait. *#1994.46.1, Whatcom Museum, Bellingham, Washington.*

for local Democrats in the next election.

Fitzhugh's primary power base remained his position over the increasingly productive coal mine envisioned by the San Francisco syndicate. This important resource gave Fitzhugh the base from which to help build a Pacific voting bloc in Congress desired by the California Democrats. The coal proved excellent for coke, manufacturing, and domestic use, though not the very best for steamship use. The Sehome Mine's production cost was $3 to $5 per ton, sold in San Francisco for $16 to $17 per ton. The U.S. Navy's patrol ship *Massachusetts* now stopped regularly to check on the community, as well as Puget Sound merchant vessels that loaded tons of coal. Crews shopped in the mine store and drank in the saloon. Fitzhugh's most important employees stayed with him. Tawes' wife Mary Bird provided the community with an on-site midwife. Tennant ran the office, surveyed, and was reading law under Fitzhugh's tutelage at the same time. Blacksmith Tom Wynn kept mine equipment in repair, forged new iron apparatus, plus made and repaired housewares.[16]

The Sehome Mine community was generally a happy, if grimy, place. Residents remained on alert for a Laich-wil-tach attack until Fort Bellingham was finished and its firepower dominated the waters, but they were already safer. Employees built houses when they married local indigenous women, and many took in boarders tired of the barracks. The bachelors could live in a family atmosphere with good food and someone to do their laundry, while the hosting couples saved up money for their future. Perennially irritating, mail never arrived regularly, but in August 1857 the all-steam *Constitution* initiated a regular route and had newspapers to Sehome in twenty-four hours, even if papers coming from San Francisco still took six days to reach Olympia. Any settler deaths on the Bay were usually from accidents or a prior condition, not diseases caught at their new home in northwest Washington Territory.[17]

By 1857 Julia and Mary managed two toddlers and kept Fitzhugh's home ready to welcome unexpected guests. When the *Pioneer-Democrat's* editor visited Sehome in November, he found that among the many tidy buildings, the "grounds about [Fitzhugh's] place are tastefully laid out, expressive of comfort and convenience." Fitzhugh's house was located toward the community's end closest to Whatcom. The other homes and mine buildings lined the "street" that followed the line of the bluff above the beach where his in-laws lived. Whatcom was also doing well by that year. The editor also counted two stores, three carpentry, and other skilled worker shops among a total of seventeen buildings.[18]

Independence Day was, from the start, the biggest community event for the bayside communities, and soon the new army fort. At first celebrations were scattered except for competitive cannon-firing. In 1857 cannoneers positioned themselves at Fitzhugh's, the Pattle Mine, Whatcom, and Fort Bellingham for a noon contest. Each team was determined to be the one who could load and fire the fastest. Fitzhugh's gunner didn't sponge out his English cannon, causing a premature discharge, though not a complete explosion. He was mortally wounded and died the next morning, which resulted in reconsideration of how the settlements would celebrate the nation's independence. What resulted was a growing county celebration that brought people together from Lummi and the new communities for food, speeches, horse races, children's games, and baseball.[19]

By late fall, miners were working a third chamber 180 feet deep under the bay, assisted by steam machinery. Fitzhugh told the *Pioneer-Democrat* editor that he usually had ten to twelve employees, including three miners and three cutters, but he still needed twenty of each. Mules drew the daily ten to twenty tons to the surface in cars on a track. They moved the coal output to the 300-foot wharf extending into deep water, and Fitzhugh planned to go to 800 feet with more funding. He believed that sixty tons a day were possible from seams as thick as twenty-six-and-a-half feet. Even at less than capacity, 4,000 tons had been dug, of which 3,000 were shipped to San Francisco and the rest sold up and down Puget Sound to heat businesses and homes. Sehome Mine's coal was particularly appreciated by women with new cast-iron cookstoves that no longer required the family to have a constant supply of kindling and wood pieces. Predictive of the mine's future, steam-powered pumps were already essential to keep salt water out of the shaft. A Sehome Mine "old timer" remembered later that the coal shafts also had a habit of catching fire when sulfur in the rocks became damp. The new danger of gas deep underground added another problem.[20]

As before, now-former county auditor Fitzhugh didn't want to pay the property taxes on the mine as assessed. The 1857 tax list issued in the fall showed him (and the mine) worth $11,000 (over $330,000 in 2021), far more than Henry Roeder and his lumber mill at $4000. Fitzhugh owed the county $109.50, about $3300 in 2021. He again protested the valuation, and the County Commission postponed collection. The taxation decision eventually went to the Territorial Supreme Court for an opinion, and the 1857 taxes were not collected until early 1859. Such was Fitzhugh's power.[21]

SPECIAL INDIAN AGENT, 1857–1858

After the Treaty War, Special Indian Agent Fitzhugh retained his lucrative $1,000 per year position (equal to about $30,000 in 2021) until April 1858, while the unratified treaty languished in Congress. As a "special" agent, his appointment required no approval from Washington, DC, and was a territorial patronage position given by Stevens, so it could continue indefinitely. While Charles Vail continued to work at the mine, as assistant agent (at only $60 a year) he spent more time than Fitzhugh boarding at one of the Lummi longhouses at Tom'whik'sen, since no agency office existed. The Nooksacks, Lummi, Samish, and small Semiahmah remnant were Fitzhugh's "charges," and in general he handled the prohibited white liquor-sellers, questions about the heavily armed military at the fort, and coordination against any Laich-wil-tach attacks. The villagers called him "Misteh Picheh."[22]

In January 1857 Fitzhugh reported on his recent visit upriver to the Nooksack villages near the foot of Mount Baker to talk to the leaders unable to get downriver and sign the treaty two Januaries earlier. Fitzhugh had made his arduous way twenty miles up the glacial river or slogged his way up the Nooksack trail full of huge fallen logs, mud, and underbrush. He met the leaders at Popehomey village located at "The Crossing." The shallow ford miles inland was essential to the movement of people or animals going north to the Fraser River or other villages. Primary leader Humptalem and other village headmen told him that they did not want a "road" into their territory to The Crossing and were "determined not to have their lands taken from them." Fitzhugh concluded that the 326 Nooksacks he counted needed a defined reservation and to receive value for land taken, regardless of not being treaty signers. Looking at the situation through lawyer's eyes, he believed they had no legal obligation to vacate any land or permit settlers in their territory.[23]

After a repeat visit six months later, Fitzhugh's letter stressed Nooksack economic independence, with the women's agriculture producing a "superabundance" of potatoes sold to settlers, as well as some of their large salmon catch. He remarked, "I think I never saw a country so well adapted for the Indians to live in as this." They had never needed supplies from him and so he had only given presents, provided aid for the sick, and hired Nooksack men. They wanted to be left alone and Fitzhugh seems to have seen himself mostly as a consultant and safety net. This unusual stance was contradictory to what the territorial and federal government saw as the future for indigenous Americans.[24]

Special Agent Fitzhugh confronted a new problematic situation when he returned from Popehomey. The Point Elliott treaty outlawed indigenous slavery, but until it was ratified by Congress two years later, the long-time custom remained a gray area of jurisdiction. Coast Salish slavery was not racial, but instead was based on capture and sale far away from home, thus causing loss of individual personal history. The enslaved people in Fitzhugh's jurisdiction were generally from Alaska or northern British Columbia—men, women, and children who had been sold and re-sold until they no longer knew where their home village was. Some had even come to the intermarriages with the wife as gifts from her parents, to help her in her new life. Fitzhugh became complicit in physical abuse when an enslaved boy broke into a cabin.

Superiors told him not to put the government to the expense of a trial. The village headman involved did not want to whip the boy and possibly cause him to run away, so he got Fitzhugh to do it. Another agent might have refused and sought some other form of discipline for a somewhat minor crime, but Fitzhugh was from a slave-owning family in Virginia. Whipping a child was routine.[25]

If Fitzhugh and the bayside settlers believed that the Army's permanent presence with their guns and warning system, in addition to visits from the *Massachusetts*, would discourage the Laich-wil-tach from invading, they were wrong. In late March 1857, raiders landed in the middle of the night without waking anyone other than Whatcom "mechanic" Louis Loscher, kidnapped from his house. Loscher may have been targeted because his wife was a northerner and he had learned enough of her language to understand the raiders' complex message. They stole blankets and other items easy to obtain in trade at the HBC forts, but they wanted to make a point with the stealthy invasion of a home without being seen. The Laich-wil-tach released Loscher at the beach and told him to stay silent until morning, on pain of death, then to take his wife and leave the area. Most threatening, the men told Loscher they were scouting the settlements for a return when they would take everything and kill Fitzhugh, Peabody, and Pickett, the men they considered important. The Laich-wil-tach planned to take Fitzhugh's head and kill any settlers at Sehome who resisted.[26]

About a week later Fitzhugh, acting as both mine superintendent and Special Indian Agent, angrily wrote to his friend Governor Stevens. He needed more than a few guns, which had been the response in 1854. At the time of Loscher's kidnapping, both communities had many families with children. "It is most unpleasant, as well as most dangerous, to remain here—the citizens are all wrangling amongst themselves and there is so much ill feeling existing, that many intend leaving if the *Hancock* does not make her appearance very shortly—as they have no confidence in one another." He called the *Massachusetts* departure in the spring when it was dangerous, an "inglorious retreat," and demanded a steamer be stationed in the area, or "we will *all* be obliged to leave." The slower, propeller and sail-driven *John Hancock* was smaller than the *Massachusetts* but it had more guns and was based out of San Francisco, so his demand for immediate presence was probably hyperbole unless it was on the Sound at the time. Fitzhugh's ten men were building a blockhouse for Sehome families to sleep in now that they had seen the stealth that could be employed by raiders, but he repeated that people were in a "stampede" and he couldn't make them feel confident because he felt none for himself or his family. He threatened to leave if no military steamer was sent to cruise the area. It is highly unlikely that Fitzhugh meant to leave permanently, even if it sounded like it, but to abandon the mine and his multiple jobs was the strongest threat he could make.[27]

While he was writing, Fitzhugh received word that a raiding party of thirteen canoes carrying 300 men was six miles out from Victoria heading in the direction of Bellingham Bay. Songhees leader Che-a-thluc ("Chief Freezy") had arrived from his village at Victoria to warn his granddaughter Jenny (Mrs. Tom) Wynn and her Sehome community. Fitzhugh included the sudden news in his letter and stressed that he knew "Freezy" well and had complete trust in Jenny's grandfather. He wrote, "We might all be killed as we expect no assistance from the military post, they having as much as they can do to protect their perimeter, their pickets not being finished and many of the soldiers being in irons in the guardhouse." He added at the end of his letter, "My Indians are terribly alarmed," which can be seen as Fitzhugh's patriarchal urges as much as a condescending label. Such huge numbers of armed warriors, like the group Che-a-thluc had seen on Haro Strait, would be difficult for anyone to hold off, but the raiding party went elsewhere that time.[28]

On May 1, 1857, Fitzhugh visited Olympia to take a howitzer back to Sehome. He handed the newspaper editor a copy of his angry letter to Stevens. That same day, Territorial Indian Agent Mike Simmons sent a letter to Governor Stevens informing him of a large meeting at Lummi that brought together men from many Coast Salish villages to "make common cause" against the northerners and keep each other defended and informed. The leaders did not want any whites to attend the meeting, but Fitzhugh and Captain Pickett went anyway. They didn't record what happened in the meeting, but they likely went to affirm cooperation against the invaders as well as spy on what the men were planning on their own. Fitzhugh was speaking Straits Salish well enough to make sure everyone understood the cooperative defense. Simmons thought it a good idea to station an army officer at the Whatcom blockhouse to assist the organization of defense, if necessary, also smart because Captain Pickett and his Alaskan Native wife lived in town, with just a small blockhouse beside their home for protection.[29]

And then, on the dark overnight of August 11, the warning given Louis Loscher the previous March came true. Kake village Tlingit raiders from southeast Alaska's Kupreanof Island arrived to exact retribution for events at Port Gamble the previous November 1856. The Kake had refused a direct order to leave Puget Sound after they raided several locations, which resulted in a battle with the *Massachusetts*. The Kake lost twenty-seven men, including a chief.[30]

The threat against Fitzhugh, Peabody, and Pickett was real, but the "important man" they found first was (militia) Colonel Isaac Ebey, Whidbey Island's first settler. He was also a former customs collector, legislator, and a recently elected prosecutor. The extended Ebey family lived on Whidbey's largest prairie, where their clustered homes were fully exposed above the bluff and beach. Because his dog seemed on edge, Ebey slept outside that night, where the raiders found him. They shot and decapitated him before leaving with his head. This grisly murder of a well-known and respected man spread terror throughout Puget Sound and north in the Salish Sea. In the aftermath, the U.S. Coast Survey's ship *Active* began visiting Sehome and Whatcom every few days to establish an armed marine presence, for which Fitzhugh had pleaded many times.[31]

Within a month of the Ebey murder, Michael Simmons asked Fitzhugh for a report describing his Indian agent duties that warranted $1,000 a year. Since Simmons already knew what he did, it was likely part of the preparation for James Naismith, his anticipated replacement in the new administration. Simmons would then return to concentrating on his mill and large family. Fitzhugh wrote that he was required to see that no "worthless white men" imposed upon the tribes, to prevent difficulties, and report any rumors of hostile intent. His job included looking after and feeding the sick, plus doing what he could "towards the amelioration of their conditions." He said he supplied medicine, blankets to elders, pipes and tobacco, cloth, and some food, though "his" tribes were generally healthy except for colds.[32]

Fitzhugh went into some detail about what his job currently meant without the Point Elliott Treaty's ratification. He had not tried to move anyone to the proposed reservation at Lummi Peninsula. He claimed to have frequently visited the resource camps in the spring and summer (unlikely given his many other activities), but food resources were so abundant that the tribes needed little from him. However in the winter, after the salmon, clams, and potatoes had been preserved, Fitzhugh said he "collected" people in the three longhouses at Sehome and Whatcom where he could prevent whiskey-sellers from getting to them. He detailed his efforts to prevent whiskey trafficking to the tribes, including getting a conviction under U.S. laws, which he called a singular accomplishment for a local agent. Fitzhugh had appointed his assistant Charlie Vail to help catch the "rum sellers" and do everything in his own power for the good of the assigned groups (Lummi, Samish, Nooksack, and the few surviving Semiahmah). Fitzhugh wrote that he found it very difficult to catch the liquor sellers because of the size of his assigned geographic region, but Vail's assistance helped him to partially stop it.

During the winter of 1857–58, while Fitzhugh's attention largely turned to politics in the new Buchanan administration, his side job as agent faced a completely unexpected challenge. In the report he wrote for Simmons earlier in the year, Fitzhugh said he provided some medical care for his "charges." His patriarchal view, though official, mimicked the way his physician father saw Falmouth residents as "his people." That was also literally true because many of the people he watched over were Fitzhugh's in-laws.

At the very end of 1857 a medical emergency that overrode everything else came to the longhouses where Fitzhugh said he gathered people in winter to keep them away from the liquor peddlers. An epidemic thought to be an influenza variant swept through. It was a type no one, including Fitzhugh, had seen before, and it still hasn't been identified. It had symptoms of whooping cough, influenza, and for some people, paralysis, especially of the tongue. In the alarm sent to Simmons, Fitzhugh said he and his assistant Charlie Vail were working "continually" to save the victims.[33]

That year salmon runs had failed and the northern raiders had stolen much of the Lummi and Samish stored foods. Fitzhugh and Vail distributed flour and other supplies the government shipped in or settlers shared, but these "white foods" did not provide the disease-fighting nutrition the gathered Coast Salish needed. As the son of a small-town doctor educated in the finest American medical school of his time, Fitzhugh arrived in the Northwest with an abundance of observed medical knowledge, if not actual experience assisting his father. His model was his father's "bleed, blister, and purge" methods and perhaps homeopathic practices from his mother. They may have helped some victims, but unknowingly worsened the condition of others. Fitzhugh and Vail provided as much medical aid as they could, but over seventy men, women, and children died by the time the epidemic vanished in the spring.[34]

Tsi'lixw's longhouse at the creek, where native mill workers lived and epidemic victims collected, was just downhill from the white-washed frame house Russell Peabody had built for Captain Pickett and his Haida wife. Having Fitzhugh's fellow Virginian live in town brought better army protection, and provided a place for dignitaries to stay, in addition to the likable Pickett's camaraderie. There, Mrs. Pickett gave birth to James Tilton Pickett on New Year's Eve, 1857. She died later during the epidemic, probably more vulnerable to infection from a visiting downhill friend. No cause of death was ever recorded, but her proximity to infectious victims makes it likely that the epidemic played a part in her death.[35]

POLITICS

After the Treaty War ended in the fall of 1856, and Fitzhugh had solidified the governor's trust and loyalty, he increasingly took a more important role in territorial politics. In January 1857 dissatisfied stirrings left from the Treaty War birthed the Republican Party in a territory far from eastern and southern regional disagreements. Gov. Stevens's martial law declaration had exacerbated the growing split in the Democratic ranks between the "Olympia Clique" and the anti-Stevens men. It left the door open for a new national party's branch to find members among Stevens's bitter opponents and former Whigs.

That same month, after Fitzhugh visited the Nooksack, he managed to be the first man to sign in at Olympia's Washington Hotel meeting room where the five members of the Democratic Party's Central Committee would make plans before the legislative session opened. They elected him chairman, and he would run the spring convention as well as be the new party liaison for the legislators. Stevens held a large party to christen his new home near the Capitol, where possible Democratic moves were inevitably discussed since they all coalesced around him.[36]

Fitzhugh worked closely with W. W. Miller, who continued to be the actual field marshal for Democratic legislation strategy, vacant patronage appointments, and for the upcoming congressional delegate election campaign for their man Stevens. By then Miller's gift for comradeship and ability to base evaluations on deeds, not words, was highly developed. He focused on how men fulfilled obligations, were personally loyal, and didn't lie to their associates. He and Fitzhugh became close even though Fitzhugh didn't always personally live up to Miller's ideals.[37]

After the 1856 national election the previous November, Democratic President James Buchanan's new administration was moving ahead with his patronage appointments and policy agenda. Miller and Stevens favored any legislative action that would improve Washington Territory, and they also knew that now-Senator Jefferson Davis continued his ambitions for the Northwest that he had shown as secretary of war. Davis was a friend in Congress who could influence others to support them. To that end, the territorial legislature quickly passed "An Act to Incorporate the Geographical and Statistical Society of Washington Territory." Fitzhugh was among the men listed in the society whose purpose was to promote general improvement and allow the taking and conveying of real estate valued at $10,000 and under. Donations to the society were to be applied specifically to the wishes of the donor. Perhaps most significantly, whatever business society members chose to do, they were free from taxation. And perhaps not coincidentally, shortly thereafter the legislature passed an act to incorporate Stevens's pet project, the Northern Pacific Railroad. Fitzhugh was listed as one of the investors along with more than twenty others. Stevens deeply wanted to get the railroad pushed through on the route he and his party surveyed before he was governor. It was to start at a Rocky Mountain pass between southeastern Washington Territory and Nevada, and connect with the route passing through Minnesota and Nebraska.[38]

When the territorial Democrats convened in mid-May, delegates unanimously elected Central Committee Chairman Fitzhugh president of the convention. He delivered Whatcom County's two delegate votes to nominate Governor Stevens for Congressional Delegate, defeating the candidates put up by the anti-Stevens men. When the Olympia paper joked that convention president Fitzhugh was fully capable of buying out Stevens if he wanted to, it implied that his financial clout that made him a political force was now so strong that he could not be unduly influenced by Stevens.[39]

DEATH IN THE GARDEN

May 28, two weeks after Fitzhugh chaired the 1857 convention and was elected Central Committee Chairman again, brought uncertainty and legal chaos to his personal and political life for the next two years. He killed employee Andrew Wilson in circumstances that were less than clear.

One of Fitzhugh's first improvements to the Sehome Mine settlement had been the only store for people at the bay, as well as the rough-hewn mine saloon. William Busey added another store and saloon on the muddy "road" later. Men collected at the little business area for fellowship, liquor, cigars, and gambling, especially at the end of the work week for mine, mill, and fort.

On a balmy Saturday evening, militia veteran and miner Andrew Wilson headed home with eight miles to walk around the point and south to Chuckanut Bay. Wilson's Lummi wife Lucy, little son John Andrew, and dinner awaited him there. He was, in the words of witnesses, "tight" and "intoxicated." Heavy-set Wilson was known to quarrel and fight with his fellow saloon patrons when he drank. When he reached Richard Williams's house, he yelled for him to come out, and the two talked for a bit by the street.[40]

At the same time, Fitzhugh walked the trail from Whatcom toward home with Francis Cooty and his boy. Julia, Mary, and the toddlers awaited his arrival, and a hot, fresh dinner was in the making. When Fitzhugh came to the men standing near his own house, he asked Williams if Wilson was "making a row," and inquired which way Wilson was headed. He told the intoxicated man to move along and not disturb the community's families.[41]

A defiant Wilson claimed he wasn't making any noise and would go where he pleased. Fitzhugh's inner sense of ownership over the situation came not only from being the ultimate authority for the land claim and mine, but was also born from generations of male Fitzhugh identity and sense of honor as protector of their property and family. In the "First Family of Virginia" culture, defiance by a trespasser was usually met with violence. Wilson, drunk, probably did not understand the seriousness of his situation.[42]

Fitzhugh told the man he didn't want to hear any more and to go. Wilson said "Where?" Fitzhugh pointed to the street through the settlement and south. Instead of taking that direction, Wilson turned to go down to the beach through Fitzhugh's family garden, saying he would go when he liked and whichever way he liked. Fitzhugh said Wilson could go down the road or around to the beach, but not to cross his garden. Wilson still did not perceive the threat, or his liquor-fueled belligerence led him to ignore it.

After a few more remarks, Wilson started for the beach again but turned after a few yards, threw his bundle down, and dared Fitzhugh to "come on." He advanced toward Fitzhugh who stood his ground as his honor required him to do. Wilson threw both arms around Fitzhugh's waist. One hand grabbed Fitzhugh's small single-shot pistol from his pocket, and they began to grapple over it. The pistol went off between the men as they struggled, though they continued to fight over it, raising the pistol over their heads.

Men came from everywhere when they heard the gunshot. Francis Cooty had been lighting his pipe down the slope, but he ran back and grabbed the pistol. Richard Williams quit watering his cabbages, and William Lueke put his book down and joined the others. They had a hard time getting the heavier Wilson to let go of Fitzhugh so they could separate the two men. Then they saw that Wilson had been shot in the groin. Cooty thought both men held the gun when it went off. Fitzhugh showed them the powder burn on his hand and said the gun had gone off accidentally. He left for his own house, perhaps to get a bandage.

The others carried Wilson into a nearby house, where they asked him "Why did you come back and attack the Colonel? If you had not done it, this would not have happened." Wilson said nothing. When Fitzhugh returned, he told Wilson that if had not been for his foolishness in grabbing the gun, it would not have gone off. "You grabbed my pistol," he said. Wilson said nothing. Fitzhugh left again.

William Lueke walked back to Fitzhugh's house, where his boss asked him if Wilson was badly hurt and said, "I did not mean to harm the poor devil. He shot himself." Looking at Fitzhugh's hand and shirt, it looked to Lueke like Fitzhugh had been the one holding the muzzle and Wilson the butt with the trigger. Richard Williams thought that Wilson held the muzzle and Fitzhugh the butt. Their inconsistent observations triggered the controversy and protracted legal proceedings that followed.

Three days after the shooting, Wilson lay dying on a floor pallet. With the limited medical treatment available, there was nothing to be done to save him from such a wound. The men later said they weren't the ones nursing him, so some of the wives must have taken charge. Probate Judge Edward Eldridge arrived and asked Wilson if he wanted to make a statement. He wrote down Wilson's words as two witnesses stood by. Wilson recounted the verbal confrontation about where he could walk on his way home. He declared that Fitzhugh came after him and shot him when he turned around. Wilson died shortly after.

Andrew Wilson's senseless death, however it happened, destroyed his family. Lucy Wilson and her little boy were left in a distant cabin without financial support. Fitzhugh was the $1,000 per year Indian agent who was supposed to look out for the welfare of the Lummi, but nothing records that he helped her. She took her little son and returned to her family on Lummi Peninsula where, in the future, John Andrew founded a large family.

A non-witness later wrote, from apparent rumor, that Fitzhugh was taken into custody. There is no evidence of that in the case file, in witness statements, or of Fitzhugh posting bond. The fort would have been the only place to hold Fitzhugh.[43]

As soon as Wilson expired on May 31, local residents organized what they called a grand jury "trial" for the next day. Justice of the Peace Russell Peabody temporarily resigned his office so he could act as an informal coroner. The next day, County Auditor John Lysle conducted the coroner's inquest into what was apparently the first death by homicide between local settlers.[44]

As soon as the ad hoc coroner's inquest concluded, the grand jury convened with Peabody back in charge as justice of the peace, for what in the future would be called a preliminary hearing, not a "grand jury trial." The county did not have a real courthouse, just the small shack for business. It is likely that to provide room for everyone, "court" was held in one of the saloons.

Whatcom County men conducted the proceedings in a way nearly unimaginable a century later. Peabody was the only person who did not work for Fitzhugh. All the jurors and witnesses worked at the mine, including Probate Judge Eldridge, now enlisted as a juror. Unlike in later times, grand jury proceedings included attendance by the accused. Territorial Prosecutor Butler Anderson did not conduct the hasty court hearing, leading to a future problem.

Fitzhugh's Virginia lawyer persona strode into "court," and stated that he was there in person to defend himself against the plaintiff, Washington Territory. The charge under consideration by the grand jury (who all worked for him) was "assault with intent to kill." After hearing the charge, Fitzhugh demanded that before he would make any further statements in his defense, the court should produce evidence of the charge.[45]

Justice of the Peace Peabody and the grand jurors considered testimony by three witnesses and the deathbed statement taken by Eldridge. Fitzhugh made no other statement. Justice Peabody ruled that he was discharging Fitzhugh because the evidence before him was insufficient to "convict" him, so no indictment from the ad hoc proceedings made its way to the District Court and to Prosecutor Anderson.[46]

The coroner's inquest and grand jury "trial" turned into a money-maker for local men. The county paid everyone. Peabody received $12.50, equivalent to over $350, for saying "He died of a gunshot wound," and then presiding as the justice. John Lysle and five jurors received $2 each, witnesses were paid $8, and Sheriff Jewett (nominally in charge of defendant Fitzhugh) received $11.75.[47]

Editor J. W. Wiley of the Olympia newspaper was a Stevens man who usually wrote positively of Fitzhugh, his fellow Mason, and member of the "Olympia Clique." He published an oddly contradictory article on the homicide, sure to be of interest to everyone in the territory. First he wrote that Fitzhugh deliberately shot Wilson without provocation. Then, he gave himself an out by adding that he had talked to some Whatcom people and "a majority…, whilst they deplore the casualty [sic] or necessity of Col. Fitzhugh's proceedings…, at the same time justify his course of conduct." Wiley accused Republicans of trying to pin the act on Fitzhugh as a crime, though he had just said "without provocation." He was a loyal Stevens man in the festering conflict among Democrats over the martial law fiasco, and the desertions of some Democrats to the new Republican party. Those men included both Edward Eldridge and Russell Peabody, who may have seen an opportunity for revenge against the Stevens man during the 1857 campaign season. (See Chapter 7.)[48]

An Aborted Duel

If Fitzhugh hadn't generated enough controversy after the shooting in May 1857, the succeeding August brought a situation in which he might purposely kill another man. And not just any man—the nephew of Senator Jefferson Davis, who as secretary of war sent the army to build Fort Bellingham and earned lasting gratitude from locals.

First Lieutenant Robert Hugh Davis had arrived a year before with Captain George Pickett's Company "D" of the new Ninth Infantry. Lt. Davis's "Uncle Jeff" had established the regiment and equipped it with the newest model guns. Robert Davis was his uncle's "citizen appointment" to the regiment's officer contingent, meaning he didn't need either West Point education or prior military officer experience, though he had served in the Mexican War. Evidence indicates that while visiting his brother in Oregon, he had served as a witness (and spy) for his uncle at some early Washington treaty negotiations. Robert was not progressing toward an adult career as the Davis men thought he should, and so his uncle appointed him to the Ninth. When new West Point graduate and Second Lieutenant James W. Forsyth met Davis, he didn't like the civilian appointee who outranked him. However, Davis was liked by most of the sixty-some enlisted men who were generally recruited off the docks and streets of New York City, and were adventurers or men who ran from their problems. Perhaps drawing on Davis's rural Mississippi hunting experience, Captain Pickett tasked the citizen appointee with teaching the enlisted men to shoot, usually with only one bullet per practice session. Like Pickett and Forsyth, Davis married an elite indigenous young woman, Tol'stola (Caroline), who was Samish-Swinomish and very likely a cousin of Fitzhugh's wife Julia, as she also was of Jenny Wynn whose grandfather had warned Fitzhugh of a possible raid.[49]

On the last day of July 1857, Fitzhugh and Lt. Davis were drinking and gambling at the same table in the Sehome Mine saloon. Fitzhugh accused Davis of cheating in their whiskey-fueled card game. The insulted Mississippian challenged Fitzhugh to a duel. Bellingham Bay men knew that Fitzhugh might often be likeable, but recent events had shown that he could also be deadly if angered. Lt. Davis had developed his own reputation for fearlessness, having only weeks before taken a whaleboat out in the dark to pursue attacking Laich-wil-tach.

A challenge by Lt. Davis complicated matters for Fitzhugh. Territorial Prosecutor Butler Anderson was planning a proper hearing on the Wilson homicide charges, and Lt. Davis was scheduled to testify. Since the Army officer had not witnessed the actual shooting, he had probably been in the saloon where Wilson got intoxicated. Whatever Davis's testimony was going to be, it would not go well for Fitzhugh to kill one of the witnesses.

For planter-class Southerners like both men, gambling had become a ritualized way to best rivals without bloodshed. Not to play when invited implied cowardice, as well as an anti-social attitude. Both men were expert gamblers, and cheating in the saloon atmosphere of "friendly" rivalry brought the highest disgrace. In Davis's own Vicksburg history, going to the dueling grounds across the Mississippi River in Louisiana settled almost every serious dispute. Southern migrants carried the custom west, as in the 1852 duel in California that included Fitzhugh as the second to a fellow Virginian. And now two prideful Southerners were about to face off in Whatcom County, Washington Territory.

Fitzhugh declined the challenge.

Robert Davis believed that his honor as a gentleman and his social standing were at stake. "Southern honor" was still based not on what a man thought of himself, but what other men around him thought. The lieutenant believed he must demonstrate his worth to civilians, his Army superiors, and the men under his own command. He ignored all military and civilian anti-dueling laws. However, this was Washington Territory where the social structure differed, because many settlers were from the Northeast. Public consensus to support the custom of dueling was absent. It wasn't Virginia, Mississippi, or even California. Apparently Fitzhugh felt that he could refuse the challenge without personally losing anything, particularly in his current legal circumstances.[50]

Before Lt. Davis could force Fitzhugh into a duel, Virginian and Captain George Pickett arrived in Sehome to intervene in the name of military law and common sense. Carried through, a Davis duel would result in a court martial. Davis could face imprisonment, the end of his career, or lose his life. Fitzhugh could kill Jefferson Davis's nephew, a witness in his criminal case. Every Washington Territory citizen wanted the appropriation support in Congress from Davis's uncle.

Pickett's arguments, and perhaps military order, won out but he might not have foreseen Davis's solution to preserve his honor.

Pickett had his own example to consider. His cousin Henry Heth had stopped one of the final Army duels by making the two adversaries stand out in the cold a good long time. Pickett had probably heard from Heth that foolish men could be stopped without weapons, but he may not have anticipated that the result would be the loss of his rifle instructor.[51]

First Lieutenant Davis resigned his commission. There was no great incentive for him to remain in the army after what he saw as a major affront to his honor as a gentleman and officer. The army had no retirement policy and seniority ruled, which meant that he could stagnate at lieutenant rank for many years, barring another war. Dueling was in Davis family history, but Robert Davis also had a family example of being angry enough to resign a commission and go home. His uncle Jefferson left the army in 1834 over a frontier outpost argument.[52]

Fort Bellingham's enlisted men and non-commissioned officers were angry at their loss of Lt. Davis, and probably angry at Pickett for intervening in a way that caused Davis to leave. They collectively wrote two unusual letters to the Olympia newspaper that brought Fitzhugh into more public controversy. The first was an open letter to Davis regretting his departure and thanking him for his "repeated acts of humanity to many in this company," and vowing never to forget him. The second letter applauded his "deeds of valor and noble daring" in the Mexican War. The men asked the editor to print the revealing letters so everyone would read them, something of a protest against Pickett for causing the loss of their officer.[53]

Civilian Robert H. Davis did not leave Caroline and go home to Mississippi. He contracted to hunt meat for the fort, then bought half of William Busey's store and saloon in Sehome. The commissioners appointed him deputy sheriff in December, on-site law enforcement for Sehome and Whatcom. The jobs Davis held after his resignation almost certainly annoyed either Pickett or Fitzhugh, or both.[54]

಄

Another series of events in the latter half of 1857 would soon bring chaos to the daily life of everyone at Bellingham Bay. During the early 1850s, while Washingtonians worked on organizing their territory and building their hoped-for wealth, the rest of the country was in a post-Mexican War economic boom. But in August 1857, just after the territorial elections and the aborted Fitzhugh-Davis duel, a massive embezzlement scandal and failure of a major financial institution shocked the nation. They caused a domino effect that led to falling grain prices, factory layoffs, and railroad failures in an overbuilt system. Land speculation collapsed. Thirty thousand pounds of San Francisco Mint gold shipped by sea to the eastern banks was lost off South Carolina in the wreck of the *Central America*. Thousands of people questioned whether the U.S. government had the ability to back paper currency.

Rumors about gold in western Canada up the Fraser River had filtered out for years but did not tempt those obsessed with California gold, or anyone at Bellingham Bay. However, as the national financial crash increased in late 1857, that attitude changed a month after new Governor Fayette McMullen arrived. First Nations indigenous people from far up the river began to trade gold from the Fraser's sandbars at the Hudson's Bay Company's Fort Yale below the Hell's Gate rapids.

CHAPTER 7

Loyalty's Reward in the Season of Gold

IN 1856 A MAJOR POLITICAL EVENT changed Fitzhugh's life for years to come, occurring at the same time as his business activities, territorial politics, and the Wilson homicide. Voters elected James Buchanan president, and the Pennsylvania Democrat with Southern sympathies replaced northern Democrat Franklin Pierce in the White House.

Buchanan was perhaps the most qualified person ever to assume the presidency. He has also frequently been labeled the country's worst president. Born to Irish immigrants shortly after nationhood, in his twenties after college he began assuming a chain of elected and appointed positions of increasing responsibility and political influence: state legislator; five terms in the U.S. House of Representatives where he left the Federalist party for the Democrats; ambassador to Russia under President Andrew Jackson; U.S. senator; secretary of state for President James Polk; and Pierce's ambassador to England. Two presidents offered him a seat on the U.S. Supreme Court, which he turned down. He was, for his time, one of the ultimate political

Figure 13, President James Buchanan, circa 1850–1860. *Library of Congress, Prints and Photographs Division. #2002699740/LC-DIG-pga-09177.*

107

insiders who advanced through ambition, ability, and personal connections. Fitzhugh was much like him, on a smaller stage.

Buchanan also carried some political negatives. For ten years, he and fellow politician William Rufus King lived together as intimate partners and were often called derisive names by newspapers and opponents. Their affair and friendship lasted until King's death in 1853, shortly after his inauguration as Pierce's vice president. Because of Alabama-born King's influence, most of Buchanan's social circle were Southerners. He became wedded to an outdated vision of the nation as a slaveholding republic where, it was expected, the institution would fade away as it had in Pennsylvania, without needing to be rooted out. This led him to condemn slavery in the abstract while not supporting abolition, and to support the slavery compromise laws passed by Congress in the 1850s. He realistically saw slavery as the weak link in the government and nation but was afraid to touch it lest the union break apart. Worst of all, "Old Buck's" presidency was tainted by the patronage system that led to vast corruption within his government. He called the new Republican Party's members "Black Republicans" and "disunionists," unworthy of public offices he controlled.[1]

White-haired and sixty-five, President Buchanan was sworn in on March 4, 1857. His vice president, Kentucky's John Breckinridge, had been chosen to balance the Democratic ticket between regions. Under the patronage system, all positions were open for change and used to enhance political leverage, including those in Washington Territory. Buchanan, a known micro-manager, began an over-long period of nominating federal appointees down to local postmasters, then waited for Congressional approval that could drag on for several years. His goal was to shape a "reliable, popular coalition of national Democrats loyal to him and thereby defeat the Republicans" who were the new majority in Congress.[2]

Buchanan took control of the nation's federal justice system. Washingtonians wanted federal judges appointed from their territory, not men who knew little or nothing about them. After Governor Stevens was elected congressional delegate, they were unhappily looking forward to the arrival of Buchanan's new appointee, Fayette McMullen, coming straight from Virginia. Stevens had first come to Washington Territory with the railroad survey. He knew the place and the people. McMullen's unfamiliarity with local conditions, so different from the state of Virginia, meant Buchanan's judicial choices took on even more import.

A judicial system for law and order was a deciding factor that spurred the March 1853 formation of Washington Territory out of Oregon. Economic development and peaceful relations among residents north of the Columbia River was not sustainable without it. Three classes of courts had been established for the new territory: 1) justice of the peace courts and 2) probate courts, both of which had elected judges who could be non-lawyers. For example, neither Justice of the Peace Russell Peabody or Probate Judge Edward Eldridge were lawyers when they conducted the informal inquest and hearing after the Wilson homicide. The third judicial branch was three district courts whose justices were presidential appointments. Once a year in December the district court justices became the Territorial Supreme Court to hear appeals from their own district courts. The legislature tinkered with the monetary value of misdemeanor cases handled by a county justice of the peace as the population and financial arguments multiplied, so the district courts' time would not be overwhelmed by minor cases. An unacknowledged legal problem was the inclusion of district justices in the Supreme Court. All three justices had to be present for the Supreme Court to open, and they did not recuse themselves from cases they first heard. An objective review of a case was difficult, and perhaps sometimes impossible, to achieve by later standards.[3]

President Pierce's 1853 appointments, including Isaac Stevens, generally required party loyalty, the support of an influential administration member, and often service in the Mexican War. The first Washington Territory district justices were Chief Justice Edward Lander from Massachusetts, Victor Monroe from Kentucky, and Pennsylvanian Obadiah McFadden who transferred from Oregon. Lander, Monroe, and former Oregon Justice William Strong, who heard cases north of the Columbia for several years, wrote the initial legal code using New York's as a foundation revisable to fit local conditions. Monroe, an alcoholic chosen to placate the South, was removed the next year, and replaced by lawyer, and first territorial legislature Speaker of the House, Francis ("Frank") Chenoweth. As Third District associate justice, he moved to Whidbey Island where he heard most cases at Penn Cove in a Coveland cabin and occasionally in Port Townsend. The split locations annoyed everyone until 1859.[4]

Chief Justice Lander was Harvard-trained and Associate Justice McFadden attended Yale. Their scholarly approach to the law professionalized the judicial system. Associate Justice Chenoweth was informally schooled in the law, but he passed the Wisconsin bar at twenty-two. It was during the term of these three justices that Governor Stevens declared martial law, arrested Lander and Chenoweth for not supporting it, and subsequently had to acquiesce to public opinion and the rule of law. He did not forget this personal affront from the justices that made him pardon himself, and their terms were expiring. He also remembered those who had remained loyal to him.

Though almost everyone agreed that personable Stevens was brilliant with unending energy and many friends, some thought the man, standing barely over five feet tall, a "Napoleonic dictator with delusions of grandeur and a narrow egotism that brooked no criticism or opposition." Others found it odd that he achieved so much influence and notoriety despite his notorious lack of hygiene. In many ways Stevens was a perfect match for Fitzhugh's personality and family culture. They understood each other, though Stevens was from a New England founding family and Fitzhugh from a founding Virginia one. After the martial law debacle and resulting national bad publicity, it became clear to Stevens that the new president, even if he was another Democrat, would not re-appoint him, so he had run for congressional delegate.[5]

Fitzhugh, as Democratic Central Committee chairman during the 1857 territorial campaign, worked hard for candidate Stevens. He left the mine's management to his capable men there, including John Tennant who also took on the local campaign tasks when Fitzhugh was absent. Stevens constantly traveled to local communities to debate with lawyer William Wallace representing the Republican nominee, Alexander Abernethy.

After a vigorous campaign, and despite Stevens's personal shortcomings, the territory delivered 65 percent of the vote to him, including every single one of Whatcom County's votes delivered by Fitzhugh and Tennant. Not everyone in the county believed the ballot count was honest because, they said, Fitzhugh could be very intimidating when accompanied on his canvassing rounds by rough-looking bodyguards.[6]

New congressional delegate Stevens owed much to Central Committee Chairman Fitzhugh's efforts to bring in votes. When he and his family left for Washington, DC, in September after Governor McMullen arrived, Stevens mentally carried his plans to reward and punish when he presented his nominee recommendations to the Buchanan administration. As a fellow Democrat, he would play an outsized role in nominations even if he had no vote in Congress. No one was going to be more deserving of an appointment than his campaign worker and loyal former military aide, E. C. Fitzhugh.

෬෩

Stevens certainly intended to pressure Buchanan to nominate Fitzhugh to the territorial court from the start. However, in addition to the problem of Fitzhugh's martial law loyalty to Stevens, two major personal issues might interfere with congressional approval of him taking office. One was the continuing public accusations of murder, ignoring the possibility that Wilson had accidentally shot himself, and Whatcom County residents' active efforts to get Fitzhugh indicted. Two, there was the almost-duel during campaign season with the nephew of Pierce's secretary of war and new-senator, Jefferson Davis. McMullen, the new governor, knew Fitzhugh and his father from Virginia's legislature and might have his own opinion on a nomination.

In his early fifties, "LaFayette" McMullen was not from a First Family of Virginia like the Fitzhughs, though he liked hanging out with FFVs. The former Shenandoah Valley stagecoach driver and farmer served ten years in the state senate and then four terms in Congress,

Figure 14, Territorial Governor Fayette McMullen, about 1857–1859. McMullen held office during E. C. Fitzhugh's nomination process for territorial justice. *Susan Paris Photograph Collection, 1889–1990, #8681. Washington State Archives, Digital Archives.*

despite also being indicted four times for assault. Where he came from, fisticuffs replaced duels. McMullen was a delegate to the national Democratic convention that nominated James Buchanan, who then awarded the former congressman the governorship. McMullen did not see his appointment as governor in the distant Pacific Northwest as a prize position.[7]

McMullen stayed in the territory less than two years, still long enough to meddle in Fitzhugh's political life. Descriptions of him are colorful. "He was a good, staunch, southern Democrat with friends in high places" said one historian. Isaac Stevens biographer Kent Richards was more direct in his assessment, asserting that McMullen appeared to think that he could spend a couple of years in Washington, be elected congressional delegate, and take over the territory's Democratic Party. McMullen was "condescending in his personal relationships," with a "puritanical streak which led him to make a major issue of the use of the legislative hall for dances," though the town had no other large gathering space. McMullen "didn't suit the people and they didn't suit him." If citizens could tolerate the replacement governor, they were incensed that he held up the re-appointment of Territorial Secretary Charles Mason, a popular man who frequently had to take on Governor Stevens's duties. The *Puget Sound Herald* noted that the people of Washington were "deeply chagrined and mortified" at McMullen's appointment and "disgusted with his deportment" when he "did not make a single friend," only because "he showed that he despised the people to whom he owed the performance of such important duties."[8]

There were meetings among Washington Territory's central Democratic figures, including McMullen who knew nothing about local politics and events. They did not all agree that Lander and Chenoweth should be abandoned in favor of Fitzhugh and William Strong. McMullen seems to have slept at Fitzhugh's home on at least one trip north, perhaps to get a current assessment of his fellow Virginian. In addition to his personal problems, Fitzhugh had no legal experience in Washington other than two short stints as court clerk and court commissioner in the year after his arrival. He had not earned the prominent law school credentials held by others. He certainly could not be nominated for chief justice, though the *Pioneer-Democrat* reported that Stevens had offered him that post in return for his campaign support. Fitzhugh denied any offer. Associate Justice

Obadiah McFadden received the chief justice nomination. Former Oregon Justice William Strong, a Stevens loyalist who had captained a militia company and co-written the territory's legal code, would be acceptable to everyone.[9]

Fitzhugh's supporters had, in the late months of 1857, started circulating petitions throughout the Third District for the thirty-six-year-old's nomination, though many outside of Sehome and Whatcom did not take it seriously at first. However, Associate Justice Frank Chenoweth took it very seriously, and tried to pre-empt what Fitzhugh's supporters might send to Washington, DC. He wrote to U.S. Attorney General Jeremiah S. Black in December to request re-appointment and said Stevens had told him he'd "nail me to the counter and teach me whose path I had crossed." Chenoweth criticized the cronyism of Stevens's staff officers during the war, including Fitzhugh. It did not help Chenoweth's case when Attorney General Black passed the letter along to Delegate Stevens who denied the allegation, and said he'd lost faith in Chenoweth's competence because he was a "false and unscrupulous man."[10]

Stevens campaigned for Fitzhugh's appointment in Washington, DC, coordinating with W.W. Miller and other operatives around the Third District as the fight to replace Chenoweth began. The petition drive in Fitzhugh's favor went nowhere, with many voters still angry about martial law or the questionable lack of consequences for Fitzhugh killing a former militia member. Letters of recommendation and Stevens's support were always going to be the strongest factors in a personal and party loyalty patronage-driven system. Stevens sent word to Miller in mid-March that "No nominations have been sent in [to Congress]. The President assures me that no appointments shall be made from the Territory over my head...The Attorney General thinks I was *right* in the martial law matter...I have taken my ground totally and decisively and shall not falter in the least."[11]

;<>;

Opposition to Fitzhugh's likely nomination continued to grow as 1858 dawned, even as he dealt with the epidemic at Bellingham Bay. Governor McMullen wanted to take control of the territorial appointments, but his unpleasant personality and unfamiliarity with local politics gave him almost no influence. When he quietly came out for Chenoweth after the Fitzhugh nomination for the Third District was placed by

Stevens, his influence with W. W. Miller and other upper echelon Democrats was over. He cut his term short and left after obtaining a legislative divorce and marrying a young Olympia woman who apparently was eager to flee stump-strewn Olympia.[12]

Associate Justice Frank Chenoweth (age 39), originally a Wisconsin lawyer, traveled the Oregon Trail in 1849 instead of going to the California gold rush. Settling on the northern side of the Columbia River's lower rapids, he built the first railroad in the Pacific Northwest, a mule-drawn flatcar on wooden tracks. His crude five-mile-long railroad moved freight and people around the Cascades Rapids, eliminating an arduous portage and easing the burden of many exhausted Oregon Trail sojourners. Before his judicial appointment, he was Washington's first speaker of the house. His judicial integrity during the martial law episode led to massive public respect and few complaints about his court actions, but his term of office was set to expire on August 2, 1858.[13]

When men who disliked Fitzhugh's political methods spotted the petition supporting his nomination, they circulated counter-petitions. Eighteen Democratic legislators as well as Third District voters from Jefferson, Island, and Clallam Counties, signed. Nearly every settler signed, whether he be farmer, lawyer, or businessman. Current legislators in two petitions did not mention Fitzhugh, instead commending Chenoweth as a "prompt impartial and efficient officer and a sound reliable and true democrat." Petition signers said his re-appointment would "meet the approbation of his constituency and the party generally."[14]

Figure 15, Francis (F. A.) Chenoweth about 1890. Lawyer, territorial justice, and prosecutor during Fitzhugh's time in Washington Territory. *Courtesy of the Washington State Historical Society at WashingtonHistory.org, #2018.0.391.*

The opposition's petitions began to reach Attorney General Black's desk in early 1858, even before Stevens submitted his choice. So did letters to Black and Buchanan. There were many judicial nomination files, but only the files for Washington Territory centered around a legally disastrous martial law declaration by a territorial governor-turned-congressional delegate who pardoned himself.[15]

U.S. Attorney General Jeremiah Black (age 47) had left his position as Pennsylvania's chief justice to take the new office. He understood the implications of lawyer Fitzhugh's loyalty to Stevens during the 1856 events. Though Black's father had served in Congress, he was largely self-educated before he started to read law at seventeen with a local attorney. He was such a prodigy that he was admitted to the Pennsylvania bar at twenty. He and Buchanan both wanted to hold the squabbling country together. They might favor putting a Virginian on the Washington Territory bench for balance, despite Fitzhugh's lack of a prestigious law school education.

Figure 16, Jeremiah Black, U.S. Attorney General during E. C. Fitzhugh's judicial nomination process. *Brady-Handy photograph collection, Library of Congress, Prints and Photographs Division, #LC-BH826-3912.*

The Jefferson County (mainly Port Townsend) petition warned of "evil consequences to the people" if Fitzhugh was seated instead of Chenoweth and was signed by nearly sixty men. It was a template for Clallam County's petition that warned of the same dire results. Over forty Clallam County voters from the isolated settlements at Neah Bay and Dungeness ("Whiskey Flats") signed. Sixty-nine men, virtually all of Whidbey Island's male settlers, asked for Chenoweth's re-appointment on the basis of their "entire confidence in [his] ability and integrity."[16]

The petition potentially most harmful was from Whatcom County dated December 30, 1857, addressed directly to President Buchanan, and inserted into the Chenoweth file. The petition was likely organized and written by Edward Eldridge, tentative new Republican. He was the respected Whatcom County probate judge who took Wilson's deathbed statement, questioned what happened when Andrew Wilson was shot, and was leading the ongoing effort to get Fitzhugh prosecuted. Eldridge had begun to publicly question Fitzhugh's imperious methods of obtaining votes in Whatcom County elections. The third settler at Whatcom and current Fitzhugh employee, Eldridge was the first to sign, followed by thirty-nine other men. Whatcom Mill's Henry Roeder signed, as did most other prominent settlers of Sehome and Whatcom except Fitzhugh's blacksmith Thomas Wynn, who was a Quaker and mostly stayed aloof from politics. All of them were men Fitzhugh knew well. Signers included former lieutenant Robert Hugh Davis, by then a saloon and store owner at Sehome and new deputy sheriff. Fitzhugh's appointment would give Whatcom County a seat on the court, but it didn't matter to the petitioners who knew him best.[17]

The Whatcom County petition listed four specific reasons why Fitzhugh should not be appointed to Frank Chenoweth's judicial seat:

1st. "That the said E. C. Fitzhugh although long known as the leading democrat in this county, we do not consider worthy of our confidence or support for his language and actions in his intercourse with his fellow citizens plainly show that his feelings are diametrically opposed to the cardinal principles of democracy whatever his public career may show to the contrary and we consider a democrat from interest and not from principle to be unworthy of our confidence."

2nd. "That he has totally estranged the affections of a very large majority of his fellow citizens. His deplorable and reckless conduct and his intercourse with the poor also of the community."

3rd. "That we do not consider him qualified to discharge the duties of the U.S. District Court." [Author Note: What is surprising is that Fitzhugh's clerk John Tennant, who was reading law under him, signed, thereby agreeing to this criticism of Fitzhugh.]

4th. "That about six months ago, he shot a fellow citizen who died three days after for which he has yet to appear before a court of justice."

Whatcom petitioners included a fifth item, a statement of support for Chenoweth who had "discharged his duties to our full satisfaction and thereupon we hope he can be continued." Then, a final shot at Fitzhugh, saying that if Chenoweth was not re-appointed, they hoped he would be succeeded by "someone who can obtain the support and well wishes of the community."

Ironically, nearly all the future plaintiffs and defendants, whose cases Fitzhugh would adjudicate in the coming years, were opposition petition signers. If appointed, this was a case where "letting bygones be bygones" would be essential for all participants.

A letter from the territory's U.S. Attorney, J. S. Smith, accompanied the petitions opposing Fitzhugh's nomination that he collected and sent to Attorney General Black in February 1858. Smith claimed that petitioners comprised every single voter from the last election and accused Stevens of getting his nomination and election for congressional delegate "by *hook and crook*." He maintained there "was not the shadow of a necessity" for martial law. Smith concluded with the statement that Chenoweth was not a member of any party faction but was a victim of Stevens's revenge for his opposition to martial law.[18]

On March 10 Governor McMullen sent Black a letter "strongly" recommending Frank Chenoweth, a man he hardly knew, apparently bowing to what he saw as overwhelming support by Third District voters. Only a few months had passed since he went to Whatcom to confer with Fitzhugh and other politicos at Christmas. He admitted that despite the strong support for Chenoweth's abilities and integrity on the bench, "there was some dissatisfaction against him" from the martial law events that "now has subsided to a great extent."[19]

☙❧

Stevens wrote a lengthy formal nomination letter to Black on March 16 from his office in the U.S. House of Representatives. Black had it in hand before the McMullen letter could reach him. Stevens portrayed Fitzhugh as an "eminent citizen" characterized by "great integrity, public spirit, and a thorough understanding of the wants and conditions of a new country." He applauded Fitzhugh's actions during the Treaty War without mentioning martial law except to say, "he was the right arm of the defender of the Sound." Though he knew that Fitzhugh did not have an academic law education, he called him "thoroughly trained and experienced," and he had been "associated with the eminent men of his profession and can bring the most conclusive testimonials to his competency." He called the shooting of Wilson self-defense and asserted

that Fitzhugh had been exonerated by a magistrate with no other proceedings instituted, this despite moves still being made to indict him for
murder. Stevens claimed falsely that the majority of settlers supported
his innocence. Stevens lied that Fitzhugh's few enemies were mostly
men who wanted to sell liquor to the Indians, in addition to men who
"encouraged insubordination in the military service." Finally, the letter
excoriated Chenoweth as a "convenient tool of the Black Republican
party," and that the men who recommended him were mostly of that
group, also not true. He called Chenoweth's December letter "scan-
dalous and indecent." The last line said Senator William Gwin knew
Fitzhugh's personal, professional, and political character well. Gwin, as
California's first and present senator, had become an even more powerful Democrat representing the West Coast since Fitzhugh knew him
in San Francisco. Three days later, having apparently talked to the president, Stevens wrote his letter to W. W. Miller claiming that Buchanan
would not make any appointments over his head.[20]

Stevens obtained support letters from Fitzhugh's former law partner
(and coal syndicate head) Calhoun Benham, whose personal familiarity
would add weight. Archibald Campbell, head of the U.S. Northwest
Boundary Survey Commission, also wrote a support letter, although
he had only been in the county months and had little familiarity with
issues outside of getting the boundary in the islands fixed. A dissatisfied
neighbor of Chenoweth wrote that the justice told someone to kill his
neighbor's cattle. A single legislator from the south Sound wrote in
support.[21]

Justice Frank Chenoweth was not one to give up easily. He fought a
public battle for his re-appointment. In May 1858 the *Pioneer-Democrat*
printed his letter about the campaign to keep him from re-appointment.
He denied the accusation that he had written letters to Washington,
DC, trying to prevent payment of the Treaty War debts to the territory.
He claimed near-unanimity in the district for re-appointment, despite
realistically being unable to claim being a Democrat by Stevens's
requirements. A week after that, the paper printed another letter
from him that claimed his re-appointment was being held up because
opponents were calling him an "enemy of the people."[22]

Current Democratic Party chairman, the irascible J.J.H. Van
Bokkelen of Port Townsend, wrote to Miller about the dying resistance
to Fitzhugh. No admirer of Fitzhugh, his was the third signature on

the Jefferson County petition supporting Chenoweth. Despite the previous conflicts with Fitzhugh in California and the militia, his letter to Miller on May 16 said his county's opponents would do nothing more to stop the Fitzhugh nomination. Though nearly all Jefferson County men had signed the petition in support of Chenoweth, by then they thought a new judge might move the Third District Court to Port Townsend permanently, something that would inevitably advance commercial development.[23]

Justices Lander and Chenoweth made the long journey to Washington, DC, in the spring to plead their case with Black and Buchanan. Stevens wrote home to Miller on June 3, telling him that the justices made no progress for re-appointment. He reported he recently had a "full interview" with Buchanan and Black, and that was the result. "I did a good deal of good," Stevens bragged, having in his opinion also advanced the other territorial causes he had taken on as congressional delegate. The Senate confirmed McFadden, Strong, and Fitzhugh the very next day, June 4, 1858.[24]

In true Fitzhugh tradition, again the critical factor was Edmund's personal connections that had advanced him from the young lawyer who arrived in California nine years earlier. The day before Stevens presented his nomination to Black, Senator Gwin wrote a second enthusiastic recommendation outlining Fitzhugh's involvement in law and politics in Virginia and California. He concluded by saying Fitzhugh's appointment would "place an able and true man in a position for which he is fitted" and would be welcomed by his numerous California friends and himself. He didn't say that it would be another influential position secured by the men building the Democratic slavery-sympathetic Pacific bloc. Gwin's support meant everything when coupled with Stevens's support. In addition, there has been an overlooked factor— lawyer George Fitzhugh worked for Attorney General Black. In the small office, Black could not overlook the men's shared surname and home state or fail to question the bestselling apologist for slavery about his double cousin.[25]

Stevens wrote home to W. W. Miller that there had been no opposition to Fitzhugh in the Senate (probably due to Gwin's influence), and he was satisfied with the new justice's competency as well as future as a "popular judge." Stevens believed that the opposition to Fitzhugh would dissolve after his first court term. Surprisingly, he maintained that if Chenoweth had kept his mouth shut instead of writing the letters so strongly impugning Stevens's integrity, he probably would have been re-appointed.[26]

Stevens wrote a lengthier letter to Miller after receiving three that Miller wrote back in May, victims of the mail delay to and from Puget Sound. Stevens thought that if the Olympia paper published the recommendation letter from Fitzhugh's coal mine partner Calhoun Benham, it might help repair his reputation before he took the bench. Considering that Stevens had approached the judicial appointments looking for revenge, telling Miller that he had not strongly opposed Chief Justice Lander's re-appointment was ludicrous. After all, when Lander and Chenoweth spoke with Black after they arrived on their fruitless mission to derail Fitzhugh's appointment, Lander had told Black that Fitzhugh "would not answer at all, because he was not competent...and because he had killed a man." Stevens credited Senator Gwin's close friendship with Fitzhugh for overcoming any of Lander's statements.[27]

Fitzhugh wrote to Miller himself in the midst of local celebrations on July 4, after the steamer *Constitution* brought a letter from his political colleague. Official notice of his appointment a month earlier had not yet arrived, but Stevens had written him to expect its arrival. In a peculiar inclusion not discussed in any other correspondence, Fitzhugh mentioned that he had once asked Stevens to withdraw his name, but his friend wrote back that it was too late, and he wouldn't do it even if he could. Fitzhugh now wrote: "I really don't want the office but I'll accept it to a *certainty* if I am confirmed by the Senate (I have warm friends there) and as [a] compliment to Stevens after his taking the trouble to get it for me and to *oust* his *friend* Chenoweth."[28]

In mid-July Stevens wrote Miller again with his opinion that Chenoweth and Van Bokkelen would both stand by Fitzhugh's appointment now that it was no longer in question. He saw all three as "upright and honorable men," although that is certainly not how he earlier portrayed Chenoweth. Stevens conceded that Fitzhugh's style was much different, but still believed that his conduct on the bench would vindicate the appointment he had championed. On July 30, the *Pioneer-Democrat* announced Fitzhugh's appointment. Governor McMullen made a visit to Bellingham Bay, perhaps a peace-making call on his fellow Virginian.[29]

New Indictment

Though Congress approved Fitzhugh to assume the bench in the Third District from Chenoweth, he wasn't to take office until after Chenoweth's last three-week term in August. During that final term, Chenoweth and the prosecutor convened the official grand jury to consider a murder indictment against Fitzhugh. Their hearing superseded the ad hoc one conducted without Prosecutor Butler P. Anderson the day after Wilson died. However, the witnesses from the first hearing did not show up for the new one. Fitzhugh waited at Coveland five days while boarding at someone's house because there was no alternative on the island. Frustrated and angry at the waste of his time, Fitzhugh left and told people that Anderson had assured him no indictment was forthcoming. However, immediately after Fitzhugh started for the mainland, the grand jury indicted him for murder. The case was so well known by then that the grand jury took a vote without any testimony.

There may have been another factor at work in Prosecutor Anderson's actions during the term of court and for months afterward. Butler P. Anderson's brother was J. Patton Anderson, the territory's first congressional delegate, the man Stevens replaced in Washington, DC. The prosecutor's actions hint at a bit of passive aggressive retaliation against the man at the head of the 1857 election that left his brother behind.

Public criticism of the episode went on for months, until Anderson wrote to the *Pioneer-Democrat* editor in January: "I gave no such assurance; but when Judge Fitzhugh was about leaving Coveland (he was already in his canoe) he remarked to me that he had been there long enough and did not believe anything would be done with his case, and asked me what I thought. My reply was that 'I really did not know, but supposed no action would be taken.'"[30]

When the August 2, 1858, indictment came in without Fitzhugh's presence, both the grand jury and Anderson thought a change of venue to the Second District in Olympia was in order, but they did not carry through. Instead, they added a few more witnesses and issued subpoenas to appear at the Third's next term in February 1859. Edward Eldridge eluded Whatcom County Sheriff William Busey and the subpoena service at that time, surprising because it was Eldridge who had spearheaded the effort to get an indictment in the first place. Lame duck Justice Chenoweth also issued an arrest warrant, but Sheriff Busey reported back that he couldn't find Fitzhugh, who was probably already on his way to Olympia to take his oath of office and learn the job, having received his commission in the mail from new Chief Justice McFadden.[31]

Whatcom's new newspaper, the *Northern Light*, announced "Colonel Fitzhugh's" appointment in a small notice on August 6. Perhaps unwilling to annoy the powerful local, the editor from Sacramento ignored the indictment.[32]

Five days after Chenoweth signed the arrest warrant, on September 8, 1858, "E. C. Fitzhugh, Esq." wrote to Attorney General Black acknowledging receipt of his commission as "Associate Justice of the Supreme Court of Washington Territory." He added the affirmation "Acceptance" and included in the envelope a copy of his oath of office sworn before new-Chief Justice McFadden on the seventh in Olympia.[33]

Fitzhugh presented his credentials on September 17, despite Chenoweth issuing a second arrest warrant on his very last day as Third District justice. It seems he did that from Olympia because the next day Sheriff Busey arrested Fitzhugh there and handed him over to his new deputy (legislator and Fitzhugh employee John Tennant) to handle the bail. Fitzhugh had to be in Coveland in four days to conduct a special session of his Third District court. Justice Chenoweth had ordered Busey to present Fitzhugh at the next regular term of the Third in February to answer for the murder of Andrew Wilson. With no change of venue, that order meant that Fitzhugh would preside over his own murder trial, and the new district prosecutor would be none other than Frank Chenoweth. Over a year had passed since Wilson's death.

Fitzhugh was in Olympia until September 20 to celebrate his victory and learn his new job. After Sheriff Busey arrested him there, Prosecutor Anderson had his Second District grand jury consider holding Fitzhugh's trial in that Olympia court, even though Chenoweth had not issued a change of venue at the time of indictment. Anderson wanted to present evidence of Fitzhugh's unfitness to be Third District justice, but the judge ruled his evidence inadmissible for the grand jurors to hear because the Sehome witnesses couldn't arrive in time. Heading back north, Fitzhugh banged his gavel down for the first time at Coveland on September 22 to preside over the smuggling case of the Mexican schooner *Lord Raglan*, just four days after his arrest.[34]

Figure 17, The original Island County courthouse at Coveland where Justice E. C. Fitzhugh presided until the court was moved to Port Townsend in 1859. He was also indicted for murder at the Coveland courthouse. *Courtesy of Island County Historical Society, Coupeville, Washington. #2013.002.042b/#2013.002.032.*

The Third Judicial District of northwest Washington Territory was now Fitzhugh's, despite the indictment. All three districts were different. The First handled everything east of the Cascades. The Second included Olympia and the southern Sound areas. Fitzhugh's Third included the entrance to Puget Sound and customs questions, as well as admiralty cases involving vessel crews, shipwrecks, and salvage issues. There would be tribal problems, especially with liquor sellers. Lumber mills were increasing in number and their civil cases often involved contracts or insolvency, and debt collection cases were frequent. However, few cases ever involved settler against settler violence like Fitzhugh's own.

On October 10 Fitzhugh convened another special session to try a murder case. In the last business of the third day, Prosecutor Anderson, instead of new Prosecutor Chenoweth, moved for a change of venue for the Fitzhugh trial. As presiding judge, Fitzhugh issued the order to hold his own trial in Olympia. He also issued subpoenas for all the witnesses to appear there instead of at Coveland. The Second District court met in March, which gave him some time to prepare his defense, attend his first Supreme Court term in December, and hold his first regular term at Coveland in February. Andrew Wilson homicide witness Richard Williams, Fort Bellingham's Dr. Robert. O. Craig, and H. C. Page, the part-owner of the Roeder Mill, put up the $100 bail to guarantee Fitzhugh's appearance in the Second District courtroom.[35]

Sheriff Busey and Deputy Tennant noted that witness Edward Eldridge "refuses to recognize [the proceedings] or attend" despite being the instigator of the whole indictment mess. On October 15 *Pioneer-Democrat* editor Wiley put into print his own belief that Fitzhugh would be acquitted. Already rumors were circulating that Eldridge had an ulterior (political) motive in taking Wilson's deathbed statement, because he hadn't requested Fitzhugh to be a witness, even though his house was only one hundred fifty yards away. The rumor found its way into the *Pioneer-Democrat* later when the paper labeled Eldridge "malicious." Of course, Eldridge still worked for Fitzhugh and the two might have discussed the matter at the office. At the time the Eldridge couple had no other substantial source of income but their jobs at the mine.[36]

The arguments over Fitzhugh's competence continued. New prosecutor Frank Chenoweth and others wrote negative letters to the *Pioneer-Democrat* about him and new justice William Strong. Editor Wiley loyally defended Fitzhugh against his "traducers." He railed against the writer of a letter to the *New York Tribune* that called Fitzhugh "a murderer, bully and a blackguard." New Whatcom County legislative representative John Tennant (still Fitzhugh's employee) gave a speech in the House defending the appointment he had once opposed, and it was printed in the paper for everyone to read.[37]

Fitzhugh's problems hit the East Coast in a newspaper available to family in Virginia. The November 17 *New York Daily Tribune* headlined on page five: "One of Mr. Buchanan's Judges." It printed a long letter from "A.T." written from Whatcom County on September 30, after Fitzhugh had been arrested and taken his oath of office.

"A.T." attacked Fitzhugh's patronage appointment and the judicial proceedings surrounding the homicide. He told of the citizen efforts to stop the appointment, but claimed that Fitzhugh's friends in many places, including Virginia, helped push it through. He repeated Andrew Wilson's dying statement and cited Fitzhugh's anger at being indicted. The writer connected the crime with what he saw as Fitzhugh's moral failings. "Among the crimes committed by E. C. Fitzhugh…his deliberate and cold-blooded murder of Andrew Wilson, and the keeping in a public manner a harem supplied with Indian girls." He added that there were two women and several children, backing up his opprobrium with a salacious description of the local intermarriage custom. He claimed that town families were disgusted by Fitzhugh's domestic situation, failing to mention to the unknowing readers that almost all town families were cross-cultural ones. Lastly, to play into current religious prejudices, he compared Fitzhugh to Mormons with multiple wives.[38]

Controversy didn't stop until 1859, when Fitzhugh had conducted two special sessions of his court and sat on the December 1858 Supreme Court term.[39]

1858 FRASER RIVER GOLD RUSH

In 1858, while Fitzhugh watched the slow progress of his judicial nomination and confirmation, as well as that of his murder accusation, those events happened against the backdrop of the epidemic, mine business, and a new social upheaval that brought changes of a larger sort to Bellingham Bay and all the people who lived there.

By the end of 1857, when the first anti-appointment petitions circulated and Fitzhugh faced the first epidemic cases, some of Canada's *N'kla'pamux* First Nations men had been trading gold from the upper Fraser River Canyon's sandbars to the Hudson's Bay Company (HBC) at Fort Yale for months. Chief Factor (and colonial Governor) James Douglas and his fellow factors at the river forts were already writing regulations for the gold rush they anticipated when word trickled out. They made plans for a commissioner to issue mining licenses even as they avoided publicizing how good the discovery was. It wasn't until February 2, 1858, that Washington Territory's Steilacoom *Puget Sound Herald* printed an "Extra!" trumpeting the discovery, and relating that miners were making eight to fifty (U.S.) dollars a day. More headlines said territorial residents were abandoning homes and mills to go to the mines. It added that nearly everyone had already left Fitzhugh's mine, while Fort Bellingham soldiers and the Northwest Boundary Survey army escort had started deserting. All were eager to get upriver to the gold before the Californians arrived.[40]

On March 9, California's *Alta* published its own correspondent's confirmation. The new gold discovery became the chief topic of conversation among failed '49ers and younger gold seekers. Nearly every able-bodied miner with money for a ticket made plans to get on one of the rotting old ships that could still carry passengers north. The British Navy and the HBC suddenly lost large numbers of men, just as did the nearby American military. By May the major contingent of Californians was headed north, arriving at their "stopping place" of Bellingham Bay in early June. It coincided with Fitzhugh's confirmation, though he would not know right away.[41]

Once the news leaked out despite the HBC's best efforts, Fitzhugh and other Bellingham Bay owners of the land claims fronting the long beach realized there was another way to make money. Assuming that the gold rush could last for years, and more merchants and service providers would arrive, they began to see land speculation as a surefire profit venture. Russell Peabody saw that his level land claim next to Henry Roeder's mill site could be a real town and had "Whatcom" surveyed into lots. He reserved lots for his own half-indigenous children and gave some to army officers and local friends. Charlie Vail sold half (or all) of his claim next to Fitzhugh's to the coal syndicate for $500. Fitzhugh filed a "Sehome" townsite plat with the county auditor. He named all the Sehome streets for his political cronies and local friends, as well as one for himself. Just as Peabody was giving away some of his Whatcom lots to army officers and early settlers, Fitzhugh (as BBCC agent and stockholder) received permission to give away five lots of the thirty to forty already surveyed. He could sell the rest of Vail's former claim while retaining all mineral rights, with the condition that buildings had to be erected immediately. Unlike Peabody, Fitzhugh did not reserve any lots on his own land for his two children, though he had received the patent and had clear ownership. In the summer Territorial Surveyor James Tilton (the Pickett baby's godfather) and J. N. Wise (son of Virginia's current governor) bought into Fitzhugh's enterprise. The haste to record lot sales by Fitzhugh and Peabody, and subsequent re-sales, resulted in a tangle of sometimes contradictory deeds recorded at the county's office shack.[42]

A troubling sign appeared in May that went unrecognized by those in Victoria and Bellingham Bay. The earliest gold seekers were already trickling back down the river with tales of starvation, death, and no gold because spring runoff swelled the river trapped within its narrow canyon. The water kept rising as much as two feet a day with more to come while snow still covered peaks and bluffs. It would be a while before all the sandbars became visible and workable. First Nations men who discovered the gold possessed many sandbar locations and defended their traditional territory. Prospectors arriving early enough to stake a claim before the water rose tried to wait it out but buying food at Fort

Yale and drained their savings. They caused increasing trouble in the N'kla'pamux villages on the bluff above the sand bars. Some retreating miners were foolish enough to try canoeing themselves through the towering rapids and whirlpools squeezed between the cliffs at Hell's Gate. Those miners frequently ended up in the eddy dubbed "Always Horns" by the N'kla'pamux, so called for the drowned animals found there. The newcomers called it "Dead Man's Eddy" due to the fearful sight of animals, pieces of canoes, and drowned miners spit out by the river-wide whirlpool above. They should have hired the N'kla'pamux who had read and traversed the river for centuries.

In Whatcom County, either ignoring or not comprehending the import of the signs, considerable rivalry for new residents and businesses developed between the two townsites as the large wave of miners began to arrive. Fitzhugh was extending his deep-water wharf out to 800 feet to accommodate several ships at a time. Peabody had more flat land for businesses and homes, but Whatcom's wharf was new and under construction, needed to extend as much as a mile to escape the mudflats that fronted his townsite. The sound of saws, falling trees, and pile drivers was heard all day, every day, by the bay's families.[43]

As the gold rush exploded, Bellingham Bay became the American jumping-off place for the Californians, rather than British Victoria. Thousands of men waited for the river to recede and expose the sandbars. The social and economic hurricane of a gold rush fundamentally changed the small communities, as it also changed the Songhees village and small town at Fort Victoria. For example, where once a ship tying up at the Sehome Mine wharf was an irregular exciting occasion, Edward Eldridge witnessed seven steamers and thirteen square-riggers in the bay at one time, disgorging hundreds of men. Most of the gold seekers, trudging through Whatcom's mud flats or down the gangplank onto Fitzhugh's wharf, left as soon as possible on the old Nooksack trail headed northeast toward Fort Hope at the Fraser River's turn north. Overland, it was more than forty difficult miles to the river. As many as seventy canoes and other less seaworthy craft could be seen at one time fighting the Salish Sea's coastal currents as they headed twenty miles to the Fraser's delta. If they didn't sink, it was a long walk, or row, upriver on tidal waters, east to Fort Hope. Gold seekers on any route had to provision themselves for a total journey of 150 to 200 miles to the gold-bearing sandbars.[44]

In early June while Fitzhugh waited for appointment news, a California newspaper's special correspondent wrote: "Whatcom is just such a town as San Francisco was in '49. The streets are thronged with people. Merchants are busy receiving and selling goods; builders are at work erecting tenements on all sides; speculators are staking off lots; miners are discharging and cleaning their firearms; restaurants are doing a smashing business; a few gambling saloons are in operation." He thought there were four thousand people in the towns with forty to fifty houses in Whatcom and twenty in Sehome. Years later Edward Eldridge recalled the beach and bank were covered with tents "as if an invading army had taken possession of the bay." At the time, the settler population of Washington Territory may have been only four to five thousand, and the miners quickly doubled that, but concentrated in only the one place. Just weeks after houses numbered in the tens, when John Nevin King came into town from the Boundary Survey camp at Semiahmoo Bay, he saw a hundred. Russell Peabody had given him one of the new Whatcom town lots for speculation, but King wanted to wait for a more "propitious" time to sell. Copying the new businesses in town, he gambled that the town would grow indefinitely.[45]

Estimates of how many gold seekers invaded the townsites and beaches to wait for the river to recede range from five to ten thousand. They stayed in hastily built hotels or pitched tents on the beaches and every flat piece of ground. Half of the men slept in the open, enduring June's frequent rain. As they had for mine and mill workers, the mostly indigenous wives in both places took advantage of the situation to take in boarders or do laundry for cash. It is likely that many of them also cooked and sold food, considering the number of single men camped out.

While Fitzhugh's lingering murder accusation and appointment hung over his head that 1858 summer, his attention was also occupied with the gold rush concerns. Still managing coal sales, he was occupied selling lots in the new townsite while others managed the coal mine operation. Probably of more immediate concern was how to control the hordes of miners on his beach who brought chaos of every kind. As soon as the *Northern Light* started to publish, Fitzhugh placed notices directed at trespassers seeking free wood for building or for cook fires burning everywhere. He threatened prosecution for anyone cutting timber on his land claim where boundary lines were well-marked and left no excuse for any violations.[46]

CRIED

Fitzhugh was still acting as the resident Indian Agent, though he had officially left the post in March. The epidemic and gold rush apparently delayed the end. It was not a good time to bring in a new man who didn't know anyone at the villages and didn't speak Northern Straits Salish as fluently as Fitzhugh. The miners were a different kind of invasion from the men who came for the mill, mine, and army over the previous five years. The earlier settlers' relationship with local Coast Salish had become one of in-laws, friends, army messengers, and fellow mill or mine workers. The invading miners did not recognize the Coast Salish families as anything more than aggravations and hindrances, as they had in California, and Fitzhugh was in the center of conflicts.

Tribes and colonizers alike waited for the 1855 Point Elliott Treaty to be ratified and reservations to be finalized. Fitzhugh's late June report stated that without the ratification, the miners didn't respect laws, spread disease, and sold illegal liquor to the local villagers. It was leading to an increased death rate that he thought could lead to all the indigenous residents dying as a direct result of the gold rush. Fitzhugh wrote to the *Northern Light* pleading for support from the general public to help him "stop this damnable traffic." Without their assistance to stop the liquor sales, he said that he alone could do little. Another serious problem was that many Lummi were selling their canoes to miners for high prices and would not have a sufficient number available for salmon season. He had already sent Charlie Vail to stay with the upriver Nooksacks because whites wanted to control the tribe's ferry at The Crossing (today's Everson). Miners were threatening to "exterminate" the people at Popehomey so they could get to the mines overland without paying a ferry fee to the Nooksacks.[47]

In mid-summer, lame duck Territorial Indian Agent Michael Simmons traveled to the bay. He and Fitzhugh met with three tribes at Lummi to discuss the liquor problem. Fitzhugh translated as Simmons spoke about the dangers of liquor and selling the canoes to miners that would be needed for salmon harvest. He encouraged them to stay out of town, away from the miners who were a danger to all if the tribes tried to solve disputes by themselves. Simmons pointed out that Fitzhugh would help with their conflicts with miners any time they asked. For Fitzhugh, this was all in addition to the continuing intermittent problem with the northern raiders, despite the army's presence. The

Laich-wil-tach simply viewed the hordes at the bay, and miners headed north by water, as more people to harass and rob or kill.[48]

⊂᠅⊃

Despite his existing obligations and legal problems while waiting to hear about his appointment, in late May 1858 Fitzhugh had taken on yet another job—a government contract to administer. Two years earlier during the Treaty War, Congress appropriated $10,000 for a military road between Fort Bellingham and Fort Steilacoom near what would become Tacoma. If Laich-wil-tach seaborne attacks on the bay communities continued despite the army's presence, or any other attack by water, the road would make possible essential troop and ordnance movement overland. Fitzhugh and Ed Warbass, the Fort Bellingham post sutler (store manager), got the contract for the military road's northern five miles from the fort to the coal mine. Warbass's partnership may have had something to do with the fact that he owed Fitzhugh a substantial amount of money and had recently signed over collateral pending payment. Lieutenant George Mendell of the army's Topographical Engineers surveyed and laid out the road. Fitzhugh's contract allowed for hiring forty to fifty laborers to clear the often twelve-foot-diameter trees, build bridges, and then grade and plank the road. Captain Pickett's troops, now experienced in logging and building, did most of the work. Fitzhugh and Warbass finished the contract on schedule, including an extra half mile. The towns got three much-needed bridges over Whatcom Creek and two other creeks toward the fort. The government paid the pair $8,000, equivalent to about $243,000 in 2021, and Warbass probably used his portion to pay off the debt to Fitzhugh. Whatcom and Sehome now had a connecting road instead of a simple trail, even if it was muddy, narrow, and rutted. For years, it remained the only "road" in the area in the absence of many wagons. Once the anticipated Sehome school was built for the growing number of children, the bridges would enable those from Whatcom to safely reach it. The road to Fort Steilacoom was never completed once the Civil War demanded reallocation of funds, but remnants of its route, and sometimes the name "Military Road," remain.[49]

⊂᠅⊃

Colonial Governor James Douglas did not allow goods to be sold at the mines that summer. Miners would have to purchase supplies at Victoria, Fort Yale, or the little boomtown of Yale clinging to a riverside bench below Hell's Gate. As a result, miners heading north on the Nooksacks' trail from Whatcom still had to carry two hundred pounds of supplies with them, or pay Yale prices that yielded merchants a five hundred percent profit over what prevailed elsewhere. This problem, however, worked to the benefit of merchants opening stores in Whatcom and Sehome.[50]

Fitzhugh and the other locals decided that pushing an improved trail through the county's backwoods to the HBC's Brigade Trail would avoid the dangerous part of the river entirely to intersect with the gold-bearing sandbars, and it would increase commercial traffic in Whatcom and Sehome permanently. The "Whatcom Trail" project occupied much of the newspaper's summer attention that wasn't taken by the chaos. Starting almost a year earlier, the county had very roughly improved the Nooksacks' trail to the ford and ferry at Popehomey to accommodate Boundary Survey pack trains, usually led by local Russell Peabody who hired on to bring supplies from Whatcom to wherever the survey camp was. The original trail continued to the Fraser because Nooksack families also lived in that area. Going beyond that, as Fitzhugh and the other promoters wanted, proved to be an immensely difficult project. Surveyor W. W. DeLacey and his men found clearing obstructions to be slow and grueling. Just as time-consuming and difficult was locating a suitable route through mountains to the Brigade Trail on the east side of the river after its northward turn. The men worked long and hard and sent back encouraging messages, but by the time they connected to the Brigade Trail, Governor Douglas was requiring customs clearance and mining licenses obtainable only in Victoria, as well as having new trails cut through to Yale. It made the Whatcom Trail remote to men leaving from Victoria, and probably of little use to anyone in the future because their mountain route would be passable only about three months of the year.[51]

By mid-summer, Whatcom and Sehome had changed dramatically and were visually thriving. With the mine's deep-water wharf, it seemed that Sehome might become the dominant town, but with more flat land for expansion, Whatcom grew faster. The new bridges facilitated movement between. Where once everyone used Fitzhugh's and Busey's stores, now ten others competed for miners buying clothing, food, and mining equipment. Hotels included the What Cheer, named after San Francisco's famous hostelry. Restaurants, saloons, liquor dealers, and prostitutes completely re-made the atmosphere for local wives and children into one less friendly and sometimes dangerous. Fitzhugh bought newspaper ads listing himself as both real estate and coal agent, as well as one week the seller of "cured Neah Bay halibut" at his store, perhaps procured with the help of his S'Klallam in-laws. A doctor and several lawyers advertised their services, and Fitzhugh got John Jenkins appointed notary public by the governor so some minor legal activities requiring a witness could be handled by someone else. For men arriving with only a business plan, building materials were available from multiple merchants. Early Whidbey Island settler John Alexander opened the Pioneer Store and sold groceries, kitchenware, and other things women might want to buy. San Francisco merchants included chocolatier Ghirardelli and Andrometti's store stocking cigars, fruit, stationery, and "fancy goods." Sehome boasted the only bakery for treats most desired by men far from home. What seemed to put the stamp of permanency on the boomtowns was the brick T. G. Richards and Co. building, the first brick structure north of Portland, Oregon. With two floors and a damp basement barely above the high tide line, Charles Richards and postmaster John Hyatt presided over commission orders, consignments of goods, storage, mail, and the sending of packages.[52]

Outsiders were not always enamored of Bellingham Bay's new prosperity. It was the same unbridled capitalism Fitzhugh experienced in California. Treaty War veteran and Thurston County (Olympia) official Urban Hicks's mid-July letter to the *Pioneer-Democrat* described Whatcom as "Sodom and Growmorrow" that Heaven needed to strike down if the nearby volcanic Mount Baker did not. "Vice and immorality of every description is practiced there at noon-day, which will require the firm arm of a vigilance committee to arrest." By then there were one hundred stores between Whatcom and Sehome, while homely Olympia's merchants were short on goods because suppliers sent everything to Bellingham Bay for the miners. Hicks saw avarice everywhere as one merchant or town proprietor competed with the others, "everything raging, ripping, and roaring, all striving for the same thing, 'viz' the root of all evil." Hicks may not have known that Whatcom and Sehome merchants were also smuggling goods in small boats to the miners heading inland on the Fraser, without paying duty to the British. A larger smuggling effort of goods to Bellingham Bay was thwarted when the Mexican schooner *Lord Raglan* was apprehended carrying luxury foodstuffs in excess of what was on the manifest for Victoria.[53]

Despite the mountain of goods available at Bellingham Bay and the progress of the Whatcom Trail, others equally disliked what they experienced. Timothy O'Dowd, a stalled miner at Fort Hope, wrote to his brother: "As for Bellingham Bay, it is a humbugging, thieving place …gulling the people that go there that they could cross over to Fort Hope. During my stay, I have seen over twenty men who have crossed the trail and they were barefooted, their clothes torn in rags, and they half-starved with hunger, by being misinformed at Bellingham Bay."[54]

By the end of July, there was another hint of trouble to come, though it didn't discourage the Whatcom Trail project. As the river receded from the Fraser's sandbars, it became apparent to miners on-site that there didn't seem to be any large gold source like that in California, and what was there consisted mainly of fine "dust." Miners also realized that the warm-weather mining season on the river would probably always be short. A brutal conflict between Americans and the First Nations people they wanted to supplant and exterminate had broken out, called "McGowan's War" after the former San Francisco vigilante who led it. Discouraged miners straggled back into Whatcom-Sehome, often broke and not knowing how they would get home to California. While there had been many ships to take thousands north, now there were but few to take the bankrupt and defeated men south. William Bausman, *Northern Light* editor, wrote of the need for a hospital to care for the "destitute sick" after a corpse lay unnoticed in a tent for two days. Fitzhugh was later reported to have extended "many kindnesses to the miners."[55]

Waiting for the Whatcom Trail's safer route to be finished, most miners had still not left for the gold rush though winter would soon be on its way. Talking to returnees who joined the camps on the beach, the would-be gold miners also faced the reality that the Fraser River sand bars weren't going to yield their fortunes. The trickle of discouraged men leaving Bellingham Bay became a flood of miners, most unhappy that the shortcut trail was still unfinished. On August 13, a reporter observed "Business is exceedingly dull…and there are not a thousand people in the two places…The merchants here are gradually working off their stocks of goods having long ago stopped ordering fresh supplies." A few buildings were still going up and work on the long wharf at

Whatcom approached 2,500 feet, but "it seemed as if all life had been knocked out of the people." Still, in anticipation of the Whatcom Trail's completion to circumvent the British monopoly, everyone remained hopeful and patriotic. "Almost every building in the place flies the 'red, white, and blue' and in all the gambling houses bands of music were continually playing the national airs."[56]

A week after that observation, Benjamin Shaw brought word from DeLacy that the Whatcom Trail was through. In celebration, Whatcom and Sehome held a first—a large "sumptuous" dinner at one of the new hotels, attended by eighty celebrants and several territorial officials. Fitzhugh chaired the dinner and was master of ceremonies for the speeches, singing, and lengthy list of toasts raised to everyone involved, including the long-suffering local women. One toast bringing particular acclaim was "American soil, first, last, and all the time." Celebrants piled unanimous criticism on the Pacific Mail Steamship Company for obtaining an exclusive contract to transport miners from San Francisco to Victoria, instead of supporting the ambitions of their fellow Americans.[57]

Fitzhugh and the others who were permanently committed to the new towns did not see the Whatcom Trail as a failure. Even though it hadn't turned out to be a finished route to the Fraser gold diggings in time, they had a permanent way to reach the Fraser and tributary Thompson River without portages, a dangerous river, or Salish Sea navigation. The year 1858 had brought them that infrastructure addition, as well as their new local road and bridges whose contract Fitzhugh had administered. Some gold seekers decided to give up their long-held dreams of going back to their hometowns with a fortune and settled in Whatcom County where they became some of its most prominent citizens. Future sheriff and superintendent of schools Frederick F. Lane, from maritime Massachusetts, said later that some miners were "more susceptible to the allurement of a life on Puget Sound."[58]

Perhaps not a complete coincidence, shortly after the dinner Fitzhugh organized and emceed for the locals, his tax assessment on the mine and his property were once again postponed, pending legal opinions.[59]

And what of John Nevin King, the Boundary Survey employee waiting for the most "propitious" time to sell the lot Peabody gave him? He waited too long. By the last day of August, he knew he would only make $25-50 on the still-empty lot, instead of the $500 he thought he would profit. A week later, he wrote home optimistically: "Whatcom is dead, but I think it will be resurrected in the spring. I can hardly realize that it could die as it had come into existence." But it did.[60]

A special correspondent for the *San Francisco Herald* wrote on September 22, the same day Fitzhugh opened the special session of his new court: "Whatcom...is nearly deserted, and the stampede from it is quite as thoughtless and inconsiderate as was the headlong rush to it.... Two thirds of the tenements in town exhibit on the door the significant signal 'This cabin for sale'—'This store to let.' ...but although apparently dying, Whatcom is not dead. No town ever died...in a country possessing such resources and advantages." Almost all storekeepers had packed up their goods, even the buildings, and moved to Victoria or back to San Francisco, but a few permanently joined the little business center along Sehome's only street. The weatherproof brick Richards building in

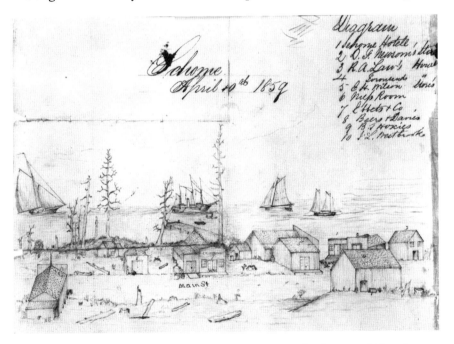

Figure 18, Sketch of Sehome by Captain George E. Pickett, April 10, 1859. Although drawn months after the Fraser River Gold Rush ended, many store buildings remained though the owners had left. The Sehome Coal Mine wharf is visible at the center, and E. C. Fitzhugh's residence was farther to the right along "Main Street." Pickett, drawing from Sehome Hill behind the mine settlement and Sehome townsite, included typical vessels that called at Bellingham Bay, as well the ever-present tree stumps, many of which were eight to twelve feet in diameter. *#1994.46.2, Whatcom Museum, Bellingham, Washington.*

Whatcom became a gathering place for the entire bay community as well as home to a few merchants and professionals.[61]

One bankrupt store had an inventory that speaks to the unreality of the hopes of residents and newcomers alike, including Fitzhugh. Its San Francisco wholesaler filed suit when it heard that the merchant was going to pack everything up and flee his creditor to Victoria to open a new store. The storekeeper had few building or mining supplies left, but the bulk of his remaining merchandise would never fit the current reality of life in isolated Bellingham Bay. It included multiple cases of sauterne and claret wines, champagne and Hennessey brandy, four dozen wine glasses, eleven sugar bowls, and some "fine" tea pots. None of it was very useful to the small group of families who remained, with husbands who liked their whiskey.[62]

As for the gold rush, almost four thousand miners stayed at the sandbars over the winter and continued to dig. They either had a producing claim or they had purchased enough provisions to last them over a harsh winter of snow and unrelenting Arctic winds sweeping down the canyon. The First Nations families and their miners went into their warm *kikwillies* sunk partially down into the ground until spring.[63]

By November, there was no more news of the gold rush or Bellingham Bay's towns in the San Francisco papers. The *Northern Light* editor had long since packed up his press and returned to Sacramento after only eleven issues, citing "dullness."[64]

CHAPTER 8

Sometimes Judge, Sometimes Defendant

WITH THE END OF THE GOLD RUSH, life that autumn of 1858 in Sehome and Whatcom almost went back to pre-invasion normal for the few dozen people left, centered around mill and mine. Normal, perhaps, except for dealing with the mountains of trash that remained from the tent-dwellers and de-construction of the buildings taken to Victoria and beyond.

Fitzhugh remained one of the territory's "hip pocket bankers" with cash to loan, though his mine shares had not paid off yet. Through assorted real estate deals with Vail and Tilton, Fitzhugh was part-owner of the entire Sehome townsite formed from multiple land claims, and he remained the sole real estate agent.

An Oregon reporter wrote in late October that the Sehome Mine had "meagre and insufficient facilities for making excavations and hoisting the coal," and that the California owners were making bigger plans. Fitzhugh's responsibilities at the Sehome Mine decreased as court business took more of his time. The now-expanded BBCC syndicate received a large contract and decided to invest more money in the mine. They (perhaps with input from shareholder Fitzhugh) made mine clerk J. R. Tompkins, a Pennsylvanian with coal mine experience there, the manager to nominally work under Fitzhugh. Tompkins and mining engineer McKinney Tawes were well able to run the mine alone. If the syndicate's original plan was to have Fitzhugh open the mine while helping forge the Democratic Pacific bloc, then this move four years later to change management loosened Fitzhugh to spend more time on Democratic politics, as well as his judicial duties.[1]

THIRD DISTRICT COURT JUSTICE

At thirty-seven, E. C. Fitzhugh was a new Washington Territory Associate Justice and member of the Supreme Court. His ambition had

brought him a long way since leaving Falmouth for the California Gold
Rush only nine years earlier.

Figure 19, Territorial Associate Justice Edmund
C. Fitzhugh, probably his official portrait about
1858. *Military Records Collection, Washington
State Archives, no assigned number.*

All three justices on
the new panel had studied
law independently, rather
than at a university law
school. Fitzhugh was the
only one who, by the lack
of records, may have never
been formally admitted to
the bar. Neither California
nor Washington Territory
had a bar association when
he arrived. Virginia's bar
association records burned
in the Civil War. Everyone
was well aware that the
youngest justice owed his
new judicial career to a
political payoff.[2]

Pennsylvanian Obadiah
McFadden at forty-three
had been on the Oregon
Supreme Court for a year
before President Buchanan
assigned him to the new territory's court system. He took over the
Chief Justice chair temporarily after Lander's term ended in 1857,
getting the permanent appointment at the same time Fitzhugh and
Strong received theirs. Eccentric about his given name, he disliked it
so much he refused to give his children names when they were born.[3]

William Strong (age 41), was a Vermont minister's son and
Yale honors graduate. He'd both taught school and practiced law in
Cleveland until appointment to the Oregon bench in 1849. Replaced in
1853, he moved north and helped write Washington's legal code before
he was Governor Stevens's legal advisor during the Treaty War, led a
militia unit, and was elected to the legislature.

Washington Territory's three judicial districts stretched from
western Washington east to Montana, and by the time Fitzhugh took

Figure 20, Washington Territory Chief Justice Obadiah McFadden. *Brady-Handy photograph collection, Library of Congress, Prints and Photographs Division. #LC-DIG-cwpbh-04605.*

Figure 21, Territorial Associate Justice William Strong. *Courtesy of the Washington State Historical Society at WashingtonHistory.org. #C2015.0.75.*

the bench the court calendar and locations had been tinkered with to fit local conditions. There was generally no regular transportation system in place, and people often caught whatever vessel might be going their direction on Puget Sound. The Supreme Court's annual December session met in Olympia, when the three district justices changed titles to Supreme Court Justice and acted as the appellate court for their own cases. Conflict of interest seems to have been considered only in who wrote the final opinion for the Supreme Court.

The district courts were required to meet no longer than three weeks, twice a year. Fitzhugh's court convened the second Monday in February and the first Monday in August, hearing cases from the northern counties. Sometimes a special session had to be held, as Fitzhugh had done in September and October shortly after he took the oath of office. For civil cases in the territory, litigants could appeal any case valued at more than $2,000 to the Supreme Court. Those were few and generally business-related. Fitzhugh didn't have to bother with civil cases under $200 as those were heard by a county's elected justice of the peace. When the first legislature met, they allocated money for a state library, available to Fitzhugh for legal research beyond his personal law books.

Fitzhugh heard somewhat over two hundred cases for the Third District, split almost evenly between civil and criminal cases with scattered admiralty cases. He dispensed with some cases in minutes, and others bore great regional and territorial import. The criminal cases infrequently involved serious injury or death, but those became feverish territorial newspaper fodder. Many civil cases were odd, even funny by today's standards, but were important to the plaintiffs who filed them in a region where bartering still was part of the economy and cash scarce for the average settler. Examples discussed here by no means span the breadth of cases over which Fitzhugh presided.[4]

Fitzhugh only recused himself from one case at the end of his appointment. Cases before him usually involved people he knew from Sehome-Whatcom, business dealings, or politics. Other people crossed his path during the Treaty War. One case came from the coal discovery that brought him north. All the lawyers who appeared before him, including Frank Chenoweth, were already known to Fitzhugh as political friends or opponents. Chenoweth served as prosecutor for a time and also appeared frequently as a litigant's counsel during Fitzhugh's years. In 1860, when Chenoweth was sued for nonpayment of a judgment, Fitzhugh granted his old nemesis a restraining order to give him more time to pay and stipulated there would be no further court actions if he did so within the limit. Sometimes an individual was the plaintiff in the morning, and defendant in the afternoon. Or the man might be on the jury after his own case was decided. Conditions in the lightly-settled Third District superseded any modern ideas of how a court should be administered.[5]

There was the jail problem, too. The so-called county jails, like that at Whatcom, were generally small log shacks suitable for short detention. If genuine incarceration was needed, prisoners had to be transported to the army's Fort Townsend or Fort Bellingham. The fort commanders did not want to do this for free, and arguments about payment resulted. After the court moved permanently to Port Townsend, the grand jury reported that a better local jail was the next critical need after equipping the courtroom.[6]

Like legislative sessions, the three-week sessions of both District and Supreme Courts developed in the 1850s into getaways for some men to leave home and socialize. The weeks were formally judicial, but at night there was gossip, politics, and business to discuss in the social atmosphere of dinner and drinks, as well as some (officially illegal) gambling thrown in for diversion. During the Supreme Court term in December, lawyers and the justices from around the territory socialized in Olympia's establishments. Fitzhugh did not isolate himself during his Third District Court terms. This behavior was little different from "Court Days" in Virginia when people isolated on farms and plantations looked forward to gathering at the two-room Stafford County Courthouse or Dr. Alexander Fitzhugh's Magistrate's Court in Falmouth.[7]

⚜

After Justice Chenoweth signed his last action on September 4, 1858, Fitzhugh held court at Coveland or Port Townsend for the intersession cases needing immediate action until the February 1859 term. Coveland and Coupeville, across Penn Cove, were very small, yet were important maritime settlements on Whidbey Island, otherwise dominated by large donation land claims and villages of the Lower Skagit tribe. The court location had been placed at the first Island County seat and Port of Entry until U.S. Customs moved to Port Townsend. Coveland was central between the Bellingham Bay settlements and Port Townsend in what was essentially an east-west business neighborhood that ended at Victoria. Settlers voyaged south to Olympia or Steilacoom almost entirely for politics or sale of commodities, not shopping, and Seattle was still of little importance. At Coveland Fitzhugh held court upstairs in Thomas Cranney's store (also the site of his murder indictment). Built in 1855 to replace a log cabin, the sizable two-story building stood alone above the beach, and served as the Island County courthouse, post office, and general store. People with business before the court had to board in private homes or camp out together nearby.[8] (See figure 17.)

Justice Fitzhugh opened his court for the first time on September 22, 1858, four days after his arrest in Olympia. It was also the day after Whatcom's *Northern Light* editor announced the end of the Fraser River gold rush, packed up his press, and left for California. Fitzhugh might have been garbed with judicial robes obtained in Olympia, but just as likely in his best suit after the hasty trip north. His first business was to appoint court commissioners for each county, his court clerk, and deputy clerk.

An appointed court commissioner for each county handled emergency intersession business that couldn't wait for the next district court term. Most court commissioners were decently educated men, even a non-practicing lawyer with access to some law books, like Fitzhugh had once been for Justice Chenoweth in 1855 before they clashed. Sometimes Fitzhugh filled the Jefferson County court commissioner office with his militia irritant, former San Francisco vigilante, and short-time mine employee, Jacobus Jan Hogerworth (J.J.H.) Van Bokkelen. In Port Townsend he had previously held postmaster, county auditor, and deputy court clerk offices, sometimes simultaneously.[9]

Any district's handwritten files varied with the literary skills of the man who got the job of court clerk, both in readability and in what papers were filed permanently. Fitzhugh appointed both a court clerk and deputy who varied over time. The men were important hires because of the distance from Sehome to Coveland and Port Townsend. Robert Hill from Whidbey Island had some prior management experience and lived close enough to handle court business between terms. Another who served under Fitzhugh was Port Townsend's James Seavey, business bookkeeper and superintendent of schools simultaneously with the clerkship.[10]

When Fitzhugh convened his first court term, he set the guidelines and rules for his courtroom, e.g. the order actions would be handled, decorum by litigants and spectators, time for breaks, etc. Rules remained flexible while the territory's early justices worked on efficiency amid the ever-increasing workload and variety of cases brought. Fitzhugh assigned the second day to motions, finishing previous actions, and hearing arguments for demurrers to stop litigation. Court business for the first day or two of any term was used to build a grand jury and petit jury, which sometimes meant sending the sheriff out on the street to commandeer anyone sober and male. The occasional admiralty cases would be heard first, jury trials next, and non-jury ones last. Appeals from county justice courts had to be scheduled in. If a litigant didn't appear or parties were not prepared, that case would go to the bottom of the list. All agreements and stipulations, by and between parties, had to be in writing. On a court day late in the term, new lawyers could be admitted to the bar after cursory examination by several attorneys in town for the court session, and Fitzhugh would approve naturalizations.[11]

Fitzhugh's first full case was an Admiralty Court one, *U.S. v Schooner "Lord Raglan,"* heard in his special September session. The Mexican-flagged schooner was charged with smuggling. It had been seized avoiding Customs at Port Townsend on its way to deliver goods to Bellingham Bay for gold rush miners. Fitzhugh told the Olympia paper that he would be somewhat lenient because the Italian skipper wasn't good with English, but he would also rule that his leniency should not be taken as a precedent.[12]

Later that fall Fitzhugh (ignoring the conflict of interest) doubled as both judge and the main witness for the acting prosecutor, Frank Chenoweth. The two jury trials of men accused of liquor law violations dated from Fitzhugh's service as Indian agent. Aggravating liquor law violations continued. Laws that applied included the 1855 prohibition of liquor production in the territory, sale to native people, and one that specifically targeted Hudson's Bay Company employees by prohibiting sale to Hawaiians (known as "Kanakas"). Liquor law violations brought no jail time until 1863, when Fitzhugh was no longer in office.[13]

☙❧

In mid-July 1858, during the gold rush, U.S. Deputy Surveyor Dominic Hunt was murdered. The resulting prosecution of two Coast Salish men in Fitzhugh's October special session became the first time he presided over a "hanging offense" trial.

Hunt went missing after he took to his canoe bound from Whidbey Island to Whatcom. People presumed that he drowned or was murdered by the northerners for his watch, money, and revolver. When the *Northern Light* posted a notice asking for help finding him a week after his disappearance, his body was found, shot to death.[14]

Five Coast Salish men were accused of killing him with "a $5.00 gun." Captain George Pickett dispatched a squad of soldiers to apprehend and bring them to Fort Bellingham for incarceration. Of the five, only two were indicted. Historian Brad Asher believed that this split implies that the justice system worked correctly on the basis of evidence, not just a rush to judgment against indigenous people. However, it could be interpreted differently.[15]

The problem with taking a thorough look at this case, heard by Fitzhugh, is that the files are incomplete. The file for the two who were indicted contains only the indictment, the sentence, and a note about its completion. The testimony and evidence may have been questionable. It is possible (if not probable) that the three unindicted men turned on the other two in order to get released. Without testimony to review, it is not possible to entertain the possibility that the gun in question was owned by one of the northern raiders who still roamed the waters, or someone else, even a white settler with a beef about land surveys.

Only two months after Fitzhugh's judicial debut, Frank Chenoweth prosecuted the case against the two Coast Salish men who pled guilty on the advice of their lawyer, William Wallace. That should have resulted in long-term imprisonment, but like the county jail problem, the territory itself had no prison. Instead, Fitzhugh sentenced the defendants to death. On November 5 the *Pioneer-Democrat* reported "They are said to have had a very fair trial, and every proper indulgence shown them in the presentation of their evidence and defense." According to Asher, this was true in an ideological sense, because the conviction rate of indigenous defendants was relatively low. However, the sentence led to indigenous residents' deep resentment because the Coast Salish did not see why two lives should be taken in retribution for one. Not only that, the very fact that the foreign authority (the U.S. government) was surveying indigenous territory without permission challenged their ownership when the treaties had yet to be ratified by Congress.[16]

It was a busy autumn for the new justice. Besides the Hunt case, he was still involved in getting the mine back to full speed after the end of the gold rush and turning over management to the Moody and Sinclair partnership. He spent time buying leftover merchandise from defunct gold rush stores to enlarge his store at the mine. The *Pioneer-Democrat* continued to print articles supporting him in his own murder indictment, and there was the New York newspaper item about his indictment and living circumstances with two wives. Acting-prosecutor Chenoweth was still dueling by letter with the *Pioneer-Democrat* over what he saw as prejudice against him in the judicial nomination fight.

Most important to Fitzhugh, the same day his jury convicted the men, October 10, was the day he finished up the special session by granting himself a change of venue for his own murder trial.

On December 10, 1858, Whatcom County Sheriff William Busey placed a pole between the crotches of two trees near the new bridge over Whatcom Creek. It served as gallows for the two convicted Coast Salish men. The deputy "officiated." When Busey turned in his report to the court he wrote, in what can only be described as enthusiastic script, that he had hung the men "by the neck until they were dead, dead, dead."

Another case of alleged indigenous violence against a settler occurred the following August 1859. The *Massachusetts* transported four indigenous prisoners to Whatcom for incarceration on the charge of fighting that had resulted in a white man's death. The triumphant gun salute to the judge in front of Sehome was recorded, but no judicial record of this resulted. Perhaps remembering the questionable execution, everyone realized that prosecution would be patently unfair if the white man contributed to his own death.[17]

CREW

The Supreme Court (including Fitzhugh) awarded the permanent Third District court location to Port Townsend in February 1859. It was on the mainland, though farther southwest across the Salish Sea to the Olympic Peninsula from Sehome. Fitzhugh would still need to find a local merchant vessel, Salish canoe-for-hire, or government steamer on the right day (and with the right destination) to take him there for court. The town's location on a bay off the junction of the Strait of Juan de Fuca and Admiralty Inlet leading into Puget Sound predicted long-term growth. The brick U.S. Customs House at the harbor signaled the town's permanency as a shipping and transportation hub. Chet'ze'moka, brother or cousin of Fitzhugh's father-in-law, led Kah'tai village by the lagoon at the edge of the new town. When Fitzhugh moved his court to Port Townsend, about 300 whites and 200 S'Klallams lived in the environs. In addition to the Customs House, several dozen log and frame commercial buildings lined wide, muddy Water Street that backed on the harbor. Vessels large and small usually dotted the bay in front of town and retired Captain Enoch Fowler's recently completed long wharf accommodated the largest ships bringing goods "only 135 days from Boston." The U.S. Marine Hospital, where its single doctor cared for sick and injured sailors from the docking ships, overlooked the harbor from the high bluff. Women and children coped with the disreputable, whiskey-soaked atmosphere of the seaport town where a lawyer, a prostitute, a wandering bull, and a drunken sailor might co-exist on Water Street. A visitor wrote for eastern readers that the place was a "resort for…outlaws." The liquor atmosphere was bad enough to spawn the opposite—the Dashaway Club (named for a California ship) that sought to help men stop drinking.[18]

Fitzhugh began to spend at least six weeks of his year in Port Townsend, very different from boarding in Coveland for three weeks

Figure 22, The business section (Water Street) of Port Townsend in 1862, during E. C. Fitzhugh's term of office. It was also the first town new bride Cora Bowie Fitzhugh saw in Washington Territory. *#2011.1.272 from the collection of the Jefferson County Historical Society.*

at a time. Henry Tibbals operated his Pioneer Hotel across from the waterfront to serve a diverse traveling public. An imposing wide structure with two floors, the Pioneer included a saloon, dining room, and up-to-date guest rooms. Tibbals aspired to be acceptable to people used to upscale accommodations, like Fitzhugh. Because of its location for incoming ships from the eastern states and smaller vessels from Victoria, on any day the dining room menu could include pheasant, lobster salad, bon bons, and fruit cake, as well as the usual meats and vegetables. As activity increased, Tibbals built a large addition on the back with more guest rooms, a billiard parlor, and a private dining room. Fine cigars, pipe tobacco, and any kind of liquor in which Fitzhugh might indulge himself after a long day at court were all available.[19]

Port Townsend's atmosphere took a defensive and hostile turn against Northerners in May after Fitzhugh's first term. It didn't matter if they were invaders, relatives living peacefully at Kah'tai, or working for locals. Some of the town's most prominent citizens met and veered into repeating the vigilante period in California by forming a committee. J.J.H. Van Bokkelen joined, as he had in California. Local lawyers did not. Resolutions included one to bar northerners from any employment and asking for citizen involvement to drive all of them out, including if any tried to land for any reason. The most egregious resolution stated that all men with Northern wives should be required to send them away within two weeks. The committee halted their work after the appearance of one newspaper article, probably after being informed of the conflict with the nearby army base, as well as other legal authorities.[20]

Newcomer James Swan found Fitzhugh's new permanent courtroom "comfortably fitted up" and conducive to the judge conducting business with "dispatch and decorum seldom witnessed in a frontier settlement." That description was optimistically rosy. Used for other purposes when court was not in session, it was hardly comparable to the halls of the Virginia capitol. It was twenty by sixteen feet and usually crammed with as many "Court Days" participants and spectators as could fit. At the center, a sheet iron stove provided heat in the winter, although with a sweaty crowd additional heat was likely needed only on a cold morning before court. S'Klallam woven mats covered some of the floor, but probably only where Fitzhugh and lawyers sat since dozens of muddy boots would have ruined them quickly. Sawn logs provided audience seating beneath two large chandeliers holding thirty-five candles and four holding nine candles to provide illumination, especially for the clerk taking notes on dark February days. After a year passed, Fitzhugh's courtroom had seen little if any improvement in furnishings or spectator behavior. Many left the courtroom between cases for a liquor break. The local newspaper said Fitzhugh calmly puffed on his pipe even as some spectators drank in his courtroom.[21]

C380

Animals caused much litigation because of their great value as income and food for isolated families in the Third District. One example that came before Fitzhugh was *Crockett v Wilson G. Hunt*. Walter Crockett, patriarch of one of the first Whidbey Island families, whom Fitzhugh knew well from the Treaty War, sued the *Wilson G. Hunt* during the judge's first year. Crockett shipped a large flock of sheep from Steilacoom on the small steamer, an expensive and valuable addition to his prairie ventures. When the *Hunt* neared Ebey's Landing, the crew threw the sheep overboard to swim to shore. Sheep are not good swimmers and dozens drowned, while others died under the steamer's wheel.[22]

And then there was the case of John Herring's hogs that ran loose in Whatcom. Valuable to Herring, they were nuisances to the rest of the small post-gold rush population living in a ravaged environment. Resident Moses Phillips complained that Herring's hogs constituted a public nuisance roaming the streets and breeding "filth" under the houses. He said Herring had even built a pig pen in the middle of the street. Herring maintained that the hogs weren't even his and anyway, lying under the houses was a private nuisance not a public one. He did not see his pig pen as an obstruction of the street because it didn't keep pedestrians from walking and it wasn't a wagon road anyway, just a footpath. Apparently annoyed with Herring's stubbornness, the justice of the peace fined him $5 but attached court costs of $115, an enormous sum at the time, thousands in the twenty-first century. He wound up "imprisoned" and "restrained of his liberty" by the sheriff, apparently in the local log shack jail.[23]

A few days later, Herring filed for a writ of habeas corpus in Fitzhugh's court. The case file never said why Sheriff John Jewett had felt it necessary to jail him, but possibly since Herring signed his habeas corpus request with a defiantly large signature, his anger got the best of him. He claimed that the Whatcom County Justice Court 1) did not allow his counsel to be heard; 2) had admitted illegal evidence; 3) recorded a judgment not a verdict that would result in jailing; 4) violated his rights; 5) did not call him to testify or attend the sentencing; and 6) nothing authorized the sheriff to arrest him. Fitzhugh granted the writ and a new trial after hearing the appeal in his "chambers." That was usually in the Bank Exchange, Henry Tibbals's new saloon fronting on Fowler's wharf, where manager Ben Cooper welcomed the judge and his friends.[24]

CRED

Sometimes pranks broke up Fitzhugh's court days at a time when anything funny was appreciated in the post-gold rush doldrums. At the end of one day, the bailiff's Chinese combination padlock went missing from the grand jury's meeting room. It was particularly important because it locked the tin box where Court Clerk James Swan kept safe the papers being used by the current grand jury. Prosecutor Butler P.

Anderson was very interested in the padlock and absent-mindedly put it in his pocket (or so he said). When the grand jury adjourned and the padlock turned up missing, bailiff and padlock owner Henry Webber "protested loudly." The court officers hunted, suspicious that Anderson had walked off to dinner with it, and found him at Armstrong's Hotel taking the lock apart and re-assembling it. He gave it back to Webber and apologized. The search party of Swan, the grand jury foreman, and Webber decided to go to Swan's office where they drew up a fourteen-count fake indictment charging Anderson with "the rape of the lock." The next morning, Anderson read it and thought it was a good joke. However, current Territorial Attorney Chenoweth had accidentally scooped it up with other indictments and carried it into court before realizing that it wasn't real. Since court hadn't convened yet, lawyer Paul Hubbs solemnly read it out and had just finished when he saw Judge Fitzhugh watching the fake proceeding. Hubbs was chagrined, but Fitzhugh assured him that the grand jury had a right to indict anyone for trespassing in their room and he would hear the case "in chambers" at the close of the day. True to his word, Fitzhugh held a meeting at the Bank Exchange Saloon and all the lawyers in town argued the case. Anderson was fined a basket of champagne and the "court" closed.[25]

⊗⊗

One man spent an inordinate amount of time in Fitzhugh's court. Maybe every western community had its Oscar Olney, a restless wanderer who moved between Bellingham Bay, San Juan Island, Port Townsend, and Dungeness ("Whiskey Flats"). He had what locals considered mitigating circumstances that generated patience from those who knew him. As well, there was the problem of inadequate jails for anything but brief detention, even for repeat offenders.

Olney was one of a more famous, and infamous, Rhode Island clan in the Pacific Northwest. Nathan Olney (believed to be Oscar's brother) was involved in the suppression of Yakama and other tribes across the Cascades, though he married a Yakama woman himself and became a long-time Indian Agent. One family member was an Oregon judge, while another was hung for murder. Olney himself married S'Klallam leader Chet'ze'moka's sister, which made him Edmund Fitzhugh's distant in-law. Among the Coast Salish, this relationship counted as much as it would for the Fitzhughs in Virginia. This may have been one of what the case file called "mitigating circumstances" (perhaps unvoiced) that allowed him to escape serious punishment more than once.[26]

In the Treaty War, Oscar served in Captain Isaac Ebey's militia unit from Whidbey Island and lost some of his fingers at Port Townsend when he fired a cannon that burst in saluting an incoming ship. Perhaps in recognition of giving his fingers for the cause, shortly after the war ended, he replaced Henry Webber as the customs collector on San Juan Island but soon left in fear of the Northern raiders. Despite that, one island historian called Oscar Olney a "hard-drinking, two-fisted frontiersman." He drifted over to Port Townsend, where he signed the petition opposing Fitzhugh's appointment. However, by 1860 he had worked for Fitzhugh tending bar in the Sehome Mine Saloon, and his wife had given birth to baby Thomas. After his wife apparently died, Oscar lived with Thomas and Betsy Jones in Whatcom until they became the legal guardians of his son, allowing Oscar to keep moving and drinking.[27]

Olney started his sporadic journey through Fitzhugh's court that year with six cases too serious for justice court, a few of which were heard by substituting Justice Strong. The first cases also involved the Joneses when the three planned to build a bar in San Juan Town on the island but failed to pay for a loan and materials. The most gossip-producing case was a slander lawsuit brought by Eliza Lotzgesell and her husband from Dungeness. She was the first non-native wife in the notorious settlement of land claims and whiskey smugglers at the edge of the Olympic Peninsula across the Strait from Victoria. The Lotzgesells felt Eliza had a respectable reputation to defend. Olney had said to her "You are a damned old whore. Shut up your mouth." They sued for $5000, which would be over $150,000 today. They won, but Olney had no money to pay, making his financial punishment irrelevant.[28]

Fitzhugh presided over Olney's three most serious criminal cases that were heard in a row and resulted in large fines. They involved assault and battery, waving a knife and pistol in the midst of a crowd (probably in a saloon), and assault with intent to kill. Sheriff Tom Wynn reported that Olney had no property "whatsoever." Sympathetic friends petitioned acting-Governor Henry McGill to release him from the fines because he was "crippled." Inexplicably, McGill paid the fines himself, instead of canceling the fines. When Fitzhugh sentenced Olney to forty-five days in the "county jail or someplace safe" in one case, he then reduced the sentence to one day. Irritated, Sheriff Wynn did not want to canoe back and forth the long distance from his home in Sehome to Camp Pickett on San Juan Island for such a paltry sentence. There was still no decent jail in Whatcom, and Fort Bellingham's troops were at Camp Pickett on San Juan Island since the "Pig War" (Boundary Dispute) began the previous year. The peace-loving Quaker sheriff, with a job and a smithy to tend, abruptly resigned.[29]

Oscar Olney and his legal problems might have been the type of court business that Fitzhugh was glad to leave behind when his term ended. A decade later and deep in 1871's dark rainy days of January, former sheriff James Kavanaugh wrote in his diary that Oscar had fallen dead in the Sehome Mine saloon just as he was about to take a drink. Maybe it was his first one of the day, or perhaps his fifth when he raised the glass and toppled over. Kavanaugh felt compelled to note "Society will not suffer much on account of it."[30]

SUPREME COURT JUSTICE

The once-a-year December Supreme Court term left the other months for staggered district court terms. That allowed for always having a substitute justice available for emergencies or an extended leave. If the Supreme Court needed a full three-week term, court could be suspended for a Christmas week and finish in the first week of January when all three justices would be available.

During Fitzhugh's years, the court met in the first Capitol's Territorial Library. In the five years since the 1853 Organic Act allocated $5000 for the governor to buy books, the collection under the stewardship of Librarian Bion F. Kendall grew to several thousand books, plus documents for the use of officials, lawyers, and residents. The library walls were never lathed, plastered, or painted with anything other than whitewash, so Olympia's wet climate and inadequate heating resulted in immediate deterioration of the wood foundation and carpets. Furniture was cheaply made and quickly worn out. The narrow and deep, wood-frame two-story capitol without even a cupola was an unimpressive location for a high court to gather. It was not the Supreme Court home Fitzhugh might have dreamed of as a young Virginia lawyer.[31]

கூஜி

Figure 23, First Territorial Capitol building. The Territorial Supreme Court met there during E. C. Fitzhugh's term as associate justice and it also housed the Territorial Library and Legislature sessions. *#C1982.18.30.29, courtesy of the Washington State Historical Society at WashingtonHistory.org.*

In December 1858, Fitzhugh arrived early for his first Supreme Court term, but although he was in town, a "late severe accident" kept him from court for a week, until Monday the thirteenth. *Pioneer-Democrat* editor Wiley never specified what accident had befallen Fitzhugh that kept him from the scheduled court opening, probably because his friends already knew and others didn't need to know until the gossip got to them. Evidence suggests this involved his wives' reaction to domestic violence and his need to recuperate.[32] (See Chapter 9.)

Because of Fitzhugh's absence, the delayed opening was a minor (or major) inconvenience for litigants, but also a week to party, do business, and talk politics. The newspaper editor reported the happy news that all three of the new Supreme Court judges were locals with local interests (i.e., hadn't come from outside the Northwest), and they had invested money in the territory as well as served in the Treaty War militia. Six qualified lawyers were on hand the first day of court and witnessed the division of districts and term schedules by consensus of the three judges. Fitzhugh's district included five counties: Kitsap, Jefferson, Island, Clallam, and Whatcom (including later Skagit and San Juan Counties), and his schedule was February and August. Almost no cases originated in Kitsap, without towns and the few whites living at lumber mill operations. Fitzhugh's first Supreme Court term went into recess along with the legislature on December 23 for the holidays, and concluded on January 5, 1859, after re-convening.[33]

Fitzhugh took a leave of absence twice from his judicial duties between Supreme Court terms when his Third District commissioner could handle emergency business and the clerk could take filings. After the "accident" glitch at his first Supreme Court term, he was always present on time so the court could legally convene. There seems to have been no mechanism for a quick succession to keep the Supreme Court in operation if a justice short. Fitzhugh would have had to resign if he didn't want to return for the annual term, and the appointment of a new judge would have taken a year, as it had for him.

During his judicial appointment 1858–1861, Fitzhugh heard twenty-two Supreme Court cases. Of those, only four were appeals on alleged errors from his own district court. Four more appeals from his court were carried over to the Lincoln appointees when they gathered for the 1862 Supreme Court term. Of the four Third District cases heard by himself and the other Buchanan appointees, none were overturned in their entirety. Fitzhugh wrote five opinions for the court during his appointment, the least of the three justices, but given the superior educations and experience of McFadden and Strong, that might be expected. Fitzhugh was not assigned to write the court's opinion for the most important or complicated cases. However, when read today, his opinions were the most readily understandable by non-professionals. They were clear, concise, and in more common language.[34]

ை

Perhaps not all of Fitzhugh's determination to board a steamer for Olympia that first December, even if injured, had to do with judicial responsibility. From a stump-filled quasi-street with one saloon, two stores, thirty scattered houses, and a blacksmith in 1854 when he arrived, the territorial capital had grown to an established center of government and politics by his first Supreme Court term. The Washington Hotel's large dining room was used for banquets and dances, and it had a reading room. The owner's ads targeted governmental folks coming into town. The Non Pareil Saloon touted its oysters, lobsters, and the "best" wines, liquors, and cigars. Across the street from Fitzhugh's friend and real estate partner James Tilton's home, Silas Galliher's boarding house touted its food as "the best the market affords." If Justice Fitzhugh stayed away from home and family to celebrate New Year's in Olympia, he would be a much sought-after guest at the usual public dinner and ball.[35]

Washington Territory men who gathered in one place, whether it was for court, convention, or legislature always took advantage of their time together to party. They epitomized what English journalist Frederick Marryat said about the free-flowing liquor in America: "I am sure the Americans can fix nothing without a drink…If successful in elections, they drink and rejoice; if not, they drink and swear…They begin to drink early in the morning, they leave off late at night."[36]

Between Fitzhugh's first Supreme Court term in Olympia and his arrival for the second in December 1859, a momentous hospitality change developed. Rebecca Groundage Howard and her blacksmith husband Alex arrived. They were "free blacks" from Massachusetts, and nothing annoyed her more than when Southerners, like Fitzhugh, called her "Aunt Becky" instead of "Mrs. Howard" or "Rebecca." The couple bought and improved the 1854 Pacific House restaurant and boarding house, starting Mrs. Howard on her way to wealth, and eventually becoming so famous she would host President Rutherford B. Hayes. To people like Fitzhugh, Mrs. Howard offered not only a "smiling countenance" in "spotless white," but meals touted by customers as good as what San Francisco offered. She was a large woman who could lift a man off the ground, allowing her to control the behavior in her establishment that became the headquarters of lawmakers and lobbyists. It probably was also Fitzhugh's choice, as it fit his long pattern of going where influential people gathered to enjoy whatever "finer things in life" were available. In their personal life, the Howards had no children of their own, but they adopted an abused and abandoned half-Snoqualmie son of Thomas Glasgow, one of the earliest settlers north of Oregon, but also a notoriously bad husband and father.[37]

EDMUND C. FITZHUGH, DEFENDANT

Many months passed after the second (and legitimate) grand jury indicted Fitzhugh for murder, and still the controversy continued and grew over his judicial appointment. It began to appear that every man in the territory had an opinion to share on the juxtaposition of appointment and indictment.

About twenty months after Andrew Wilson's death, a legislator from Chehalis gave a speech that first praised Fitzhugh as "a perfect gentleman." He followed with his opinion that if the criminal charges had any foundation, Fitzhugh's appointment was a "disgrace to the Territory and the man [Stevens] who would knowingly recommend such a man to this office should receive the condemnation of the people." When printed in the Olympia paper a week later, J. W. Wiley, the Democratic editor, said the Chehalis legislator had his own agenda for opposing Stevens and his friends. When the Steilacoom opposition newspaper also reprinted the speech, it included use of the word murder, as well as a disclaimer that the editor wasn't certain if Stevens knew of the crime.[38]

When Whatcom County's new legislator (and soon Whatcom County's first farmer) John Tennant delivered his own reply in the House of Representatives, the paper printed it a few days later. Tennant maintained that all proper steps had been taken, resulting in no indictment before Stevens departed for Washington, DC, as the new territorial delegate, and couldn't have known that one would come in after he left. He stated that recommendations in the District of Columbia were in favor, from Washington Territory and those who knew him there, and so Stevens could not unilaterally cancel the submission of Fitzhugh's name. Tennant stressed that the appointment was confirmed and commission issued before the grand jury brought in the new 1858 indictment. He put up a defense against the storied existence of the Democratic "Olympia Clique" from which all appointments came as long as they agreed with Stevens's positions.[39]

Shortly after Fitzhugh brought his gavel down to adjourn his February 1859 district court term, Chief Justice Obadiah McFadden presided over his murder trial in Olympia. Fitzhugh hired two now-Republican defense lawyers: William Wallace and Olympia's first mayor, Elwood Evans. The fact that Fitzhugh hired two talented

Republican lawyers instead of fellow Democrats to defend him implies that he had some doubts about how things would go, or that he didn't want an acquittal to appear to be a whitewash by Democrats and a Democrat-appointed chief justice.[40]

Fitzhugh's political views certainly did not align with Wallace, the new Republican orator and legislator who was the debate stand-in for Stevens's election opponent in 1857. Wallace had spent many years as a politician in the Midwest where his long-time friendship with Abraham Lincoln began. Despite that, Fitzhugh respected his legal expertise and that Wallace's integrity and ethics would allow him to defend a political adversary. He had been the defense attorney for Chief Leschi's death penalty trial after the Treaty War prior to defending the two native men Fitzhugh ordered hung. Two years after the trial, President Lincoln appointed him Washington's fourth territorial governor, and then Idaho Territory's first governor.

Figure 24, Governor William Wallace, photographed 1850–1870. Before he became the governor, Wallace was one of E. C. Fitzhugh's defense attorneys for his murder trial. *State Library Photograph Collection 1851–1990, Washington State Archives, Digital Archives #AR-07809001-pho04530.*

While Wallace was some years older than Fitzhugh, Elwood Evans was only twenty-nine. After coming from Philadelphia to serve as the customs collector on Puget Sound, he quickly gained a reputation for organizational and legal ability and people considered him the territory's best orator. In the years after he defended Fitzhugh, he became territorial secretary, organized the Washington

Bar Association, was territorial librarian, and became Washington's first serious historian.[41]

Figure 25, Elwood Evans, photographed 1860–1880. One of E. C. Fitzhugh's defense lawyers, he later served as the territorial librarian and was an early historian of Washington. *State Library Photograph Collection, 1851–1990, Washington State Archives, Digital Archives, #AR-07809001-ph004226.*

On March 14, 1859, nearly two years after Andrew Wilson was shot, Fitzhugh pleaded not guilty in Olympia's courtroom in the Capitol building.

Of three witnesses called by the prosecution, Wallace briefly cross-examined only one. Three others, including Edward Eldridge, attended but were never called to testify. Wallace and Evans called not a single defense witness and rested their case on the prosecution testimony. The two talented orators also declined to address the jury.[42]

The admissibility of Wilson's dying statement became a major problem for both sides. Chief Justice McFadden ruled that the prosecution had to establish a factual basis for saying that "the witness made it of his own accord and under the immediate fear of death." Perhaps the witnesses never heard Eldridge tell Wilson that he was about to die.

Facing an apparent impossibility, Territorial Prosecutor Butler Anderson then rested his case and asked McFadden to direct the jury to find Fitzhugh "Not Guilty." He said the Territory was unable to offer any further evidence and that which he had introduced already failed to establish the charge. When McFadden addressed the jury, he said that he couldn't tell them what to do, but the evidence presented did not support the charge of "murder." The witnesses failed to make out any part of the motive necessary for a murder charge of any degree, or even criminal manslaughter.

The jury retired to deliberate. One and a half minutes later, they acquitted Fitzhugh and Chief Justice McFadden discharged him, probably to the applause of his friends in a crowded courtroom.

The *Pioneer-Democrat* presented a complete account of the trial and the witness testimonies. Editor, Democrat owner, and fellow Mason, J. W. Wiley then presented some of his own opinions about what had transpired since Wilson's death on the warm late spring evening of Saturday, May 28, 1857.

Wiley emphasized that he thought Edward Eldridge had "malicious" motives, instead of "honorable, honest and disinterested" ones, or he would not have "sneaked in" to the dying man's presence and would have requested Fitzhugh's presence. He disputed the 1858 indictment, at which no witnesses appeared. Wiley believed that without the concurrent judicial appointment, no indictment would have been found at all. And he thought that the acquittal vindicated President Buchanan's appointment.

According to Wiley, during Justice Chenoweth's last term of court at Coveland, all the indictments brought in by his grand jury were later found to be faulty and thrown out. Only Fitzhugh waived his right to object to the faulty action, and instead the change of venue was allowed when he *"demanded"* a trial. That Fitzhugh demanded a jury trial instead of pursuing dismissal of a faulty indictment reflects a Virginian's defense of his personal honor.

The Olympia and Steilacoom newspapers devoted startlingly different levels of attention to Fitzhugh's trial. While the *Pioneer-Democrat* gave a complete account of every moment, Steilacoom's Republican *Puget Sound Herald* devoted only five lines buried among other judicial news: "Acquittal of Col. Fitzhugh.—This gentleman was placed on trial, last week, at Olympia, for the murder of a man named Wilson, some years since, at Bellingham Bay. The jury almost unhesitatingly pronounced him Not Guilty."[43]

After protesting Fitzhugh's appointment for two years, Frank Chenoweth continued to complain two months after the swift acquittal and editor Wiley's criticism of his own court. A Whatcom County man heard Chenoweth calling Fitzhugh a murderer far south from Bellingham Bay near the army's Fort Vancouver. He quietly asked

Chenoweth what he thought "Judge Fitzhugh" would do to him if he heard that. Chenoweth's reply was that he "did not know nor care a damn." This, in spite of the fact that he would need to appear in Fitzhugh's court in the future.[44]

Perhaps not a coincidence, barely a month later in May the BBCC syndicate leased the Sehome Mine for six years to some newer shareholders. They formed the business entity Moody and Sinclair with plans to expand the mine further and installed their own on-site manager. Fitzhugh would reap income from his mine shares if the larger contracts increased profitability, and he could concentrate even more on politics and his court. His title of "coal agent" became less and less real.[45]

POLITICS

If the murder indictment handed Fitzhugh's political enemies a weapon in 1859, there was another one. Those still angry about Stevens's declaration of martial law and incarceration of Chief Justice Lander weaponized the issues of money and corruption remaining from the Treaty War. Though Fitzhugh had inspected and discharged the last militia members in October 1856, he had in effect triple-dipped the government treasury by remaining on the payroll months more as militia inspector, military aide, and Special Indian Agent. In July the *Pioneer-Democrat* printed a complaint from one of the federal war auditors examining the records about "monstrous abuses" that Stevens allowed from his militia staff officers. Fitzhugh and the others were the main obstacle to payment of the war debt, he said, because the officers found ways to speculate, were paid for services never rendered, and Stevens had an unnecessarily ballooned staff of 179 men. Following up, the opposition *Puget Sound Herald* printed the entire auditor's report that indicated other abuses such as the extravagant number of meals and hotel rooms that "General" W. W. Miller bought without reporting the recipients. Even a year later in 1860, Fitzhugh and the other officers were being portrayed as "torpid boa constrictors" whose "vices tinge the frivolity of their follies with something more than ridicule." Hopes all over the territory continued that, with Delegate Stevens's influence, Congress would ultimately reduce Washington Territory's $6 million war debt share down to $3 million, though most knew a 50 percent reduction was probably unrealistic. The federal auditor didn't think the volunteers, who were never mustered into the

U.S. Army, had any cause at all to claim compensation, and he reduced the amount paid settlers for supplies. The claims moved to a House committee hearing in 1860, but final passage of the claim was not paid until the next year.[46]

After eighteen months away, Stevens returned from Washington, DC, in May 1859 to run for re-election in the midst of the complaints about the war debts. Criticism of him and the Democrats picked up immediately in the *Puget Sound Herald*, where editor Edward Furste wrote "very small men may sometimes secure the highest and most unqualified recommendations of the delegate; and hence the favor of the President." He called the system "toadyism" that established a man's reputation for ability simply by holding a commission, which would include Fitzhugh. He saw only "twaddle" about Stevens's accomplishments and plea for $16,000 in salary again to get more done, including reduction of the war debt. Stevens would argue that it had been approved in principle, and the next session of Congress would set the dollar amount to be paid militia veterans for expenses they paid themselves and reparations for Hudson's Bay Company lands lost, despite the increasing focus in the national capital on sectional differences. What Stevens didn't want to focus on was that Congress was debating whether or not the territory-led Treaty War was even legal.[47]

Fitzhugh was again the Democratic Central Committee Chairman. County conventions the same month Delegate Stevens returned showed that the Democrats continued to split between the Stevens camp who supported President Buchanan's policies, versus those who supported Steven Douglas's faction. However, to voters, national issues paled in importance to territorial ones, and the opposition to Stevens was mostly unorganized while Fitzhugh allies were most of the convention delegates. Under his leadership, they endorsed Buchanan's policies, applauded Stevens's work, again called for the transcontinental railroad to be built and terminate in Washington Territory, and supported an end to the Hudson's Bay Company rights connected to their fort and farm operations, which was strictly a regional issue. Fitzhugh and his committee members brought in the votes to nominate Stevens for his second term with fifty-four of sixty votes cast at the convention.[48]

The territory's new and growing Republican Party nominated Fitzhugh's former defense lawyer William Wallace as an independent to oppose Stevens, almost a sure election loss. They made martial law a big issue again. They also emphasized Stevens's drinking, using the example of his failure to make it to Dungeness for a stump speech because he had partied too much at Bellingham Bay with his friend Fitzhugh. Stevens claimed campaign exhaustion, but no one believed it. Ever more confident as the Republican opposition's voice, the *Puget Sound Herald* printed a letter about the Whatcom event when both candidates spoke. Owner-editor Edward Furste maintained that most attendees thought Wallace had won the debate and changed some minds. However, he added that some men had been "threatened with being thrown out of employment by certain Stevens men, who are foolish enough to imagine they can intimidate freemen and control their votes by such threats." This directly pointed at Fitzhugh, the Virginian slaveholder when it used terms of slavery, e.g., "freemen." Furste also wrote "When men holding high official positions seek to enslave the laboring man for daring to express his political opinions and preferences." The editor predicted that because of Fitzhugh's behavior, Wallace would win Whatcom County by a majority of twenty-five of the eighty to ninety votes to be cast.[49]

Between court terms, Fitzhugh worked hard to turn out the vote. In late June, he wrote to W. W. Miller, and added a postscript to the letter about a large loan to expand the Sehome store: "All right down here in the political line—I think we shall give the damn murderous Black Republicans hell, so that they will never kick again." In contrast, the *Herald* account of Stevens's campaign appearance at Port Townsend, shortly before Fitzhugh wrote, claimed that Delegate Stevens was received with the "utmost coldness." Editor Furste correctly predicted that a change was happening in public sentiment and cracks in the Stevens machine were growing.[50]

July 1859 was election month for congressional delegate, legislators, and county officials, and things became more heated as the election drew near. Fitzhugh went out to Semiahmoo where a precinct had been set up at Boundary Survey headquarters for the workers (mostly loggers), and he expected to bring in fifty to sixty votes for Stevens. There had already been complaints months before that a man couldn't get hired unless he declared his allegiance to Stevens. The *Herald* claimed that when Stevens campaigned there, he didn't bother to talk to the laboring men once officers told him that those workers could only keep their jobs by voting for him. John Tennant went out to San Juan Island to secure twenty votes, although it is questionable whether those were going to be committed Americans voting, or just those who hadn't decided yet to be Americans or British citizens.[51]

The *Herald* called Olympia "the hot-bed of cliques and spoils, and the emporium of political tricksters and high-toned federal functionaries" where Stevens would get only a slim majority because the Republican party was growing, despite being called "Black Republicans" by Fitzhugh and others who opposed abolition. Furste hinted at electoral cheating if the Fitzhugh and Miller-led Democrats needed it to stay in power.

When the territory's votes on the non-secret ballots were counted, Stevens won handily by at least five hundred votes. Fitzhugh wrote to Miller that if the Republicans complained about illegalities, "we don't care a damn, as the battle has been fought and won by us." Fitzhugh had delivered a vote for Stevens of 128–24 in Whatcom County, the biggest disparity in the entire territory. It helped Stevens achieve a majority vote of 65 percent.[52]

It didn't take long for accusations to fly. The *Herald* accused the Democrats of illegal voting, particularly in Whatcom County where the estimated turnout was expected to be seventy to eighty voters and instead, Fitzhugh delivered 128 votes. Furste published a letter about election day from Henry Barkhousen (writing as "H.B."), still a mine employee, who said "Fitzhugh made himself mighty busy that day, being the first time that he has been seen in town for some time, strongly guarded by his coal miners." Barkhousen, an election judge whose ethics would lead him to the post of county auditor the next year, claimed there were bogus voters, and it was made clear to him that it was dangerous to challenge one. When elderly lawyer Henry McNair brought up the law and how the election was to be conducted, Fitzhugh told him to "dry up," insulted him, and made an implied threat. Barkhousen claimed that the ballot box's cover was secured only with tacks before it was taken to another building rather than the courthouse and returned much later.[53]

Barkhousen and McNair were not the only ones to accuse Fitzhugh of voter intimidation. He threatened his longtime mining engineer, McKinney Tawes. Still with some major authority at the mine as titular coal agent, shareholder, and Sehome townsite owner, as well as judicial authority, Fitzhugh told Tawes that if he didn't vote for Stevens, he'd lose his job. Tawes quit on the spot.[54]

Still angry in November, Furste couldn't let it go. He wrote and published a long front-page article about the folly of choosing judges because of their political affiliations, directly addressing the Third District citizens of the northern territory.[55]

SUPREME COURT, DECEMBER 1859

At the end of 1859, the Supreme Court justices heard nine cases. The first one on the docket was perhaps the most significant for Fitzhugh's legal legacy in Washington Territory. That was Fitzhugh's own *Benjamin Madison v Lucy Madison* divorce, in which Benjamin Madison appealed Fitzhugh's decision that he must share the first Clallam County land claim ("Groveland Farm") and his other assets with his indigenous wife when he divorced her through the legal system. Fitzhugh's divorce decree seems unique for the territory because he treated indigenous testimony equally with that of a white man, despite it being illegal to do so.[56]

Madison's original divorce filing earlier that year admitted that he treated their 1854 tribal custom marriage equal to a legal one and did not deny that she was his wife. He admitted that he treated her like the Northerner slave from the nearby S'Klallam village that he claimed she had been. Witnesses had observed a tumultuous marriage with spousal abuse and infidelity by both parties. Fitzhugh knew many of the Dungeness men who testified, several of whom, like himself, were married to S'Klallam women, some of whom were likely cousins of his wives Julia and Mary. Nominally farming, Madison sold contraband liquor from British Victoria to all comers in his store at the mouth of the Dungeness River, which had led to the place being called "Whiskey Flats." Nearly every witness testified that Lucy was frugal with the couple's money and a hard worker who was as responsible for the farm's economy as he was. While some said she had a hot temper, the witnesses had seen Benjamin treat her horribly, including hog-tying and beating her with a board until she fled to another home.[57]

It was yet another court event that brought together old combatants. One of Benjamin Madison's two attorneys was Frank Chenoweth. The other was the respected B. F. Dennison who practiced in Whatcom after his arrival during the gold rush. Lucy Madison's attorneys were also well-known and respected: future congressional delegate Selucius Garfielde and Territorial Librarian Bion F. Kendall. All four attorneys had faced each other many times. Though juries adamantly opposed acceptance of indigenous testimony against a white man under territorial law, Fitzhugh allowed Lucy to testify, which may have been ground-breaking and not confirmed by a new law until the 1870s. With no jury for a divorce case, Fitzhugh had decided to accept whatever testimony he wanted and make whatever financial arrangements he wanted, subject to appeal. He awarded Lucy Madison one-third of Groveland Farm as a legal co-owner, despite indigenous wives in tribal custom marriages being ineligible. He awarded her a trust fund that would yield annual income, and ordered that Benjamin pay her court costs and attorney fees. Finally, Fitzhugh ordered that when Lucy Madison died, the trust fund would revert to her ex-husband, instead of any children she might have. That proved to be a mistake for Lucy Madison's future in the long run.

Benjamin Madison could not accept that Lucy should receive any benefit from his assets—no alimony, no court costs, no interest in his land claim, no trust fund. Just before he filed for divorce, Madison hid his major asset by selling the farm to his lawyer Frank Chenoweth. Fitzhugh stopped Chenoweth from paying over any money to Madison until Lucy's rights from his decree were taken care of. Benjamin Madison ended up as plaintiff in both the original divorce case and the appeal.

When the 1859 Supreme Court heard the appeal, Justice William Strong wrote the opinion affirming everything Fitzhugh ruled, except for preventing Chenoweth from paying Madison for the farm, because he was not a party to the divorce case. Benjamin Madison repeatedly went back to District Court in the coming years, in a series of moves that tied up the funds until Lucy died, never having had access to the monies Fitzhugh awarded her.

CRWO

The second appeal out of Fitzhugh's court was also heard during the 1859 term: the murder conviction and death sentence appeal, *Yelm Jim (Wahulet) v Washington Territory*. [Wa-he-let is the preferred anglicized spelling now.] This historic and notorious case came out of the Treaty War and the controversial murder conviction and execution of Nisqually war chief Leschi. Wa-he-let was another Nisqually war chief who subsequently killed a third, Slugia, for betraying his uncle Leschi. He carried out Coast Salish justice while Leschi still lived, and his case was being fruitlessly appealed. Wa-he-let's lawyers, members of the usual group of reputable lawyers that handled cases at both levels, appealed his conviction on the basis of eight errors by Fitzhugh and his court. The appeal centered on jury selection, the charge, and jury instructions, but the final error that Fitzhugh and his colleagues examined was whether or not Wa-he-let's people were in a war with the United States. The panel ruled that no defined war occurred at the time of the homicide that would give immunity. The three justices let Wa-he-let's conviction and death sentence stand. However, eight months later Territorial Governor Henry McGill pardoned Wa-he-let, and he lived out a long life in Nisqually territory.[58]

Fitzhugh wrote the 1859 court's opinion for three cases, all of lesser importance than the Yelm Jim appeal. Fred Clarke appealed his assault and battery conviction for jury mistakes and a bad indictment, but the Second District's verdict was affirmed. John Freany appealed his attempted rape conviction and that was affirmed. The third opinion Fitzhugh wrote was surprisingly a case that originated in his own court and among people he knew well: Winfield Ebey and two other Whidbey Islanders. Ebey appealed his loss of a $280 case and disputed that he should pay costs. Fitzhugh's opinion for the court affirmed the original decision and added in the extra costs for bringing the case to the Supreme Court.[59]

Chief Justice McFadden wrote the last opinions that term. Those cases involved slaughtered cattle not paid for, but without a contract; a jurisdictional problem about taxes rendered; two cases appealed by the Hudson's Bay Company's Puget Sound Agricultural Company (PSAC) against the ruling in favor of Pierce County; and an admiralty case of cross-complaints.[60]

○3∞

After Fitzhugh had been on the bench for his two special sessions, first regular district court term, and first Supreme Court session, the *Pioneer-Democrat* reported on his performance in March 1859. Editor Wiley wrote that despite the continuing war of letters and speeches against him (including the one in the *New York Tribune*), he had given "general if not universal satisfaction" in his rulings, especially supportive since Frank Chenoweth had been the acting prosecutor. Fitzhugh's reputation among the Third District's general populace continued to rise as long as he was the justice, and complaints grounded in earlier events ceased.[61]

CHAPTER 9

Cards and Candidates

I N A ROUSING END TO FITZHUGH'S district court term in February 1860, thieves broke into his commissioner J.J.H. Van Bokkelen's office above the post office late at night after the last day of court. They used ether to incapacitate him and escaped with money on the local steamer *Eliza Anderson* in the morning before anyone discovered the crime. People proclaimed it a "grand finale" to the court term and the usual extended male gathering.[1]

ANOTHER TRIAL

Some days after the "grand finale," on March 12 Olympia's Second District territorial court indicted Fitzhugh and Justice William Strong for gambling during the previous December Supreme Court term. It proved to be one of the odder cases during the years before statehood.

Despite the Supreme Court's crowded docket in December 1859, there had been plenty of time for the usual socializing by attendees and justices. On the fifteenth, Justices Fitzhugh and Strong probably ate a fine dinner at Rebecca Howard's or one of her competitors, and then they gambled at one or more of the local places that allowed it, despite the law. It was not the only occasion. Mrs. Howard did not permit gambling at her respectable establishment. Perhaps the judges gambled at the Washington Hotel where many government types stayed in Olympia. Or maybe at the Non Pareil Saloon across the street from Rebecca Howard's restaurant and hotel. The Non Pareil had a new "ball alley" and billiard table for more entertainment. It didn't "do credit," which meant gamblers made loans of treats, oyster dinners, or cash to keep the game going among friends.[2]

Someone who didn't much like the court (or maybe just those two judges) took notice of the pair flagrantly violating the territorial gambling laws. That two Supreme Court justices displayed such arrogance would bring new trouble for Fitzhugh some months later.

The Territory had a love-hate relationship with gambling. Everyone seemed to do it, and everyone knew about it. It went with the whiskey and cigars during an evening at local saloons. And yet, the first legislature decided to take a respectable stance by trying to control how gambling occurred. Legislators passed the first law (#23) in 1855, then amended it in 1857 (#25) under the rubric "Gaming and Gaming Contracts." The amended law imposed fines and court costs for "every person who shall suffer any gaming table, bank, cards or gambling device, etc." The 1855 act already specifically forbade betting on card games in its first section. Citizens largely ignored both.[3]

In 1858, a year before Fitzhugh's holiday gambling, Steilacoom's *Puget Sound Herald* editor Edward Furste wrote a lengthy piece entitled "Public Gambling." He did not hold the territory's Democratic administration's lucrative printing contract that stifled any dissent in the *Pioneer-Democrat*, leaving Furste to be a strident voice about anything he wanted. He wrote that for several months public gambling had been going on in Steilacoom "to a fearful extent." He blamed it on the Fraser River gold rush that brought "hordes of gamblers from California" to Bellingham Bay where they "spread their tricks and pursued an uninterrupted career of midday plundering of the unsophisticated." He claimed that the "vultures" headed for Steilacoom's major settlement and army fort "when the light went out and Whatcom went in." Furste maintained that his town was actually against gambling, but no arrests were being made and gambling was being publicized. He contrasted what was happening on Puget Sound to Hudson's Bay Company-dominated Victoria where he naively claimed (or purposely lied) that gambling laws were so well executed that it was non-existent. He appealed to the public to at least think of their national pride and realize the "degradation to which we have allowed ourselves to be reduced."[4]

Furste's words might have seemed hypocritical to many, especially women readers. He, along with Democratic Party leader W. W. Miller and other prominent men, gambled and borrowed money from each other to stay in their games. Nothing resulted from Furste's appeal to respect the law. By early 1860, when the legislature passed another amendment adding prosecution to simple fines, the *Pioneer-Democrat*'s editor said he thought half the inhabitants of Olympia and Thurston County could be put in the new territorial prison for gambling.[5]

The March 1860 grand jury in Olympia indicted Justices Fitzhugh and Strong for playing "Hazards" on December 15, 1859, and the following days. The indictment made clear that the two justices continued to play, even the very same day the grand jury considered the charges. Hazards was the parent game to "Craps," and originated in the fourteenth century. Players bet against one or more opponents or the house, and threw cards into a central pot called the "main chance." The new gambling law amendment granted immunity to witnesses in exchange for required testimony. They included Fitzhugh's long-time friend and business colleague, Territorial Surveyor James Tilton, and the previously incensed newspaper editor Furste. The indictment did not accuse the men of gambling for money, only for "things to represent value," contrary to the law and "against the peace and dignity" of the territory. That probably meant drinks or the usual oyster suppers.[6]

Justice William Strong, the minister's son and Yale honors graduate, had little in common with relatively amoral Fitzhugh beyond militia experience until their appointments to the bench brought them together. Playing cards together enabled them to voluntarily exclude some individuals who might be scheduled to appear before them in court and were looking for some favoritism by socializing with the justices.

Another type of experience also might have bonded the two judges from such different backgrounds. Justice Strong's son wrote that when his mother needed help on their Cathlamet land claim in southwest Washington, Strong negotiated a large payment to a Yakama chief for his daughter, Wah-kee-nah, to come live with them. The Yakama lived a long way from Cathlamet, but Strong had earlier been in their area as an Oregon justice. Strong's son characterized her as a "domestic servant" who carried her own revolver. It is difficult to believe that this important young woman's father did not believe she was marrying another important man. Even if he knew Strong had another wife, this might not have deterred the arrangement given some indigenous customs for wealthy men, similar to Fitzhugh's marriages. Whatever her arrangement was, Wah-kee-nah left for home several years later.[7]

Fitzhugh himself had presided in a similar gambling case the previous year. The civil lawsuit concerned who was supposed to pay when a Port Townsend saloon ordered breakfast brought over from a restaurant for six players. The men had avoided betting scarce cash the previous night by playing for booze, oysters, and breakfast. The litigation ignored the illegality of the game.[8]

There is nothing in Fitzhugh's criminal gambling case file to indicate that he and Strong were arrested at any time under the new gambling law amendment passed in January between their offense and the indictment. No notice of arrest, no bonds posted. The file is missing many common filings, perhaps because it was all so ridiculous. The pair's colleague Chief Justice McFadden presided over the proceedings, and he almost certainly had been in many card games himself. That was just part of male socializing in Olympia.

Fitzhugh and Strong's legal team included Frank Clark, Territorial Librarian Bion Kendall, William Wallace, and Selucius Garfielde, all lawyers who had appeared in the courts of all three justices. Once more, Fitzhugh as a defendant faced Prosecuting Attorney Butler P. Anderson who had tried him for murder. As before, Anderson's motive to prosecute two sitting associate justices for being scofflaws may have had political overtones. He had joined the "Douglas Democrats" in the previous election cycle, and now called the "Stevens Democrats" a "sham democratic organization." Prosecutor Anderson also acted under the January amendment passed *after* the alleged December offenses, which was bound to cause trouble in court. It said that gamblers could be indicted and tried, not just fined as before. It required other participants in the game to testify under immunity about betting something of value. When court costs were added to an increased fine, it was a substantial slap. By putting the justices on public trial, Anderson made a statement about how he would enforce the new rules while also publicly deriding the Democratic appointees.[9]

When Fitzhugh and Strong's trial started on Monday, March 19, it was probably in a crowded courtroom eager to see how the chief justice would handle the legal maneuvering that started immediately. The defense filed a motion for no further proceedings, citing two major legal problems. First, the four lawyers said the grand jury had not been selected and empaneled according to the law. Second, they accused the grand jury of misconduct by admitting an unqualified person into the jury room. They also claimed that there was unlawful discrimination between Fitzhugh and Strong by the grand jury, though they never specified which man it was. Chief Justice McFadden overruled the motion, but then reversed himself and allowed the objection regarding discrimination against one defendant.

Later the same day, the defense team filed a motion to quash the indictment completely. It said vague language made no allegation that the betting was made with any individual or that anything of value was bet. Second, that the indictment did not state the specific time the offense was committed. Indeed, no specific place was identified. The non-specific general terms of the gambling indictment smelled of politics. McFadden overruled the motion, but once again allowed an exception that reversed his decision. One unnamed defendant was released for want of evidence.

The trial proceeded but the jury failed to agree on the charges against the second defendant, still unnamed, but likely Fitzhugh the Democratic activist. McFadden and Anderson brought in a new jury to try his case. The new jury had only eleven members after it proved impossible to find a twelfth "competent" person to serve, usually meaning sober. By a vote of nine to two, the result was the same lack of consensus. Prosecutor Anderson then dropped the case. The *Pioneer-Democrat's* Wiley wrote that Anderson's action saved Thurston County "a heavy expense in prosecuting cases based upon the most frivolous pretexts imaginable."[10]

Wiley excoriated the grand jury in the next issue. He estimated that nine-tenths of the territory's men gambled, and the jurors had indicted "our very best and most law-abiding citizens." He questioned with astonishment why the jurors singled the two justices out when most card players were from "the best and most intelligent class of our community," and almost no one saw himself as a lawbreaker. Wiley adamantly maintained that "card-playing is pre-eminently the national American amusement" and source of "innocent enjoyment in the family circle" as well as saloon. Surely, he said, betting cigars, oyster suppers, apples, and drinks was the case across the nation. He made clear that there were citizens who liked to gamble as amusement and also "GAMBLERS" [his capital letters] everyone loathed.[11]

Wiley contrasted the small offense of gambling that had exploded into such a huge mess to the more important issues causing sectional conflicts on the other side of the country. He claimed he didn't want to cast a bad reflection on individual grand jurors but, in the future "a few grains of common sense will materially help to construe law properly." Wiley didn't support literal interpretation in every case. In other words, let the men (and the justices) play cards.

The controversy on the streets did not stop. Wiley defended his editorialized article. Some people, he claimed, had "tortured [it] into a defense of gambling." He solemnly declared it a vice he did not support.

He wasn't blaming Chief Justice McFadden, who couldn't discriminate between "bosom-friend or the most implacable enemy." Wiley said he just wanted everyone to think about the issues before finding bills of indictment which couldn't be sustained in court. He mentioned seven current other gambling indictments, but the absence of case files for the others indicates that proceedings came to a halt.[12]

None of it seemed to affect Fitzhugh's growing reputation as a respected territorial justice. It did not affect his deep involvement in Democratic politics, despite Furste's accusations the previous July of ballot-stuffing in Whatcom County.

A few weeks after his acquittal, Fitzhugh, still one of the informal money men of the territory, lent $1,000 to former Whatcom County Commissioner (and 1855 sheep raid companion) William Cullen. The loan was in the form of a mortgage on Cullen's Donation Land Claim on Whidbey Island. Only a year later, this mortgage would figure into Fitzhugh's plans for his Northwest future as his appointment drew to a close.[13]

Politics

Fitzhugh's political career took another turn in late spring 1860 when party conventions met at every level. Congressional Delegate Isaac Stevens left Washington, DC, in late April for South Carolina and the Democrats' national convention in Charleston. It dissolved in hostility between northern and southern Democrats, just as the presidential campaign would fracture the nation into multiple political factions. The gambling trial may have been a minor Northwest expression of that growing acrimony if adversarial politics had entered the proceedings. Two sitting justices, of all the men gambling in the city of Olympia, were targeted by the new "Douglas Democrat" prosecutor who publicly derided the territory's "Stevens Democrats."[14]

As the country's parties split apart over slavery, most Washingtonians' interest in that issue only involved the implications affecting territorial popular sovereignty, their right to make governmental decisions for themselves. Fitzhugh's political cronies and others were far more interested in building their own fortunes, new communities, and infrastructure that would come with funds allocated by Congress. Advancing those priorities was Congressional Delegate Stevens's job. The territory had always been a Democratic stronghold, even if a few were defecting to the anti-slavery Republican party whose members were labeled "Black Republicans" for their support of freedom for enslaved African Americans. The average former Southerner in the territory had been interested in abolition news, but it was a distant interest connected only to the state of one's birth and family, not current life in the far Northwest. For Fitzhugh and other men allied with the California Democrats who wanted to build a slavery-neutral Pacific voting bloc, their interest in the issue had a different underlying tone.[15]

The country was coming apart, and President Buchanan was not up to the job of saving the union with a strategic policy to diffuse the situation. His close friendships with Southerners tilted his own beliefs about slavery toward a likely natural demise. It was the same attitude that Washington Territory's Democrats largely held. Very soon, both sides of the conflict would reject Buchanan. Yankees called him a Southern "toady" while the Southerners would blame him for not facilitating secession.[16]

Stevens left for Charleston a month after Fitzhugh's entertaining gambling trial. When he arrived, he optimistically wrote home to W. W. Miller that he thought Oregon's Senator Joseph Lane had a good chance of being nominated for vice president over the current one, Kentucky's John Breckinridge. He thought northerner Douglas had a chance, but Lane was "decidedly in the best position." In that moment, Stevens did not anticipate the convention dissolution, or the ultimate rise of Steven Douglas over Buchanan's re-election bid. In a local sign of what was to come nationally, the Washington Territory Democrats were beginning to split almost evenly between supporters of Douglas and those who still supported Buchanan and his men.[17]

Multiple divisive events in eastern states and between factions in Congress occurred in the run up to the Democrats' convention. When the convention delegates rejected a pro-slavery platform, eight Southern states walked out. After the remaining delegates could not agree on a candidate, they also went home. After the adolescent Republican Party nominated Abraham Lincoln for president, the Democrats re-convened on June 18 in Baltimore. Without delegates from the eight southern states, they nominated Steven Douglas for president.

The breakaway Southern-led Democrats scheduled their own June "Peace Democrat" convention, also in Baltimore. Isaac Stevens would attend to support the conciliatory policies of Buchanan, the president who had appointed him and so many of his Treaty War loyalists. Fitzhugh joined him in that support.

Complicating things, a fourth political party founded mostly by former conservative Whigs, the Constitutional Union Party, nominated John Bell of Tennessee for president. Their vague platform supported the Constitution, the Union, and law enforcement.[18]

୯୫ୠ

On May 23, 1860, Fitzhugh wrote Miller that he would leave for Washington, DC, in June to work with Stevens on the Peace Democrats' presidential campaign. He now held only the flexible title of "resident agent" at the Sehome Coal Mine, and townsite sales had mostly evaporated, taking up minimal time. He firmed up his travel plans and obtained a six-month leave of absence from court. Justice Strong would preside over his August district court term, while his commissioner and clerk would take care of other court business. Fitzhugh would be free until after the presidential election, though he could not be absent when the Supreme Court opened in December.[19]

Planning to leave for the East in June, Fitzhugh's journey by steamer would not get him to the Peace Democrat convention in time, so he would join Stevens in Washington, DC, shortly after. Six months leave included enough time for a visit with his remaining sisters, Rosalie having died in his absence.[20]

After Fitzhugh chaired the territorial Democratic convention in Olympia, the *Pioneer-Democrat* told readers that "the Colonel" left June 11 for the states "on a visit to his friends and relatives, from whom he has now been absent for some 11 years." Editor Wiley extolled Fitzhugh's good cheer, hospitality, affability, gentlemanliness, and agreeableness before saying "The fog of prejudice with which he was once looked upon by some, has long since been lifted, and those who then beheld him as an arrogant, overbearing man, are now his admirers, and find him the modest, forbearing and religiously upright and honest man on all occasions." The editor said he heard praise for Fitzhugh's legal opinions, knowledge of the law, and dignity of his courtroom. Such praise, he said, came from some of Fitzhugh's former legal enemies. Fitzhugh's complex personality was encapsulated in Wiley's paragraph. There was no mention of the voter intimidation accusations. The mention of a religious Fitzhugh in the *Pioneer-Democrat* was a first by anyone.[21]

Wiley's article concluded with the information that Fitzhugh wanted readers to know he would be in the capital city for some time, and if anyone had business to transact with governmental departments, he could assist. In other words, Fitzhugh announced that he was ready to make money as a lobbyist or mediator for Washington Territory interests.

There was a gap of some weeks before Fitzhugh actually left for Washington, DC. His activities were probably related to his wives and children. (See "Family" below.)

Before he left Port Townsend to catch a steamer out of Victoria in early July, local Democrats threw a dinner for him. He replied to toasts with "oratorial elegance," despite reportedly being choked up. The attitude was far different when those same men signed a petition opposing his appointment.[22]

Steamers bound for San Francisco had dropped their frequency drastically after the gold rush ended, so Washington Territorial Governor Richard Gholson likely took the same one Fitzhugh boarded for his own six-month leave of absence. The two Virginia-born Democrats would have had much to talk about. The territory's third governor, Gholson, was another Buchanan loyalist like Fayette McMullen, and a slave owner in Kentucky and at his Texas ranch. His 1859 address to the legislature had been a blistering defense of keeping the union together, also Fitzhugh's stance. Gholson railed against what he considered treasonous talk from abolitionists, agitators, and reckless Southerners alike. He wrote to current Secretary of State Jeremiah Black (the former Attorney General who handled Fitzhugh's appointment) that he would not serve even a day under a Republican president.[23]

The Peace Democrat convention settled on Vice President John Breckinridge for their presidential candidate and Oregon's Senator Joseph Lane for vice president. Breckinridge agreed with Stephen Douglas on most things, except his favoring federal protection for slavery. The new party viewed federal interference as a trespass of private property. Breckinridge, at thirty-nine the same age as Fitzhugh, came from a prominent Kentucky family. He was a university-trained lawyer before he served as a major of Kentucky volunteers in the Mexican War. In Congress for five years before his election as Buchanan's vice president, Breckinridge supported the Dred Scott decision that no

Figure 26, Democratic Ticket for President, John C. Breckinridge and Joseph Lane. Broadside published in 1860 by Hayer & Ludwig of Richmond, Virginia. It included the names of fifteen Virginia electors at the Peace Democrats convention. *Broadside Collection, Portfolio 187, no. 1. Library of Congress, Prints and Photographs Division, #LC-USZ62-79543.*

African American could ever be a citizen, which was contributing to the nation's turmoil. By this decision, Olympia's prominent restauranteur Rebecca Howard could never claim Constitutional rights.

Senator Joseph Lane of Oregon was much older, but he was the first Northwesterner to be on a national ticket. Raised in North Carolina, he was an unpolished Eastern stereotype of a frontier politico. Lane had been a long-term Indiana legislator and farmer before service as a brigadier general of volunteers in the Mexican War. Afterward he was appointed Oregon Territorial Governor and Superintendent of Indian Affairs. Leading armed forces against a local revolt by indigenous tribes made him a colonizer hero, their elected congressional delegate, and fighter for Oregon statehood. When Oregon became a state in 1859, Lane was elected one of its first senators. He supported the right of a slaveholder to bring slaves into any territory (which included Washington Territory).[24]

Slavery had existed among the Coast Salish until the treaties that outlawed it were confirmed in 1859, but their version was never race-based, only on loss of personal history due to capture. A few early Washington settlers brought a slave with them, most notably Territorial Surveyor James Tilton, who preferred to call young Charles Mitchell his "ward."

The platform adopted by the Peace Democrats (taking the name "National Democrats") agreed for the most part with the Douglas wing's platform and affirmed Buchanan's earlier 1856 platform. For the new campaign, they added a few "explanatory resolutions," mostly supporting non-interference with slavery in territories and popular sovereignty over the issue for new states. The platform supported the Fugitive Slave Law in every state. If one sought to defeat it, that would be considered hostile, subversive to the Constitution, and "revolutionary." While supporting the exclusion of blacks from citizenship, one of the resolutions affirmed the equality of naturalized and native-born citizens. The platform also pledged support for Isaac Stevens's pet project, the earliest possible construction of a railroad from the Mississippi River to the Pacific Ocean. Lastly, the platform added Buchanan's own pet project, the acquisition of Cuba.[25]

The convention selected Isaac Stevens to chair the Breckinridge campaign after he helped get the candidates nominated, though (or maybe because) he was from a distant territory that could not vote for president. Fitzhugh was almost bound to stay in the capital after Miller wrote asking him to keep an eye on Stevens, and to write back about his behavior while Stevens managed two roles instead of just representing the territory. Miller told Fitzhugh that he would handle the political fight in Washington Territory, where it would become centered on the popular sovereignty issue. There, it soon grew into a fight between the Breckinridge supporters and a temporary coalition between the Republicans and the Douglas Democrats. Though Democrats still controlled the Washington legislature, only twenty-one percent of all Pacific Northwest residents in 1860 were from slave states, while Midwesterners were heavily contributing to the population growth. It would be a fight to keep political control in the hands of the Democrats.[26]

Without Fitzhugh to influence voters in Whatcom County's election, the political split there was visible. The post-gold rush population totaled 205, including the Fort Bellingham soldiers, but excluded the many settlers' indigenous wives and their children. Whatcom County voters came from twenty-seven states and eight foreign countries. Bad news for Democratic dominance, some of the most influential people in the county had turned Republican.[27]

A recurrence of Fitzhugh's "Panama Fever" malaria felled him by the time he arrived in the capital after his second trip across the isthmus, though by rail this time. The relapse left him in bed for much of the following month. Rather than stay with his sister Mary Eliza and her husband in the Georgetown neighborhood where he had once attended school, Fitzhugh boarded in the Cross home just outside the capital city in Fairfax County, Virginia, while the relapse was its worst. Not surprising for Fitzhugh, Mrs. Benjamin Cross was a cousin. When the 1860 census taker came to their house, Fitzhugh stated a personal value of an astonishing $20,000, probably counting his townsite, but not the mine as before. It was the equivalent of nearly $600,000. Though he was absent, the Whatcom County census taker also counted him and estimated a personal value of only $400.[28]

There were many old Fitzhugh acquaintances in Washington, DC, including a friend and mentor, California's Senator William Gwin. In the following year, men would choose their own paths in the wake of Lincoln's election. Gwin was a staunch defender of slavery, the issue tearing California Democratic Party state politics apart. The next year, he and Calhoun Benham (Fitzhugh's syndicate and former law partner) would carry their politics farther, becoming leaders of the separatist Knights of the Golden Circle (KGC) in California. Subsequently, they would be arrested together on their way to buy arms in Cuba for the Confederacy. Benham's wife was arrested as a spy. Fitzhugh probably also crossed paths in the capital with his Falmouth neighbor James Seddon, a delegate to the Peace Democrat convention before joining the Confederacy a year later and becoming Jefferson Davis's Secretary of State.

In typical fashion, Fitzhugh's association with Stevens, within political and social activities with the sixteen other members of the campaign committee, widened his personal connections, including a new one with the powerful Bowie family of Maryland. Fitzhugh and Stevens worked out of the National Democratic Executive Committee offices at #28 on 4½ Street in Washington. Not far from the Capitol, it was an attractive street of one and two-story brick buildings that housed offices and businesses. Chairman Stevens's tasks were to produce and distribute literature, do publicity, give some speeches himself (few of which he did), and schedule rallies and speeches for Breckinridge and Lane. Stevens was not very interested in the prodigious detail work needed to build a national campaign, but detail-oriented lawyer Fitzhugh was someone to help with the work after he sufficiently recovered from his illness.[29]

Vice President John Breckinridge was an attractive candidate to handle. He was a Mexican War veteran, the youngest vice president in the nation's history, had earlier served in the House of Representatives, and had never been defeated. Once a slaveholder, he currently owned none after a bank in which he was heavily invested collapsed and financially ruined him. Best of all, Breckinridge was called charismatic, personally charming, and a stump speaker who was a "clear, vibrant, expressive" orator.[30]

Shortly after his arrival at the end of July, Fitzhugh wrote Miller about the problems he was encountering with Stevens. Though he was sick, he had found ways to gather information from others about Stevens's behavior. He opined that Stevens might die within a year, judging from his appearance. He drank, hid it, and appeared drunk in front of others both then and at the convention, often at the worst times. Stevens never paid much attention to his appearance, so he must have looked much worse. When his bills for Washington Territory came before Congress, he was at the convention and failed to appear to promote them, resulting in Congress dropping the measures. It was a political disaster for his constituents at home. Fitzhugh said he planned, as soon as he was well enough, to stay with Stevens for a week or so and try to get him to stop drinking. However, he told Miller that because of the long duration of his friend's drinking habit, he thought that his efforts would probably be futile. Fitzhugh saw that Stevens only drank copious amounts of water when they were together, but the alcoholism was obvious.[31]

There was another somber message from Fitzhugh in his letter to Miller. He believed that by then—the end of July—the election of Lincoln was already a "*foregone* conclusion" [his emphasis].

Fitzhugh told Miller there was no Democratic Party anymore— that it was "bursten open." He was angry that the party that had "stood the test of ages" should split up on the slavery question. He warned that "fears are entertained here about the continuance of the Union, by the oldest and wisest heads. Many think we will never be united again—that there are eight states now virtually out of the Union, that will never come in again and that seven more will follow in their lead. It is predicted that we shall split up into several small republics and have more—like the South American Republics did formerly."

As the summer wore on, Fitzhugh wrote more critically of his friend Stevens. One nearly unintelligible letter Stevens wrote to Miller included a laughable claim that he never made loyalty to himself a requirement for a "good word in appointments to office." Fitzhugh's opinion of the claim was that Stevens was leaving too many enemies from the Treaty War in their positions after they joined the Republican Party, e.g. Michael Simmons, longtime territorial Indian agent for whom Fitzhugh had worked. He told Miller that Stevens continued his heavy drinking while he ignored his duties and wouldn't listen to advice. Stevens's biographer Kent Richards theorized that Fitzhugh had his own ambitions to be congressional delegate and his critical letters were intended to boost his own chances. Perhaps, but alcohol was already a known problem for Stevens back home and Fitzhugh described the new problems it caused on the wider stage.[32]

Breckinridge tried hard to be a moderate who wouldn't completely alienate voters in both North and South, but it did not work. In the

November election he came in second with seventy-two electoral college votes to Lincoln's one hundred eighty, with Douglas and Bell trailing substantially behind. However, the popular vote illustrated the depth of the national divide. Lincoln received nearly thirty-nine percent of the votes, Douglas had ten percent fewer, with Breckinridge a distant third at eighteen, which gave the combined Northern unionists almost sixty-nine percent of the national vote. After the election news made its way slowly to Olympia, the *Pioneer-Democrat* published the dismal election results on page two and downplayed the significance of the undeniable Democratic Party loss.[33]

Justice Strong substituted for Fitzhugh during an additional October term of the Third District Court before he started home after the early November election. Stevens stayed on, attempting with others to prevent secession of the southern states. The *Pioneer-Democrat* noted on December 7 that "We are happy to welcome among us again Judge Fitzhugh, who arrived here this week direct from the states. He is just recovering from an attack of the Panama fever. His many friends will be pleased to hear of his safe return." It is possible that Fitzhugh's malaria relapse lasted in lesser intensity the entire six months he was gone from Washington Territory, but he managed to arrive home in time for the Supreme Court term that month. He also carried eastern newspapers to share the magnitude of what was happening.[34]

Democrats still were the legislature's majority party, but the Republicans took control after the self-preserving Douglas Democrats formed a coalition with them. When Isaac Stevens finally arrived home in April 1861, a contemporary said he looked "grave and careworn, for he had taken deeply to heart the troubles between the North and South." Shortly before the next territorial Democratic convention met, one man who saw him in Vancouver on the Columbia said he was "treated with an indifference amounting to contempt." Stevens withdrew his name from consideration for re-election to prevent a further breakup of his territorial party. After secession of southern states, the territory's Democrats officially backed the Lincoln government, even if all their federal appointees who hadn't turned Republican were about to lose their jobs. By the time Stevens arrived in Olympia, Fitzhugh had already left for Virginia again on April 5. The two friends never saw each other again.[35]

Absent from the Democrats' territorial convention where he had been chairman, Fitzhugh's name was put up for congressional delegate candidate with eight other men, but he failed to gain support. Douglas man Selucius Garfielde was nominated on the twenty-fifth ballot. Ultimately, the intra-party split destroyed their chances to hold the congressional delegate office. William Wallace, Fitzhugh's former defense attorney and newly-appointed Republican governor who had resigned to run, was elected delegate.[36]

Supreme Court 1860

Once Lincoln was elected, Fitzhugh became a lame duck appointee with his fellow justices, and any other Buchanan appointee. Governor Gholson resigned as soon as Lincoln was elected and never returned to Olympia, leaving Territorial Secretary Henry McGill in charge until Lincoln's appointee would take over. The process of nomination and confirmation for Republican-approved justices moved just as slowly as it had for Fitzhugh, a two-year-long process. Fitzhugh remained the presiding justice in the Third District until after the August 1861 term.

The 1860 Supreme Court convened days after his return from the campaign and heard ten cases. Fitzhugh's skills as a legal writer must have grown stronger since he wrote the court's opinion on four, including more complicated ones. Perhaps indicative of Fitzhugh's growing legal skills in his own courtroom, only two of his decisions were appealed.[37]

The first case for which Fitzhugh wrote the opinion was more complicated than his previous assignments because it involved the assertion of eleven errors out of the Second District. It started as a probate case argument over the disposition of a donation land claim estate. Another appeal had just been heard by the justices that involved pre-emption land claim rights. These were the harbingers of more land claim cases to follow as ever more land was settled, boundaries were disputed, and estates of the original claimants had to be settled when inheritance became acrimonious. Fitzhugh's opinion would be widely read by landowners.[38]

The second Fitzhugh-written opinion was another estate case which had gone to arbitration and the decision then disputed. The defendant in both district and supreme court cases was William H. Wallace. Fitzhugh's prior experience with Wallace as his defense lawyer, and their conflicting political views, did not deter him from hearing the appeal of the distribution of William Slaughter's estate, because the justices never recused themselves. Slaughter was a well-known victim of the Treaty War. Fitzhugh wrote the court's affirmation of the original decision—that it was not necessary to pass on all the alleged errors because they were minor complaints, and an estate award should not be disturbed for minor complaints.[39]

Another Fitzhugh-written opinion was for an unusual intergovernmental dispute seeking a final ruling that would have far-reaching consequences. Lewis County's residents south of Puget Sound did not like it when the legislature taxed them in order to build a better territorial (versus county) road. Their county government subsequently refused to pay the assessed cost for their portion of the road from Olympia to Monticello (today's Longview). Fitzhugh wrote the court's decision affirming that roads were rightly a legislative function when they passed through several counties. It was likely a precedent for years to come and on into statehood for a territory with scattered growing communities.[40]

The final case of the 1860 term came from Fitzhugh's district court and again involved people he knew well. The opinion was written by Strong. Henry Roeder and Russell Peabody of the Whatcom Mill had not always approved of Fitzhugh's heavy-handed methods to influence Whatcom County voters and local government. The circumstances of the case went back to Samuel Brown and Henry Hewitt's discovery of the coal vein under an upturned tree that led to Fitzhugh's arrival in Washington Territory. Loans and payments among the principals had followed with numerous twists and turns. Fitzhugh's first alleged error happened when he told Roeder and Peabody to amend their answer to Brown's complaint or he would disregard it. The second error examined was Fitzhugh's overruling of a motion for continuance. The third alleged error was that Fitzhugh overruled a motion for a new trial. The Supreme Court ruled for Brown, who was charged an illegal interest rate on his loan, and affirmed the overall decisions made by Fitzhugh in his Port Townsend courtroom.[41]

While Fitzhugh prepared for the 1860 Supreme Court term, something happened in another place that would prove to be his biggest case during his lame-duck 1861 District Court term—one that would be found in Washington historians' books and articles over 150 years later. Up the barely-colonized Snohomish River, a trader named Carter died instantly from a stab wound. Local whites accused E'lick, a Coast Salish man from the upper Skagit River, of the murder which set off legal proceedings that stretched over three years.

FAMILY

What of Fitzhugh's wives Julia and Mary, and his children at Sehome during his time working in national politics?

Before Fitzhugh could leave for six months in 1860 to work on the Breckinridge campaign, there was his family to consider. He made what was a cruel and inhumane decision.

In the years since his early 1854 arrival, Fitzhugh built an unusual family life with two wives and two small children. He learned his wives' Northern Straits Salish fluently enough to be a government interpreter. He had been publicly accused in a New York newspaper letter of being a "practical Mormon" during the years when that church still included polygamous marriages. Wealthy Coast Salish leaders of the time often had more than one wife, but Fitzhugh was the only Bellingham Bay settler who was comfortable enough with the custom to take the widowed Mary as a secondary wife. Julia and Mary kept the only home, other than Captain Pickett's, deemed comfortable enough to host visiting overnight dignitaries and military officers. The Fitzhugh house contained a large kitchen, dining room, big living room and two large bedrooms upstairs, better than Pickett's attic accommodations.[42]

When military commanders or territorial officials divided between the Pickett and Fitzhugh homes to sleep, the family went down to Seya'hom's longhouse on the beach to visit. Perhaps Julia and Mary cooked dinner for the men before leaving them to their conversation, cigars, and whiskey unimpeded by the presence of small children and their mothers. One overnight guest wrote that he found the family to be living very well and Fitzhugh's hospitality "genuine." Along with his more imperious and intellectual traits, the Roeders described Fitzhugh's "many kindly impulses" and called him "generous" and "hospitable." However, there was a completely different and violent side to Fitzhugh, usually only seen by recalcitrant voters, Robert Davis, and the ill-fated Andrew Wilson.[43]

Fitzhugh's cousin George Fitzhugh, besides trying to justify slavery in his widely read *Sociology for the South*, also promoted the "cult of domesticity" which balanced a woman's right to protection with her obligation to obey. It was an influential patriarchal philosophy that transcended race and class, but E. C. Fitzhugh's slave-owning background certainly affected his behavior toward the women he married and his expectations for them. For example, to him they were not "ladies" and so probably not considered to be suitable hostesses for dignitaries. Neither wife was familiar with the cooking and housekeeping style he thought civilized by Virginia standards. His precise demands had already contributed to the misery felt by the pregnant teenaged Julia that led to her aunt Mary becoming Fitzhugh's secondary wife. The safety and protection Seya'hom believed he was getting for his family's women in a period of drastic cultural and authority change, as well as Northerner raids, was not the same as that provided by Coast Salish husbands.[44]

When Olympia's newspaper had succinctly noted in 1858 that first-year Justice Fitzhugh had arrived late for the Supreme Court term after a "severe accident," the editor provided no further details. Like many involved in domestic violence, Fitzhugh may have been reluctant to give details for public consumption, or perhaps the editor loyally euphemized the event, making it sound like the judge fell or something equally innocuous. Generally speaking, the *Pioneer-Democrat* and the *Puget Sound Herald* reported grisly details of real accidents almost like entertainment, so this points to the possible time of this incident that was a life-long memory for Julia and Mary. They did not come from a culture that accepted domestic abuse.

Fitzhugh demanded that his evening meal was to be ready and hot at the same time every day, and no re-warmed leftovers. One day the young women were giggling as they did housework in the midst of little Julianne and Mason. They failed to notice the time on the dining room clock. When Fitzhugh walked in the door, they had just started to stir up the kitchen fire. Seeing that dinner was not ready for him, he hit both young wives.[45]

Julia did not get over the assault. Fitzhugh came home after work in an angry mood the next day and pointed his anger at his wives even though dinner was almost ready. He was very particular about how the table was to be set. He owned good dishes and a "beautiful coffee pot that he wanted on the table in a certain place." While Fitzhugh sat down to eat, Julia picked up one of the smallish pieces of stove wood while still in the kitchen and said, "I'm going to kill him." She was less than five feet tall, but she was strong, according to her niece. Julia walked back into the dining room and hit him on the head. Moaning, Fitzhugh fell from his chair.

The two women stood over him, petrified. Mary said, "You killed him!" and Julia replied, "I don't care!" She hit him again in the face before Mary could stop her, but then realized what she had done. Fitzhugh looked dead. They fled with the children to relatives a few miles south at Chuckanut Bay, instead of down to the longhouse. According to her sister, Julia told the family she didn't care what happened to her, but "Nobody is going to slap me around."

The Seya'hom family members downhill from the house watched as Fitzhugh boarded a ship soon after, dressed in a high hat and satin waistcoat. His head was bandaged, he had a black eye, his face and jaw were swollen and bruised, and he limped painfully with a cane. It is likely that this is the December 1858 occasion when Fitzhugh arrived in Olympia dressed for court business but badly injured from his "accident." The women and children subsequently returned to the Fitzhugh home where they stayed for another two years.

The final and most abusive incident occurred in 1860, given that the women's account said it was about six years after Julia married Fitzhugh, and he left town at that time. The family said the women had gone berry-picking after recently angering Fitzhugh by speaking their own language around Julianne and Mason. Fitzhugh wanted his children to learn English. He was preparing to leave for the Breckinridge campaign and expected to be gone for six months. When Julia and Mary came home, Fitzhugh and the children were gone. He took them far south on Puget Sound to live permanently with a white, English-speaking family who would functionally strip the small children of their own language and mothers' Coast Salish culture. Julia and Mary walked out on Fitzhugh and never returned. They were unable to locate their children, and never knew what happened to them until many years later when they were reunited. (See the Epilogue.)[46]

No woman of the time, white or indigenous, had a legal right to custody of her own children in event of a marital breakup, unless her husband agreed. An indigenous woman had no chance of taking them back into a tribal life unless her husband allowed it or abandoned his family.

Almost a hundred years later, in 1954, Julia's niece Harriet Shelton Dover (daughter of her younger sister Ruth Seya'hom Shelton) wrote: "I have shrieked to high heaven every time I hear this story of Fitzhugh and my aunts. I vow I'll look for him, and beat his head off by bits—tear him to shreds—and my mother smiles and says, 'Why he must have died long ago.' And I say I'll tear his grave apart and kick his head to bits anyway. I wonder where he came from? And where did he go?... Life is so fascinating—even while your heart aches for the people who get hurt in it."[47]

CHAPTER 10

Courts and Cora

A s Fitzhugh and the other Buchanan-appointed colleagues concluded their last Supreme Court term in December 1860, their world was descending into turmoil. Newspapers published articles and bulletins from the East and South, usually a month late, still a small timely improvement from news delivery in the territory's earliest days. Since April, the Pony Express brought the most urgent bulletins to California in ten days, where a steamer carried them to Puget Sound in a few more. As 1861 progressed and the nation crumbled, there were more and more urgent bulletins.[1]

After the election, the territory's Democrats became the opposition party. There would be no more Democratic government patronage for small jobs to provide cash, influence votes, and support the party. Steilacoom's Republican *Puget Sound Herald* took the lucrative official government printing contract. Now financially struggling and trying to mollify Republicans, the *Pioneer-Democrat*'s articles began to include information on what territorial offices were up for grabs by Republicans (old ones and new) and front-page articles on secession meetings in the East and South.[2]

If Fitzhugh had ever entertained hopes of being the next congressional delegate if Stevens did not run, they were dead. South Carolina seceded before Lincoln even took office. Four days after the inauguration, the *Pioneer-Democrat* printed urgent news of interest to Fitzhugh. Union men had carried the Virginia secession convention for the time being. The paper also accused outgoing Justice Strong of being a secessionist. Isaac Stevens returned home with his rumored hopes for a judgeship dashed like Fitzhugh's.[3]

Preserving the union became the goal. Governor Gholson followed through with his threat to never serve a day under Abraham Lincoln and resigned from his home in Kentucky on February 14, 1861. Lincoln appointed the territory's first Republican governor, Fitzhugh's former lawyer William H. Wallace, but he soon resigned to run for congressional delegate. The territory would have to adjust to the next governor, William Pickering, an outsider originally from England and close friend of Lincoln. Like McMullen, he was unimpressed by the locals and so leery of Northwest rain that he wore rain gear and carried an umbrella even on sunny days. The locals he disdained called him "Pickwick."[4]

Respected "Big Mike" Simmons was soon removed from his territorial Indian agent job. Other Democrat lame-duck office holders and hangers-on had to decide if they would stay and become Republicans, leave for an army, or stay and remain Democrats. If they chose the last, they would endure ridicule while they tried to think up ways to get back in power. Fitzhugh's political career was over if he couldn't adjust to being a minority organizer supporting an unpopular position as the war loomed. He was no longer even the chair of the Democrats' Central Committee, replaced by J.J.H. Van Bokkelen.[5]

It may also have been a lonely time for Fitzhugh back in his comfortable home in Sehome. The mine had been leased out and his judicial appointment was ending, taking away most of his influence over the county and its votes. He heard no more laughter of small children, nor the talk of their mothers. Nothing records who took care of his home, did his laundry, or made his meals, but he had the means to hire other women to do that without becoming a boarder in another man's home. Or, if he did become a boarder, he turned his house over to the new mine management.

DISTRICT COURT

Fitzhugh did not show up at his courtroom on February 11, 1861, when he was to open his next court term. Whether the weather affected transportation from Bellingham Bay, or he was sick or hungover that day, he convened court the next. Port Townsend, with its hotels, saloons, and shops, still welcomed the lame duck justice. An early businessman recalled later (with some exaggeration) that the town was strongly "Copperhead" at the time with only three Republicans in the whole settlement and they were still keeping quiet. Across the North, Peace Democrats were now ridiculed as "snakes" for wanting a settlement with the South rather than war, but in Port Townsend they were, for the time being, still the majority.[6]

After Fitzhugh convened the court at ten a.m., procedural court business waited. He admitted his legal protegee John Tennant to the bar the next day after a lengthy examination by three of the best lawyers.

Tennant had studied Fitzhugh's law books well. After serving for a time as the Third District prosecutor in the new Republican justice's court, Whatcom County would elect him their probate judge.[7]

One of Fitzhugh's first cases that final term was the grand jury hearing to indict Republican Edward Eldridge for "marking a ticket" (voter fraud) during the July 1860 territorial elections. It may have been a bit of Democratic political revenge encouraged (or engineered) by Fitzhugh, going back to the Wilson deathbed statement Eldridge recorded and the subsequent two-year path to put Fitzhugh on trial. Though witnesses Eldridge and his wife Teresa were two Whatcom people Fitzhugh had known the longest, it may have been a source of satisfaction for him to preside over the grand jury's proceedings. The case against Eldridge never went beyond the 1861 indictment, but it does not seem to be a coincidence in the time frame. Fitzhugh had previously overseen two aborted cases filed, but never continued against Eldridge, also a prominent signer of the petition against Fitzhugh's judicial appointment. Instead, it seems indicative of the animosity that had grown between the two in the aftermath of Wilson's death and local elections, and some urging of the prosecutor to bring the case up.[8]

◌◌◌

Fitzhugh's most important case in his final year, and in the territory's legal history, was *Territory v E'lick (aka Harry Peeps),* the capital murder trial of a Coast Salish man accused of killing the white trader on the Snohomish River a few weeks after the 1860 election. Few settlers had ever been murdered, except by the Northern raiders, so a perceived threat of violence by the dominant indigenous population caused such cases to take on a larger importance to the scattered white colonizers outside towns. The *Puget Sound Herald* noted that the case had caused alarm two counties away when rumors circulated that the killer had fled there.[9]

Frank Chenoweth prosecuted the case against able territorial lawyers Selucius Garfielde and B. F. Dennison for defendant E'lick (called Harry Peeps by many whites). Though it was later claimed that E'lick had no interpreter, Charles Bradshaw, currently studying law and married to a S'Klallam woman, interpreted for the trial. Like Fitzhugh, Bradshaw may have spoken decent Northern Straits Salish, at least the S'Klallam dialect. The problem was that E'lick spoke Lushootseed language and may not have known any Straits Salish. While there are similarities due to geographical proximity, the languages are still different, which made Bradshaw or Fitzhugh poor interpreters of complex legal language for E'lick. Neither Garfielde nor Dennison was intermarried, and they were probably limited to Chinook trading jargon (chinuk wawa) with their client.[10]

The grand jury brought in an indictment after hearing from three witnesses. They included two native men who were not indicted after giving evidence against E'lick, even though they were also involved in the crime. The native witnesses were remanded to the custody of "the chief and principal men in their tribe for their appearance" after Fitzhugh continued the case until the August term.[11]

Other important cultural issues that were only implied when the case entered the legal system with Fitzhugh's grand jury have given it enduring interest. What was "Indian country" where indigenous justice might prevail? Did indigenous people receive an equal sentence for killing a white man as a settler would for killing a Native?

Politics

The same day Fitzhugh continued E'lick's case to August, the *Puget Sound Herald* published "Union Resolutions" adopted by the new legislature. The third one stated: "That we utterly discountenance, as fraught with incipient treason, and as the insidious offspring of reckless aspirations and disappointed ambition, all projects of a Pacific Confederacy. Washington Territory covets only the distinction of exhibiting, first and last, her devotion to the entire Union." It was ten days before Lincoln's March fourth inauguration, and rumors were coalescing on the West Coast around the Knights of the Golden Circle's (KGC) secessionist goal, particularly since in 1860 California's entire congressional delegation supported that goal. That radical splinter group's seemingly unattainable dream had morphed into a suspected real drive to secede from the Union and form the "Pacific Confederacy." Fitzhugh's friend Senator William Gwin was a leader of the shadowy group, as well as Calhoun Benham and his wife who were among the most active members. More than two thousand KGC members lived in southern Oregon. If Fitzhugh stayed in Washington Territory, he would have to make hard choices about where he stood.[12]

Two weeks after Lincoln's inauguration, the *Pioneer-Democrat*'s J. W. Wiley, once so supportive of Fitzhugh and the Southerner-dominated territorial Democrats, reprinted an attack on Southern honor from a

Northeastern abolition newspaper. Though the article softened the blow with praise for Virginia's place in history, it condemned Fitzhugh's home state by mentioning the New England blood shed at Harper's Ferry. Finally, the abolitionist writer insulted loyal Virginians by saying that their present production was "negroes, demagogues and half-breeds, traitors, applejack and tobacco." Fitzhugh must have been appalled at what his long-time friend Wiley had put in his newspaper to pander to local Republicans whose ads and subscriptions he badly needed to survive.[13]

A week later on April 5, Wiley announced that Fitzhugh had left for the States. He headlined that Fitzhugh was opposed to "secesh" and strongly in favor of the Union. Virginia was still hoping for the same.[14]

Fitzhugh thus took another leave of absence until his August court term and the important E'lick murder trial. When Fitzhugh left Washington Territory on the Steamer *Panama* for home, he couldn't predict how fast events would unfold while he was on the way: the attack on Fort Sumter, the formation of the Confederate Congress, and most importantly, Virginia's secession on April 17. It wasn't until May 3 that the *Pioneer-Democrat*'s headline said "Civil War Commenced" after Fort Sumter.[15]

Isaac Stevens was on his way back to Olympia from the District of Columbia in April, still offended that Fitzhugh had ambitions to take his delegate job. He wrote from his own steamer on April 15 to W. W. Miller: "Fitzhugh claimed to be my earnest and strong friend… He more than comes within the category of prominent friends who have been lukewarm." Fitzhugh had told another man that Stevens had little or no support on the Sound, and that man told Stevens. The oncoming war did not put them in the same place again and prevented any reconciliation.[16]

CORA WEEMS BOWIE

In addition to his Copperhead status in an increasingly pro-Union area, Fitzhugh had another reason to head for home. There was a woman he wanted to marry. Based on later evidence he probably really loved her. Cora Weems Bowie was from a prominent colonial Maryland family of influence and wealth—just the type of woman Fitzhughs married, whether they were indigenous like Julia and Mary, or from one of America's first families.

Cora Bowie came from a powerful Democratic family from the border state, where political loyalties were split along slave ownership lines. Almost certainly, Fitzhugh met the hopelessly unmarried thirty-year-old during the Breckinridge campaign. For elite women, to be thirty and a "spinster" was social death. Such a woman often had to marry a man with great flaws, rather than never marry at all. Such was Cora.

During the 1860 election, when Fitzhugh was keeping an eye on Stevens and working in the Breckinridge campaign, there were social and political gatherings when ladies also attended, and Cora had several close relatives in the new political party. Now that Julia and Mary had left Fitzhugh and their tribal custom marriages, the territorial justice turned to the life of an older eligible bachelor of means and importance. With bushy beard and perhaps a hint of the violence that lay underneath his charm, forty-year-old Fitzhugh was charismatic with his many tales of life in the West to tell a spinster flattered by his attention.

In addition to her connections, Cora was from a familiar slave-owning culture and political history going back to colonial days, like Fitzhugh's own. The two had some ancestral cross points that added the desirable relationship web both understood, irrespective of any mutual attraction. Cora descended from some of the earliest Maryland colonists after Lord Baltimore's granddaughter married Dr. John Bowie. By the Revolution and shortly after, the Bowies had so built their relationship web that the family and their in-laws controlled most of Maryland. Cora's family branch settled between Washington, DC, and Annapolis on the Chesapeake Bay.[17]

Eighteenth century Bowies served as Revolutionary War army and naval officers, congressmen, and state legislators. Cora's great-grandfather, Robert Bowie, was an early republic governor of Maryland, and her step-uncle Reverdy Johnson was both a senator in the 1840s and the U.S. Attorney General. Her uncle General Thomas Fielder Bowie was a congressman from 1855 to 1859 and may have been the conduit for Cora and Fitzhugh to meet the following year at the convention, if not one of her cousins attending. As one of the great slave-holding planter families of Maryland, where almost half the African American population was free, the Bowies were Unionists sympathetic to the South. For Fitzhugh, the Bowies were both conveniently influential, wealthy, and of the same Copperhead political mindset.[18]

Cora's father, Robert W. Bowie, and mother Margaret French Bowie, lived at "Cedar Hill" where Cora was born in the hilltop house that looked down on the slave quarters below. It came into the family when Margaret inherited it and the prosperous plantation from her own father. She died when Cora was seventeen, leaving behind at least seven children. Since Cora's older sister was married, it fell to the teenager to stay home with her father and care for the younger children, one of which was only four. Robert Bowie was a busy father, prominent in ways other than politics. He was one of the founders of three important Maryland entities: the Agricultural College, the Baltimore and Potomac Railroad, and the Jockey Club for racehorse owners. In Cora's social circles, with no matrimonial prospects when Fitzhugh entered her life, her future was only many years of caring for her aging father and her siblings at Cedar Hill.[19]

Fitzhugh's arrival in Virginia at the start of the war enabled him to check on his two sisters still in the Falmouth area, and what he saw at home had to be deeply disturbing. After Virginia's secession, men from Stafford County were joining the Confederate army in numbers that before long were at 40 percent of the white male population. Confederate troops were camping around Falmouth, needing firewood, food, and forage for their horses. Nearly half of the county's people were slaves, and as soon as the Union Army arrived in the area, they began to cross the lines. Those from across the river forded shallows near Fitzhugh's childhood home to reach the Union lines and continued in ever-increasing numbers. The area's future would be one of Union occupation and four battles nearby at Fredericksburg that left one hundred thousand men dead.

Fitzhugh returned to Cora, and Reverend H. Smiley married them on May 25, 1861, at Cedar Hill. On the same day, the fight for the railroad hub at Chesapeake Bay's Aquia Landing, twenty miles north of Falmouth, began. The *Fredericksburg Star* announced Cora's marriage to "Judge E. C. Fitzhugh" at the bottom of the paper's last column, after the news that the battle at Aquia Creek was the first on Virginia soil. The landing would never leave Union hands.[20]

Maryland's split loyalties led to turmoil, especially over the Union occupation of Baltimore. The April 19 riot between soldiers and citizens had resulted in twelve deaths and numerous injuries. General Benjamin Butler and his troops took possession of the city ten days

Figure 27, Fugitives fording the Rappahannock. Escaping their captors, enslaved people crossed the river at Falmouth and many other shallow fords along the river as soon as Union troops controlled the northern shore. Stereograph by Alexander Gardner, c. 1862. *Brady's Album Gallery no. 518. Library of Congress, Prints and Photographs Division, #LC-DIG-stereo-1s02891.*

before the Fitzhugh wedding and held it for the rest of the war. Other units moved into smaller towns, signaling the militarization of rural Maryland life. That brought a loss of slaves at the Bowie plantations and others as hundreds ran away to the Union army and many enlisted. If Fitzhugh and Cora stayed in Maryland, they would find themselves in the midst of war-long disputes between friends and family over ideological differences concerning slavery and the war.[21]

Virginia's new secessionist treason law made things clear: "That any man whose conscience won't allow him to vote for separation from the Union, must leave the state." In other words, any Copperheads from the Breckinridge Democrats (like Fitzhugh and Cora) would no longer be welcome in Virginia unless they wholeheartedly threw their support behind the Confederacy.

On July 18 the Port Townsend paper, *The North-west*, included a notice that Judge and Mrs. Fitzhugh were on the passenger list of the Steamer *Northern Light* that left New York City on June 11, bound for Panama. It reassured locals that the judge's August term would probably start on time. Even as they married, it was obvious that there would be no comfortable place for the Fitzhughs in either Maryland or Virginia, where Richmond had been designated the Confederate capital four days before the wedding. They committed to Washington Territory despite the problematic atmosphere also found there. For Cora, it meant abandonment of her family and comfortable home for a completely foreign atmosphere. At forty, Fitzhugh was little interested in joining either army, though age hadn't stopped his friend (and West Pointer) Isaac Stevens from rejoining the U.S. Army officer corps. Fitzhugh still had his personal connections in Washington Territory even if the Republicans, now including many former Democratic colleagues, ran things. He must have desperately believed that, as a lawyer, he could start anew with Cora after his judicial salary ended when his Republican replacement arrived.

ᑲᔆᖇᑭ

Cora and Edmund Fitzhugh arrived at Port Townsend many weeks after departing New York City. Although Cora was probably deeply grateful to disembark, the town was unlike Baltimore or the District of Columbia in every way. With luminescent Mount Baker towering in the east across the salt water, the town had about three hundred residents and sixty buildings, mostly wooden storefronts that constantly changed names and owners. Only the brick U.S. Customs House, the U.S. Marine Hospital, and the army's nearby Fort Townsend stayed the same. Kah'tai village of about two hundred S'Klallam was just west of town on their lagoon. Fitzhugh probably did not mention that it was the home village of his former wife Mary, if he ever mentioned her and Julia at all. He introduced his bride to people they met and took her to see what paltry goods and services were available without going to Victoria. He needed to check on the courthouse and what his commissioner and clerk did in his absence. There were two options for where Cora could live while Fitzhugh conducted court. They could board at one of the better homes or live at one of the hotels. That would likely have been the recently expanded "upscale" Pioneer Hotel that was always occupied by lawyers, litigants, jury members, and observers during the court sessions.[22]

ᑲᔆᖇᑭ

While Fitzhugh and his new wife traveled to Puget Sound, the atmosphere in Port Townsend and the territory became distinctly different after two battles were fought in Virginia. Isaac Stevens was gone, and William Miller was recruiting for Washington Territory's volunteer Union regiment. In June fellow Virginian and friend Captain George Pickett finally came to terms with the inevitability of leaving the U.S. Army and his small half-indigenous son behind to join the Confederate army. Fitzhugh's murder indictment adversary, Territorial Prosecutor Butler P. Anderson, left for British Columbia after he was hounded out of the territory when people heard that his brother, J. Patton Anderson, the territory's first congressional delegate, had joined the Confederate army. The *Pioneer-Democrat* accused the former prosecutor of helping set up an insurrection for British Columbia to secede from the British empire, i.e., to join the KGC plot for a Pacific Confederacy. The situation was uncomfortable for Fitzhugh and Cora after they arrived from San Francisco, but not compared to the turmoil of the military conflict at home.[23]

Judge Fitzhugh arrived in Port Townsend in time to open his August term promptly, unlike in February. With little to occupy Cora's time in a now-enthusiastic Union town, she may have filled her days by attending court, even if a murder trial and hot room were not to her liking. One of Fitzhugh's first actions was to issue a summons for the sheriff to search out and bring in the three E'lick trial witnesses from distant Snohomish County. Fitzhugh presided over the delayed murder trial and again dismissed the charges against one native man who testified against E'lick.[24]

The jury convicted E'lick of murder and asked that he "suffer death." On August 18, Fitzhugh sentenced him to hang at Coveland on November 21, "any time between 10 a.m. and 6 p.m." Before he adjourned his final court term as the associate justice, Fitzhugh sent one case on to the new justice, since he had already expressed an opinion on the case publicly.[25]

Five days after the death sentence was issued, E'lick's lawyers filed their motion for a new trial. Fitzhugh overruled (denied) it. The lawyers excepted to it, and then Fitzhugh allowed the motion because of the errors they cited as reasons for a new trial. He rescheduled the execution for December so as "to give Counsel an opportunity for the Supreme Court to pass upon it." The most important problem the lawyers raised was who had jurisdiction over a tribe "in amity" with the U.S., since "Indian Country" was under the jurisdiction only of the federal government, not a local one. That would mean that the territory and Judge Fitzhugh had no legal authority to bring criminal charges or apply territorial laws. Fitzhugh ruled two days later that E'lick was to be kept in "close confinement" at Fort Townsend, citing the original November death sentence. He sent the death warrant to the Supreme Court after E'lick's lawyers gave him notice that their appeal would be heard in December.

Fitzhugh's conduct of the E'lick trial seems to have been singularly careless. Perhaps it was because his attention was split, or because he had no reputation to worry about anymore. Few of his cases in earlier years had been appealed, but in 1861 the E'lick case and three more from Fitzhugh's court were on the Supreme Court docket.

With that, Fitzhugh brought his gavel down for the last time. He would be replaced in early September by Associate Justice Ethelbert P. Oliphant (age 58) who was singularly unimpressed with Port Townsend when he saw it. He had joined the Pennsylvania bar when Fitzhugh was seven, was a Black Hawk War veteran, and served in various legal offices before his new appointment. James E. Wyche, only 33, was the other new associate justice. Despite his youth, he had a solid law education and practiced in Chicago until he was appointed. The new chief justice was Christopher C. Hewitt (age 52) from Ohio. He'd crossed the Plains to Oregon in 1852, practicing in Steilacoom and Port Madison before becoming Seattle's second lawyer in 1855. He had won an admiralty case against the Pacific Mail Steamship Company before the U.S. Supreme Court. The three were all solidly educated and experienced judges. None were Southerners.[26]

By October, Dennison and Garfielde had filed all the materials necessary for the new panel to hear their appeal of E'lick's conviction. They followed those up with a brief of their arguments and legal citations for examination as new precedents by the Lincoln appointees. Perhaps in an effort to sway the newly-arrived justices, the *Puget Sound Herald* published an article that encouraged whites to kill Indians if it seemed necessary because the government didn't, and they should use the same blood-for-blood law of the Coast Salish peoples. It defended the efforts of citizens, instead of the sheriff who had gone after E'lick and the others.[27]

When the new Supreme Court panel took up E'lick's appeal, Dennison and Garfielde pointed to eleven errors that Fitzhugh and his court allegedly committed. The first ones concerned the fact that E'lick did not get to plead to the charge in person, only by his counsel. They saw illegal evidence, an improper oath given to the jury, unqualified jurors, absence from court of E'lick when his death sentence was read, testimony by whites not properly interpreted, and a vague indictment missing the victim Carter's full name and date of death. Most important for precedent, they added that there was no legal authority for the grand jury to inquire into Carter's death because it occurred in "Indian Country" under the guardianship of the U.S. government, not territorial authority. The eleventh one simply stated there were other "manifest errors."

Prosecutor Frank Chenoweth defended his conduct of the case, which meant defense of his old appointment opponent Fitzhugh's rulings, too. The Supreme Court justices made it clear that their decision had to be based on statutory law, not what might be seen as custom or questions of location, etc. They could not rule on whether evidence was relevant or not. They questioned allegations that E'lick was not present for the important moments when the written record said he was. Most important, they ruled that everyone, white or indigenous, was subject to be indicted for indictable offenses. What was very important to the unanimous decision was that they said E'lick did not have competent interpretation, and so could not understand when he decided to object or decline to plead. In short, because the plea and arraignment were in error, everything else that followed was in error.

Months later, in February 1862, Justices Hewitt, Wyche, and Oliphant ruled unanimously to grant a new trial due to "manifest error." By that time, Fitzhugh protegee John Tennant was the new Third District prosecutor. After Justice Oliphant received the mandate, Tennant failed to assemble a full jury for the new trial. Charles Bradshaw was again appointed interpreter, something that had already caused trouble.[28]

This time E'lick was in the courtroom to plead. On February 20 he stated that he had never severed his tribal relations and been subject to tribal justice until he was arrested by the whites. He asked for dismissal of his case. The next day Prosecutor Tennant exhausted the jury pool and "bystanders in town" in an effort to get a full jury to hear the case. Justice Oliphant decided to continue the case (again) until the August term. It was also getting costly to keep the defendant in jail.

On March 1, with Tennant's agreement, "for good reasons and causes" Oliphant placed E'lick in the custody of three chiefs from different Lushootseed-speaking inland tribes. They pledged to bring him back for trial in August.[29]

Oliphant issued another continuance in August 1862, for a February 1863 trial because E'lick had not appeared as promised. Two years after the first trial in Fitzhugh's court, in October 1863 the sheriff made another try to find him. In February 1864 the clerk placed a note in the court journal that the sheriff of Snohomish County still could not find E'lick and the chiefs had not produced him in court. They never did. They hid E'lick until he could live out his life in peace, away from a white government's case that began in Fitzhugh's court four years earlier.[30]

WHIDBEY ISLAND

Luckily for a newlywed couple seeking a permanent residence after Fitzhugh closed his court, Port Townsend's paper *The North-West* was advertising a farm for sale on Whidbey Island. It was William and Eliza Cullen's donation claim of 160 good prairie acres north of Penn Cove, the same farm for which Fitzhugh held an unpaid mortgage. Former judge and prosecutor Frank Chenoweth was the selling agent.[31]

After William Cullen chaired the first Whatcom County Commission and went with Fitzhugh on the 1855 sheep raid, he moved his family to San Francisco, then returned in 1858. He served as bailiff for Fitzhugh at Coveland that year, and as a grand juror in the Dominic Hunt murder case before he bought Levi Ford's original land claim about a mile north of Penn Cove in 1859. Before long Cullen was deeply in debt, unable to pay Ford or the farm's expenses. He went to Fitzhugh for a "hip-pocket" loan in the continued absence of banks. Fitzhugh loaned the Cullens $1,000 at two percent interest a month and they agreed to repay the large loan no later than January 1, 1860, only seven months later. For a farm family to gather the current equivalent of about $30,000 in such a short time was going to be difficult. They put up their 160 acres and buildings as collateral. Fitzhugh filed the mortgage in Coupeville a week before he left for Washington, DC, to work on the Breckinridge campaign. The Cullens were unable to pay him back the rapidly accumulating debt when he returned, and he extended the deadline by nearly a year. During that time, they abandoned the farm to go to the distant Cariboo gold rush in British Columbia in a last effort to make a fortune in the mines. In the meantime, Fitzhugh had tended to court, married Cora, and returned from the East Coast again. Cullen's ad to sell the farm had already been in the newspaper while Fitzhugh was in Maryland, without takers. However, after Fitzhugh's final court term closed, he and Cora needed a permanent home, so he foreclosed on the farm without an acrimonious lawsuit. William and Eliza Cullen deeded over their land claim and its buildings to him for $1,500, erasing the debt and possibly leaving them with a little cash. Fitzhugh registered the new deed, though unlike most men with white wives, he did not make Cora co-owner of the property.[32]

Narrow and thirty-eight miles long, Whidbey Island had been colonized for about ten years, and Island County established for eight, before Fitzhugh took over the Cullen farm. After the first visits in 1848 by land-hungry men who were quickly turned away by the four Coast Salish groups who shared the island, the men told others of the three large fertile prairies left behind by melting Ice Age glaciers. For thousands of years Coast Salish families from many villages on and off the island hunted game, harvested shellfish, used temporary summer camps for salmon fishing, cultivated food and medicinal plants, and burned the prairies to increase yields. What the whites saw was that there was no forest to clear. Starting in 1850, nearly all the first colonizers settled on the prairies, and once all three were claimed, new settlement slowed. Newcomers, like Fitzhugh, who wanted some prairie land had to buy it.[33]

The only business on the north side of Penn Cove was in the single building at Coveland where Fitzhugh first held court. Storekeepers had come and gone more than once, and the summer Cora and Edmund arrived, merchant vessel Captain Eli Hathaway had opened his own. All the others had disappeared, drowned, or moved across the cove. Those who relocated rightly concluded Coupeville would survive because it was the Island County seat, had a deep-water landing, and Puget Sound's civilian ship captains were making it their home.

In 1860 the island's scattered 294 whites came from a variety of states and backgrounds. Fitzhugh already knew many (if not most) from court, county business, or politics, and some were friends from his earliest days at Sehome and Whatcom. He and Frank Chenoweth would be legal competitors with a grudging camaraderie from their shared experiences over the years. They weren't the only educated professionals living on the north half of the island. County surveyor, the Reverend George Whitworth, was a teacher and minister. Dr. John Kellogg owned a land claim and tended to patients as far away as Bellingham Bay. Some of the island's men, including Captain Edward Barrington, had indigenous wives, which introduced Cora to the region's unique social structure. By the time the Fitzhughs arrived, as the Civil War gained momentum, there were both Republicans and Democrats on the island, and a few young men had left to join both Union and Confederate armies, as they had in Maryland.[34]

സ്ജാഠ

Moving to Whidbey Island, the couple first had to find transportation for goods Cora brought from Cedar Hill and any purchased in San Francisco for her eventual new home. The previous year Coupeville's founder, Captain Thomas Coupe, started using his twenty-seven-foot sloop to ferry people and cargo between Port Townsend and Ebey's Landing on the west side of the island. The *Maria* ran fast around the point out of Port Townsend across Admiralty Inlet under 150 feet of sail. Fitzhugh paid $1.50 per person plus the cargo charge. Coupe dropped anchor in front of the beach below Ebey's Prairie south of Penn Cove. To complement the new business, two of the late Isaac Ebey's sons had built "Ferry House" up the long, steep bluff-side trail. Its so-called tavern had liquor and a place to sleep on the floor or up the ladder, as well as hot food from the kitchen out back. The Ebeys served people waiting to take the ferry, as well as incoming travelers who couldn't make it home before darkness fell. From Ferry House, the Fitzhughs and their goods still had to take a long trail north to their newly-acquired farm set back from the shore. Transporting goods by land or canoe was a business of the Coast Salish across the region and men were available at the Penn Cove villages to help.[35]

The scattered sights that met Cora's eyes after she hiked over the lip of the bluff, and when she walked or rode a horse the few miles north to Penn Cove and her new home, bore no resemblance to anything she'd seen before: Ferry House standing alone across open prairie; Lower Skagit village longhouses; the lone Coveland Store/Courthouse; and more-settled Coupeville on the south shore. Penn Cove was a densely populated Coast Salish center for many other activities, in addition to cultivating the nearby prairie. Near the cove's head was a horse clam beach and close to the trail to Cora's new home was a year-round longhouse and others used in the summer during the clam and mussel harvest. A larger village, Cekwola, spread along the north shore, led by treaty-signer Go-liah, and long fortified against Laich-wil-tach raids. Another major village was around the point.[36]

The other thing that Cora saw on the prairie were some of the Treaty War blockhouses, especially the Ebey one built after their family patriarch was murdered by the Kakes from Alaska. She would soon hear endless stories about Isaac Ebey's horrific death and other raids by the Laich-wil-tach coalition. Only weeks before the Fitzhughs arrived, a Haida "hunting party" had been turned back by Captain Pickett's troops keeping watch from San Juan Island for raiders.

When the Fitzhughs arrived, Coast Salish people from lower British Columbia to the Columbia River were in the midst of a period of deep change to their accustomed culture. Though area Indian Agent Robert Fay and his wife lived at Coupeville, he supervised a wide area. The Penn Cove Lower Skagits had not been forced, or even strongly urged, to leave their homes for the mainland after the Point Elliott Treaty was signed. The disparate groups that now co-existed around Penn Cove had few serious conflicts despite the colonizing settlers taking land claims that included longhouses within their boundaries. Fay and other whites believed that Penn Cove would eventually become its own reservation, and his mandate had been to supervise "for the maintenance of friendly relations with the Indians on Penn Cove Reservation." Fay's main job was to watch for settlers violating the laws in their interactions with their native neighbors, and if any goods arrived to distribute, he gave them over to the leaders. However, the year the Fitzhughs moved in, Fay's superiors told him to close his small office at Penn Cove because there would be no reservation. The longhouse families began to disburse, and those that stayed often worked on the farms and other operations that had overtaken their territory and traditional economy. However, longhouse families continued to host traditional potlatch gatherings with drumming and singing whose sounds carried far across the water, and perhaps a mile north to Cora's new home.[37]

Island newcomer Cora Bowie Fitzhugh might have been sophisticated in her plantation Maryland world, but she was hopelessly naïve in her new one. Perhaps she had an adventurous heart that had never been allowed to bloom, but she could as well have been completely terrified by her new surroundings, and life with a former Virginian she did not really know.

Cora's new home would be a shock compared to Cedar Hill. There was a "dwelling," which may have still been a log house given the short periods the Fords and the Cullens lived there. There was an outside kitchen, a log barn, outhouse, and some other structures, as well as a rail fence to optimistically keep in livestock. Unlike Maryland's carefully organized plantations that dominated the rural landscape, Whidbey's pigs, cattle, and sheep saw crude fences as minor inconveniences. Some cattle even went dangerously feral. Wolves preyed upon animals that left their fences, with piglets a preferred delicacy. What was familiar to Cora was how far away neighbors were, since her Maryland plantation home was about the same size as Whidbey's land claims. Buggy-smooth dirt roads were rare there, too.[38]

Unclaimed land lay on two sides of the Fitzhugh farm, but to the east was a lake where the Scots-Welsh Hastie family lived. Former stonecutter Thomas was the current Island County sheriff and married to an Irish nurse. Another prospective friend for Cora, New Brunswick-born Irishwoman Margaret Power lived south on the trail from Penn Cove. Power was an Island County commissioner when Whatcom split off and County Auditor Fitzhugh would have known him from then, plus Power was a founding member of the Olympia Masonic Lodge. He had raised (likely wandering) cattle and started the island's first blacksmith shop prior to his death two years before Cora arrived. Since then, self-reliant Margaret ran the farm alone with her six children. If anyone could help Cora through her adjustment to living on an island with a demanding husband in a crude home, on a land claim, and without her family or the slaves who did menial chores, it would be Margaret Power.[39]

Two occasions that united scattered settlers around Penn Cove were Christmas and July Fourth. Islanders, like other Washingtonians, celebrated Independence Day as an occasion to gather with people they saw infrequently. They feasted together, played games, raced horses, and danced at the Ferry House. Both occasions took months of planning and fundraising to make them the memorable events they became. Cora and Edmund missed July 4, 1861, but their first Christmas was similar with some overnighting after the feasting and dancing.[40]

CRBO

After Fitzhugh's appointment ended with Justice Oliphant's arrival, he was available to handle legal problems on Whidbey Island, in addition to attempting to farm in some way. His active connection to the coal mine was nearly gone, other than keeping an eye on Moody and Sinclair for his partners. Land sales at the Sehome townsite were still stagnant.

The Fitzhughs do not appear in the public record until Cora's father Robert Bowie filed a compensation petition on their behalf with the federal government in Washington, DC, on July 12, 1862. In a reminder of the war they left behind, they had to swear allegiance to the United States for eligibility.[41]

Three months earlier on April 16, 1862, President Lincoln freed 3,100 enslaved men, women, and children in the District of Columbia. It was five months before he issued the national Emancipation Proclamation. He had realized the hypocrisy of fighting a war that would end slavery in the nation, while the U.S. government allowed slavery to exist in the federal district. Under the emancipation act for Washington, DC, slaves as it was passed by Congress, slave masters would be compensated for each individual they legally owned.

The compensation petition signed by the Fitzhughs, with James Tilton a witness, was filled out in Washington Territory and sent to Cora's father. She had inherited enslaved people from her grandmother Mary Weems, and the group apparently moved to Robert Bowie's second home in Washington with him. Cora still owned six slaves, one of whom was an infant. The others ranged from age two to thirty-five. Ellen, Robert Bowie's cook, was described as "not particularly robust" and required extra care to keep her out of wet weather. She had four generally healthy children, though her papers said eleven-year-old John had lost the sight in his left eye after a bout with rheumatism following a spring cold. Annie was thirteen but was not Ellen's child. All six were mixed-race, which could mean that Cora's grandfather, or another male in the French family, was Ellen's father, given that she inherited from her grandmother. The fact that one of Ellen's children was an infant and others were born after Cora inherited her, might also mean that Robert or another Bowie family member was their father. The real nature of paternity was not spoken of in slave-owning families, to keep family women from embarrassment about the forced sex actions of their menfolk. Whatever the relationships, there was a strong possibility that all were related to Cora in some way, even half-siblings.

While Cora and Edmund Fitzhugh would have benefited financially from the emancipation compensation, the date of application makes the incident murkier. Whether it was accidental because of the distance and time it took for the signed papers to reach Cora's father, or whether Bowie purposely filed it on July 12, 1862, is not noted. On that very day, Congress passed an addendum to the April act which, if the former owners had not yet filed, allowed the freed District of Columbia people to do so on their own behalf, and personally receive the $300 per person compensation. Today that amount would equal well over $8000. Therefore, Ellen and her four children would receive the equivalent of almost $42,000, enough to start a new life. Young Annie's compensation would also help her to start over when she was old enough.

It is tantalizing to speculate on what might have happened in the District of Columbia with the petition in Robert Bowie's hands. He may have had advance notice that the bill would pass and held onto it until July 12 to give the family's newly-freed slaves (and relatives?) a start in their new lives as free people, by turning it in as soon as word came in that the bill passed. Or did the Fitzhughs know in advance that the bill was in the offing, and chose not to profit from the new freedom of Cora's enslaved people when they had little need of that money themselves? The other possibility is that it was just the last date for the Fitzhughs to claim the money and Bowie was a procrastinator, waiting until the last minute before the bill passed. There is no indication in the papers of who received the money.

掀

Cora probably looked forward to the chance to dress up and be among a group of women at her second Christmas celebration, no matter how different from herself they might have been. She never attended. She died on November 1, 1862, in Victoria. Fitzhugh may have taken her there to see Dr. John Helmcken, who had trained at the prestigious medical school in Edinburgh. No cause of death was stated in any record and it's possible Cora died in childbirth, from an injury, typhoid, or had caught pneumonia or another infection.[42]

Fitzhugh buried her in Victoria's little cemetery. Reverend Edward Cridge presided over her burial, using the Anglican rites and prayers familiar to Cora and her husband. Perhaps she had a small funeral in the church on a hill overlooking the fort and town. That Fitzhugh made sure Cora was properly buried in Victoria's cemetery points to the depth of his love for her, as later evidence would show. Any burials on Whidbey were still on land claims, as they had no cemetery there. Cora's obituary appeared in the *Alexandria (Virginia) Gazette* after Fitzhugh wrote to her father. It said tersely "On Whitby [*sic*] Island, Washington Territory, the first of November instant, Cora, the wife of Judge Edmund C. Fitzhugh, and daughter of Robert Bowie, Esq. of Cedar Hill, Prince George's County, Maryland."[43]

◌ঙ৾৹

Long-time acquaintances Orrington Cushman and Benjamin Shaw, to whom Fitzhugh owed money, pounced immediately after Cora's death. A month to the day after she died, neighbor Sheriff Thomas Hastie nailed a summons to Fitzhugh's door that ordered him to appear at district court. Hastie appears to have resigned the same day, perhaps displaying discomfort with his task so soon after Cora died. Fellow members of Isaac Stevens's Treaty War staff Cushman and Shaw had filed a lawsuit to collect two long-overdue promissory notes. Fitzhugh had pledged to repay Cushman's February 1859 loan for $210 the next day but did not. Left unpaid by Fitzhugh ever since, interest accumulated at two percent a month. Though well-aware that Fitzhugh hadn't repaid that loan, Cushman and Shaw still loaned him another $500 the following November 1860, a few weeks before Fitzhugh and Justice William Strong gambled their way to an indictment. Judging from similar language in other lawsuits, with a one-day term these notes "for value received" were for gambling debts. By 1862 Fitzhugh had managed to pay back $406.50, while at the same time loaning money to others instead of paying his own debt. It was an example of how, without a banking system, money for gambling and wealth-building projects moved informally among acquaintances and friends, tying them together with debt.[44]

Shaw apparently paid attention to rumors, because at the same time he filed the lawsuit to recover $740 on behalf of himself and Cushman, he filed a Request for Attachment. Knowing that with Cora's death nothing held Fitzhugh to the local community, Shaw said he was "convinced and verily believes that Defendant is about to sell and convey his property with intent to hinder and delay his creditors." When Sheriff Hastie had nailed the summons to Firzhugh's door on December 1, he had some time to come up with the cash before the court term, but Shaw's action negated that. Subsequent to Hastie's resignation, on the fourth, the newly-appointed sheriff rode out, handed Fitzhugh the Writ of Attachment, and took over the land and buildings valued at $1400. Old friend John Lysle rode out with the sheriff, perhaps to defuse a flammable situation. It must have been humiliating for the former justice who once held so much political and economic power in Whatcom County to face Lysle under the circumstances. The forced "sale" to former colleague Shaw left $1,000 with Fitzhugh after he signed over everything four days later. Shaw (without Cushman listed) apparently settled for $400 of the remaining debt, though the papers are confusing.[45]

CR80

As 1863 dawned, Fitzhugh had a dilemma. The transcontinental telegraph had been transmitting bulletins to San Francisco for a year, where they were sent on to Puget Sound with a steamer, as were San Francisco newspapers. The detailed war news that arrived in bulletins and newspapers gave Fitzhugh enough information to compare events at Falmouth and Fredericksburg with those in Washington Territory, and make an informed decision about his next move. He was going to be forty-two, no longer a young man by military standards. Cora was dead. His former wives Julia and Mary were remarried, and the children he abducted were in the hands of others. There were no personal ties to keep him in Washington, as Shaw had correctly believed.

Republicans controlled every appointive position in territorial government and there were other disturbing developments for Fitzhugh to consider. Pointed directly at Copperhead Democrats like himself whose loyalties remained suspect, the U.S. Land Office had ruled in 1862 that no claim patents or final titles would be issued to people who did not sign an oath of loyalty to the Union. It echoed the pledge Fitzhugh and Cora signed in order to submit the emancipation compensation petition. The Democratic *Pioneer-Democrat* had folded, leaving only the Steilacoom Republican Edward Furste's *Puget Sound Herald* to influence political opinion. Former Chief Justice Obadiah McFadden had successfully run for office as a new Republican, but then faced attacks that underneath he was still a secessionist, and so would be anyone who voted for him again. Emblematic of the intolerant political atmosphere, the accusations continued as long as the respected former justice served in the wartime legislature.[46]

The *Puget Sound Herald* reprinted an old eastern paper's assessment that "the greatest crisis of this war" was happening on the Rappahannock where both armies were massing at Fredericksburg. On December 11, a week after Fitzhugh's property was confiscated, the paper re-printed an earlier Philadelphia reporter's account from Falmouth about the oncoming Battle of Fredericksburg with the massing of hundreds of thousands of troops around Fitzhugh's vulnerable hometown. As of late November, all business in occupied Falmouth had ceased. Fitzhugh's Boscobel birthplace was now U.S. General Daniel Sickles's headquarters, but reporters said nothing about the Fitzhugh women who lived there. There were multiple items delayed from November in that issue. General Bayard had occupied Falmouth with gun emplacements behind the town, probably on the hill with a spring that Fitzhugh remembered. Fredericksburg residents fled and the Confederate army destroyed $100,000 worth of tobacco to keep the profitable commodity out of Union hands. Two weeks later the paper reported "a severe battle." Dispatches gave accounts of the Battle of Fredericksburg, with its great losses, especially among Confederate officers. They included General Ewell, whose West Point seat Fitzhugh had "inherited."[47]

By the end of the year, some of Fitzhugh's Northwest and California colleagues and friends had fared poorly also. The same month in 1861 that Fitzhugh took over the Cullen land claim, Union forces had apprehended KGC members Calhoun Benham and Senator William Gwin on the way to Cuba to buy guns for the Confederacy. Former Virginia governor Henry Wise, whose son had invested in the Sehome townsite, was another purported leader of the separatist organization dedicated to forming a slave-friendly Pacific Confederacy. Northwest members now met openly at the Confederate Saloon in Victoria. The national KGC headquarters occupied the former office where Fitzhugh toiled during the 1860 Breckinridge-Lane campaign, and former Vice President John Breckinridge was consistently named as a member. Fitzhugh's political colleague W.W. Miller was by then the quartermaster for the territory's new Union volunteer militia. Perhaps worst of all, Fitzhugh's longtime friend Isaac Stevens died leading his Union troops in the Battle of Chantilly two months before Cora's death.[48]

Fitzhugh knew that with the delay in getting news from home, and letters out of the Confederacy no longer delivered by the post office, the situation for his family was inevitably worse. It was time for him to go home. And even though only men up to forty were being drafted, at forty-two he needed to join the Confederate Army where so many of his kin already served. Fitzhugh disappears from the record for some months during which he may or may not have made arrangements to pre-pay the board for Julianne and Mason and make some arrangement in case he was killed. He traveled home to Virginia to once again seek out his distant cousins and personal connections who might help him find a suitable assignment in the Confederate Army.

CHAPTER 11

"Poor Fitz"

INTO THE CONFEDERATE ARMY

FITZHUGH MADE HIS WAY HOME TO VIRGINIA. Over forty with no wife and children, no viable political or economic base in Washington Territory, and once a vocal opponent of secession but supporting slavery's continued existence, he was adrift. Newspaper reports said the Union army occupied Falmouth to prepare for another battle. His long journey in early 1863 was probably in company with many other Westerners in the same predicament. He had plenty of time to consider his next move. The Confederate States Army (CSA) started drafting adult males under forty while Fitzhugh was en route. Professional men like himself and other wealthier men could still buy a substitute until late in the year, but surprisingly, he did not avoid enlistment.

Fitzhugh's older sister Mary Eliza and her much older husband, Dr. Hezekiah Magruder, were safe in Washington, DC, but it is likely that he checked on the location of his two unmarried sisters as soon as he got home. Virginia (age 31) and Helen (age 29) were almost certainly with his father's elderly sisters, including Henrietta Fitzhugh, the current owner of Boscobel. But the family home now housed General Daniel Sickles and his staff as their "headquarters." Sometimes owners stayed to assure good treatment of their home, but it is unlikely that Fitzhugh's unmarried sisters and aunts stayed in what became overwhelming male surroundings. They probably moved out to a safer Fitzhugh clan home unless they were with Mary Eliza.[1]

If Fitzhugh had found Falmouth changed in the spring of 1861 shortly after the war started, his hometown's condition was exponentially worse when he arrived in 1863. The previous April 1862 the Confederate army abandoned Stafford County, burning the wooden bridge to Fredericksburg as they went. Over the winter of 1862–63, while Fitzhugh mourned his wife and traveled home, more than one hundred thousand Union troops erected their tents at "Camp Fitzhugh Farm," on Boscobel's fields. The troops stripped the countryside of all vegetation for food, forage, and fires, their tents eventually spreading north to the edge of the Potomac Creek. While General Sickles took over Boscobel house for his headquarters, Union General Irvin McDowell was nearby at Chatham above the burned bridge, neither currently Fitzhugh properties. Edmund's other relatives living in Falmouth fled their homes along with other county residents who feared the troops would kill them, despite the area's lukewarm attitude toward a war. Many had been Unionists like Fitzhugh. As the planters and merchants fled south, hundreds of slaves from south of the river continued the move north across Falmouth's shallows to seek sanctuary with the Union army, using wagons and mules their slave masters left behind. Boscobel slaves found themselves already across the Union lines.[2]

As the 1863 campaign season started, the Union Army repeatedly assembled forces at Falmouth for new battles that made Virginia the war's main conflict region. Stafford County historian Homer Musselman called the county a "desolate wasteland of war." In early April President Lincoln reviewed thousands of troops gathered in the fields before Boscobel and attended a party in the home, hosted by General Sickles and other commanders. It was the first of six visits Lincoln made to the troops occupying the Falmouth area during the war.[3]

The repeated occupations and need for command headquarters had one beneficial result. Many of Falmouth's major buildings, as well as Boscobel and Chatham, were spared. Toward the end of the war, a Union colonel called Falmouth a "wretched straggling old place, very dirty, and now deserted almost." Some civilians in Falmouth who had nowhere else to go were nearly starving by mid-1863, but sometimes the Union soldiers far from home were kind to them. One four-year-old daughter of an absent Confederate soldier wanted a doll for Christmas. Union soldiers camping on her farm found out and presented her with a whittled wooden doll dressed in clothing sewn from bandages and someone's blanket.[4]

If Fitzhugh was surprised by what had happened to his Washington and California friends, he might have been equally surprised that his Falmouth neighbor James Seddon, who he'd surely met again at the Peace Democrats Convention in 1860, was now the Confederate secretary of war.

As Fitzhughs had always done—as Edmund C. Fitzhugh had always done—he turned to his personal contacts to help him land where he wanted. The search took months. If the Confederate army was drafting anyone forty and under, then it wouldn't be long before they wanted everyone forty-five and under, given how defensive the war had already become in early 1863. Fitzhugh had limited time to obtain a preferable position before he was drafted and given little choice over his assignment. He had a web of influential men in Virginia who could assist him. He also had a web of men from the Pacific Northwest to contact, like now-Brigadier General George Pickett. On August 8, a month after the Battle of Gettysburg, Fitzhugh dined in Washington, DC, with six men he knew from Washington Territory, among them Winfield Ebey from Whidbey Island, two colonels, a major, and another judge in the mix. They were not all Confederates or even participating in the war yet. One, Major Granville Haller, had been dismissed from the Union army after Gettysburg and would soon retreat with his family back to Whidbey Island, where he'd been during the 1859 "Pig War."[5]

At his age Fitzhugh's preference would be a desirable staff appointment that kept him out of battle unless dire circumstances required. In the heat of battle, a Confederate staff officer might lead troops, carry verbal orders to and from the front, go on a special mission, or personally guard his commander, but normally, a staff officer stayed behind the lines and relatively safe. Assistant adjutant general (AAG) was the best option for Fitzhugh.[6]

Fitzhugh could argue his personal qualifications to any commanders considering him for a staff appointment. Already a lawyer (the basic AAG qualification), he'd been both a judge and a military aide-de-camp before. He was mature and intelligent. If he was willing to tell of his aborted West Point experience, it would tell them he understood military discipline and West Point graduate officers' mindset. He also knew both the terrain and the people who remained around Falmouth and Fredericksburg.

The Confederate army remained more traditional about staff selections than the Union army, leading to frequent complaints of nepotism, favoritism, and lack of prior military experience. Confederate West Point graduates soon recognized a clear problem—the academy did not train cadets to be staff officers. Commonly, commanders hoped to get the best combination of talent and personality so they could get along together while running the war. Most often that meant hiring relatives, old friends, or just acquaintances they thought would be courageous in battle. Usually the top staff appointees proceeded to get their own relatives and friends appointed to serve with them at some level. For example, Fitzhugh's friend George Pickett's staff included his brother, his cousins, and his sister's husband on several levels. President Jefferson Davis told his generals to make experimental appointments and see what happened. Incompetents could be dismissed or demoted. If commanders wanted a "boon companion" during the long months of living in close quarters, Fitzhugh could be very "boon."[7]

Fitzhugh took about seven months after his return to Virginia to achieve a position he wanted and could have used some of that time to look after his family. However, he also worked his connections to the men who would eventually be his commanders at every level. While seeking an appointment, he had many names to drop. He likely told interviewers that he knew Jefferson Davis's nephew, Robert Hugh Davis, in Washington Territory, although he might have left out the almost-duel incident. He could also mention that Secretary of War Seddon had been his Falmouth neighbor. Fitzhugh's strategy worked. Ultimately, by the time he received an AAG appointment after the Battle of Cold Harbor, all four officers in his higher chain of command were connected to him by family or friendship.[8]

He first went to his relative General Robert E. Lee (or his staff) for an appointment. Lee's mother and mother-in-law were both Fitzhugh kin. Edmund got his old friend (and very distant cousin) George Pickett to write a letter of recommendation for brigade inspector, and on August 22, 1863, First Army Corps commander Lieutenant General James Longstreet approved the appointment, and Fitzhugh was to report to General Lee's twenty-five-year-old adjutant general, Colonel Walter H. Taylor. The age difference between the two, for one who had been the man in charge for many years, surely took some attitude adjustment on Fitzhugh's part.[9]

General Lee and Secretary Seddon were informed of the appointment. By order of the adjutant's office, Fitzhugh assumed a captain's rank on November 2. He reported in for brigade inspector duty with his friend Pickett's division on the nineteenth after two weeks' training. His new duties were much different from judicial ones or even those he expected to do. Gettysburg took a serious toll on Pickett, and his mental and physical health started a long decline. Fitzhugh reminded Pickett of happier times and the comradeship between officers in Washington who now opposed each other.[10]

While the Confederate army rebuilt after Gettysburg, they had a dire need for inspectors during the steady influx of new men, both enlistees and draftees. Just two weeks after Fitzhugh reported, the government ordered an end to allowing men with financial means to hire substitutes to serve in their place. It allowed those who had already done so until February 1, 1864, to choose their branch of service and report. Some newcomers became excellent soldiers, while others were of little use. A Virginia regimental historian noted that "many were so old they looked like they had been resurrected from the grave, after laying therein for twenty years." Fitzhugh, at forty-two, was no young man either. By a few days before the deadline, an estimated ninety-five percent of eligible Virginians were in the army. Fitzhugh had made the right decision when he arrived in Virginia early in 1863 with time to seek an assignment that fit his skills and civilian status.[11]

Confederate inspectors came from the same pool of men as the assistant adjutants. Men moved between the two jobs as needed, which caused occasional confusion. Field commanders and soldiers widely disliked the arrival of an inspector, but those who did the job temporarily, like Fitzhugh, could earn some respect by doing the unpleasant duty well. His two prime duties included evaluation of a unit's readiness for battle, and enforcement of discipline and regulations. In reality, both duties also meant being the commander's eyes and ears as well as an enforcer. A formal inspection allowed Fitzhugh to look at anything—men, equipment, kitchens, horses, etc.—then pass along his recommendations to the commander.[12]

After joining Pickett's decimated division of Virginians, Fitzhugh reported to Brigadier General Junius Daniel on December 7, 1863. An assignment usually put the inspector with troops from outside his own state of origin and Daniel's brigade was composed of his fellow North Carolinians. They performed heroically in the Confederate success on the first day of Gettysburg, and subsequently transferred into Pickett's Division. West Point graduate Daniel, like many Confederate officers, came from a prominent family in his own state. His father had been North Carolina attorney general and a member of Congress. His Virginia-born mother was a Randolph, probably a cousin of Edmund Randolph who gave Fitzhugh his first law firm job in California.[13]

Less than a month later, Fitzhugh joined Brigadier General Eppa Hunton's brigade as the permanent inspector. He remained with Hunton, and Pickett, to the end of the war. Like Lee, Hunton had relatively close Fitzhugh relatives, and the transfer into his brigade was unlikely to have been a coincidence. A few years younger than Captain Fitzhugh, Hunton was a prominent Virginia lawyer and prosecutor from Loudoun County whose wife was a Fitzhugh. He had been an elector for the 1860 Breckinridge ticket, at a time when he and Fitzhugh probably crossed paths. For the entire war the indomitable Hunton suffered with a fistula (abnormal connection between two abdominal organs) and had more than one surgery. He was wounded at Gettysburg, which led to his promotion to brigadier general, but also to his dislike of his commander, Pickett. Hunton's integrity and moral character were unquestioned.[14]

Figure 28, Eppa Hunton, Virginia senator and Confederate Brigadier General. E. C. Fitzhugh served as his second Assistant Adjutant General. Photographed 1865–1880. *Brady-Handy Photograph Collection. Library of Congress, Prints and Photographs Division, #LC-DIG-cwpbh-04813.*

In 1863 General Lee issued a special manual for Confederate army lawyers that spelled out the difference between military law and civil law. Improvisation had come too often with untrained military lawyers. This impacted Fitzhugh when his inspector duties changed in the new year.[15]

1864

Winter encampment for Hunton's Brigade was at Chaffin's Farm between Richmond and Petersburg on the north side of the James River. The commissary officer issued Fitzhugh a tent and firewood for a half-cabin, half-tent combination of low log walls and tent top. He requisitioned a blank book for personal use, perhaps a journal. Over the winter when active combat campaigning ceased, the brigade worked on the concentric circles of Richmond's permanent defenses. Campaigning resumed in March and the brigade, with Fitzhugh, left their winter cabins and fireplace-warmed tents.

An order in 1864 brought expanding duties to the inspectors for brigades that usually numbered up to five thousand officers and soldiers in four or five regiments but were no longer at full strength. Fitzhugh took charge of questioning prisoners, inspecting hospitals and guard houses, as well as examining all camp records to see if officers were implementing orders given them. Three times a month he was to do a formal inspection using the expanded list and submit the proper report. On the battlefield, his job was to be the direct link between commander, provost marshal, and guard, riding his horse between them with orders and reports. Increasingly, all the brigades needed to prevent straggling and looting. Reflecting the growing discontent that came with multiple defeats, some soldiers drifted to the rear, especially if they were escorting the wounded out of harm's way. Then they never returned to the lines. Fitzhugh also took charge of inspecting guards, paroling prisoners, and certifying any volunteer or militia units that arrived for national service. His most onerous new duty that year was to supervise a firing squad or hanging if a court martial ordered an execution. As a judge, he had sentenced men to death, but he didn't have to attend an execution. Now he did.[16]

The war turned into a "grim, hate-filled struggle that knew few rules and no niceties," according to historian Edward Longacre. Desertion increased as men completed their three-year enlistment and families begged them to come home. Once new conscripts had arrived at the winter encampment to train and saw the realities, they sometimes bolted at the first chance. Those numbers continued to increase during the 1864 combat season.[17]

April 4, 1864, was a day of fasting and prayer for the Confederacy, which meant no food rations were issued. Not only did rations often decrease by as much as three-quarters that year, but precarious Confederate Treasury reserves meant Fitzhugh received his $140/month pay intermittently, usually months late until, finally, nothing at all. What he was able to get every month until records ceased was forage for his horse: corn and hay, plus oats when he was at Chaffin's

Farm over the winter. When pay ceased, in addition to grazing, army horses still needed eight pounds of corn and fourteen pounds of hay each day, paid for with Confederate dollars, by IOU, or stolen from a luckless farmer. After the winter, horses no longer got any oats.[18]

From the first week of May to the end of June, the brigade fought almost constantly in the fields and woods surrounding central Virginia's smallest settlements. In early June, Brigadier General Hunton's AAG Charles Linthicum was killed during the short-lived Confederate victory at Cold Harbor, one of five thousand lives lost. He was Hunton's hometown Methodist minister and Loudoun's regimental chaplain, and the loss of his favorite staff member devastated the general. Fitzhugh got the job of AAG, but Hunton could not bear to give him the official title until months later on November 4, 1864, almost a year after his first commission as an inspector. As unit consolidation continued, Hunton's infantry brigade joined Major General Wade Hampton III's Cavalry Corps in August, when Fitzhugh requisitioned a second horse for use "in the field." At full strength, "Hampton's Legion" had included four companies of infantry, equaling four hundred men. Hunton's original four-thousand-man infantry brigade may have been down to as few as four hundred itself at that time, at least temporarily. Hampton's men were already famous for their daring raids behind enemy lines. Hampton's own courageous actions had earned him command of the cavalry corps but cost him the lives of two sons.[19]

Wade Hampton came from a wealthy planter family in South Carolina. A manager of plantations, he had been in the legislature, but was without military experience. His other experience was seen as evidence of leadership skills, and he also had social standing. Fitzhugh's association with Hampton did not last long. When Lee's army stalled in the Siege of Petersburg, in January 1865, Hampton left to recruit more men in South Carolina, a desperate mission to find anyone willing to join what was clearly a lost cause. Fitzhugh returned with Hunton to his friend Pickett's Division.[20]

Fitzhugh's role as AAG was much different from that of brigade inspector, though as the army shrank from death, capture, desertion, and wounds, his orders also included the inspector's tasks. He became the general-purpose officer on Hunton's field staff with some specified duties, but also many informal assignments by default if assigned to no one else. Having run a court and managed paper movement, Fitzhugh was well able to coordinate the movement of his brigade's official correspondence and orders up the chain of command to General Lee, and down the chain to the company level. Fitzhugh published brigade orders under Hunton's name, and managed the incoming reports and correspondence from brigade subordinates. He was responsible for maintaining Hunton's own headquarters records and logs. Everything had to be indexed. Even though supervision of the postal system was never a formal assignment, for the ordinary soldier as well as the commanders, Fitzhugh had the most important duty of all—the distribution of mail to the smallest units. One AAG said "I cannot be absent for even one day." Despite that assessment by a fellow AAG, Fitzhugh did take leave.[21]

Fitzhugh wielded an inordinate amount of power outside of battle, something he had always sought, because the AAG managed both personnel and paper. Fitzhugh remained the supervisor of executions, when all troops would assemble in a hollow square with the scaffold in the middle. He also worked on unit strength reports directly after battles, as well as generating paperwork for promotions, the all-important reward for bravery and competence. As well, he could hold an examination board to eliminate unfit officers for any reason.

For the command structure of the army, there was another issue. In June 1864, while one hundred twenty thousand men were in the CSA army, only fifty thousand were present and ready for combat. By early fall, it was down to one hundred thousand men with only thirty-eight thousand combat ready. Making that type of depressing observation and report for the brigade was Fitzhugh's job.[22]

All summer, Confederate soldiers and slaves continued to work on defensive trenches known as the Howlett Line south of Chaffin's Farm. The preparations were part of a plan to protect against invasion of the capital at Richmond and the important manufacturing town of Petersburg, Virginia's second largest city. In September a battle included the farm and 1700 Confederate men were killed, but it remained the designated winter quarters for General Hunton, his staff, and his remaining troops for the 1864-65 winter. By the encampment, about the number in one full regiment (one thousand men) composed Hunton's brigade after more consolidation and adding new men. During the Siege of Petersburg, Hunton's troops spent eight months with others defending the seven miles of fortified line. Men gathered materials and constructed better housing for themselves, even digging out caves fitted with fireplaces in the trench wall. There were more rainy days than snowy ones and mud was a constant, as were wet or spoiled rations. It is unlikely that Fitzhugh's assignment was by then the "clean hands" one he had once anticipated.[23]

That winter of the siege, life at the trenches was described by one of their officers as "endurance without relief; sleeplessness without exhilaration; inactivity without rest; constant apprehension requiring ceaseless watching...Not the least of the evils encountered was the unavoidable stench from the latrines." There were ration shortages of medicine, clothing, and equipment.[24]

Gloom infused the soldiers in Hunton's encampment on the Howlett Line. Men would be away from home for the holidays again. Regular pay was a thing of the past. More demoralizing even than the winter conditions was the knowledge that Lincoln had been re-elected and the war might continue for another four years. News reached the trenches about Union General William Sherman's destructive march across Georgia, and that General Phil Sheridan took the Shenandoah Valley, west of the Blue Ridge. The many deaths in combat, and now in the trenches from disease, led men to become numb to horrific war deaths, and those who died were mourned only for moments by most.[25]

Virginia's governor had previously built some cabins for the men building the defensive works, and the house of the Chaffin Farm's overseer became Hunton's headquarters, a more comfortable situation for the staff. For officers, life was different because some wives joined their husbands in the house or cabins for the winter. Fitzhugh could attend some diversions like dances and musicales, which seems contradictory to maintaining morale among the troops who couldn't have their wives there or "musicales."

In late October AAG Fitzhugh received a general order clarifying punishment for deserters because penalties had been inconsistent. There was a combination of losing leave or pay, wearing a ball and chain, or wearing a placard that said "Deserter." Fewer men were sentenced to be shot or hung, but numbers punished increased as the army sought to scare men into staying. It was a grim duty for Fitzhugh.[26]

Ann Fitzhugh Grayson

Fitzhugh had personal business on his mind that winter of 1864–65. Winter quarters was also the regular season for happier personal events

for those officers and soldiers lucky enough to get leave to go home and
marry, but only if their homes were north of the Carolinas. General
Hunton granted Fitzhugh leave in October to head to Falmouth, and on
northwest to the general's own Loudoun County. Even if Fitzhugh and
his horse took a train to Richmond, it would take over a week by back
roads, while avoiding any Union troops, to get to his destination. Apparently leaving all the AAG duties in the hands of someone else, his leave
lasted until early January.

Edmund Fitzhugh was not done with women, particularly women
from important, monied families. His first two wives, Julia and Mary,
had been from an elite Coast Salish family whose wealth was in salmon,
resource territories, leadership status and connections. Likewise, Cora
had been a member of one of Maryland's wealthiest and most influential
families.

Soon E. C. Fitzhugh would marry for the fourth time in ten years,
this time to his first cousin. She was Ann Fitzhugh Grayson, the
daughter of Richard O. Grayson and Edmund's Aunt Margaretta, his
father Alexander's younger sister.

After Fitzhugh joined General Hunton's staff in 1863, he accompanied
his commander on at least one trip to his Leesburg home in Loudoun
County when Union troops were not there, and it was leave season for
those in winter camp. In addition to Hunton's Fitzhugh-family wife,
Edmund Fitzhugh had his own connections to Loudoun's rolling
farmland and the small towns in the shadow of the Blue Ridge because of
his aunt's marriage. After Ann Fitzhugh Grayson's brothers and cousins
joined Hunton's Eighth Virginia Infantry, it led to visits by Hunton and
his staff to Elizabeth Carter at "Oatlands Plantation" where Ann lived.[27]

Loudoun was a border county in a Confederate state where sentiment
was deeply divided, and friend sometimes fought against friend. Then-
Colonel Eppa Hunton recruited the county's Confederate Eighth
Virginia Infantry, who served with him to the end. Other young men
slipped away and joined the Union infantry or the "Loudoun Rangers,"
the Union's only regular Virginia cavalry unit. Leesburg itself was at the
junction of two main roads, the end of an important railroad line at the
Potomac River, and site of the main fords and ferries over the upper river
to Maryland, all of which made it a communications and transportation
hub. Consequently, Loudoun County civilians, including Ann's family,
suffered as both armies crossed or occupied it repeatedly, even though

Figure 29, Oatlands Plantation in Loudoun County, Virginia. E. C. Fitzhugh's first cousin and fourth wife Ann Fitzhugh Grayson grew up at the home of her aunt Elizabeth Osborne Grayson and her second husband George Carter, descendant of "King" Carter. *Photograph by Candace Wellman.*

only one major battle (Ball's Bluff) was fought there. By the war's end, the county would be nearly stripped of crops, wood, and livestock, leaving only its fertile soil, similar to conditions at Falmouth.[28]

છગ્ગૃ

Edmund's aunt Maria Margaretta Fitzhugh Grayson gave birth to Ann Fitzhugh Grayson on October 5, 1829, at Boscobel, where Edmund had also been born. The Fitzhugh-Grayson marriage was another example of the FFV goal of keeping land and money within the tight web of families who founded Virginia. The original Grayson was a 1600s immigrant Scot baker who built a fortune with his biscuits and married President James Monroe's aunt. His son, William Grayson, was General George Washington's aide-de-camp, delegate to the Continental Congress, and a Virginia senator in the first United States Congress. Each succeeding male generation married women from prominent colonial families until Ann's grandfather married a Stafford County woman, leading to Grayson-Fitzhugh ties.[29]

Ann and Edmund probably attended many of the same large family gatherings at Boscobel, but he might have overlooked the first cousin who was about eight years younger. Ann lived at the Grayson family's "Newstead Farm" in Loudoun County until her parents died when she was eleven. She and her five siblings went to live with their father's sister Elizabeth O. Grayson Lewis Carter at nearby Oatlands, owned by Elizabeth's second husband George Carter. He was a descendant of one of Virginia's largest landowners, Robert "King" Carter, and had developed Oatlands into a plantation of over 3,400 acres with at least 120 enslaved people before the Grayson children moved there. After Ann and her grieving siblings were enfolded into their aunt's family, they joined their Carter cousins in the little schoolhouse. When their aunt's husband died five years after the Grayson children arrived, Oatlands included a brick manufactury, church, store, and large grist mill in addition to other outbuildings and slave quarters. With the labor of his slaves, George Carter had remodeled his home into an airy Greek Revival showcase surrounded by four acres of terraced gardens.[30]

Ann's aunt Elizabeth Grayson Carter owned, in her own right, "Bellefield Farm" that adjoined Oatlands. In the years after George Carter's death, Ann's kindly-faced aunt managed both Oatlands and Bellefield herself. In an unusual will for Southern elites, her own father had divided his Grayson lands and houses at the foot of the Blue Ridge among all his children. Ann's father inherited Newstead Farm a mile away from Bellefield and her uncle took it over after her parents died. Each Grayson property had its own enslaved community.[31]

By 1850 twenty-one-year-old Ann's Aunt Elizabeth was Loudoun County's largest slaveholder, her lands so vast that escaped slaves from other places could hide there. Oatlands was virtually self-sufficient and exported goods and services to the coast. Its greenhouse even had a hot water heating system that allowed it to produce bananas and strawberries in mid-winter. When the war began in 1861, Elizabeth Carter was the wealthiest *person* in the county (not just the wealthiest *woman*) with the largest landholdings, worked by her 133 enslaved people. The northern part of the county above the Grayson-Carter lands was dominated by pacifist and abolitionist Quakers who started to help local runaway slaves get to the Union lines. Three hundred of them subsequently fought for the Union.[32]

෴

While Edmund Fitzhugh married Cora Bowie and returned to Washington Territory during the first year of the war, Ann's life at Oatlands changed rapidly. At first the family carried on as usual. Her aunt's diary noted Ann's recurring medical problems, which seem to be from migraine headaches or her menstrual cycle. By the end of May 1861, Union soldiers were coming around, commandeering food and horses, and threatening people. As military operations continued into the coming months, Oatlands Plantation began to have problems continuing its usual economic activities, probably as slaves ran to the Union lines.

By June 1861 as Cora and Edmund Fitzhugh journeyed to the Northwest on a strife-free ocean, the Grayson-Carter family's life centered around the war. Two of Ann's brothers and three cousins, all in their twenties, enlisted, including her cousin Dr. John Grayson, though at forty-six he was exempt from service. Four joined Loudoun County's Eighth Infantry Regiment under Colonel Hunton, while Ann's older brother Richard joined the cavalry. Her brother Thomas left medical school to enlist, then was wounded and captured in the First Battle of Bull Run (First Manassas) in the southern part of Loudoun County. He was taken to Washington, DC, but released shortly, as was Ann's cousin Fitz Grayson. An example of the complexity of loyalties during the war, Ann's brother Ben Grayson had migrated to booming Iowa six years earlier and did not return to Virginia to enlist in the CSA. Like other Iowans, he joined the Union army and became an assistant paymaster working out of New York City. It did not tear the family apart.[33]

Bull Run was a Confederate victory, but on July 7, 1861, Colonel Hunton arrived at Oatlands to personally tell his friends that Ann's brother Richard had been killed. The terrible news made it chillingly real to the women that they could lose all their sons, brothers, and cousins who said goodbye with such excitement and optimism. Young Ben Carter had also been briefly captured with Thomas, and when his mother Elizabeth heard what happened, she made him return to the university he'd left to enlist.[34]

Two days after the Battle of Ball's Bluff, only eight miles from Oatlands, Elizabeth Carter's slaves loaded wagons with the family's important belongings. She moved twelve miles to her Bellefield house with family and household slaves. It was further away from the Potomac River's nexus of fighting, and closer to Ann's uncle at Newstead. Elizabeth's son George Carter II buried the family silver and stayed behind to run Oatlands. With Elizabeth's departure, Confederate district commander Colonel Nathan "Shanks" Evans made Oatlands his headquarters for the next ten days, while his troops camped on the expansive grounds. After Ball's Bluff, he was promoted to Brigadier General, and his assignment was to guard the upper fords of the Potomac ten miles away. The West Point graduate from South Carolina had served out west until his state seceded, and he was already a hero from First Bull Run, brave and a good tactician. However, he was also an alcoholic with an abrasive personality whose aide carried his small barrel of whiskey everywhere. He may have been abrasive, but he respected Elizabeth Carter's home and left it untouched.[35]

While former Justice Edmund Fitzhugh was contemplating a move to peaceful Whidbey Island with his third wife Cora that fall of 1861, his future fourth wife's life grew increasingly harrowing. Elizabeth Carter's diary recorded the confusion and stress the family endured as the war intensified. Their homes at Bellefield, Newstead, and Oatlands lay almost literally in the center between battlefields and campaigns of the Confederate counteroffensive: the Shenandoah Valley, Antietam, Manassas (Bull Run), Harpers Ferry, and Ball's Bluff.

In late October 1862 Major General Jeb Stuart and his Confederate cavalry camped at Newstead. Stuart had a distant family relationship with the Graysons, which may have influenced where he camped and where he went to eat dinner. After Stuart left, the Union army began to pass in front of Bellefield after the Maryland campaign, which included the war's deadliest day at Antietam. The commissary officer posted a guard to protect the Grayson-Carter family and home that night from "marauders." Elizabeth Carter spoke cordially enough to discover Captain George Corkhill was from Iowa where her nephew Ben had enlisted, and found that Corkhill cared that thousands of men not loot her farm. The next day, General Winfield Scott Hancock sent a major to formally call on Carter to say guards would continue to protect Bellefield from the long column. On the march's third day passing by, Brigadier General (and Doctor) Nathan Kimball sent guards. The Union army could have stolen Bellefield's corn, but instead, Kimball bought it with an IOU. Once the massive Union army was gone, Confederate General Stonewall Jackson's battle-worn troops moved through. Ann and her family hosted dinner for Jackson's staff that night. Through all the area's near-daily changes between Union and Confederate control, Elizabeth,

Ann, and the others remained cordial to everyone in order to save their home from looting and burning. Many were not as fortunate or as savvy.[36]

While Edmund Fitzhugh traveled home to Virginia in the winter of 1863 and sought out contacts that would help him find a favorable commission in the army, Ann's family members filtered in from other homes seeking a wartime refuge. She still suffered nearly every month with her chronic physical problems. On June 21, 1863, the Battle of Upperville (part of the Gettysburg Campaign) was fought in drought-ending heavy rain about four miles from Bellefield. Iconic Confederate cavalry commanders Wade Hampton, Jeb Stuart, and John Mosby (the "Grey Ghost") were all involved. Ann's cousin Robert and brother Thomas, who by then had joined Mosby's Rangers with hundreds of other men, were both invaluable in their familiar neighborhood.

After the Battle of Gaines Mill six days later, General Hunton started to use the term "Bloody Eighth" for the Loudoun men he believed would fight no matter the odds, but July first brought the hellish days of Gettysburg. After Hunton's brigade was in the front line of Pickett's Charge, ninety percent of the "Bloody Eighth" were killed, wounded like Hunton, or missing. Only twenty men remained of about one thousand who started with him. Ann's cousins Captain Alexander Grayson and Dr. John Grayson both died. At the time, Edmund Fitzhugh was still seeking an appointment and escaped the carnage.[37]

Fitzhugh joined General Hunton and some of his cousins in a rapidly shrinking brigade, his life centered around battle after battle, but Ann's life at Bellefield centered around the civilian chaos of war and her personal medical problems. Intermittently, soldiers arrived for good or for bad. In late winter, Ann's brother and cousin arrived with hundreds of Mosby's Rangers, who were dominating the area General Lee called "Mosby's Confederacy." The Union army considered them guerillas. The family was able to visit when Colonel Mosby came to dinner one night and had his band serenade Ann and her family. If his habit of seeking out a house continued, he also slept at Bellefield. Another evening, the family hosted a dance for Mosby and his officers, a rare moment of peace and frivolity for everyone. Three months later, Elizabeth Carter wrote that other troops "robbed" Bellefield, which usually meant taking all a family's food, chickens, bedding, clothes, and any valuables they found, unless a commander arrived to stop the looting of civilians.[38]

C3ЄᎾ

Edmund Fitzhugh re-connected with his cousin Ann while a member of Hunton's staff. By that time, she was in her thirties and the "spinster" companion of her widowed aunt and older family refugees at the Grayson-Carter homes. Ann had few prospects in life beyond remaining in the First Families of Virginia (FFV) world of the Grayson, Carter, and Fitzhugh families where she would always have a home even if finances were ruined. Her circumstances were much like those of ill-fated Cora Weems Bowie when she married Fitzhugh three years earlier in Maryland.

During Fitzhugh's winter leave, on November 15, 1864, the Loudoun County clerk issued a marriage license to Edmund and his first cousin, Ann Fitzhugh Grayson. He listed himself as forty-three and a widower living "in camp." She listed herself as thirty-four and single, living at Newstead, where she had been caring for her uncle George Grayson's widow. The times Ann lived in were desperate for all civilians in her border county, and the clerk noted at the bottom of the license: "The minister can keep this and return it to me when this cruel war is over."[39]

Six weeks later on December 28, Elizabeth Carter noted in her diary "Dear Anne [Ann] married to Edward [sic] C. Fitzhugh at Newstead." There may have been a chapel on the grounds of her childhood home, as there were at other family houses, or they married in Newstead's parlor in a typical evening ceremony conducted by the Rev. Walter Williams.[40]

1865

The newlyweds went to Bellefield days later to say goodbye to Elizabeth Carter, Ann's sister Mary Stuart Grayson, and the family's war refugees. The couple returned to Newstead to pack and leave for Chaffin's Farm. Carter sent her (officially at least) ex-slave Sarah with Ann's clothing and a gift of chickens and sausage for their final dinner. When they left the warmth of Newstead on the morning of January 6, it was snowing and windy in the rolling countryside.[41]

The long journey to Chaffin's Farm was miserable, and Ann had no idea what she was to experience as an officer's wife and "camp follower" in the coming months of 1865. She knew only that her new husband and men from her family would be there. Fitzhugh may not have told his new bride exactly what the conditions were for the officers' wives at the winter encampment, even those toughened by wartime conditions.

By October 1864, when Hunton's Brigade had gone back into winter camp, it consisted of only five officers (including Fitzhugh), and its numbers plummeted to 104 soldiers, even after combining with other units. Ann may have still envisioned the four thousand men of the Hunton brigade, whose commander Loudoun County citizens called their own. Or Loudoun County's thousand-man Eighth Regiment that had included her excited brothers and cousins going off to defeat the invading Yankees. Or the heroic "Gray Ghost" Mosby's cavalry with her brother Thomas when he last was home. What she saw at the Howlett Line defenses and Chaffin's Farm in January 1865 was the reality of the oncoming Confederate total defeat. Her new husband may have moved her to Richmond at that time where many officers' wives were living, although others chose to stay at the camp. If Ann went to Richmond, as long as the capital city remained in Confederate hands she would be safe, and Fitzhugh could ride the ten miles to visit her. Hunton's brigade received orders to help defend the city, which may have enabled him to see her even after spring combat began. If he didn't move her to the city in January, her living conditions at Chaffin's Farm were horrendous for a woman who had always lived in comparative comfort. If she was there, she had a log hut to make into her first home without help, unless invited to live in Hunton's headquarters house.

When Fitzhugh returned to AAG duty, he dealt with ever-increasing desertions as the inevitability of defeat became clear to everyone. He received a new order to grant amnesty to deserters who returned, or were apprehended, instead of punishing or executing them. Fitzhugh became one of the "thousands who resolved that neither hunger nor cold, neither danger nor the bad example of feebler spirits could induce them to leave 'Marse Robert,'" his relative. Deserting his Fitzhugh relatives Lee, Pickett, and Hunton, his fellow staff officers, Ann's family men, and the rest of the brigade remnant was ultimately unthinkable for Edmund either as a man of honor or a Fitzhugh.[42]

February 1865 brought Robert E. Lee to the command of the entire Confederate army in all theaters of war. On the same day of that appointment, Fitzhugh's presidential candidate John C. Breckinridge became Confederate Secretary of War, coincidentally replacing his former Falmouth neighbor James Seddon. The desertion rate continued to rise, including almost 1,100 in one February week, the largest number from Fitzhugh's own Pickett's Division.[43]

To counter the negativity in camp, General Hunton and other commanders gathered their remaining men to draft resolutions supporting the Confederacy on February 7. Hunton's tattered soldiers met in the log brigade chapel where their officers spoke for hours. They certainly included the experienced and persuasive public speaker Fitzhugh, after Hunton kept his own remarks brief.[44]

Influenced by these morale-building meetings, most men looked forward to the 1865 combat campaign with pride, resignation, and dread. They knew that their defensive battles would decide the outcome of a terrible war so different from what anyone anticipated in 1861's spring and Virginia's secession. By March, rations often consisted of "pickled beef" from London or no meat at all, just coffee, molasses, and sugar. There was plenty of food in Virginia, but the Yankees interfered with its transportation.[45]

৩৪৬৩

At the end of March Pickett's Division left the protective Howlett Line between the James and Appomattox Rivers in the hands of another division and boarded an aged train for the Five Forks intersection of major roads and the Southside Railroad. Sally Ann ("LaSalle") Pickett left for Richmond with any other wives still at Chaffin's Farm, including Ann Fitzhugh if she had persisted.[46]

Virginians dominated the assembled forces, torn by wanting to go home to protect their families, yet knowing they were defending Virginia against an enemy who had made their state one vast battlefield. The day after they left winter quarters, Hunton's brigade lay in trenches along the White Oak Road. Torrents of spring rain fell, the creeks were rising, and deep mud grabbed at men and horses everywhere. Fitzhugh's friend General Pickett had about 19,000 men under his command after brigades rendezvoused. There was nothing to eat but dry corn roasted over a fire. Men hoped that rations lay ahead in a coming train.[47]

On April 1 the battle for the crossroads began. General Hunton's decimated brigade was ordered to combine with two other remnants to guard one road and keep communication with General Pickett open. As the AAG, carrying orders between the generals and unit commanders was Fitzhugh's battle job, though armed only with his revolver and a short field sword or a saber. When fighting began, Hunton's men and the others drove Union troops back a mile to a creek called Gravelly Run. Hunton took a minie ball across his coat that hit his sword scabbard but did not injure him. He later described his men's actions as heroic, every man.[48]

A minie ball found Fitzhugh while he ran through the woods chasing the bluecoats. He may have heard it coming. Men described the sound like wounded men crying, bees humming, or just a 'zip'-like noise. The nature of the stubby, thick, pointed soft minie ball was that it expanded in the muzzle-loaded rifled musket and was effective over a long distance. When it hit, a minie ball splintered bone and tore up tissue despite being fired from far away. The minie ball that hit Fitzhugh's forehead was fired from at least three-quarters of a mile away, but only stunned him and produced a bloody wound without piercing his skull.

Figure 30, Reproduction .58 caliber Minie ball that traveled as far as 1500 yards, the most likely model to have wounded E. C. Fitzhugh in the forehead without killing him. *Photograph by Candace Wellman.*

The astonishing Fitzhugh incident that followed lived on in the writings of his fellow soldiers. General Hunton said in his memoir: "As we were driving the enemy, Captain E. C. Fitzhugh, my Adjutant, who had succeeded Linthicum, was struck in the forehead and down he fell. Colonel Green, of the 56th Regiment, said, 'Poor Fitz! Forward, Boys!' and on we went; but not long afterwards we were joined by Fitzhugh, who was only stunned, and he continued in the charge." The 56th Regiment's historian said the men were "happily surprised when he caught up with them."[49]

When Fitzhugh regained consciousness some minutes behind the confusion and tumult of battle, he could have stayed on the ground, feigning death. Instead, he picked himself up, dizzy, bleeding, and in pain. At forty-four and wounded, Fitzhugh's courage was clear when he still ran toward his fellow Virginians fast enough to catch up to them in the woods. The concussion of the minie ball slamming into his forehead may have done permanent damage, but it didn't stop him that day.

Fitzhugh was among the very few who avoided capture and survived the hand-to-hand combat in thrown-up rifle pits that continued into the next days. General Ulysses Grant's forces captured over 4,500 Confederates who they lined up virtually back to chest, the captives not knowing what was to happen to them next. General Lee dismissed Pickett from the army for dereliction and general incompetence, but Fitzhugh's friend never left his troops. Three to four thousand Confederates died at Five Forks, but not Fitzhugh.[50]

One historian said Pickett's forces had been "mauled" and the five depleted infantry brigades "cut to pieces." Five Forks was the beginning of the end for Lee's army, and the beginning of total victory for Grant's. Fitzhugh and Hunton's small remnant struggled on to the railroad stop that should have food waiting in the middle of the night, after they marched twenty-four hours without food. They found the vital Southside Railroad line had been cut and the food lost. On April 2 there were few more than one hundred men in Hunton's consolidated brigade, unbelievable losses from his early four thousand. The Confederate Army had one final torturous week to exist.[51]

That night the Confederate government abandoned its capital where Ann was staying. The depleted units tasked with guarding Richmond and Petersburg could not hold the miles of defense lines. Chaos took over with looting and burning of the city whose panicked residents and refugees fled across bridges and down roads before the towering flames, extinguished only the next day by Union soldiers.[52]

A "turgid little stream" called Sayler's Creek gave its name to the last major battle of the war. Fitzhugh fought hand-to-hand after eating only parched corn in the last two days, and without any sleep. The men left in Pickett's Division became surrounded, but once again Fitzhugh somehow managed to escape capture or death. Humiliated, General Hunton and seven other Confederate commanders threw down their weapons and surrendered before the Union army took possession of three hundred wagons with eight hundred mules and horses. Nearly one-fourth of Lee's remaining army was killed or wounded. One of the surgeons commented, "That hideous day ended at last."[53]

Most of the remaining Hunton brigade was captured at Sayler's Creek, along with their commander and about six to seven thousand other men, but not Fitzhugh. Pickett had escaped the disaster and, ignoring his dismissal, he rode at the head of what was left of his

Virginians, perhaps beside his family members. Only eleven survivors of Loudoun County's original "Bloody Eighth's" one thousand men trudged on, led by Fitzhugh. With them were the 56th Virginia's survivors. Both units officially were led by Major Michael Spessard, who just two years before cradled his dying son's head on the field at Gettysburg.

AAG Fitzhugh was now one of only two surviving officers in Hunton's Brigade, in an army that was irretrievably broken. Some men started for home in despair as soon as their column passed a road headed in the right direction. Though he probably had at least a concussion, Fitzhugh stayed with the rest struggling on over muddy roads with nowhere else to go, and loyal to the other despairing men they knew as friends and family. It was April 6 and unconditional surrender was only days away while Fitzhugh rode on, pursued by Grant's army. Rations at Farmville were captured on the eighth, marking the end of any continuation.

೦೪೫೦

On April 9 in the pouring rain, (former General) George Pickett surrendered his division's remaining 1,031 men in dirty, tattered butternut or gray uniforms, only sixty of whom still bore weapons. He wasn't their commander anymore, wasn't even in the army after Lee's dismissal, but he couldn't emotionally abandon the role, his family members, and his brave Virginians. At the end, Captain Edmund Clare Fitzhugh was second in command of Hunton's few remaining troops when they shuffled into Appomattox. Major Spessard, who like Fitzhugh was in his late forties, shared Fitzhugh's determination to keep going. Following them were 149 exhausted survivors of the consolidated brigade. Loudoun County's "Bloody Eighth," first organized by Hunton, now included Pickett's own brother-in-law, Dr. Blair Burwell, when they surrendered. General Grant mercifully ordered that rations be issued to the starving Confederates immediately.[54]

General Robert E. Lee rode out among his troops to their cheers while officers and soldiers alike cried. Fitzhugh may have cheered his distant cousin with extra feeling. As night fell, young Virginian James Whitemore said: "The moon, watery and pale, is up. Last night we were free soldiers of the Southern states; tonight, we are defeated men, prisoners of war of the Northern states." Men lay in camp with nothing to do but eat. Fraternization between the Confederate and

Figure 31, The rural road into Appomattox, site of the Confederate Army's surrender. The National Park Service keeps it looking much like it did when E. C. Fitzhugh passed with the remnant of General Hunton's brigade. *Photograph by Candace Wellman.*

Union soldiers started immediately as old acquaintances were renewed, and all were relieved it was over. In the coming days, Fitzhugh likely spoke with his Fort Bellingham acquaintance Colonel James Forsyth on General Phil Sheridan's staff. Pickett and Fitzhugh certainly talked more, probably at length. Perhaps they even traded a few words in "chinuk wawa" as veterans of the Pacific Northwest had done in notes across the lines during the war, until respective commands heard about it and feared spying in the language they didn't speak.[55]

It only drizzled on the tenth. Once official paroles were printed, Spessard and Fitzhugh started signing them for soldiers. Pickett also signed paroles for his men, though officially he was no one's commander. Fitzhugh's own parole had been signed by Lee's copyist earlier when he promised he would not take up arms against the government again. The valuable paper proved that an ex-Confederate was a paroled prisoner entitled to free transport on trains and boats if he had to cross federally occupied territory to get home, and ordered that he be left undisturbed in his journey.[56]

Fitzhugh's parole said: "Belonging to Pickett's Division, Army of Northern Virginia, this day surrendered by General R. E. Lee, CSA, commanding said Army to Lt. General U. S. Grant, commanding

Armies of the U.S. Done at Appomattox Courthouse, Virginia, April 9, 1865." Each prisoner of war had a property list, and Fitzhugh's was two horses and personal baggage. Part of that personal baggage was Fitzhugh's copy of the first issue of Whatcom's *Northern Light* from the Fraser River Gold Rush summer. He had carried the memento of happier times through the entire war and kept it for a future return to Sehome.[57]

On April 12, Lee held the formal surrender. The defeated army marched between two columns of Union soldiers who offered silent respect for the bravery the Confederates had displayed. If Fitzhugh still had his staff officer's revolver, he stacked it with the others. The ceremony lasted from six a.m. to four p.m. Pickett's Division marched in last. Fitzhugh and Spessard led the 149 men of Hunton's Brigade who had waited for many hours, less any who were in such poor physical condition they couldn't participate. Missing were Ann's family members in Mosby's Rangers because they disbanded only on April 21, without ever surrendering.[58]

On the thirteenth, the former Confederates started home with three day's rations and their protective parole. The service record is not clear about Fitzhugh's two horses that he still had with him at surrender. General Lee knew that farmers needed a horse to get crops in and feed their families, so it is likely that Fitzhugh kept one while the other went to a horseless farmer-turned-soldier. Union soldiers offered money to many for the trip home and were often refused. The Confederates believed that the Yanks didn't understand Southern hospitality, and that they would be helped along the way. Of course, along the way home, many houses had nothing left to share.[59]

Two days after the formal surrender, Lincoln was assassinated.

War deaths totaled 618,000 men. Fitzhugh was not among them. Wounded and courageous to the end, he was among those who survived to start over.[60]

CRBO

What were Captain Edmund Clare Fitzhugh's thoughts when he rode his starving horse into Appomattox? As he took the tangle of roads that would finally lead him up the lane to Ann?

He had enlisted at a time when men of his age did not have to, and many planter-class men paid substitutes. He took on the inspector and assistant adjutant general duties at a time when desertions increased exponentially, and what had seemed like the prospect of routine legal work changed drastically to include presiding over executions. To return to Virginia and fight with his family and friends whose lives and property were in danger meant alienation from his friends in Washington Territory.

Good men died of disease and wounds, while the living experienced extreme fear, depression, and hopelessness in the last year of the war. Fitzhugh had to maintain optimism and determination to help soldiers carry on, and not desert or collapse as rations ran out and anger with officer mistakes took over. Despite that, he could take pride in staying until the end when he was forty-four with a serious head wound. He had acted heroically in battle when others did not, despite being shot and left for dead. He had gone from being the brigade "paper pusher" to fighting hand-to-hand alongside the privates. He led the desperate remnant of a once-proud Virginia brigade into the unknown at Appomattox. He had done all he could to protect Virginia, Stafford County, and his Fitzhugh and Grayson-Carter families, while undergoing the extreme mental and physical stress of the end. His head wound hurt, and his financial future was uncertain. He didn't know what had happened in the last days to his younger sisters.

There was much to occupy Fitzhugh's thoughts and emotions as he rode out of the village of Appomattox Courthouse, put the Blue Ridge on his left and started on the circuitous route home, and hopefully to "Nannie." He had married only months earlier and now he didn't know where she was or even if she had survived Richmond's end.

CHAPTER 12

Retreat to Iowa

FORMER CAPTAIN "ED" FITZHUGH left Appomattox Courthouse on
April 13 with thousands of other paroled men heading home peacefully to resume their civilian lives. He had long hair, a dirty beard, and
dried blood on his head. Unless a Union doctor found time to help, he
had a dirty bandage over the wound on his forehead. After multiple
battles and little food in the last weeks, his gray officer's uniform hung
loosely, tattered, torn, and filthy. His horse was dirty and thin, too.

Taking the shortest route north to Loudoun County meant a
network of dusty country roads with no straight way home. Keeping
the Blue Ridge always on his left horizon, Fitzhugh and the remaining
few men from Hunton's Eighth Regiment trudged home. The former
soldiers were aided with directions and after their three days of rations
were gone, perhaps some food from local people, if they had anything
left to share. Fitzhugh rode about two hundred miles through the
foothills to get to Bellefield and Newstead. It took six long days, but
many more for those on foot.[1]

On April 19 Fitzhugh rode up Bellefield's lane. Ann wasn't at
Newstead or Bellefield. Elizabeth Carter wrote in her diary: "Captain
Fitzhugh came from the Army. Left his wife in Richmond." Was this
statement judgmental when it emphasized "his wife" instead of using
Ann's name? There are no entries that show her presence until much
later. She had her own stories to tell of privation, fear, and a desperate
flight from Richmond to sanctuary. Her brother Richard, and cousins
Alexander and Dr. John Grayson, were not there to greet them, all dead
on the battlefields. Her brother Thomas and cousin Robert would come
after Mosby's Rangers disbanded without surrendering on April 21 but
leaving four hundred imprisoned. On May 24, five weeks after Fitzhugh
arrived, Elizabeth Carter's diary entry finally included Ann, who with
her sister Mary and "Captain" Fitzhugh came to Bellefield for dinner.
Their aunt served a "large dish of peas" and "fried chickens." It was very
different from the sumptuous meals once served from Oatland's bounty

that included the winter bananas and strawberries from the plantation's greenhouse. Still, the family had enough to eat when many did not.[2]

Though Oatlands, Bellefield, and Newstead were largely intact, troops from both armies had taken animals and crops. The family economy was not completely ruined, as most former slaves had stayed to the war's end. Ann's brother Thomas was quoted later that the "Graysons lost everything in the great war of the rebellion." The Confederate veteran's perspective came from the past he had fought so hard to preserve. It is worth noting that the Grayson-Carter family still had enough money for him to return to medical school in Pennsylvania immediately and graduate the next year. Elizabeth stayed at Bellefield, leaving Oatlands in the care of its future heir, her son George Carter and his wife. It wasn't long before impoverished and homeless Carter relatives turned to the family base and found sanctuary living at Oatlands. Their financial support would inevitably drain the plantation's income.[3]

E. C. Fitzhugh was never a farmer, but now he had to help. After the war, planter-class people who had never done physical labor had to do housework, cook, and labor in the fields. Fitzhugh still had his legal and financial skills, and on June 12, 1865, he "walked off to Washington to see how things lay." He walked because any horse the family had was needed for the fields or to pull a buggy for aging relatives. Why did Fitzhugh go to Washington? It is difficult to believe he walked over fifty miles in the summer heat and humidity unless he had a definite goal in mind. Former General Hunton was imprisoned in Fort Warren on a Boston Harbor island. The former Leesburg lawyer could be of no assistance in getting Fitzhugh started again in a legal practice. Perhaps Fitzhugh went to see some of the Union officers and others he had known in the Northwest, many now working in the federal government. They might have a position for him or know of other jobs. No employment offer was forthcoming. He stayed in the Washington area for a month while he accessed his contacts, probably boarding at his sister's home. When Fitzhugh walked up the Bellefield lane again a month after he left, he brought Elizabeth Carter a gift, an expensive gallon of whiskey purchased with scarce U.S. dollars.[4]

Four months after Fitzhugh returned from the war, newly-released former General Hunton came calling. The pair rode over to

Bellefield for tea with Elizabeth and Ann's sister Mary, now her aunt's companion. Thirty-six-year-old Ann did not go, perhaps suffering with morning sickness or a migraine. Pregnancy news would not have been shared with an unrelated man. The conversation at tea that afternoon probably centered around war stories fit for ladies' ears, and perhaps the job outlook.[5]

At the same time, the former Grayson-Carter slaves who had stayed to the end of the war were making decisions for their own futures. The relationship between the two groups who called Bellefield and Oatlands home seems complicated. By August they were leaving family by family, though not all. Seventy to eighty adults and children stayed. One group started their own community on a corner of Oatlands and called it Gleedsville for its ex-slave new landowner. Men worked the Carter's farm to keep it afloat while some women still worked in Elizabeth Carter's home. She paid wages, gifted new dresses at Christmas, and recorded the births of their children. On Christmas Eve 1862, Jacob and Sophy Howard had been married by Elizabeth's minister in the Bellefield dining room, a week before Lincoln issued the Emancipation Proclamation. They continued to work for wages after the war, purchased some of the Bellefield land, and founded Howardsville.[6]

Fitzhugh fell from his horse and was "badly hurt" a month after Hunton visited, according to Elizabeth Carter's journal. She recorded no additional details, but if he suffered another head injury so soon after the war wound, it might explain some of his erratic life over the next twenty years. He may have also been drinking heavily, as army officers and "Southern gentlemen" were well known to do, and as bored Washington Territory men did with any excuse. However bad the accident was or its cause, he recovered enough to leave for Washington, DC, again three weeks later on October 15, so he did not have a major broken bone.[7]

Part, or all, of the reason for October's trip seems to have been the first congressional hearings about compensating the Hudson's Bay Company (Puget Sound Agricultural Company unit) for the agricultural land peremptorily seized by Washington Territory. Their reparation lawsuit had no priority during the war but was reactivated, and former territorial justice Fitzhugh would testify. In Washington Fitzhugh was away from Ann's illnesses and the tedium of a rural post-war plantation while he also job-hunted. It was another fruitless effort.

1866

By January 1866 the Fitzhughs' lives seem centered around Ann's difficult pregnancy. At thirty-six with a first pregnancy during post-war disruption, she was in considerable danger and was constantly sick, if not in pain. Her aunt frequently sent her former slaves Sarah and midwife Fann(y) to Newstead to check on her. Ann didn't sleep well, and Fitzhugh sometimes brought her breakfast from Bellefield, at least once her favorite Sally Lunn bread and hot tea made by ex-slave Hannah.

When Ann was eight months pregnant, Carter sent Fann to Newstead with a vial of myrrh. The valuable remedy was difficult and expensive to obtain. Probably used as an antiseptic for childbirth in this case, it was also used for stomach problems and congestion.

Despite Ann's difficult pregnancy, that same month Fitzhugh went to New York City to testify at the congressional hearings about the value of the Hudson's Bay Company's Puget Sound Agricultural Company lands. He was a valuable witness available on the East Coast, having been the governor's military aide during the Treaty War, and on the territorial Supreme Court during some of the earlier litigation. Fitzhugh was apparently in touch with people from his old days in Washington Territory who knew where to find him. They were most likely John Tennant, his friend James Tilton (who was now the secretary of the testimonies), or George Gibbs, former treaty negotiator who wrote to W. W. Miller about Fitzhugh's appearance at the hearings.[8]

In May 1866 the family readied Ann for her first childbirth. Her aunt sent whiskey, an iron bedstead, and bedding to Newstead with former slave Jacob Howard. Ann could grasp the birthing bed's iron bars during labor. Carter also had a small bag sewn and filled with bran for her niece to place between her teeth during labor. She checked on Ann herself and sent caregiver Milly several more items for the event: a bottle of fine wine, candles, and bread. On May 16 Ann Fitzhugh Grayson Fitzhugh gave birth to "a very fine large daughter" at 10:30 a.m. on a sunny morning.[9]

In Fitzhugh's world, a father did not have to consider his wife's wishes for a new baby's name if he did not want to. He named his Northwest son with Mary for Territorial Secretary Charles Mason instead of his father or another ancestor. Southern men in the early territory who initially did not intend a son born to a tribal custom wife to inherit their estate commonly chose a non-family name. For example, George Pickett named his son after his friend Territorial Surveyor James Tilton. It implies that they were still hoping for a later all-white child who would be their legitimate heir. Within a few years, the men often changed their minds, which in turn led to a series of marriage law amendments that would legitimize their children to make them legal heirs for probate. In the case of the baby girls there initially was more variety in how they were named. For example, Julianne's name came only through her mother's line.

However, when Fitzhugh used his right to name Ann's daughter, he did something incomprehensible to modern sensibilities. It is difficult to believe that Ann favored the name given to her newborn daughter. Fitzhugh decided his little girl would be Cora Bowie Fitzhugh, named for his dead third wife, Ann's predecessor.

The new father didn't linger at home while Ann went through the hard first weeks with a newborn. He left for Washington, DC, before the month was out, again apparently in relation to the Hudson's Bay Company hearings. There he met with his old friend James Tilton, still the secretary for testimonies, and former Territorial Chief Justice Edward Lander, the attorney representing the Hudson's Bay Company in the reparations dispute. While Tilton was an old personal friend, Lander's conversations with Fitzhugh were probably strained due to the martial law arrest of the former chief justice. Dinner conversation topics with Tilton probably included the ongoing Congressional debate about how to conduct Reconstruction, including restoration of rights to former Confederates like Fitzhugh. Once again, no job offer resulted from his meeting with the former associates or other contacts.[10]

Falmouth was far out of Fitzhugh's way, and he may not have gone there, but Mary Eliza and Dr. Magruder probably knew about its post-war situation, if he even briefly considered moving back where he still owned a house. Stafford County was under military law and would be for at least another year, though Falmouth was being called a Union-sympathetic town. Still, authorities might not be professionally friendly to a former Confederate AAG. Eleven thousand slaves had been freed, and the population of all races there declined by over twenty-six percent by 1870.[11]

The county was economically devastated after the armies left. The lumber industry was gone. There were few horses and untilled fields abandoned for four years were weeds and brush. The large landowners were not used to laboring for themselves, so they planted easy crops of corn for hog feed, but that depleted the soil. Stafford County became known as Virginia's poorest until the ruined economy recovered when Quantico Marine Base was built during World War I. Until then, Falmouth was stuck with the nickname "Hogtown."[12]

North in Loudoun County, the Grayson-Carter clan still had fertile land and adjusted to their new reality. Elizabeth Carter kept records of the wages she paid her former slaves, now essential employees. That 1866 summer, the families who worked for her went over to Upperville for a picnic and game day, a large social gathering that would not have occurred before freedom came.

During the summer of 1867 Ann had a terrible spell of migraine headaches. While they incapacitated her at Newstead, Fitzhugh lay ill in Baltimore. It was most likely a return of his "Panama fever," leading to a much longer stay, and he ran short of money. Ann had to ask her aunt for eighty dollars to send him, a very substantial amount in the post-war economy. Why was he in Baltimore? Probably to make a long-delayed visit to his late wife Cora's Maryland family. He was back home about two months after he left Ann and baby Cora. The Fitzhughs seemed to be in a holding pattern without a stable income, but a new opportunity presented itself.[13]

IOWA

In a stiff wind off the Appalachians' Blue Ridge after a night of snow, the Fitzhugh family left for Iowa on November 12, 1867. With them went Ann's cousin "Fitz" Grayson and former slave Dora, whose motivation to go far from anyone she knew might be a story in itself, unless the aged former slave woman in Iowa was her family.[14]

Ann's brother, Benjamin ("Ben") Grayson IV, had at twenty-one in 1855 carried their famous ancestor's name to Iowa when the land office opened. By 1867 he had a growing family and solid real estate business in Fort Dodge. As soon as Ann and Ben's brother Thomas finished medical school, he joined Union veteran Ben in the booming central Iowa town. The men were an example of brothers on different sides in the war, but when reunited they left it behind. Many enthusiastic letters must have passed back and forth between the Grayson brothers and the Fitzhughs until they convinced Ann and brother-in-law "Ed" to join them for a new beginning where destruction and despair would not surround them.

The U.S. Army established Fort Dodge in 1850 on the Des Moines River, upstream from the new state's capitol. Though it was built to defend the western edge of white settlement, nothing happened that needed defending. After thirty months the army sold the fort to the post sutler and left. He turned the parade grounds into the town square and a public park as soon as he took possession. The army had discovered coal nearby, and soon gypsum to make plaster was found, triggering railroad barons' interest in building a spur line to the new town. After the land office opened, it attracted speculators whose profits from town lots and surrounding land fueled non-agricultural growth. Many Virginians and other Southerners moved to Iowa in the 1850s, and the state remained slavery-sympathetic Copperhead until Republicanism took over in 1860. By then a thousand people lived in the riverside town, including at least one lawyer, enabling them to start a municipal court.[15]

When Ann's brother Ben moved to Fort Dodge for a civil engineering job in 1855, there were no Iowa towns west of it until distant Sioux City was founded in the northwest. He had worked for a railroad and located "land warrants" before becoming the local agent

Figure 32, Fort Dodge, Iowa, in 1860. The town probably looked somewhat improved when Edmund and Ann Fitzhugh arrived in 1867. Photograph by Samuel Rees, now in the public domain. *Old Fort Dodge Facebook page and State Historical Society of Iowa.*

for several eastern land agencies and a speculator himself. In the war his job had been distribution of wages, but perhaps for a health reason he returned to Fort Dodge in 1864 before the war ended. It is worth noting that Nancy Robinson, a blind one-hundred-year-old former slave, lived in his home at the time of the 1870 census, and probably when the Fitzhughs arrived with ex-slave Dora. Ben, his wife, and their Irish housekeeper probably cared for the elderly woman who likely came as a slave to Fort Dodge with Ben's Virginia wife.[16]

Iowa sent over 76,000 men into the Union Army; 13,000 of them died (usually of disease), and 8,500 wounded returned home. No other state had a higher percentage of young men in the military. In Fort Dodge it was almost every young man, organized into two companies. This would be the local population that Confederate Captain E. C. Fitzhugh and his family would join after their long winter journey from Virginia.[17]

Another economic boom started after the war, bringing in several former Union army surgeons as well as ex-Mosby's Ranger Dr. Thomas Grayson. Ann's brother told people in Fort Dodge that he believed in abolition but fought out of "chivalrous love of his state." This is an interesting tale he told, because the woman whose home he grew up in was Loudoun County's biggest slave master. When he said the Graysons had been impoverished by the war, it may have been true to the extent that most of the family's ex-slaves left, and they could not support young men when elders were in need. However, Elizabeth Carter had still been able to pay wages, medical school tuition, and send a large sum to Fitzhugh when he was ill in Maryland. Dr. Grayson moved to the town his brother was so enthusiastic about and served the residents and homesteaders for thirty-six years, until his death. One of his fellow doctors had fought on the Union side in the Battle of Bull Run when Thomas was wounded. Despite that, and probably some other grievances among local Union veterans, Thomas was so well-liked that he was voted into the local Grand Army of the Republic post, the organization of *Union* veterans.[18]

◌◌◌

If the war had not happened, it is unlikely that all three siblings from an elite Virginia clan, with thousands of acres of land and comfortable homes, would have moved to Iowa. As well, there is no easy explanation for why the Fitzhughs, a baby, and Ann's cousin left the comfort of

Newstead and Bellefield that wintry day to go to a place on the midwestern plains subject to tornadoes and blizzards, even if money and sometimes food staples were scarce in Virginia. It seems more likely that they would have waited until spring, but they didn't. Elizabeth Carter's journal does not make clear the reason for the late fall departure in miserable weather. Her lack of entries in the days leading up to their departure might indicate that there was some dissention, and Elizabeth did not want to include such personal information in her journal.

When the Fitzhugh party arrived in the Iowa cold, the group had crossed the Des Moines River by ferry after a stagecoach or wagon journey from Des Moines, since the railroad spur from the main line had not been completed. When Fitzhugh took his late wife Cora Bowie to Washington Territory, it was a completely foreign geography and atmosphere from Maryland for the new bride. Fitzhugh again took a once-sheltered wife to a place far removed from any cities, as well as foreign in population and post-war atmosphere. Her only concrete impression of Iowa life when she was still in Virginia had been a set of enormous elk horns that Ben sent home to be hung over the Oatlands drawing room door. For most of Ann's life, she had also been used to house slaves taking care of her needs, and the presence of former slave Dora only reminded Iowans that Ann was a Virginia woman from a slave-holding Confederate plantation.[19]

During the next half-dozen years Fort Dodge grew economically and culturally. Fitzhugh's law practice was one of nine that served the town and thousands of homesteaders. Entrepreneurial ventures surrounded the town square, and mining became the dominant economic driver when the coal and gypsum discoveries were followed by gravel, clay, and limestone. All were supported by a bridge over the river that supplanted the ferries, and the joyous completion of the railroad into town in August 1869. Ann's sister Mary Stuart Grayson then left Virginia and "went west" to join her three siblings in the less-isolated town where she would soon marry an Episcopal minister. Veterans introduced baseball, a well-known artist moved into town, and newspapers arrived weekly.[20]

There were a few jarring developments for the Virginian newcomers. Large Memorial Day parades honored the town's Union veterans who quickly took over the county's elective offices. Unlike other states, Iowa voted to give black men the vote in 1868. They also voted to allow black children to attend the public schools, though there were only a few at new Lincoln School when Cora Fitzhugh was old enough to join her cousins. And if Wing Lee, Chinese owner of the laundry, had children they attended the school also.[21]

Between the Fitzhughs' arrival and 1872, Ann gave birth to three more children: Mary in 1868, Alexander three years later, and Margaretta in 1872 when Ann was forty-three. Fitzhugh named his son for his father this time, and the others were also Fitzhugh and Grayson family names. In 1874 when Margaretta was two, the Fitzhugh marriage between the two first cousins broke. It had produced four children in the space of about six years and survived the post-war devastation, Fitzhugh's injuries, and the move into an uncertain financial future in Iowa. Ann was fortunate to have so much family in Fort Dodge to support her and the children, but she was not a fragile Southern belle. She had been through her parents' deaths as a child and the terrible war years when her familiar world collapsed. Ann Fitzhugh Grayson Fitzhugh had the strength to guide her four children in a fatherless future—a strength she might not have recognized as a young woman. Ann and the children moved back to Elizabeth Carter's home in Virginia sometime during the next five years.

There is only one hint about the events that sent Fitzhugh back to Bellingham Bay and his family back to Virginia. A year before the marriage ended, the *Bellingham Bay Mail* reported on July 19, 1873, that there was a rumor among the "old settlers" that the absent judge had gone insane in Iowa. Apparently John Tennant, now U.S. Deputy Surveyor, superintendent of schools, probate judge, and farmer, was in touch with him by mail, and two months later he told the newspaper that the rumors were false. However, a drinking problem in combination with being shot in the forehead and the horseback accident only months apart, may have affected Fitzhugh's cognition and emotional stability. Having demonstrated a dangerous temper in the past, he could have been physically abusive to Ann as he had been to Julia and Mary. Alternatively, he may have simply abandoned his family. It is equally possible that Ann (or her brothers) told him to leave.

CHAPTER 13

What Cheer

F ITZHUGH HAD BEEN GONE FROM Washington Territory almost eleven years following Cora's death, his farm being seized, and his quick departure for the war. There had been no local newspaper reports of his whereabouts or situation until the 1873 article containing the insanity rumor, debunked shortly after by John Tennant.

After Tennant passed the bar, he became the only lawyer in post-gold rush Bellingham Bay. After serving as prosecutor for a short time, the now-Republican lawyer, mentored by Fitzhugh in the coal mine office, had been elected county commissioner and legislator, as well as probate judge. By 1873 Tennant was hugely successful as the county's first agriculturalist, Deputy U.S. Surveyor, superintendent of schools, and still probate judge. Virtually a territorial Renaissance man, he'd been one of the first party to summit Mount Baker, and in the summer of an eruption at that. To locals, Tennant's word was gold when he denied the insanity rumor, and yet there was some truth to the rumor because Fitzhugh's life had apparently started its long downward spiral.[1]

Over a year passed without more news of Fitzhugh at Bellingham Bay, until the December 1, 1874, *Bellingham Bay Mail* reported that Sehome's founder had died. However, before the next issue was printed for the entire county, Fitzhugh arrived in town on a Puget Sound steamer, and showed up at the newspaper office's door. He hadn't gone home to Falmouth after leaving Iowa. The couple had sold his father's house four years earlier and there was no place to live. His younger sisters had moved on with their lives. And so, he journeyed across the country and north from San Francisco by sea to Bellingham Bay.[2]

The *Mail*'s editor James Power wrote that the man he'd never met had been in "excellent health during his long absence," contradicting his prior statements that Fitzhugh was insane, and then dead. He vaguely implied that Fitzhugh had left his family permanently, rather than just taking a long trip. Fitzhugh presented the surprised editor with what he said was the first copy of the *Northern Light* issue number one, printed during the 1858 gold rush summer. Fitzhugh said he kept it because he had helped "the enterprise in a most liberal manner," but it seems to have taken on the aura of a talisman for him. Apparently treasuring the landmark issue's characterization of him as known for "veracity, fidelity and ability," he carried that worn newspaper through the Civil War and the next nine years.[3]

Whatcom and Sehome in 1874 were in poor economic condition and without prospects. The area had never recovered from the gold rush crash in either population or commercial vigor. Four years before Fitzhugh arrived, only 534 people lived in all of Whatcom County, including the San Juan Islands (now officially U.S. territory) and what would become Skagit County. By 1874 Roeder's lumber mill was in ashes, and rebuilding was questionable due to seasonal low water that couldn't power the machinery. As well, Russell Peabody had died in 1868, and his birth family continued to fight over his land claim. The present owners of the much-expanded Sehome Mine had flooded it with salt water after workers were killed in several underground fires and cave-ins. With the only local industries in shambles, employees of both fled to the new Stikine River Gold Rush upstream from the town of Wrangell, Alaska, where William King Lear (Mary Fitzhugh's former husband) welcomed them. Some went to other logging operations, and others took out homesteads near John and Clara Tennant around the lower Nooksack River. The only brick building in Whatcom, the former T.G. Richards & Company store, housed the county courthouse, jail, a few small businesses, and served as the waterproof community gathering place. There were only a few other stores dotting the sad landscape and the newspaper would abandon the town for growing LaConner on Swinomish Slough a few years later. Edward Eldridge, Henry Roeder, and others were desperately strategizing how to attract new residents.

Editor Power concluded his article about Fitzhugh with a stilted regret that "the present outlook at this point does not offer sufficient inducement for the location among us of a man of the Judge's well-known energy and enterprise." In other words, no job existed. Not for an aging lawyer with a drinking problem.

Fitzhugh had not come all the way to Whatcom only to visit the "old settlers" like Tennant and Roeder, but Power didn't mention his other mission. He wanted to connect with his now-grown son Mason who he had abducted and abandoned at least fourteen years earlier.

The children had a terrible foster family experience, and had been dumped on the streets alone for a time until John and Mary Campbell, homesteaders west of Olympia, took them in. Fitzhugh had apparently been informed by someone, perhaps James Tilton, that his children were there because John Campbell's journal recorded at least one letter after the war ended. Living with the Campbells, Julianne and Mason became inlet "neighbors" with James Tilton Pickett, son of Fitzhugh's friend and Confederate commander General George Pickett. "Jimmie" was informally adopted by his loving foster parents after Pickett was impoverished by the war and could no longer pay his son's board, able only to correspond. The two biracial boys born above the Bellingham Bay beach were nearly the same age.[4]

As a young adult Mason had found his mother on Orcas Island with husband George Phillips. After the long absence from his eldest son's life, Fitzhugh found him in Sehome, and apparently thought the young man would be thrilled and receptive to a reconciliation. He asked Mason if he'd like to move with him to San Francisco. Mason replied, "Go to Hell."[5]

Figure 33, Mason Fitzhugh, son of E. C. Fitzhugh and Mary (Qui'las) Fitzhugh Lear Phillips. E. A. Hegg, photographer, c. 1880–1900. *Howard Buswell Papers and Photographs, #bus0052, Western Libraries, Archives and Special Collections, Western Washington University.*

☙❧

Teenager Lottie Roeder Roth met Fitzhugh during the 1874 visit, and she later summed up what was happening: "he returned to the scene of his early adventures...Poverty and dissipation clouded the last years of his once brilliant career." In other words, alcoholism was destroying him.[6]

Fitzhugh left Bellingham Bay for San Francisco alone. For a new resident instead of a traveler, he found the city of his memories much changed since his original 1854 departure for Bellingham Bay. San Francisco's population reached about fifty thousand and continued to grow despite economic downturns and the repeated fires that boosted the Northwest lumber market. By the 1870 census one hundred fifty thousand people crowded around the most important harbor on the West Coast.[7]

Where once scores of beached sailing vessels turned mud flats into a collection of ad hoc stores and hotels, larger buildings now rested on top of foundations made of the abandoned hulls. The uncoordinated private timber wharves had produced a mess of rotting shanties and ships extending out from the city. Public outcry demanded a proper seawall that would protect and enable a modern port. By Fitzhugh's arrival, a state commission controlled the port with major plans to construct a modern seawall that would complement ongoing post-war improvements to the military defenses of San Francisco Bay.[8]

As always, Fitzhugh sought to move ahead with personal connections. It hadn't worked in Washington, DC, and it didn't seem to work for several years after his arrival in San Francisco, though he certainly sought out old California, Washington Territory, Virginia, and Confederate acquaintants in the city. William Winlock Miller, his former Democratic Party crony and friend in Olympia, was spending increased time in San Francisco where he had many investments. However, if Miller could have been of help with a job in either location, he died within months of Fitzhugh's arrival without steering his old friend to an employer.[9]

Fitzhugh found that the city's cadre of influential men he once knew had greatly changed with the passage of two decades and the Civil War. Law partners Edmund Randolph and A. P. Crittenden, who had given him his first attorney job in the city, were both dead. Randolph died in San Francisco as the Civil War began, and Crittenden's extra-marital lover Laura Fair killed him in a sex and murder scandal that riveted the nation five years before Fitzhugh returned. Sehome Coal Mine syndicate member Charles Minturn, the transportation magnate, died the year before Fitzhugh's return. Former syndicate member R. P. Hammond lived in the city and had risen to president of the California-Pacific Railroad, but if Fitzhugh contacted him, he was apparently not interested in providing a long-term job to his alcoholic former associate.[10]

One person stands out from the others: Calhoun Benham. Fitzhugh had many connections with Benham, whose mother-in-law was Fitzhugh's cousin. The men had been law partners before Benham led the coal mine syndicate that sent Fitzhugh to open the Sehome Mine. Like Fitzhugh, Benham became an Assistant Adjutant General in the Confederate army and both men also had stories to tell of being duel seconds for the late politico David Broderick. Post-war, despite Benham's imprisonment for gun running, involvement with the Knights of the Golden Circle, and staff service under Confederate generals Patrick Cleburne and Braxton Bragg, he was once again a prominent San Francisco lawyer. Despite their relationship that spanned over two decades, Benham did not offer Fitzhugh a partnership, or even an associate's job.[11]

Politically, post-war Democrats had resurged on a white-supremacist, states-rights platform to again control the state. The mass migration of Southerners into the state, hoped for by the Knights of the Golden Circle, never materialized, but both city and state were friendly to ex-Confederates like Fitzhugh. Former senator and KGC leader William Gwin, who spent most of the war imprisoned on suspicion of treason, unexpectedly returned. He lived on a farm, invested in mining, and rose to Democratic powerbroker and San Francisco society leader again. Fitzhugh's longtime mentor also did not give him a job.[12]

Fitzhugh managed to arrive on the cusp of a general economic upheaval. Eight months later in August 1875 there was a run on the Bank of California, forcing its closure that triggered financial turmoil lasting several years, part of the nationwide depression that had begun in October 1873. A disastrous fire in Virginia City, Nevada, virtually destroyed the center of the Comstock mining area and greatly reduced gold shipments to San Francisco's mint.[13]

Fitzhugh did not appear as a lawyer, or anything else, in the 1876 or 1877 city directories, which were each based on information collected the previous six months or so. Finally, in 1878 Fitzhugh had a listing. The "Great Register" indicated that he had registered to vote that May, and his occupation was now "clerk," a humiliating come down for a former Washington Territory Supreme Court justice and General Eppa Hunton's Assistant Adjutant General. Fitzhugh had found his way to acquaintances from Washington Territory who gave him an opportunity to stabilize, with a job at the beginning of "The Great Seawall Project" that would not be finished until 1908. When completed, the project would round out the shoreline, add acreage to the city, and provide a solid foundation for construction of modern long concrete piers to replace the haphazard rotten wooden ones. Fitzhugh lived in an area of small residential hotels close to his old Portsmouth Square haunts, and only a block away from the harbor improvement project offices. Two years later, he was still living in that neighborhood, at the boarding home run by Anna Daley and her deputy sheriff husband.[14]

Fitzhugh knew the man in charge of the entire harbor project from their Bellingham Bay days. Well-liked young topographical engineer Lieutenant George Mendell designed Fort Bellingham and then Camp Semiahmoo for the Boundary Survey Commission. He also laid out the military road section between town and fort and gave the construction contract to Fitzhugh. Known as a "painstaking and conscientious" engineer, the West Point graduate from Pennsylvania took on increasingly important projects in the Corps of Engineers, but was teaching philosophy at West Point when the war started. He left to supervise construction of Baltimore's defenses, and then Massachusetts' coastal defenses. These projects led to the post-war assignment to expand and repair the critical defenses of San Francisco Bay, including Lime Point, Fort Point, and Alcatraz Island. Mendell was the obvious choice to organize the long-desired modernization of the city's harbor and that of smaller harbors around the Bay.[15]

Project clerk Fitzhugh almost certainly worked with, and probably under, Isaac W. Smith. Born in Fredericksburg across the river from Falmouth a few years after Fitzhugh, the two may have known each other in their small riverside world. In Washington Territory they served together on Isaac Stevens's Treaty War staff. Civil engineer Smith headed several lighthouse construction projects, respected enough that "Isla de Bonilla," a small island in the Strait of Juan de Fuca, was re-named for him. During the Civil War Smith became a Confederate engineer on the defenses of Richmond and Petersburg where Fitzhugh's brigade worked and quartered during the final winters, and where the two probably met again. After the war, Smith returned to Washington Territory and surveyed the prime meridian for surveying townships in Whatcom County to Canada. After engineering jobs in the expansion of railroads to the West and others up and down the West Coast, in 1876 Smith began to work with now-Lieutenant Colonel Mendell on water issues in San Francisco. In 1878 the State Harbor Commission made him the chief design engineer for the San Francisco seawall. It was then that Fitzhugh became a clerk in the project's office. Two thousand feet of the project were finished in the first three years after Fitzhugh joined the office crew.[16]

Fitzhugh was dismissed or resigned from the seawall project about the same time as Smith's design job ended. He again listed himself as an attorney in the 1881–82 Langley's directory, continuing to live at Anna Daley's West End House. Calhoun Benham apparently still didn't want to bring Fitzhugh into his firm.

At age sixty-two when the next directory was published (with information from late 1882–early 1883), Fitzhugh had "no profession" and had moved out of the Daley boarding home into another, probably cheaper one, much farther from downtown. Edmund Clare Fitzhugh's life was winding down in a manner the Virginia blueblood probably never anticipated. He was, after all, a First Family of Virginia, Stafford County, "Boscobel" Fitzhugh.[17]

◇✿◇

Sometime in 1883, Fitzhugh moved to the gold rush-era What Cheer House, still carrying the name of the sailing ship that brought smallpox to the S'Klallam people of his former wives and father-in-law. In the 1850s, professional men like Fitzhugh made the What Cheer House near Portsmouth Square their own. Built to last of brick and masonry even before fires tore through the city, it boasted fireproof doors between floors and water forced to the roof where owner Robert Woodward stored hoses, buckets, and axes to fight any blaze that threatened. He built a four-story addition to the swanky hotel so he could house six hundred men, even though he forbade alcohol consumption. Illustrated ads presented clients who appeared to be sophisticated, well-dressed people with carriages at the ready, a group of men like Fitzhugh in the 1850s that the hotel sought to attract. That was then.[18]

By the 1870s, grander hotels existed. Railroad baron and former coal syndicate member R. P. Hammond lived downtown at The Palace Hotel, which covered nearly an entire block in Italianate magnificence and trumpeted itself as equal to the best hotels in New York City. In contrast, already by 1861, a small What Cheer ad in the *Daily Alta* had proclaimed "Better and cheaper than ever." Woodward's temperance hotel for the city's prosperous had sunk to second tier before the war.[19]

In 1883, thirty years after its ballyhooed construction, the street in front of the What Cheer was still dirt and the sign under its awning advertised twenty-five cent baths. A liquor store was next door, handy for alcoholics. A photograph makes it painfully obvious that the What Cheer had entered "fleabag" status. The small gold rush-era rooms had been designed for one man with a single bed, marble washstand, mirror, and dresser. Fitzhugh's life had shrunk down to his tiny dingy room with its aged furnishings and sheets that were probably threadbare and stained. Now sixty-two, Fitzhugh led a life of alcoholic poverty.[20]

Figure 34, The What Cheer House on Sacramento Street in San Francisco. Visible next door in this 1866 photograph by Lawrence & Houseworth, publisher, are the liquor store and bath house that signaled its downward spiral. Those enterprises remained as the hotel deteriorated; E.C. Fitzhugh died there in 1883. The What Cheer House was destroyed in the 1906 fire; its site is now marked by a plaque and it is registered as a historical landmark. *Library of Congress, Prints and Photographs Division, #LC-USZ62-17738.*

On November 24, 1883, hotel staff found Edmund Clare Fitzhugh dead of a stroke ("apoplexy") in bed. The death certificate listed him as a lawyer and married.[21]

Two days later, the *Evening Bulletin* ran a paragraph about "ex-judge" Fitzhugh's death, with information supplied by someone who had clearly known him for a long time, probably Calhoun Benham. It was placed between a piece about the hard-working ladies of the upcoming "Flower Fete" benefit, and a notice about the quarantine of two immigrant "lepers." The abbreviated obituary recounted his term in the Virginia legislature, law partnership with Crittenden and Randolph, job with the coal mine, and appointment to the bench by President Buchanan. There was no mention of his law firm partnership with Benham or his work on the harbor project. It concluded with "during the past year his health had been failing." Most city deaths deserved only a line or two in the paper, so the *Bulletin* acknowledgement of his death gave it at least some minor importance. There was no notice of a funeral or where Fitzhugh would be buried. The *San Francisco Call* printed a nearly identical obituary.[22]

Fitzhugh's obituary falsely said he had moved to Virginia where his wife died before he entered the Confederate Army, and then said he left a wife and children living in Iowa. Neither woman was identified by name, nor were the children. His children Julianne and Mason were ignored entirely. Besides the erroneous information supplied to the paper that Cora had died in Virginia, it was apparent that Fitzhugh had no idea that his fourth wife Ann and the children had returned home some years earlier.

News reached Washington Territory within a week of the San Francisco newspapers' announcement of Fitzhugh's death. A short obituary appeared in Olympia's current newspaper, the *Washington Standard,* on December 7, 1883. Two days earlier, the *New York Times* had already reprinted the *Call*'s obituary. Because Fitzhugh had been a federal judge, the East Coast's premier newspaper saw fit to notice his death. Via the paper the news would eventually reach aging Confederate officers, Virginia acquaintances, and probably Ann.[23]

Someone who knew that Fitzhugh was a Mason arranged for his burial in the Masonic Cemetery, probably the friend who spoke to the newspaper. The cemetery was located far inland in a cluster of four, but in 1901 the growing city needed that acreage and emptied all of them.

Fitzhugh's remains and all the others were removed to Woodlawn Cemetery in the town of Colma, where he was re-buried with other Masons. If Fitzhugh ever had a tombstone, it was likely used as fill in the construction of the Golden Gate Bridge approaches.[24]

Epilogue

Lottie Roeder Roth's 1926 vivid description of Edmund Clare Fitzhugh that began this book reveals the complexity of his character and his life. Sometimes he rose above his identity and personality, and sometimes he failed miserably. She afforded no other person such a detailed introduction in her county history. He was not a forgettable man.

Fitzhugh's personal life included four women he married in the space of just ten years: Julia, Mary, Cora, and Ann. Each brought him different kinds of power and wealth, just as generations of Fitzhugh wives had before them. The time they and their children spent with Fitzhugh changed all of their lives negatively.

Julia Seya'hom Fitzhugh Barkhousen

Samish-S'Klallam Julia did not stay single for long after she tribally divorced Fitzhugh. She found a man of her own choosing, a special man who already knew the young woman in Sehome. He was County Auditor Henry C. Barkhousen, gold rusher and mine employee.[1]

The scrupulously ethical Barkhousen ran afoul of Fitzhugh's election tactics more than once and was unafraid to publicly protest them. Like Julia, he knew tragic and unexpected loss. His father and brother died in a cholera epidemic in Rushville, Illinois, when Henry was an infant. While Julia dealt with the knowledge that her daughter would grow up without her, if she was safe at all, Henry had grown up never knowing his father or brother. Every walk in the small town took him past the cemetery where a mass grave without markers held his lost family members. Another child of the same years, newspaper chain founder James Scripps, described the marker-less place as a daily reminder to the children of the "dark uncertainties of life."[2]

Julia married Barkhousen by tribal custom, and forevermore her kind and loving husband called her his "happy whirlwind." Their first child was born while Henry served in the legislature and as probate judge, before the couple took a land claim at Padilla Bay in what is now Skagit County. Their neighbors were other cross-cultural couples, generally with Samish wives Julia already knew, probably cousins. There in a spacious farmhouse they raised seven children while Barkhousen farmed, served as county commissioner, justice of the peace, and local postmaster for ten years.[3]

In 1878 their happy marriage was threatened by a criminal indictment for "fornication," brought against Barkhousen and eight other "Old Settlers." After long experience with Hudson's Bay Company "country marriages" (i.e. tribal custom), Catholic missionaries left couples to make their own decisions when, or if, to obtain a "legal" marriage. However, new Protestant missionaries and families who moved into the territory in the 1870s were not as accommodating and pushed the indictments in several counties. The indictments were also politically motivated, as evidenced by the prominence of the intermarried men singled out for prosecution among the many other long-time husbands. Barkhousen fought pressure to say his tribal custom marriage to Julia was not legal, saying he held the relationship both legal and sacred. He argued that to call it otherwise would dishonor Julia and brand their children illegitimate. While some of the other defendants got "officially" married to avoid prosecution, Henry and Julia instead obtained a marriage license from the county auditor to have some related official paper. Territorial Supreme Court Chief Justice Roger Greene published his legal opinion on the issue before any trials could take place. The Sunday School teacher referenced the original marital contract between Adam and Eve without any human officiant. He declared all tribal custom marriages to be binding legal contracts between two people equal to county or church-sanctioned marriages. If they weren't, he wrote, then all business contracts subsequent to Adam and Eve would be void, including those in Washington Territory. The indictments were quietly dropped. Julia and Henry's great-great-granddaughter said, "All my life I have been told what a wonderful man Henry Barkhousen was."[4]

Julia and Julianne reunited after many years. All but one of Julia's eight children married non-tribal people, and neither she nor her children officially enrolled in the Samish or S'Klallam tribes, though she continued to participate in traditional culture.[5]

Julia died a widow in 1934, cared for by her nearby family, and some of her many descendants still live in that area.[6]

MARY FITZHUGH LEAR PHILLIPS[7]

Edmund Fitzhugh's S'Klallam secondary wife's future was much different from the "happy whirlwind" Julia. Mary's was marked by survival, not happiness with a loving new husband. She returned to work in settler homes at the bay for a few years until she married entrepreneur William King Lear, the caretaker of deserted Fort Bellingham where he also ran a small store on the trail to the Nooksack River. Son of a famous early army officer, Lear had already abandoned an indigenous wife and child at Fort Cascades on the Columbia River where he ran the fort's store. After the U.S. bought Alaska, Lear abandoned Mary and his son Billy to buy former Russian Fort Wrangel and found the town of Wrangell. He married at least twice more, each time abandoning his wife after she had a baby.[8]

Mary's last husband was George Phillips, a Welsh barrel-maker at the Orcas Island lime kiln. Their two little boys died in an explosion after they dropped a match into a blasting powder container. Mary was never the same. She had a little girl named Maggie and was pregnant again when she shot and killed her alcoholic, abusive husband on Christmas Day 1878. She gave birth to her son Thomas in the Port Townsend jail after she was charged with murder, a hanging offense. With community support, the former judge's wife was only convicted of manslaughter and sentenced to two years in the distant territorial prison where she was its first woman prisoner. Maggie and infant Thomas went with her as "boarders," while her son Billy Lear went to his father in Alaska. The prison's name "Seatco" was from the Lushootseed word meaning "devil place," and so it was. Though its second female prisoner killed herself after two weeks, Mary survived with what a historian called "critical grit." Mary and both children were forbidden visitors while they lived in a shack built against the outside wall for them. Mary often sacrificed her own food rations for her babies.[9]

After Mary's release, Mason took over as guardian from the court-appointed one. He sent five-year-old Maggie (who probably spoke little English) to the Tulalip Indian School where she soon died. After living for a time with Mason and his wife, Mary spent the rest of her life with her son Billy Lear and family at Lummi Reservation. She died between 1920 and 1922 and was buried on Orcas with her little boys, or at the reservation. She has hundreds of descendants in the Northwest.[10]

Ann Fitzhugh Grayson Fitzhugh

By at least 1880, fifty-year-old Ann and her children were back in Virginia with her elderly aunt at Bellefield and four black "servants," including cook Hannah Warner (age 70) who had made breakfast for the miserably pregnant Ann in 1866. She never divorced Fitzhugh, responding "married" on all records. She died in her seventies in 1905 and was buried in Portsmouth, Virginia, where two of their daughters lived.[11]

∽

Which mother a Fitzhugh child had made a difference. Mason and Julianne, children of his cross-cultural marriages, dealt with identity questions that never rose for his children with Ann Grayson. These dilemmas of Fitzhugh's mixed-blood Northwest children were typical in the late 1800s and their choices had consequences.[12]

Julianne Fitzhugh Reid

Julia's daughter Julianne Fitzhugh's descendants' knowledge about her parents became muddled as the years passed. As one great-great-granddaughter said, "I know nothing about Julia Sea'hom (sp) and next to nothing about Edward (sic) Fitzhugh, only that he was from Virginia and that the Fitzhughs were related to the Lees… Our native heritage was not part of my growing up. It was never mentioned by my grandmother, grandfather, or mother." Julianne's daughter Christina's version was that her mother grew up in the South until Fitzhugh brought her and her brother to California after the Civil War. One hundred years later, a family member did know that Julianne was "an Indian." In the racially biased atmosphere at the end of the nineteenth century, rather than feeling pride, much of the Reid family's indigenous heritage through Julianne had been changed, denied, or nearly erased.[13]

Julianne had been deposited with a white family on the south Sound with Mason. Her aunt Ruth Seya'hom Shelton believed that the foster father died, and his widow put the half-native children out on the street, corroborated by what both of them said. By summer 1869 the pair lived with Mary and John Campbell on Kamilche Inlet west of Olympia. They had a stable family home, education, and farm chores. Since Mary Campbell sent a letter to Fitzhugh in Iowa in June of 1870, he was at least minimally interested in his children, if not sending money to board them after the war's end.[14]

Mary Campbell trained Julianne to be a nurse, and probably a midwife like herself. Coincidentally, Julianne cared for Aaron Collins, the terminally ill foster father of Fitzhugh's friend (and war commander) George Pickett's son James Tilton Pickett.[15]

In her teens, Julianne had a stalker until newcomer Reuben Reid helped drive the man away. On October 15, 1870, Julianne married widower Reid under sunny autumn skies with Mason and all the neighbors there to celebrate the match.[16]

As a logger's wife, Julianne moved with her husband a number of times, first to Sacramento, California (perhaps near his older children), then Idaho for twelve years and a series of western Washington logging towns.[17]

Figure 35, Reuben Reid and Julianne Fitzhugh, daughter of E. C. and Julia Seya'hom Fitzhugh Barkhousen, probably photographed about the time of their marriage in 1870. *Collection of Candace Wellman, gift of descendant Julie Chandler Owens.*

The family lived in Quilcene (population fifty-three in 1880) on the Olympic Peninsula's Hood Canal off and on for a number of years. One of the other women there at the same time was Julia Yesler Intermela who Julianne inevitably knew well. Also the daughter of a tribal custom intermarriage, Julia Intermela's father was Henry Yesler, one of Seattle's founding fathers. Her mother was Susan, daughter of Suquardle (Chief "Curley") of the Duwamish village where Yesler put his mill. After Yesler's white wife arrived from Ohio, he sent Susan away and kept Julia in the home as a "maid." The Intermelas and Reids moved to Port Townsend and left logging behind. Reid worked as a carpenter before starting a delivery business, and Charles Intermela became sheriff and county treasurer.[18]

When Julianne moved to Port Townsend, she lived near her S'Klallam grandfather's extended family longhouse at Kah'tai lagoon. She may have known some of her nearby S'Klallam relatives after her reunion with her mother, but it would have been typical of the period for her to have been so fully immersed in white society that she wanted no public relationship. The Port Townsend newspaper included features on the Reids in its "society" news.[19]

By 1900, Julianne and her eight children were counted as "white" in the census. It listed Julianne's birthplace as California, with both parents born in Virginia. That was unlikely to have been a mistake. Her daughter Christina described Julianne as a "peppery" woman who controlled her family, not that different from Fitzhugh's approach.[20]

Julianne died at age 97, survived by six of her children, along with ten grandchildren, nineteen great-grandchildren, and two great-great-grandchildren who were Fitzhugh's great-great-great grandchildren. Descendants continue to live in Port Townsend and elsewhere in the Northwest.[21]

Charles Mason Fitzhugh

Mason's life was the most difficult and complex of the children after he was taken from Mary and ended up on the streets with Julianne.

At thirteen he repeatedly ran away from John and Mary Campbell's farm where he and Julianne had found a permanent home. One time Campbell found him in distant Olympia at the home of Rebecca Howard, the renowned African American restauranteur. Mason may have already known the Howards' adopted mixed-blood son, who was about the same age and also the grandson of a Coast Salish leader. Both boys were fathered by abusive men and lost their mothers in similar ways.[22]

After Mason ran away three more times to the logging settlement of former Territorial Indian Agent Mike Simmons, the Campbells let him live with young C. C. Simmons and his half-native wife and attend school there. Mason struck out to find his mother a few years later and moved to the Orcas lime works where he learned the cooperage trade from George Phillips and witnessed the horrific death of his little half-brothers. His temper could get the better of him as a young man, evidenced by an altercation when he started a fight in Sehome that ended in a minor stab wound and coverage in the newspaper.[23]

In 1878 Mason witnessed the shooting death of his stepfather and had to testify at his mother's murder trial. By the time Fitzhugh's eldest son was twenty-three, both of his parents had committed homicide. Both had been tried for murder, a hanging offense.[24]

Within months of his mother's incarceration, Mason married. His bride was sixteen-year-old cousin Mary Pearson, daughter of his mother's niece Sarah Seya'hom and coal miner Charles Pearson. The pair bought land on Orcas Island where the surrounding families were mostly cross-cultural, or Coast Salish ones living at the remaining longhouses. Mason farmed while he worked as a cooper and, after having their daughter Laurinda, they buried more than one small child in Madrona Cemetery at the head of East Sound.[25]

Mason's wife contracted breast cancer and he went to Port Townsend to ask Julianne to help care for her. Although his sister was a nurse, she was pregnant, and a "lady" didn't talk about such things openly. She told him she could not help. He believed it was because Julianne was a snob who thought Mary was living more "Indian" than she was. His wife died, leaving him alone with his seven-year-old daughter. He never spoke to his sister again.[26]

Mason did not abandon his child as his own father had done and raised Laurinda alone. S'Klallam cousins frequented the island, and the pair were drawn into his mother's family circle, as well as keeping a relationship with Julia Barkhousen's family. Laurinda married Richard Squi'qui, son of a Point Elliott Treaty signer, and they moved to Lummi Reservation for a more traditional life near her grandmother Mary Fitzhugh Lear Phillips and uncle Billy Lear.[27]

Mason married widow Maggie Anderson when he was fifty-six. She was the daughter of Tom She'kle'malt, owner of the only 1884 law Indian homestead in the San Juan Islands. His longhouse and 160 acres lay along San Juan Island's northern coast where his family had lived for centuries, and he still hosted large potlatch gatherings. The couple lived there with their daughter Pearl and Maggie's previously adopted son. Their home was a frame house, but She'kle'malt refused to leave his longhouse. As well as farming, Mason transitioned to tribal fisherman, and reef netted with his S'Klallam relatives near Stuart Island,

She'kle'malt's hereditary fishing location. The She'kle'malt homestead became known as the "Fitzhugh Place."[28]

By then, Mason's identity confusion showed. Island cross-cultural families found themselves increasingly a minority among often prejudiced new settlers. The census in 1900 and 1910 counted him as "white," yet a year later on his 1911 marriage record, he listed himself as mixed white and Indian, as he had in the 1880 census. After some years, he enrolled himself and his daughters in the Jamestown S'Klallam tribe. Half-Hawaiian acquaintance Charlie Kahana said that Mason's looks enabled him to "pass" as white if he wanted to, and no one would see his mixed heritage if they did not know him. Mason had inherited the fairness and light eyes of his grandmother Elizabeth Clare Fitzhugh.[29]

Three years before Mason died, he and Maggie signed a community property agreement, an unusual document for its time, but it may have related to the Indian Homestead Law rules of inheritance if she died first. Mason died of heart failure at age seventy-three and was buried near his small children on Orcas. When Maggie died, Pearl and other relatives buried her in their ancestral cemetery on the homestead.[30]

If anyone inherited E. C. Fitzhugh's personality besides his "peppery" daughter Julianne, it was his son Mason's daughter Pearl. Local residents described her as having a great sense of humor, but she was feisty if you said or did the wrong thing. She once berated the manager of a local resort near her land about "white privilege." Pearl became a commercial fisherman with Mason's half-brother Tom Phillips, who lived with her after she was widowed, and he'd been divorced. Because she had no children when she died, the pristine waterfront She'kle'malt homestead became the subject of a years-long contested probate case that captured regional headlines.[31]

Cora Bowie Fitzhugh (the daughter)

Edmund and Ann Grayson Fitzhugh's first child knew her father for only eight years. A brilliant student, Cora graduated from the University of Virginia at fourteen, and earned a master's degree at seventeen before teaching Latin at the University of Texas. For more than fifteen years she was the principal of St. Andrew's Select School for Girls, a college preparatory day school in Fort Worth. Cora died unmarried in 1945 and was buried in Portsmouth, Virginia, near her mother Ann.[32]

MARY GRAYSON FITZHUGH

Born three years after the war, Mary was Fitzhugh's first child born in Fort Dodge. Her husband, Reverend Arthur Conover Thomson, spent most of his childhood in Shanghai, China, where his father was a missionary. A University of Pennsylvania alumnus, he wed Mary after graduation from Virginia Theological Seminary. They moved to Fredericksburg just downstream from her father's hometown, where she had her own duties as the Episcopal priest's wife. In an area heavy with Fitzhughs, she may have crossed paths with relatives, especially if she visited Aquia Creek Episcopal Church where her ancestor had contributed to its construction. The Thomsons served in Cincinnati, Ohio, before he became rector of Trinity Church in Portsmouth, Virginia, where Mary's mother Ann moved. After nearly forty years of service, he became the Diocesan Bishop of Southern Virginia. Mary returned to Portsmouth after her husband died and lived into her late eighties.[33]

ALEXANDER FITZHUGH

When Fitzhugh left Iowa in 1874, his son Alexander was three. When he was fourteen, the teenager with his father and grandfather's thick black eyebrows and darkest eyes moved from Virginia back to Iowa where his uncles lived and completed his education in Des Moines. He knew about his father's war service and judicial position but did not follow in Fitzhugh's destructive footsteps. As a history of Iowa stated, he had a "great interest in constructive civic affairs."[34]

After owning a printing company, for twenty-five years Alexander was the highly visible Executive Director of the Greater Des Moines Committee and manager of the Des Moines Coliseum. He appeared in the newspaper frequently, including after he led the Bureau of Municipal Research supporting a multi-state effort to name a "mostly hard-surfaced" highway from Massachusetts to Colorado the "Roosevelt Highway" and promote its towns. The Republican, Bridge-playing Rotarian and golfer's public life could not have been more different from his father's, except for his Masonic membership and Episcopalian church membership.[35]

Alexander married kindergarten teacher Leone Lippincott and raised two daughters, one named after his mother and the other after his father's sister Virginia. That implies a continuing relationship with the Fitzhugh family in Virginia despite Edmund's absence from his children's lives. Alexander died in Des Moines in his late eighties after a long, respectable life.[36]

Margaretta Fitzhugh

Margaretta was born only two years before her father left, leaving her with no memory of him. She was named for Margaretta Fitzhugh Grayson, both Edmund's aunt and Ann's mother. Margaretta's life left little public notice, and when she died unmarried in her seventies, she was buried in Portsmouth, Virginia, near her mother and sisters Cora and Mary.[37]

 ∞

As Fitzhugh's progeny and their children carried his genes (and sometimes his fierce eyebrows) into the future, they did not carry his name there. Mason and Alexander had only girls survive to adulthood, so the "Fitzhugh" surname of Edmund's branch of the storied family ceased to exist, though Edmund has hundreds of descendants.

Notes

INTRODUCTION

1. "Roisterer" means a partier who often takes it too far; Roth, *History of Whatcom County,* 1: 38.

2. Fischer, *Albion's Seed,* 214–16; Bernard Bailyn, *The Barbarous Years: The Conflict of Civilizations 1600–1675* (NY: Vintage Books, 2013). 184–86; George H. S. King Papers, Fitzhugh-Ficklin files; Rasmussen, "First Fitzhughs of Virginia," 81; *PSH,* 10/2/1862.

3. Jerrilynn Eby MacGregor to author, 9/23/2022.

4. Sally Lee Fitzhugh to author, 9/24/2000, Stafford County, VA.

5. Rasmussen, *First Fitzhughs of Virginia,* 82; "The Fitzhugh Family," *Genealogies of Virginia Families, v. II,* 838–61. *Virginia Magazine of History and Biography,* 1982; Isabella Grant of "Oatlands" to G.H.S. King, 10/25/1953 and genealogical charts. George H. S. King Papers, VHS.

6. Felder, "The Falmouth Story," 10/1981, 11/81, 12/1981, 1/1982; HistoryPoint.org 5/30/2003.

7. Homer D. Musselman, *Stafford County Virginia Veterans and Cemeteries* (Fredericksburg: Bookcrafters, 1994); George H. S. King, *Register of St. Paul's Parish 1715–1798* (Fredericksburg: GHS King, 1960).

8. MacGregor, *They Called Stafford Home; The Free Lance* (Fredericksburg), 9/14/1901. George H. S. King Papers.

9. Boscobel Chain of Title, 6/1986. Fitzhugh Family File. Virginia Room, Fredericksburg Public Library.

CHAPTER 1.

1. R. Bolling Batte Papers, biography card files, Library of Virginia, Richmond.

2. Will of Thomas Fitzhugh of "Boscobel," Stafford County, VA. George H. S. King Papers, Fitzhugh File #7, VHS.

3. Newspaper notice, George H. S. King Papers, File 37.

4. Master Alumni file, and history of the medical school, University Archives and Record Center, Univ. of Pennsylvania Archives. www.archives.upenn.edu; Steele, *Bleed, Blister, and Purge,* 47–48.

5. Dr. Alexander Fitzhugh portrait in private hands, viewed by the author; Mark McCutcheon, *A Writer's Guide to Everyday Life in the 1800s* (Cincinnati: Writers Digest Books, 1993), 169.

6. Stephen Fried, "A New Founding Mother," *Smithsonian Magazine* (9/2018), 16–22; Steele, *Bleed, Blister, and Purge,* 2, 48.

7. Mutual Assurance Society, Policy #274 (1811) MF reels 6, 9, 11. Central Rappahannock Library; Regimental history compiled by M.E. Lyman, Sr. 1/8/2002, www.vagenweb. org.; 1815 List of Stafford County merchants, www.departments.mwc.edu.

8. www.colonial-settlers-md-us; www.sedgwick.org; Frederick County Wills and Administrations 1795–1816 (Genealogy Pub., 1983), 14.

9. Declarations of the Mutual Assurance Society, MF reels 6, 9, 11. # 274, 2449. Central Rappahannock Library, Fredericksburg. Jerrilynn Eby MacGregor to author, 1/13/2019; Schools, *Virginia Shade*, 33.

10. *Political Arena*, 9/18/1827, 2.

11. Will of Thomas Fitzhugh of Boscobel, 9/4/1815, codicil 2/26/1819. Typescript, George King Papers.

12. George Washington's childhood home, Ferry Farm, was a mile out the river road; Myrtle Estelle Skinker, "Fourscore Plus: Stories of Thomas Julian Skinker II (unpub., 1932), 72; Schools, *Virginia Shade*, 4.

13. Schools, *Virginia Shade*, 5, 7–8, 10; Sallie French Fitzhugh to Larry Evans, 1976. Unpub. ms., Fredericksburg Public Library.

14. Schools, *Virginia Shade*, xvii.

15. The highway's name referred to "King" Carter, not the British king; Schools, *Virginia Shade*, 7–8, 16, 23, 25–26, 29–30, 112.

16. This part of Falmouth's past during Edmund's life did not appear in any local histories prior to Norman School's 2010 history of its slave community; Schools, *Virginia Shade*. 33–35.

17. Schools, *Virginia Shade*, 38, 129, 226.

CHAPTER 2

1. Steele, *Bleed, Blister, and Purge*, 5.

2. Schools, *Virginia Shade*, 34; Stowe, *Intimacy and Power*, 132.

3. 1835 Georgetown College Prospectus. Georgetown Univ. Archives, Lauinger Library; Jonathan Elliott in Grace Dunlap Ecker, *A Portrait of Old Georgetown*, Project Gutenberg release 1/6/2009. No original date. n.p.

4. 1835 Georgetown College Prospectus (Georgetown University Archives, Lauinger Library); Stowe, *Intimacy and Power*, 134.

5. www.slaveryarchive.georgetown.edu.

6. Georgetown College Entrance Book 1834–35, Georgetown Univ. Archives, Lauinger Library, 43.

7. Stowe, *Intimacy and Power*, 131.

8. Georgetown College Entrance Book, 43; 1835 Georgetown College Prospectus.

9. Eliza died on 4/17/1836; *Political Arena* 4/22/1836; *Alexandria Gazette* 4/26/1836.

10. Fox-Genovese, *Within the Plantation Household*, 197, 202, 228, 230.

11. Lynn Conway, Georgetown Univ. Archives to author, 10/19/2000 re dismissal records.

12. Georgetown University Alumni Directory card. Ledger E, 20. Georgetown Univ. Archives.

13. U.S. Military Academy Cadet Application Papers, 1805–1866. File #247, Edmund C. Fitzhugh (1838). NARA MF 688; *Encyclopedia of Virginia Biography,* vol. 2 (Richmond, VA, 1915). n.p. Online at ancestry.com.

14. USMA Cadet Application #247.

15. *Virginia Magazine of History and Biography* (1901) 8: 431.

16. Leonard, *The General Assembly of Virginia,* 39.

17. James L. Morrison Jr. *The Best School: West Point, 1833–1866* (Kent, OH: Kent State Univ. Press, 1986), ix.

CHAPTER 3

1. Sheila Biles, USMA to author, 12/5/2000 re arrival date; Waugh, "What in the World," 33.

2. Waugh, "What in the World," 35.

3. Alan and Barbara Aimone, "Much to Sadden—and Little to Cheer: The Civil War Years at West Point." *Blue & Gray Magazine* (12/1991); Waugh, "What in the World," 37; Biles to author, 12/5/2000, re dismissal date.

4. Roth, *History of Whatcom County* 1: 38.

5. No existing Virginia record indicates admittance to the bar; *Democratic Reporter,* 9/29/1843.

6. Bryson, "The History of Legal Education in Virginia," 180–81.

7. Leonard, *The General Assembly of Virginia,* 390; William Gwin to U.S. Atty. General Black, 3/15/1858.

8. Leonard, *The General Assembly of Virginia,* 423; Kimball, *American City, Southern Place,* 6–7.

9. Kimball, *American City, Southern Place,* 58.

10. *Biographical Directory of the US Congress, 1771–present.* Online at Infoplease; Richards, *Isaac I. Stevens,* 304; Phillips, "Fayette McMullen."

11. Kimball, *American City, Southern Place,* 35.

12. Virginia Auditor of Public Accounts, Claims for Payments of Militia fines Collected, RG 48, Box 1354, #477, Library of Virginia; Jerrilynn Eby MacGregor to author, 1/11/2019; "Virginia Militia," www.staffordcountymuseum.org.

13. Detailed election records no longer exist. Stafford County Land Tax Records 1834–1850, MF, Library of Virginia.

14. E. C. Fitzhugh to R. H. Dickinson, 2/16/1846. Slavery in the U.S. Collection, American Antiquarian Society; Michael B. Chesson, "Richard Henry Dickinson," *Dictionary of Virginia Biography,* Library of Virginia, www.lva.virginia.gov.

15. Kimball, *American City, Southern Place,* 156; C. B. Dew, *The Making of a Racist: A Southerner Reflects on Family, History, and the Slave Trade* (Univ. of Virginia Press, 2016), 127–28.

16. "Lumpkin's Jail" and "R.H. Dickinson," www.encyclopediavirginia.org (Virginia Humanities); "Lumpkin's Jail," wikipedia.

17. *Richmond Enquirer,* 3/10/1846.

18. Stafford County Deeds, Book oo, pp. 270–72. 6/12/1847, Stafford County Circuit Court records.

19. Alexander's death, 8/12/1847, noted in *Alexandria Gazette,* 8/19/1847; *Richmond Enquirer,* 10/29/1847.

20. Fannie Brown quoted in the 1930s, in John Hennessey, "The Slave Auction Block at William and Charles." https://npsfrsp.wordpress.com/2017/09/14/the-slave-auction-block-at-william-and-charles/. Accessed 8/15/2022.

21. In 2020 the slave auction block used by Edmund C. Fitzhugh in 1847 still occupied the same Fredericksburg corner. The city finally removed it that summer when official and popular consensus was reached after a century of debate. Removal had been complicated by its inclusion on the National Register of Historic Places. The stone was placed in the local museum with explanatory context. Descendants of the people sold on the stone no longer had to pass by the reminder of their family's pain caused by Edmund Fitzhugh and others. Stafford County Personal Property Tax Books, 1850; Stafford County Minute Book 1852–1867, 205. Stafford County General Index. All MF at Library of Virginia; City of Fredericksburg official website, www.fredericksburgva.gov.

22. Fox-Genovese, *Within the Plantation Household,* 200.

23. Jane Conner (Stafford Museum and Cultural Center) to author, 11/15/2015; Fitzhugh Family File, Central Rappahannock Public Library; George H. S. King Papers.

24. Barry McGhee, clerk, Fredericksburg Circuit Court, interview 10/2/2000; "A List of the Taxable Town Lots in the County of Stafford made by Travers D. Moncure, Commissioner of Revenue, 1850." www.departments.mwc.edu.

CHAPTER 4

1. Jackson, *Gold Dust,* 18, 62, 119.

2. Joseph Glover Baldwin, *The Flush Times of Alabama and Mississippi* (London: D. Appleton, 1854), 212.

3. Jackson, *Gold Dust,* 70, 72.

4. Jackson, *Gold Dust,* 119.

5. *New York Herald,* 12/18/1848; Delgado, *To California by Sea,* 48, 51; Jackson, *Gold Dust,* 77, 78, 82, 113.

6. *New York Times,* "The Mosquitos Are Coming for Us," 7/28/2019; Steele, *Bleed, Blister, and Purge,* 87; Jackson, *Gold Dust,* 80; Fitzhugh to W. W. Miller, 7/22/1860, WWM Papers.

7. Kimball, "A Brief Sketch of San Francisco"; Muscatine, *Old San Francisco,* 106.

8. *Philadelphia Public Ledger,* 10/15/1849, in Browning, ed., *To the Golden Shore,* 412.

9. Kimball, "A Brief Sketch of San Francisco"; Robert Phelps, "All Hands Have Gone Downtown: Urban Places in Gold Rush California" in Starr and Orsi, eds., *Rooted in Barbarous Soil,* 129.

10. Bancroft, *History of California,* 7: 229.

11. Levy, *They Saw the Elephant*, 54–55.

12. Asbury, *The Barbary Coast*, online, n.p.

13. Kimball, "A Brief Sketch of San Francisco"; Bancroft, *History of California*, 7: 778.

14. Browning, *To the Golden Shore*, 349.

15. Asbury, *The Barbary Coast*, online, n.p.; Bancroft, *History of California*, 7: 237–42; Gary F. Kurutz, "Popular Culture on the Golden Shore" in Starr and Orsi, *Rooted in Barbarous Soil*, 281.

16. Jenny Lind was a famous actress of the time; Janet Marschner, *California, 1850: A Snapshot in Time* (Sacramento: Coleman Ranch Press, 2000), 126, 130; Bancroft, *History of California*, 7: 237–42.

17. Christopher Herbert, *Gold Rush Manliness, Race and Gender on the Pacific Slope* (Seattle: Univ. of Washington Press, 2018), 140; *Philadelphia Public Ledger*, 1/15/1850; *New York Evening Post*, 11/15/49; Browning, *To the Golden Shore*, 386, 406, 412.

18. Shuck, *Bench and Bar*, 261–69.

19. Lockwood deserted his family to go to sea, then was in and out of law until he died in a shipwreck; Shuck, *Bench and Bar*, 277–79, 577–80; Robert Hastings, "Rufus Allen Lockwood," *California Historical Quarterly* 34 (1955): 243–48.

20. Mary Floyd Williams, *Papers of the Vigilance Committee 1851, 1, no. 7* (Academy of Pacific Coast History, 1919), 210; Bancroft, *History of California*, 7: 679.

21. Benham's mother-in-law was Susan Fendall Marbury. Charleen Oerding to author, 11/1/2001; Doug Fendall to author, 2004.

22. Lotchin, *San Francisco 1846–1856*, 18, 214, 217, 300.

23. Howard A. DeWitt, "Senator William Gwin and the Politics of Prejudice" www.ohlone.edu.

24. William Gwin to U.S. Attorney J.S. Black, 3/15/1858. E.C. Fitzhugh nomination file. Dept. of Justice R660, MF 1343, Roll 1. NARA; Muscatine, *Old San Francisco*, 357.

25. Bancroft, *History of California*, 7: 230.

26. Roth, *History of Whatcom County*, 1: 38; Washington Territory, 3rd Judicial district journal, 1859. WSA, NW.

27. Wells, "The End of the Affair?," 1807, 1810, 1817.

28. Wells, "The End of the Affair?," 1819, 1821.

29. Quinn, *The Rivals*, 127–28.

30. Wells, "The End of the Affair?," 1822.

31. Charles Duane in Shuck, *History of the Bench*, 232–33.

32. Muscatine, *Old San Francisco*, 263; Duane in Shuck, *History of the Bench*, 232–33; George H. Tinkham, *California Men and Events* (Panama-Pacific Expo Edition, 1915), online. www.usgennet.com, ch. 7.

33. Wyatt-Brown, *Southern Honor*), 357.

34. Bancroft, *History of California*, 7: 732.

35. Kimball, "A Brief Sketch of San Francisco," n.p.

36. Heinrich Schliemann in Lotchin, *San Francisco 1846–1856*, 175–76.

CHAPTER 5

1. LeCount and Strong, comp., *1854 San Francisco Directory* (San Francisco Herald). Digitized by San Francisco Public Library, 24, 54; www.britannica.com.

2. Levy, *They Saw the Elephant*, 209, 217; Muscatine, *Old San Francisco*, n.p.; www.californiahistoricallandmarks.com. #650.

3. *New York Times*, 9/29/2019.

4. Buse, "Machine of Manifest Destiny," 22, 26; Trowbridge, "Journal of a Voyage," 393–94.

5. Taylor, *The Quadra Story*, 28–29, 36; H.R. Crosbie, "The San Juan Difficulty," *The Overland Monthly* 2, no. 3 (1869): 202.

6. The PSCC was formerly known as the Puget Sound Coal Mining Association; Haight, "The Story of Bellingham," 29; Roeder, Narrative; Lawson, *Autobiography*, 27.

7. Roth, *History of Whatcom County* 1: 22,23; Trowbridge, "Journal of a Voyage," 401.

8. Roeder, Narrative; Hewitt documents in *WHQ*, 133–48.

9. Hewitt documents, *WHQ*, 142; Historylink.org; Alonzo Poe to William W. Miller, 12/8/1853. WWM Papers; *Samuel Brown v Roeder, Peabody & Company* #185. 3rd District, WA Terr., #185 (1859), Appeal #210.

10. Lotchin, *San Francisco 1846–1856*, 71.

11. Vigilante Committee Log Book, Box 1, Folder 2. San Francisco Library; www.findagrave.com; www.joincalifornia.com

12. www.penelope.uchicago.edu; *Morning Union*, 12/1/1891; William Ellison, "Memoirs of the Honorable William Gwin," *California Historical Quarterly*, 19: 256; Roeder, Narrative.

13. Roeder, Narrative; Wikipedia; www.findagrave.com.

14. 1850 San Francisco Directory; Meany, "Captain William Hale Fauntleroy," 289–300; Wallace, "The Fauntleroy Family," 2–18.

15. *Washington Pioneer*, 1/28/1854.

16. Washington Territorial Legislature, Act of 7/17/1854; Whatcom County Claims book, 1, #329; 1850 Oregon Donation Act; Whatcom County Deeds A, 3; Whatcom County Claims 1, 7. All in WSA, NW.

17. Robert A. Bennett, *A Small World of Our Own* (Walla Walla WA: Pioneer Press, 1985), xiv.

18. Used as a community cemetery, Poe's Point became known as Dead Man's Point; Tim Wahl to author 2/25/2002, re Fitzhugh affidavit.

19. A. M. Poe to W. W. Miller, 11/3/1853, WWM Papers.

20. Derrick Pethick, *Victoria: The Fort* (Vancouver: Mitchell Press Ltd, 1968), 90.

21. Island County Land Claims 1, 2/23/1854, 3/2/1854; Island County Land Claims 2, 5/1/1854. Both at WSA, NW; Wahl to author, 2/25/2002; *P-D*, 9/16/1854.

22. George Gibbs, "Report of Mr. George Gibbs to Captain McClellan, on the Indian Tribes of the Territory of Washington, March 4, 1854." Northwest Ethnohistory Collection, Box 42. CPNWS, WWU.

23. *P-D*, 9/28/1855; 11/6/1857; *Alta*, 10/7/1857.

24. Wellman, *Peace Weavers* and *Interwoven Lives*.

25. Sheffer, "A Story of Pioneering," serialized in *Lynden Tribune*, August 1909; Jeffcott Papers, WWU.

26. Ruth Shelton to P.R. Jeffcott, 2/5/1954. Jeffcott Papers.

27. Barrett family genealogical research; Sampson, *Indians of Skagit County*, 25–26; Ruth Shelton to Wayne Suttles, Suttles to author, 5/5/2000.

28. Contradictory sources say Chet'ze'moka was Seya'hom's brother or cousin; Lambert, *The House of the Seven Brothers*, 5, 12, 15.

29. William Jarman v Alice Jarman (Skagit County Civil Case #89, 1879), WSA, NW; Susan and Fred Miller, *Samish Island, A History from the Beginning to the 1970s* (Mount Vernon, WA: F and S Miller, 2007), 68.

30. Ruth Seya'hom Shelton to Percival Jeffcott 11/18/1953, 2/5/1954; Harriet Shelton Dover to Mrs. R.S. Simpson, 4/28/1941. Both in Jeffcott Papers.

31. Shelton to Jeffcott; Dover to Simpson. Both in Jeffcott Papers; Clinton, *Plantation Mistress*, 84, 179; George Fitzhugh quoted in Butruille, *Women's Voices from the Western Frontier*, 79.

32. Wayne Suttles, notes; Shelton to Jeffcott, 2/5/1954.

33. Suttles, notes; Shelton to Jeffcott, 2/5/1954; Roth, *History of Whatcom County*, 1: 957.

34. Emma Balch to Wayne Suttles, 9/1950, re first marriage; Dorothy Kennedy, "Quantifying Two Sides of a Coin: A Statistical Examination of the Central Coast Salish Social Network," *BC Studies* 153 (Spring 2007): 26.

35. Mason Fitzhugh stated the same date on many documents.

36. John Nevin King, 12/7/1858. King Family Papers.

37. Elwood Evans in Miles, *Michael T. Simmons*, 140; Gibbs, "Report of Mr. George Gibbs"; Teresa Eldridge, "Fifty-five Years on Bellingham Bay," *American Reveille* 6/14/1908.

38. Evans in Miles, *Michael T. Simmons*, 139, 140; Roeder, Narrative; Eldridge, "Sketch of Washington Territory."

39. Evans in Miles, *Michael T. Simmons*, 141; Roeder, Narrative; Eldridge "Sketch of Washington Territory."

40. Eldridge, "Sketch of Washington Territory."

41. Michael Simmons to Fitzhugh, 3/19/1855. Records of the Washington Superintendency, Reel 1, NARA.

42. The Peabody land claim still must remain the site of the county courthouse or by his will, the land returns to present-era heirs; William Fauntleroy to Fitzhugh, 3/2/1854. Quit claim deed, Island County, WSA, NW; Edson, *The Fourth Corner*, 44; *Evening Herald*, 3/14/1903, 7/3/1858; County Commissioners Proceedings 1, 59; and Book of Liens "H"; Whatcom County Deeds "A," 8.

43. Whatcom County Commissioners Proceedings 1, 5, 35, 40. WSA, NW.

44. Whatcom County Commissioners Proceedings 1, 10/17/1854, 12/26/1854.

45. Thompson, "Historic Resource Study of San Juan National Historic Park," 5–7.

46. William Cullen Narrative; *Sumas Vidette*, (1893) quoted in Roth, *History of Whatcom County* 1: 77–78; Charles Griffin journal entries in Thompson, "Historic Resource Study of San Juan Island," 9; Mike Vouri to author, 8/20/2020.

47. Thompson, "Historic Resource Study," 9; Cullen, Narrative; *Sumas Vidette* in Roth, *History of Whatcom County,* 1: 77–78.

48. Cullen, Narrative.

49. Cullen, Narrative; *Sumas Vidette* in Roth, *History of Whatcom County,* 1: 78; Griffin's inventory of the sheep in his official report, 7/26/1855, reprinted in *P-D,* 4/30/1858.

50. Cullen, Narrative.

51. Roth, *History of Whatcom County,* 1: 78; Cullen, Narrative.

52. Cullen, Narrative; Charles Griffin to James Douglas, 4/2/1855, in Thompson, "Historic Resource Study," 10.

53. Griffin, 7/26/1855, report reprinted in *P-D,* 4/30/1858; *Sumas Vidette,* in Roth *History of Whatcom County,* 1: 78; Michael Vouri, "The San Juan Sheep War," *Columbia* 14, no. 4 (2000–01): 22–30. Cullen, Narrative; Letter re oats, James Douglas to Charles Griffin, 7/5/1856. Courtesy Mike Vouri.

54. Cullen, Narrative; Douglas to Griffin, 7/5/1856.

55. Whatcom County Commissioners Proceedings 1, 4/1855.

56. Mike Vouri, *The Pig War,* 2nd ed. (Seattle: Discover Your Northwest, 2013), 45; James Douglas to Isaac Stevens, 4/26/1855. UW Library, courtesy of Mike Vouri.

57. Whatcom County Commissioners Proceedings 1, 20, 34, 40.

58. *P-D,* 8/24/1855, 8/31/1855; *Fredericksburg Star,* 9/3/1855.

59. Washington Territorial Court, 3rd District Journal A, 3/1855, 4/16/1855.

60. 1850 U.S. Census of Washington Territory was 1201, growing to 4000 in the territorial count three years later; Smiley, *Abraham Lincoln and the Washington Territory,* 17–18.

61. Blankenship, *History of Olympia Lodge #1;* www.olympiahistory.org, and other sources contributed to the list of Masons.

62. Lang, "Ambition has Always Been My God," 101, 107.

63. Lang, "Ambition has Always Been My God," 102–4.

64. Blankenship, *History of Olympia Lodge #1.*

65. Blankenship, *History of Olympia Lodge #1,* William Lang to author, 4/6/1999.

66. For an expanded discussion of the marriage law problem, see Wellman, *Peace Weavers,* many references; Roger Newman, personal research on marriage laws; Newell, *Rogues, Buffoons, and Statesmen,* 23.

67. Lang, *Confederacy of Ambition,* 72; Johannsen, *Frontier Politics,* 11, 83.

68. *P-D,* 5/14/1855 and other convention entries; Stella Pearce, "Suffrage in the Pacific Northwest," *WHQ* 3, no. 2 (1912): 112–13; *PSH,* 8/10/1859; *American-Reveille,* 12/12/1918; Emily Tawes Mohrman to Percival Jeffcott, in Jeffcott, *Nooksack Tales and Trails,* 387.

69. Fischer, *Albion's Seed,* 395; Lang, *Confederacy of Ambition,* 22, 51–52, 55.

70. Knight, "Early Washington Banking," 252–53; Glen Hyatt interview, *American Reveille,* 6/14/1908; Roth, *History of Whatcom County,* 1: 39; Fitzhugh to Miller, 6/28/1859, and Miller to Fitzhugh, 7/11/1859. WWM Papers, MF 1; Donation Land Claims, Certificate #329, WSA, NW.

71. Percival Jeffcott, *Bellingham Herald,* 5/11/1958.

CHAPTER 6

1. Copies of both treaties are widely available online and in archival collections; Billy McCluskey to Sr. Mary Louise (Nellie) Sullivan, 7/19/1932, in Sullivan, "Eugene Casimir Chirouse O.M.I. and the Indians of Washington." Master's Thesis (UW, 1932), 103.

2. George Suckley to Rodman Price, 7/22/1856. Bache Papers.

3. Michael T. Simmons to E. C. Fitzhugh, 3/19/1855. Records of the Washington Superintendency, Reel 1. NARA, NW.

4. For a longer explanation of the family relationships, see Wellman, *Interwoven Lives,* ch. 2.

5. "Muster Roll of the Staff of the 1st Regiment of Washington Territorial Volunteers, 10/14/1855–2/11/1856," Washington Territory Volunteer Records, WSA Olympia; Isaac Stevens to Lt. Col. James Doty, 3/8/1856. Adjutant General, WA National Guard. *The Official History of the Washington National Guard vol. 2—Washington Territorial Militia in the Indian Wars of 1855–56* (Camp Murray, WA, undated); Col. Benjamin Shaw, Annual Address to Oregon Historical Society, WWU Ethnohistory Coll., Box 34. CPNWS, WWU.

6. Lang, *Confederacy of Ambition,* 104.

7. General Order #3, 2/1/1856, Adjutant General, *Official History,* 60–61.

8. Vigilance Committee 1851, Log Book, Box 1, Folder 2; Van Bokkelen v Van Bokkelen #2-237. (3rd District Territorial Court, 1879.) WSA, NW.

9. Natalie Roberts, "A History of the Swinomish Tribal Community," Ph.D. dissertation, UW,1975, 204; Phillip Wahl to author, 6/16/2003.

10. Richards, *Isaac Stevens,* 259.

11. Newell, *Rogues, Buffoons and Statesmen,* 28–30; Isaac Stevens to Sec. of War Davis, 5/24/1856. Adjutant. Gen'l, WA National Guard, *Official History,* 86–93; Dr. George Suckley to Rodman Price, 7/31/1856, Bache Papers.

12. Stevens, 3/9/1856 to Sec. of War Jefferson Davis; Stevens to Fitzhugh, 6/4/1856; both in Adjutant Gen'l, WA National Guard, *Official History,* 94; Suckley to Price, 7/22/1856.

13. Fitzhugh to Stevens, 6/20/1856. Adj. General, WA National Guard, *Official History.*

14. *P-D,* 5/27/1859.

15. *P-D,* 4/11/1856, 5/2/1856.

16. *P-D,* 8/28/1857.

17. *P-D,* 9/1857, 11/6/1857, 11/27/1857.

18. *P-D,* 11/6/1857.

19. *P-D,* 9/4/1857.

20. *P-D,* 11/6/1857; *Bellingham Herald,* 1/30/1949.

21. Whatcom County Tax List, 1857, WSA, NW; Whatcom County Commissioners Proceedings vol. 1, 40, 41, 72, 77. WSA, NW.

22. Ledger, 9/30/1857, Reel 17, Records of the Washington Superintendency. NARA, NW Region; Tim Wahl, 6/23/2000, re Fitzhugh letter at longhouse residence; August Martin to Wayne Suttles, 1947/48, Suttles Research files.

23. E. C. Fitzhugh to Secretary of the Interior, 6/18/1857, reprinted in Roth, *History of Whatcom County*, 1: 52; Allan Richardson and Brent Galloway, *Nooksack Place Names: Geography, Culture & Language*, (Vancouver BC: UBC Press, 2011), 17.

24. E. C. Fitzhugh to Secretary of the Interior, 6/18/1857, in Roth, *History of Whatcom County*, 1: 52.

25. Asher, *Beyond the Reservation*, 110.

26. Fitzhugh to Stevens, 4/5/1857, in *WHQ*, no. 2 (Jan. 1907), 56; *P-D*, 5/1/1857, 9/4/1857; J. Ross Browne, report in *San Francisco Herald*, reprinted in *P-D*, 11/6/1857.

27. *P-D*, 5/1/1857.

28. For Jenny Wynn's biography, see Wellman, *Interwoven Lives*, ch. 1; *P-D*, 5/1/1857.

29. Michael T. Simmons led the first group of settlers into what became Washington, starting a lumber mill at Tumwater near Olympia; Simmons to Stevens, 5/1/1857. Correspondence, Washington Superintendency of Indian Affairs. NARA, NW; Richard H. Dillon, *J. Ross Browne, Confidential Agent in Old California* (Norman: Univ. of Oklahoma Press, 1965), 176; HBC Trader Charles Dodd, Journal of the S.S. Labouchere, 10/8/1859. Victoria: BC Archives.

30. Buse, "Machine of Manifest Destiny," 28–29

31. Winfield Ebey "Diary" quoted in Kellogg, *A History of Whidbey's Island*, 68–71; Cook, *A Particular Friend*, 19–21;

32. Fitzhugh to Simmons, 9/12/1857, Tulalip Papers, Box 1, WSU Library, Pullman, WA.

33. Fitzhugh to Simmons, 1/5/1858, Tulalip Papers, Box 1.

34. Fitzhugh to Simmons, 1/5/1858, Tulalip Papers, Box 1.

35. For Mrs. Pickett's biography and that of their son, see Wellman, *Interwoven Lives*, ch. 4

36. *P-D*, 1/10/1857, 1/18/1857, 1/22/1857.

37. Lang, *Confederacy of Ambition*, 50, 113–15.

38. Lang, *Confederacy of Ambition*, 65; 4th Regular Session, 1856–57, in T. O. Abbott, *Real Property Statues of Washington Territory from 1843–1899* (Olympia: State Printing and Publ. Co, 1892) 75, 872–73; Georgiana Blankenship, *Early History of Thurston County, Washington,* facsimile edn. (Seattle: Shorey Bookstore, 1972), 35.

39. *P-D*, 5/11/1857, 5/15/1857, 5/29/1857, 6/12/1857.

40. Unless specified, accounts of the homicide, indictment, and trial are from the case file. Territory v E. C. Fitzhugh, #211 (3rd District, Washington Territorial Court, 1858), WSA, NW.

41. Territory v Fitzhugh.

42. Fischer, *Albion's Seed*, 403.

43. Winfield Ebey "Diary," 6/4/1857.

44. Whatcom County Commissioners Proceedings 1, 30–31, WSA, NW.

45. 3rd District, Washington Territorial Court, Journal A, 253.

46. 3rd District, Washington Territorial Court, Journal A, 253.

47. Whatcom County Commissioners Proceedings 1, 30–31.

48. *P-D*, 6/19/1857.

49. "Robert H. Davis" is listed on the Puget Sound treaties as a witness. His brother lived in Oregon and the author has found no other man by that name in the territory; Capt. Fred R. Brown, *History of the Ninth Infantry, 1799–1909* (Chicago: R.R. Donnelley, 1909), 84; Lt. James W. Forsyth to James H. Forsyth, late fall 1856, Forsyth Family Papers courtesy of family; Fort Bellingham Post Returns, 8/1856–4/1860, MF at WSA, NW.

50. Wells, "The End of the Affair?," 1810, 1818, 1822–24.

51. Francis B. Heitman, *Historical Register and Dictionary of the U.S. Army, 1789–1903* (Washington DC: Government Printing Office, 1903) 1: 360; Edward M. Coffman, *The Old Army: A Portrait of the American Army in Peacetime, 1784–1898* (NY: Oxford Univ. Press, 1986), 68, 70, 81.

52. William H. Cooper Jr., *Jefferson Davis, American* (NY: Vintage Books, 2000), 69.

53. *P-D*, 8/21/1857, 8/24/1857.

54. Whatcom County Commissioners Proceedings 1, 12/1/1857; Whatcom County Auditor, Deeds A, 25, both at WSA, NW; Wellman, *Peace Weavers*, ch. 2.

CHAPTER 7

1. Baker, *James Buchanan*, 19, 33, 56, 71, 113; Bordewich, "Digging Into a Historic Rivalry," 98, 99; Balcerski, *Bosom Friends, the Intimate World of James Buchanan and William Rufus King.*

2. Baker, *James Buchanan*, 87.

3. Washington Organic Act, sec. 9, 10 Statute 172 (1853) cited in Beardsley and McDonald, "The Court and Early Bar of the Washington Territory," 72, 76; Mary W. Avery, *History and Government of the State of Washington* (Seattle: Univ. of Washington Press, 1961), 309.

4. Richards, *Isaac Stevens*, 147-51.

5. Richards, *Isaac Stevens*, xiii, xiv; John Nevin King to family, 8/13/1857. King Family Papers.

6. Richards, *Isaac Stevens*, 298, 302.

7. *Biographical Directory of the U.S. Congress 1771-present* (Infoplease online); www.swvamuseum.org; Phillips, "Fayette McMullen."

8. Smiley, *Abraham Lincoln, and the Washington Territory*, 20; Richards, *Isaac Stevens*, 304; *PSH*, 10/28/1858.

9. Archivist Barry McGhee, Fredericksburg Circuit Court, VA, to author re Virginia bar, 10/6/2010; Fayette McMullen to James Buchanan, 10/20/1857, in "Notes and Documents," *PNQ* 36 (1945): 73-78; Washington Territory, Third District Court, S.D. Howe for estate of B.P. Barstow #97(1858). WSA, NW; Fitzhugh, commissioner appointment, 4/16/1855, Third District Court Journal A, WSA, NW; John N. King to family, 12/25/1857. King Family Papers; *P-D*, 6/26/1857.

10. Winfield Ebey, "Diary," 12/21/1857, UW Library Special Collections; Frank Chenoweth to Jeremiah Black, 12/26/1857, in Richards, *Isaac Stevens*, 303; Lang, *Confederacy of Ambition*, 97.

11. Isaac Stevens to W.W. Miller, 3/19/1858. WWM Papers.

12. Lang, *Confederacy of Ambition*, 121-22; Richards, *Isaac Stevens*, 304.

13. Encyclopedia Britannica online; Wikipedia.

14. Ebey, "Diary," 12/21/1857.

15. F.A. Chenoweth nomination file (1857) and E.C. Fitzhugh nomination file (1857), U.S. Attorney General (USAG), Records Relating to the Appointment of Federal Judges and U.S. Attorney and Marshals for the Territory and State of Washington, Department of Justice RG60, MF 1343, Roll 1, 1853-1861. NARA.

16. Francis Chenoweth file, USAG records.

17. Chenoweth file, USAG records.

18. J. S. Smith to Atty. Gen. Black, 2/24/1858. Chenoweth file, USAG records.

19. Fayette McMullen to Atty. Gen. Black, 3/10/1858. Chenoweth file, USAG records.

20. Isaac Stevens to Atty. Gen. Black, 3/16/1858. USAG Records; Isaac Stevens to W.W. Miller, 3/19/1858. WWM Papers.

21. Sawamish County's William Morrow.

22. *P-D*, 5/21/1858, 5/28/1858.

23. J.J.H. Van Bokkelen to W.W. Miller, 5/16/1858. WWM Papers.

24. Isaac Stevens to W.W. Miller, 6/3/1858. WWM Papers; Appointment Book, USAG records.

25. Sen. William Gwin to Black, 3/15/1858. Fitzhugh file, USAG records; "George Fitzhugh," by Calvin Schermerhorn, *Dictionary of Virginia Biography*, Library of Virginia, online; *Encyclopedia Virginia*, online; *Virginia Biographical Dictionary 2*, (Richmond, 1915) n.p.

26. Stevens to Miller, 6/17/1858. WWM Papers.

27. Stevens to Miller, 6/19/1858. WWM Papers.

28. Fitzhugh to Miller, 7/4/1858. WWM Papers.

29. Stevens to Miller, 7/18/1858. WWM Papers; *Northern Light*, 7/31/1858.

30. *P-D*, 1/7/1859.

31. Washington Territory v E. C. Fitzhugh #211. (Third District Territorial Court, Journal A 1858). WSA, NW.

32. *Northern Light*, 8/7/1858.

33. Fitzhugh nomination file. USAG records.

34. *P-D*, 11/5/1858.

35. Third District Court, Journal A, 250.

36. Third District Court, Journal A, 250; *P-D*, 10/15/1858, 3/25/1859.

37. *P-D*, 10/15/1858.

38. *New York Daily Tribune*, 11/17/1858.

39. *P-D*, 12/31/1858, 2/4/1859.

40. James Douglas to William Tolmie, 2/25/1858. Lytton Museum and Archives *Newsletter* 4, no. 3 (2003): 3; *PSH*, 2/2/1858.

41. Swindle, *The Fraser River Gold Rush of 1858*, 22; Joseph H. Boyd, "Reminiscences" *WHQ* 15, no. 4 (1924): 247.

42. Whatcom County "Claims" 1, 7; *P-D*, 5/14/1858; Whatcom County "Deeds" A, 36-37 (3/27/1858), 65-67 (5/21/1858), and "Deeds" D, 103; *Northern Light*, 8/7/1858.

43. Letter to *San Francisco Bulletin* in Swindle, *The Fraser River Gold Rush*, 103.

44. Donald Hauka, *McGowan's War* (Vancouver: New Star Books, 2003), 29; Edward Eldridge in Edson, *The Fourth Corner*, 75; Lawson, "Autobiography," www.history.noaa. gov; *P-D*, 4/9/1858.

45. *Daily Union*, 6/22/1858; Edward Eldridge in *Blaine Journal*, 10/17/1899; John N. King to family, 7/3/1858. King Family Papers.

46. *Northern Light*, 7/1/1858.

47. In 1859 Vail obtained a territorial license to run the ferry; M.T. Simmons to Department of the Interior. Annual Report for the Puget Sound District, Indian Agency, #81, 6/30/1858; Fitzhugh to the editor, *PSH*, 6/25/1858.

48. Roth, *History of Whatcom County*, 1: 101-2.

49. *P-D*, 5/28/1858; Edson, *The Fourth Corner*, 60-61.

50. T. D. Woodward to *Daily Union*, 6/25/1858.

51. *PSH*, 5/11/1858; Edson, *The Fourth Corner*, 78-79; *Victoria Gazette*, 8/14/1858.

52. Ads, *Northern Light*, issues #1-11; Fitzhugh to Gov. McMullen, 7/11/1858.

53. U.A. Hicks, 7/17/1858, in *P-D*, 8/13/1858; *Victoria Gazette*, 9/4/1858; Washington Territory v 'Lord Raglan,' #103. (Third District, Admiralty Court, 9/23/1858).

54. Swindle, *The Fraser River Gold Rush*, 155.

55. *San Francisco Herald*, 7/28/1858; *Northern Light*, 7/10/1858.

56. *Daily Mail*, 8/13/1858.

57. *Northern Light*, 7/24/1858, 8/21/1858, 8/28/1858.

58. Roth, *History of Whatcom County*, 1; 105.

59. Whatcom County Commissioners' Proceedings I, 72, 9/13/1858.

60. John Nevin King, letters, 8/30/1858, 9/8/1858. King Family Papers.

61. Swindle, *The Fraser River Gold Rush*, 264.

62. E. Fitzgerald & Co. v O.P. Davis, #126. (Third District Territorial Court, 1858). WSA, NW.

63. Swindle, *The Fraser River Gold Rush*, 288.

64. Swindle, *The Fraser River Gold Rush*, 288.

CHAPTER 8

1. *Oregon Times*, 10/30/1858, reprinted in *P-D*, 11/26/58, 7/22/1859.

2. David Hastings (Washington Secretary of State office) to author, 12/3/2001; Barry McGhee (Fredericksburg Circuit Court), interview 10/2/2000, letter to author 10/6/2010.

3. Wikipedia.com; Charles Prosch, *Reminiscences of Washington Territory*, reprint edn. (Fairfield WA: Ye Galleon Press, 1969), n.p.

4. The author read and analyzed all of Fitzhugh's court cases; Washington Territory, Third Judicial District, "Journal A," 441–610. WSA, NW.

5. William Rutledge v Francis Chenoweth #269. (W.T. Third Judicial District, 1860). WSA, NW.

6. *P-D*, 3/18/1859.

7. Fischer, *Albion's Seed*, 394; Swan, "Washington Sketches."

8. The Cranney Store-courthouse can be seen across from the beach at San de Fuca, the former site of Coveland; W.T. Third Judicial District "Journal A," 237, 240; *P-D*, 1/28/1859; Arthur Beardsley, "E. C. Fitzhugh, A Colorful Figure," in "Legal History of Northwest Washington." Unpub. Mss, 157, Beardsley Collection, Box 1, WSA, Olympia; Beardsley and McDonald, "The Court and Early Bar of the Washington Territory," 71; Cook, *A Particular Friend, Penn's Cove*, 136; F. F. Lane in Roth, *History of Whatcom County*, 1: 105.

9. Camfield, *Port Townsend: An Illustrated History*, 55–57, 189; Jefferson County Historical Society, *With Pride in Heritage* (Port Townsend: JCHS, 1966), 404, 414–15; Cook, *A Particular Friend*, 48–49.

10. Camfield, *Port Townsend: An Illustrated History*, 55–57, 189; Jefferson County Historical Society, *With Pride in Heritage* (Port Townsend: JCHS, 1966), 404, 414–15; Cook, *A Particular Friend*, 48–49.

11. W.T. Third Judicial District, "Journal A," 324.

12. U.S. v Schooner 'Lord Raglan' #103. (W.T. Third Judicial District, 1858); *P-D*, 10/8/1858.

13. U.S. v Matthew Baker #112; U.S. v James Smith #113; U.S. v Daniel Kaffe #114. (All in W.T. Third Judicial District, 1858), WSA, NW; Anna Sloan Walker, "History of the Liquor Laws of the State of WA," *WHQ* 5, no. 2 (1914): 116–19.

14. *Northern Light*, 7/17/1858, in Edson, *The Fourth Corner*, 87.

15. Territory v Squitlam and Sy-a-ham #130; Territory v "Three Indians" #131. (Both in W.T. Third Judicial District case files, 1858), WSA, NW; Asher, *Beyond the Reservation*, 135; *P-D*, 9/24/1858.

16. Asher, *Beyond the Reservation*, 135–36.

17. *PSH*, 8/19/1859.

18. 1860 U.S. Census, Jefferson County, WA; J. Ross Browne, quoted in Naylor, *Frontier Boosters*, 50; Camfield, *Port Townsend, An Illustrated History*, 191; Hermanson, *Port Townsend Memories*, 1.

19. Allen Weir in Camfield, *Port Townsend: An Illustrated History*, 64; Hibbard v McDaniel and Olney #82. (W.T. Third Judicial District, 1857), WSA, NW.

20. *PSH*, 6/3/1859.

21. *Northwest Register*, 1/18/1860, in Naylor, *Frontier Boosters*, 122–23; Camfield, *The City Whiskey Built*, 17–18; Hermanson, *Port Townsend Memories*, 55; Camfield, *Port Townsend: An Illustrated History*, 70.

22. Walter Crockett v Steamer 'Wilson G. Hunt' #188. (W.T. Third Judicial District, 1859). WSA, NW.

23. John Herring v J. E. Jewett, Sheriff of Whatcom County #157. (W.T. Third Judicial District, 1859). WSA, NW.

24. Swan, "Washington Sketches."

25. Henry Webber was the customs collector alone on San Juan Island before the 1855 sheep raid; Swan, "Washington Sketches."

26. Lambert, *House of the Seven Brothers of Ste-tee-thlum*, 9–12, 14.

27. Washington National Guard, Adjutant General, *Washington National Guard Pamphlet: The Official History of the Washington National Guard*, v. 3 (Tacoma: Camp Murray Adjutant General, undated); Kellogg, *A History of Whidbey's Island*, 59; David Richardson, *Pig War Islands* (Eastsound: Orcas Pub. Col., 1990), 41–44; 1860 U.S. Census, Whatcom County, WA; Whatcom County "Probate Journal D," 56. WSA, NW.

28. John Herring v Thomas Jones, Betsy Jones & Oscar Olney #196; Isaac Higgins v Thomas Jones, Betsy Jones & Oscar Olney #221; G. H. Lotzgesell & Eliza Lotzgesell v Oscar Olney #222. (All W.T. Third Judicial District case files, 1860). WSA, NW.

29. Territory v Oscar Olney #245, #246, #247. (W.T. Third Judicial District, all 1860). WSA, NW; Whatcom County Commissioners Proceedings v. 1, 9/8/1860, 12/26/1860, WSA, NW.

30. James Kavanaugh, "Daily Record of Current Events," 1/22/1871. Unpublished transcription by MaryEllen Mulcahy.

31. Washington Secretary of State, "Historic Sites of the Washington State and Territorial Library: 1853 to the present," www.sos.wa.gov.

32. *P-D*, 12/17/1858.

33. *P-D*, 12/17/1858.

34. John B. Allen, *Reports of Cases Determined in the Supreme Court of the Territory of Washington from 1854–1879*, v. 1, new series (San Francisco: Bancroft-Whitney Co., 1891), 30–114.

35. Sheffer, "A Story of Pioneering"; *P-D*, issues from 1856–1859; *PSH*, 2/1859.

36. Frederick Maryatt, quoted in Michael Vouri, "Scofflaws & Moonshine: San Juan Island's Stormy Joint Occupation," 12/18/2020 online. Mss copy courtesy of Michael Vouri.

37. The boy, renamed Frank Howard, grew up in the wealthy home and in adulthood became a well-known Olympia real estate agent; *P-D*, 9/9/1859; Butruille, *Women's Voices from the Western Frontier*, 181; P. D. Moore, oral history @1914, Washington Biographies Project, online, 5/2007; Henry Roeder "Diary," 1859. UW, Special Collections; Newell, *Rogues, Buffoons & Statesmen*, 47, 54; *PSH*, 1/17/1861; Crooks, "Rebecca Howard"; R. L. Polk, *Gazetteer of Oregon, Washington, Idaho* (Portland: R.L. Polk Co., 1891), 906.

38. *P-D*, 1/21/1859; *PSH*, 1/28/1859.

39. *P-D*, 2/4/1859.

40. Washington Territory v E. C. Fitzhugh #211. (W.T. Third Judicial District, 1859); W.T. Third Judicial District "Journal A." Both at WSA, NW; W.T. Second Judicial District "Minute Book," 1859. WSA, Olympia; Steilacoom Historical Museum, "A Friend of Lincoln," *Town on the Sound, Stories of Steilacoom* (Steilacoom: SHMA, 1988), 37–40; MacEachern, "Elwood Evans, Lawyer-Historian," 15.

41. MacEachern, "Elwood Evans," 15–23; Thomas B. Rainey, "Tribune of Manifest Destiny," *Columbia* 4, no. 3 (1990): 9.

42. Terr. v Fitzhugh #211; *P-D*, 3/25/1859.

43. *PSH,* 4/1/1859.

44. Thomas Fletcher to W. W. Miller, 5/8/1859. WWM Papers.

45. *P-D,* 5/25/1860.

46. *P-D,* 5/27/1859, 7/1/1859; *PSH,* 4 issues in 6/1859; 5/4/1860; Richards, *Isaac Stevens,* 322–23.

47. *PSH,* 5/13/1859; Richards, *Isaac Stevens,* 342.

48. Richards, *Isaac Stevens,* 342–43.

49. Richards, *Isaac Stevens,* 344; *PSH,* 5/31/1859.

50. Fitzhugh to Miller, 6/28/1859. WWM Papers; "Mudsill" to editor, *PSH,* 5/31/1859.

51. John Tennant to W. W. Miller, 7/4/1859. WWM Papers; *PSH,* 5/31/1859, 7/8/1859.

52. Fitzhugh to Miller, 7/17/1859. WWM Papers; Richards, *Isaac Stevens,* 298.

53. *PSH,* 8/19/1859; Henry Barkhousen to editor, *PSH,* 7/15/1859.

54. Jeffcott, *Nooksack Tales and Trails,* 387.

55. *PSH,* 11/18/1859.

56. Benjamin Madison v Lucy Madison #169. (W.T. Third Judicial District, 1859). WSA, NW; Allen, *Reports of Cases,* 60–63; U.S. v Thomas Jones and Michael McNamara #144. (W.T. Third Judicial District, (1859). WSA, NW.

57. Gorsline, *Shadows of Our Ancestors,* 224; Virginia Keeting, ed., *Dungeness: The Lure of a River* (Port Angeles: Sequim Bicentennial Committee & The Daily News, 1976), 4.

58. Territory v Yelm Jim. (W.T. Second Judicial, 1858). WSA, Olympia; Yelm Jim v Washington Territory. (Supreme Court, 1858). WSA, Olympia; *P-D,* 8/24/1860; Allen, *Reports of Cases,* 63–69; Kluger, *Bitter Waters,* 229–30.

59. Allen, *Reports of Cases,* 69–73; W.T. Supreme Court cases: Clarke v Territory (2nd District); Freany v Territory (1st District); Ebey v Engle & Hill (3rd District). No numbers assigned. All at WSA, Olympia.

60. Allen, *Reports of Cases,* 74–83; Supreme Court Cases: Meeker v Wren (2nd District); Puget Sound Agriculture Company v Pierce County (2nd District)—two cases; Meigs & Talbot v Steamship 'Northerner' (Admiralty, 2nd District). No numbers assigned.

61. *P-D,* 3/18/1859.

CHAPTER 9

1. Camfield, *Port Townsend: An Illustrated History,* 141.

2. *P-D,* 1/2/1857.

3. "An Act to Amend an Act Entitled 'An Act Relating to Gaming and Gaming Contracts.'" Passed January 28, 1857. Acts #23 (1855) and #25 (1857); Richard A. Ballinger, *Ballinger's Annotated Codes & Statutes of Washington,* vol. 1 (Seattle: Bancroft-Whitney, 1897).

4. *PSH,* 12/17/1858.

5. Lang, *Confederacy of Ambition,* 218; *P-D,* 3/16/1860.

6. Washington Territory v William Strong and E. C. Fitzhugh #465. (W.T., 2nd Judicial District, 1860). WSA, Olympia.

7. Harry M. Strong, "The Adventures of a Pioneer Judge and His Family," *Columbia* (Winter 2002–2003): 18–23.

8. William Bowen v James Lambert and John Appelton, #187. (W.T. 3rd Judicial District 1858). WSA, NW.

9. MacEachern, "Elwood Evans," 15–23; Lang, *Confederacy of Ambition*, 142.

10. Washington Territory v Strong and Fitzhugh; *P-D*, 3/23/1860.

11. *P-D*, 3/23/1860.

12. *P-D*, 4/13/1860.

13. Island County, "Deeds & Mortgages, Record Book 2," 73–75, 265–67.

14. The Anderson brothers later became avowed secessionists, and Patton a Confederate general. Lang, *Confederacy of Ambition*, 142.

15. *Northern Light*, 8/28/1858.

16. Bordewich, "Digging Into a Historic Rivalry," 101, 102; Baker, *James Buchanan*, 35, 151.

17. Isaac Stevens to W. W. Miller, 4/19/1860. WWM Collection; Johannsen, *Frontier Politics*, 83.

18. Stephen T. Moore, "Cross-Border Crusades," *PNQ* (Summer, 2007): 54.

19. E. C. Fitzhugh to Miller, 5/23/1860, WWM Collection; *P-D*, 5/25/1860; Edson, *The Fourth Corner*, 187–188; *P-D*, 5/25/1860; Arthur Beardsley, "Legal History of NW Washington: Edmund Clare Fitzhugh—a Colorful Figure." Unpub. Mss, 169–70, Beardsley Collection, WSA, Olympia.

20. Fitzhugh to Miller, 5/23/1860. WWM Collection; *P-D*, 5/15/1860.

21. "Gone East," *P-D*, 6/15/1860.

22. *The North-West* (Port Townsend), 7/5/1860.

23. Legacy Project, Washington Secretary of State; Wikipedia.com; Richard Gholson, message to the 7th annual session of the legislative assembly, 12/7/1859, in Charles M. Gates, ed., *Messages of the Governors of the Territory of Washington to the Legislative Assembly, 1854–1889* (Seattle: Univ. of Washington Press, 1940), 65; Edmond Meany, "Richard Dickerson Gholson," *WHQ* 8, no. 3 (1917): 182.

24. www.oregonencyclopedia.org; Richards, *Isaac Stevens*, 327.

25. J. C. Buttre, *Portraits and Sketches of John C. Breckinridge and Joseph Lane* (NY: J. C. Buttre, 1860. Reprinted London: Forgotten Books, 2018), 10.

26. Johannsen, *Frontier Politics*, 7–8, 120.

27. 1860 U.S. Census, Whatcom County, WA.

28. 1860 U.S. Census, Fairfax County, VA.

29. Address taken from official letterhead stationery; Johannsen, *Frontier Politics*, 80, 130.

30. *PSH*, 1/3/1861; Kleber, et al., eds., *The Kentucky Encyclopedia*, 117.

31. Fitzhugh to Miller, 7/22/1860. WWM Collection.

32. Stevens to Miller, 8/8/1860. WWM Collection; Richards, *Isaac Stevens*, 351–52.

33. Kleber, *Kentucky Encyclopedia*, 118; David H. Donald, "1860, The Road Not Taken," *Smithsonian* (10/2004): 55; *P-D*, 12/7/1860.

34. *P-D*, 12/7/1860; Johannsen, "National Issues," *PNQ*, 42 (1/1951): 22.

35. Johannsen, "National Issues," 22–23.

36. Johannsen, "National Issue," 24, 29.

37. Allen, *Reports of Cases*, 99–101.

38. Ward v Moorey, adm'r (2nd District), in Allen, *Reports of Cases*, 104–8.

39. Bachelder, adm'r v Wallace (2nd District), in Allen, *Reports of Cases*, 108–10.

40. Lewis County v Hays and Kennedy, in Allen, *Reports of Cases*, 110–11.

41. Roeder, Peabody & Co. v Samuel Brown, #185. (3rd District Court, 1859), in Allen, 110–14.

42. Dover, *Tulalip from My Heart*, 72.

43. John Nevin King, 12/7/1858, King Family Papers; Roth, *History of Whatcom County*, 1: 1, 38.

44. George Fitzhugh quoted in Butruille, *Women's Voices from the Western Frontier*, 79; Dover, *Tulalip From My Heart*, 72.

45. Dover, *Tulalip from My Heart*, 72–73.

46. Harriet Shelton Dover to P.R. Jeffcott, 2/5/1854. P.R. Jeffcott Collection, Center for PNW Studies, WWU.

47. Mary's complete biography is in Wellman, *Peace Weavers*; Dover to Jeffcott, 2/5/1854.

CHAPTER 10

1. The Pony Express operated for 18 months, 4/3/1860–10/26/1861, from Missouri to California. www.Wikipedia.com.

2. *P-D*, 12/14/1860, 12/28/1860.

3. *P-D*, 3/4/1861; Lang, *Confederacy of Ambition*, 133, 139.

4. Richard D. Gholson to Jeremiah Black, 2/14/1861. NARA microcopy 26, Roll 1. WSA, Olympia; William Pickering took a square of wallpaper from the theater box where Lincoln was shot, and it became a family heirloom. *Journal of the Illinois Historical Society* 9, 496 at www.sos.wa.gov; Newell, *Rogues, Buffoons and Statesmen*, 41.

5. *P-D*, 1/15/1861; Lorraine McConaghy & Judy Bentley, *Free Boy: A True Story of Slave and Master* (Seattle: UW Press, 2013), 61–62.

6. *P-D*, 2/25/1861; 3/8/1861; 3/22/1861; Loren Hastings in Loutzenhiser, F. H. and J. R., eds, *Told by the Pioneers: Reminiscences of Pioneer Life In Washington, Vol. 2 Tales of Frontier Life As Told by Those Who Remember the Days of the Territory and Early Statehood of Washington*, (WPA, Project 5841, 1938), 125.

7. Washington Territory Third Judicial District "Journal A," 509, WSA, NW; see also Wellman, *Peace Weavers*, for a biography of John Tennant.

8. Washington Territory v Edward Eldridge, #287. (W.T. Third Judicial District, 1861), WSA, NW.

9. Washington Territory v Elick (Harry Peeps), (W.T. Third Judicial District, 1861). No Third District Court case number. Files from both courts are in Supreme Court holdings under #34. At the district court level, at WSA, NW Region, a record of the case is accessible in Court "Journal A," beginning on page 582; *PSH*, 1/3/1861.

10. Sampson, *Indians of Skagit County*, 27.

11. W.T. Third Judicial District, "Journal A," 599.

12. *PSH*, 2/13/1861; Keehn, *Knights of the Golden Circle*, 4, 82, 103, 129, 130, 135, 233n15; Waite, *West of Slavery*, 189.

13. *P-D*, 3/29/1861.

14. *P-D*, 4/5/1861.

15. *P-D*, 3/29/1861, 4/5/1861, 4/15/1861, 5/3/1861.

16. Isaac Stevens to W. W. Miller, 4/15/1861. WWM Papers.

17. Part of Cora's family land became the city of Bowie, Maryland. The famous Jim Bowie of Bowie knife and Alamo fame was Cora's 3rd cousin, once removed; Pete McLallen genealogical research; McLallen to author, 11/15/1999.

18. Will of Mary Hall Weems, 1840. www.rootsweb.com; Prince George's County History, www.pghistory.org; History of Maryland, Wikipedia.

19. Cora Bowie birthdate, 4/21/1830; Today "Cedar Hill" is part of Bowie, Maryland, near Washington, DC; East Central Prince George's County National Register, Historical survey #PG #74A-8. Online.

20. *Fredericksburg Star*, 6/7/1861.

21. Claudia Floyd, *Union-Occupied Maryland: A Civil War Chronicle of Civilians and Soldiers* (Charleston: The History Press, 2014), 22, 26.

22. Camfield, *Port Townsend: The City that Whiskey Built*, 16–19.

23. *P-D*, 8/28/1861.

24. W.T. Third Judicial District, "Journal A," 8/6/1861, and 583.

25. W.T. Third Judicial District, "Journal A," 582, 589, 609.

26. *P-D*, 9/19/1861; Judge E.P. Oliphant, *The Republican Standard* (Uniontown, PA), 5/22/1882, reprinted in *WHQ* (1920), 254–65; Donald McDonald and Arthur Beardsley, "Territorial Judges of Washington, 1853–1889," in *Building a State*, (WSHS,1949), 547; James E. Babb, "Judge E.P. Oliphant," *WHQ* (1920): 254–65.

27. *PSH*, 8/29/1861.

28. W.T. Third Judicial District "Journal B," 44, 46.

29. Asher, *Beyond the Reservation*, 138.

30. W.T. Third Judicial District "Journal C," 156.

31. *The North–West*, 7/18/1861.

32. W.T. Third Judicial District "Journal A," 251–65; Island County Auditor, "Deeds and Mortgages Record Book 1," 39–40, and "Book 2," 73–75, 265–67. Both at WSA, NW; Cullen, "Narrative."

33. Theresa Trebon, "Beyond Isaac Ebey," *Columbia* (Fall 2000), 8; White, *Land Use, Environment*, 55.

34. White, *Land Use, Environment*, 37; 1860 U.S. Census, Island County, WA.; Kellogg, *A History of Whidbey's Island*, 43, 77; South Whidbey Historical Society, *Whidbey and its*

People v.1 (Greenbank: Five Center Pub. Corp., 1983), 57, 62. Whitworth later founded Whitworth University, Spokane, WA; "George A. Whitworth," historylink.org

35. Cook, *A Particular Friend*, 34; Sally Hayton-Keeva, *Ancestral Walls, Old Abodes of Central Whidbey Island* (Sagn Books, 2003), 22.

36. Deur, *An Ethnohistory*, 82, 84, 85; George Pickett letter 6/1/1861, courtesy of Mike Vouri.

37. Deur, *An Ethnohistory*, 124, 126, 127, 133, 134, 135; Kellogg, *History of Whidbey's Island*, 80.

38. Orrington Cushman and B. Franklin Shaw v Edmund C. Fitzhugh. Series 1, #367. (W.T. Third Judicial District, 1862). WSA, NW; White, *Land Use, Environment*, 49.

39. Cook, *Penn's Cove*, 59.

40. *The Sounder*, v. 12, 145; Ebey, "Diary," Christmas 1862.

41. Petition #907 (7/12/1862) by Edmund Fitzhugh and Cora, his wife. Filed under "An Act for the release of certain persons held to service or labor in the District of Columbia." Slave Emancipation Records 1851–1863. Department of the Treasury. NARA, DC. Courtesy of Kellen Diamanti.

42. www.findagrave.com, memorial ID #122915044, from an Anglican church record; Stephen Ruttan, "The Battle of the Bishops," *The Victoria Times Colonist* 10/14/2012.

43. The cemetery took on the name "Old Burying Ground" until renamed Quadra Cemetery; www.findagrave.com, memorial ID #122915044; *Alexandria Gazette*, 1/3/1863, which got the location of her death wrong.

44. Cook, *A Particular Friend*, 142; Cushman and Shaw v Fitzhugh (1862); William Lang to author, 4/6/99.

45. E.C. Fitzhugh to B.F. Shaw. Island County "Deeds and Mortgages, Record Book 2," 258–59.

46. *PSH*, 7/31/1862, 1/2/1864.

47. *PSH*, 9/4/1862, 12/11/1862; *P-D*, 10/18/1862.

48. Keehn, *Knights of the Golden Circle*, 82, 103, 129–30, 233n15; *P-D*, 10/18/1862.

CHAPTER 11

1. nprsfrsp.wordpress.com 4/7/2013; *PSH*, 3/12/1863.

2. Selcer, *Faithfully and Forever Your Soldier*, 19; *Yankee Gazette*, 6/19/1863.

3. Musselman, *Stafford County in the Civil War*, 18, 46–47, 56–57.

4. Col. Charles S. Wainwright quoted on www.historypoint.org; Marion Brooks Robinson oral history, Stafford County (VA) Museum and Cultural Center.

5. The other men at the dinner went unnamed. Major Granville Haller to Winfield Ebey, 8/8/1863, UW.

6. Bartholomees, *Buff Facings*, 264.

7. Bartholomees, *Buff Facings*, 147, 151, 154, 155, 158.

8. Robert Hugh Davis served as a Confederate army captain before his capture at Vicksburg. He spent the rest of the war in an Ohio prison before release due to his poor physical condition.

9. George H. S. King Papers. VHS, Richmond; Fitzhugh, Compiled Service Record, "Compiled Service Records of Confederate General and Staff Officers and Non-regimental Enlisted Men." Reel 94, Library of Virginia, Richmond.

10. Longacre, *Pickett*, 135.

11. William Blair, *Virginia's Private War: Feeding Body and Soul in the Confederacy, 1861–1865* (NY: Oxford Univ. Press 1998), 102–3.

12. Bartholomees, *Buff Facings*, 35–36.

13. Fitzhugh, service record; Junius Daniel. Wikipedia.

14. Hunton, *Autobiography*; Selcer, *Faithfully and Forever*, 38–39, 44.

15. Bartholomees, *Buff Facings*, 60.

16. Bartholomees, *Buff Facings*, 37, 40, 41.

17. Longacre, *Pickett*, 141; Power, *Lee's Miserables*, 6–7.

18. Power, *Lee's Miserables*, 7; E. C. Fitzhugh, Service record, pay vouchers, and requisition record.

19. Hunton, *Autobiography*, 112; U.S. War Department, *The War of the Rebellion: A Compilation of the Official Records of the Union and Confederate Armies* (Washington: Gov't Printing Office, 1880–1901), Series 1, v. XLII/3. S#89. Paragraph VI, General Orders #44. NARA.

20. Wikipedia.

21. Bartholomees, *Buff Facings*, 17–19, 21.

22. Bartholomees, *Buff Facings*, 212.

23. Power, *Lee's Miserables*, 220; Longacre, *Pickett*,160.

24. Noah Andre Trudeau, *The Last Citadel: Petersburg, Virginia June 1864–April 1865* (Baton Rouge: LSU Press, 1991), 289; Leslie J. Gordon, *General George Pickett in Life and Legend* (Chapel Hill: UNC Press, 1998), 143.

25. Power, *Lee's Miserables*, 116.

26. Power, *Lee's Miserables*, 214.

27. Grayson Family Bible. Grayson-Carter Family Papers, Oatlands Plantation, Leesburg, VA.

28. Loudoun County Civil War Centennial Commission, *Loudoun County and the Civil War, a History and Guide* (Leesburg Potomac Press, 1961), 13, 18.

29. Grayson Family Bible, 11/25/1828; Eugene M. Scheel, *The History of Middleburg and Vicinity* (Warrenton: Piedmont Press, 1987), 11; Charleen Oerding to author, 9/5/2000; Patricia Fitzhugh to author, 7/28/2001; Peter and Lund Washington, "Benjamin Grayson's History," no date. www.doctorgrayson.com.

30. www.oatlands.org.

31. www.oatlands.org.

32. *Loudoun Times-Mirror*, 10/3/2017.

33. Carter, "Journal," 7/1/1860–10/31/1872.

34. Carter, "Journal," 7/24/1861.

35. Carter, "Journal," 10/23/1861; Wikipedia.com.

36. All events taken from Carter, "Journal," October 1862.

37. John Divine, *The Eighth Virginia Infantry* (Lynchburg: H.E. Howard, 1983), 26; Carter, "Journal," 1863.

38. Carter, "Journal," 2/3/1864; 7/18/1864.

39. Edmund Fitzhugh and Ann Grayson, Loudoun County Marriage license, 11/15/1864. Courtesy of Charleen Oerding, 2/3/2005.

40. Carter, "Journal," 12/28/1864; Index to Marriage Bonds, Loudoun County Clerk, 204; Grayson Family Bible.

41. Carter, "Journal," 1/2/1865–1/6/1865.

42. Douglas Southall Freeman in Power, *Lee's Miserables*, 312.

43. Power, *Lee's Miserables*, 242; Longacre, *Pickett*,161.

44. Power, *Lee's Miserables*, 247, 252, 267.

45. Power, *Lee's Miserables*, 291.

46. Longacre, *Pickett*, 168.

47. Longacre, *Pickett*, 163–64, 168; Power, *Lee's Miserables*, 306; Divine, *The Eighth Virginia Infantry*, 34.

48. Hunton, *Autobiography*, 118.

49. Hunton, *Autobiography*, 118; William A. and Patricia C. Young, *56th Virginia Infantry* (Lynchburg: H.E. Howard, Inc., 1990), 100; Walter Raleigh Battle in Power, *Lee's Miserables*, 30.

50. Power, *Lee's Miserables*, 272.

51. Ed Bearss and Chris Calkins, *The Battle of Five Forks* (Lynchburg: H.E. Howard, 1985), 113; Hunton, *Autobiography*.

52. One lesser-known historically valuable loss was the entire Confederate archives evacuated from Richmond with the retreating troops; Power, *Lee's Miserables*, 319.

53. Divine, *The Eighth Virginia Infantry*, 38; Longacre, *Pickett*,170; Calkins, *The Final Bivouac*, 111–12, 114; Power, *Lee's Miserables*, 277; William Marvel, "Retreat to Appomattox," *The Blue and the Gray*, 28, no. 4 (4/2001), 19.

54. Calkins, *The Final Bivouac*, 207; Longacre, *Pickett*, 170.

55. Power, *Lee's Miserables*,181, 282, 283.

56. Calkins, *Final Bivouac*, 186, 207; www.nps.gov, "The Printing of the Paroles."

57. E. C. Fitzhugh, Service Record, item #5.

58. Calkins, *Final Bivouac*, 192.

59. Calkins, *Final Bivouac*, 2.

60. Calkins, *Final Bivouac*, 193.

CHAPTER 12

1. Route assistance courtesy of Joseph Rizzo, Loudoun County (VA) Museum and Cultural Center.

2. Carter, "Journal," 4/19/1865, 5/24/1865; Clarke Pub. Co., *Biographical Record of Webster County, Iowa*, 352–53.

3. Dr. Thomas Grayson obituary, *The Weekly Messenger* (Fort Dodge, IA), 11/1903; www.wolfsrunstudio.com.

4. Carter, "Journal," 6/12/1865, 7/12/1865.

5. Carter, "Journal," 8/17/1865.

6. Carter, "Journal," 1860–1872; 1880 U.S. Census, Loudoun County, VA; Enslaved archives, Oatlands Plantation; Kevin Dulaney Grigsby, *Howardsville: The Journey of an African-American Community in Loudoun County, Virginia* (Loudoun County: Kevin Grigsby, 2008), 17, 18, 90.

7. Carter, "Journal," 9/27/1865; 10/15/1865.

8. George Gibbs to W.W. Miller, 4/24/1866. WWM Papers.

9. Carter, "Journal," 5/6/1866, 5/7/1866, 5/12/1866, 5/15/1866, 5/16/1866.

10. *Walla Walla Statesman*, 6/15/1866.

11. Musselman, *Stafford County in the Civil War*, 78; Barry McGhee to author, 10/2/2000.

12. Miller, "Stafford County History."

13. Carter, "Journal," 12/1866–7/4/1866.

14. Carter, "Journal," 11/12/1867.

15. Maj. William Williams, *The History of Early Fort Dodge and Webster County, Iowa*, Edward Breen, ed. (Fort Dodge: KVFD-KFMX, 1962), 53; Natte, *Images of America: Fort Dodge 1850–1970*, 7, 23.

16. Clarke Pub. Co., *Biographical Record of Webster County*, 352–53.

17. Fort Dodge, Iowa. Wikipedia.

18. Dr. Thomas Grayson Obituary, *The Weekly Messenger*, 11/1903.

19. Carter, "Journal," 1/1/1861.

20. Natte, *Images of America: Fort Dodge*, 18, 20, 38, 51, 91, 107; Grayson family file #6, Thomas Balch Library, Loudoun, VA.

21. Tom Morain, in "Iowa Pathways," www.iowapbs.org.

CHAPTER 13

1. For more information on John and Clara Tennant, see Wellman, *Peace Weavers*, ch. 4; *Bellingham Bay Mail*, 7/19/1873, 9/13/1873.

2. *Bellingham Bay Mail*, 12/1/1874; 12/7/1874; Edmund and Nannie Fitzhugh to Moses Wilson, 7/5/1870. Stafford County Circuit Court, "Deeds TT," 424–25.

3. *Bellingham Bay Mail*, 12/7/1874; *Puget Sound Mail*, 1/13/1883.

4. See Jimmy Pickett's updated biography in Wellman, *Interwoven Lives*, ch. 4; John Campbell, Diaries, 1860s entries. UW; Robert Reid in Reid Family Papers, courtesy of Julia Reid Owens.

5. Archdiocese of Seattle Archives, Sacramental Records v3, 103, 78; Ruth Shelton and Harriet Dover to Percival Jeffcott, 2/5/1954. Center for PNW Studies, WWU.

6. Roth, *History of Whatcom County*, 1: 38.

7. 1870 U.S. Census, San Francisco (CA).

8. Hubert H. Bancroft, *History of California*, 7: 637.

9. Lang, *Confederacy of Ambition*, 225.

10. *California History* 73 (Fall, 1994): 200; Edmund Randolph obituary, *PSH*, 9/26/1861; Quinn, *The Rivals*, 301; N. Gray & Co., San Francisco area Funeral Home records, www.findagrave.com; *Cullum's Register*, www.penelope.uchicago.edu.

11. Virginia Schluetz, Fairfax genealogy, ancestry.com; Charleen Oerding to author, 2004; Doug Fendall to author, 2004; George Wilkes, "David C. Broderick." Speech 7/9/1859, reprinted in *California Historical Quarterly* 38: 214; Calhoun Benham obituary, *Daily Alta*, 6/13/1884.

12. Waite, *West of Slavery*, 209, 213–14.

13. Lang, *Confederacy of Ambition*, 225.

14. *Great Register,1878*. California Information File, San Francisco Library; Daniel Bacon, *Walking the Barbary Coast Trail* (San Francisco: Quicksilver Press, 2002), 181.

15. *San Francisco Call*, 10/20/1902; www.findagrave.com.

16. Jerry Olson, "Colonel Isaac Williams Smith (1826–1897), from *Transactions of the American Society of Civil Engineers*," 2008. Online.

17. Directory Publishing Co., *Langley's San Francisco Directory*, 1881–82, 358; 1883, 966.

18. Whatcom had its own What Cheer House during the Fraser gold rush. In just a few years, the name was emblazoned on a Seattle hotel; Directory Pub., *Langley's San Francisco Directory*, 1883; Gorsline, *Shadows of Our Ancestors*, 205.

19. *Daily Alta*, 4/12/1861.

20. John Kiest Lord, *The Naturalist in Vancouver Island and British Columbia*, (London: Richard Bentley, 1866. Reprint, Elibron Classics, 2005), 1: 221; Photo Collection, UCB.

21. San Francisco County Dept. of Health, "Record of Deaths 1882–1889," v. 3, San Francisco Public Library.

22. *Evening Bulletin*, 11/26/83.

23. "A California Pioneer Found Dead," *New York Times*, 12/5/1883. Reprinted from *San Francisco Call*.

24. Fitzhugh is buried in plot Sycamore North 60. "Masonic Cemetery Removals," and "Interments Transferred from Masonic Cemetery." Both in San Francisco County Cemetery Records, San Francisco County Health Dept., and Masonic Cemetery Association. San Francisco Public Library.

EPILOGUE

1. Whatcom County "Deeds F," 10. 7/9/1860. WSA, NW.

2. Interstate Publ. Co., *An Illustrated History of Skagit*, 638–39; Vertical Files, compiled by Schuyler County Genealogical Society. Schuyler County Museum, Rushville, IL; James Scripps, *Schuyler Citizen*, 8/8/1858.

3. Territory v William Wallace #206. (W.T. Third Judicial District, 1860.) WSA, NW; Interstate Pub. Co., *History of Skagit*, 638–39 and other sources on www.skagitriverjournal.com.

4. Territory v Henry Barkhousen. (Skagit County #51, 1878). WSA, NW; Chief Justice R.S. Greene, "Judicial Review of the Marriage Laws." *Bellingham Bay Mail*, 6/14/1879.

5. Roblin, "Schedule of Unenrolled Indians," Julia Barkhousen affidavit, Roll 1, MF 134-3. U.S. Dept. of the Interior, Office of Indian Affairs. NARA, NW.

6. Claudia Ebsworth and Mildred Collett, eds., *The Pioneer Book of Skagit County* (Conway: Skagit Valley Genealogical Society, 1989), n.p.

7. For a complete biography, see Wellman, *Peace Weavers*, ch. 3.

8. Personal Lear family and Wrangell research by Carol Ericson, Martha Holcomb, and Patricia Neal.

9. Washington Territory v Mary Phillips #1070/45 Series 2. (W.T. Third Judicial District, 1879.) WSA, NW; Thomas Phillips, Delayed Birth Certificate, Washington State Dept. of Health, 4/18/1942; Emma Balch to Wayne Suttles, 1950; Anne M. Butler, *Gendered Justice in the American West: Women Prisoners in Men's Penitentiaries* (Urbana: Univ. of Illinois Press, 1997), 84.

10. Suttles research files, UW; Tulalip School census 1906, typescript at WSA, NW; Archdiocese of Seattle, "Sacramental Register" 4, 127.

11. 1880 U.S. Census, Loudoun County, VA; Ann Fitzhugh death, 10/24/1905, Oak Grove Cemetery records, Portsmouth, VA. Findagrave.com.

12. Gretchen Battaile and Kathleen Mullen-Sands, *American Indian Women: Telling Their Lives* (Lincoln: Univ. of Nebraska Press, 1984), 124.

13. Reid Family papers; Julie Chandler Owens to author, 9/8/2000, 9/10/2000; Helen Peach Monell interview by James Hermanson in Hermanson, *Witness to the First Century*.

14. Harriet Shelton Dover letter to Percival Jeffcott, 2/5/1954. Percival Jeffcott Collection, CPNWS, WWU; John Campbell, "Diary," 8/22/1869; 6/24/1870. UW.

15. For more information on Jimmy Pickett's time on the south Sound, see Wellman, *Interwoven Lives*, ch. 4; Campbell, "Diary," 12/1869–1/15/1870.

16. Campbell, "Diary," 1/13/70; 7/24/70; 7/27/70; 7/28/70, 7/31/70, 8/1/70, 10 /10/70, 10/11–10/15/70; Helen Peach Monell interview in Hermanson, *Witness to the First Century*; Reid Family papers.

17. Reuben Reid obituary. *Port Townsend Leader* 7/12/1934. "Four Generations of Reid Family Take Part in Reunion." *Port Townsend Leader*, 7/12/1934.

18. Kathie Zetterberg to author, 3/8/2020, and other personal research re Julia Yesler Intermela.

19. *Sunday Leader*, 9/27/1903.

20. 1889 Washington statehood census; 1900 U.S. Census, Jefferson County, WA; Julie Owens to author, 9/12/2000.

21. *Port Townsend Leader*, 5/10/1951.

22. Campbell, "Diary," 4/22–23/1869; Crooks, "Rebecca Howard." 1870 U.S. Census, Thurston County, WA.

23. Campbell, "Diary," 7/11/69, 7/14/69, 7/31/69, 8/9/69, 11/29/69, 4/4/70, 9/5/70, 9/13/70; Wellman, *Peace Weavers*, 99; Roth, *History of Whatcom County*, 1: 196; *Bellingham Bay Mail*, 5/22/1876.

24. Territory v Mary Phillips (1879); For a full account of the events, see Wellman, *Peace Weavers*, ch. 3.

25. Mary Pearson and Mason Fitzhugh, San Juan County "Marriages," v. 1, 17; 1889 Washington Statehood census; Lummi Reservation Cemetery stone, birth 7/14/1882; Compilation of Shattuck homestead land sales, Orcas Museum; 1885 Orcas Island census; 1887 state census, San Juan County; 1887 *Puget Sound Directory*, 531; Archdiocese of Seattle, "Sacramental Register" 4, 27; www.glorecordsfs.blm.gov, Homestead #3348, 8/4/1891; Woodlawn Cemetery, Orcas Island record. Whatcom County Genealogical Society Bulletin vol. 12, 133.

26. 1889 Washington Statehood Census; Julia Owens to author, 9/12/2000.

27. Laurinda Fitzhugh and Richard Squi'qui, Whatcom County "Marriage Returns," Box 1, #1176.

28. The homestead site is sacred to the Lummi people as part of the place where they originated; Maggie Anderson and Mason Fitzhugh, San Juan County Marriage Certificates, v. 2., San Juan County Courthouse, Friday Harbor, WA. Index at WSA, NW; *San Juan Islander* 1/25/1900, re She'kle'malt's death; Roblin, "Schedule of Unenrolled Indians, Roll 3, MF 1343. Maggie Fitzhugh, Affidavit, 3/1916.

29. 1880, 1900, 1910 US Census, San Juan County, WA; Kathy Duncan, Jamestown S'Klallam Enrollment Office to author, 1/14/2007; Charlie Kahana to Howard Buswell, Reel 4, Howard Buswell Oral History Collection, CPNWS, WWU.

30. Jo Bailey, "Pearl as a Child with her Aunt and Grandmother," *Friday Harbor Journal* 7/20/1983; San Juan County Mechanics Lien, "Miscellaneous Records Book 6," 292; "Northwest Pioneer Summoned by Death," *Friday Harbor Journal*, 10/18/1927; San Juan County "Death Certificates," 24. Mason Fitzhugh death, 10/7/1927; "Island Pioneer Lady Summoned by Death," *Friday Harbor Journal*, 11/18/43; Winona Rouleau statement, 10/8/1984, in the Pearl Little Probate Case #2088.

31. Bob Guard to author, 7/24/2022; Estate of Pearl Little probate case file #2088, filed 8/4/1983, San Juan County, WA. WSA, NW.

32. www.findagrave.com.

33. 1880 U.S. Census, Loudoun County, VA; James T. White, "Bishop Thomson Dies," *The Living Church* 113, no. 26 (12/1946): 3; James T. White, ed., "Arthur Conover Thomson," *The National Cyclopaedia of American Biography* 1 (J.T. White & Co., 1891), 72.

34. Peterson, *The Story of Iowa*, 57.

35. Peterson, *The Story of Iowa*, 157.

36. *Des Moines Tribune*, 2/6/1941; findagrave.com.

37. Patterson, *Patterson's American Educational Dictionary* v. 60 (1904), 556; Findagrave.com.

Bibliography

Some sources mentioned only once in the endnotes do not appear in the bibliography.

Abbreviations

CPNWS, WWU = Center for Pacific Northwest Studies, Western Washington University, Bellingham, WA

KGC = Knights of the Golden Circle

MF = microfilm

NARA = National Archives and Records Administration

P-D = *Pioneer-Democrat* (Olympia, WA)

PNWQ = *Pacific Northwest Quarterly*

PSH = *Puget Sound Herald* (Steilacoom, WA)

SFPL = San Francisco Public Library

UCB = University of California, Berkeley

USMA = United States Military Academy

UW = University of Washington Libraries, Special Collections, Seattle, WA

VHS = Virginia Historical Society

WHQ = Washington Historical Quarterly

WSA, NW = Washington State Archives, Northwest Region, Bellingham, WA

WSA, PS = Washington State Archives, Puget Sound Region, Bellevue, WA

WSA, SW = Washington State Archives, Southwest Region, Olympia, WA

WSHS = Washington State Historical Society

WSU = Washington State University, Pullman, WA

WWM = William Winlock Miller Papers, Bienecke Library, Yale University

WWU = Western Washington University, Bellingham

 ೦ঙৎ

Abbott, T.O. *Real Property Statutes of Washington Territory from 1843–1899.* Olympia: State Printing and Pub. Co., 1892.

Alexander, Chief Justice Gerry L. (retired). *The Courts of the Washington Territory 1853–1889.* www.wsba.org (Washington State Bar Association), 2003.

Alexandria (VA) Gazette

Allen, John B. *Reports of Cases Determined in the Supreme Court of the Territory of Washington from 1854–1879, vol. 1 (new series).* San Francisco: Bancroft-Whitney Co., 1891.

Archdiocese of Seattle Archives. Sacramental records. Seattle, WA.

Asbury, Herbert. *The Barbary Coast: An Informal History of the San Francisco Underworld.* NY: Alfred A. Knopf, 1933.

Asher, Brad. *Beyond the Reservation: Indians, Settlers, & the Law in Washington Territory, 1853–1880.* Norman: Univ. of Oklahoma Press, 1999.

Babb, James E. "Judge E.P. Oliphant." *WHQ* (1920): 254–265.

Bache Papers. Smithsonian Institution Archives. RG 7053. Washington, DC.

Baker, Jean H. *James Buchanan.* NY: Henry Holt, 2004.

Balcerski, Thomas J. *Bosom Friends, the Intimate World of James Buchanan and William Rufus King.* NY: Oxford Univ. Press, 2019.

Balch, Emma. Interview by Wayne Suttles, 9/1950 re Mary Phillips.

Bancroft, Hubert Howe. *History of California, vol. 7.* San Francisco, The History Co., 1884. Reprinted Santa Barbara: Wallace Hebberd, 1963.

Bartholomees, J. Boone Jr. *Buff Facings & Gilt Buttons: Staff & Headquarters Operations in the Army of Northern Virginia, 1861–1865.* Columbia: Univ. of South Carolina Press, 1998.

Beardsley, Arthur. "The Bench and Bar of WA." Unpubl. mss. Beardsley Collection, WSA, SW.

Beardsley, Arthur & Donald McDonald. "The Court & Early Bar of the WA Territory," *Washington Law Review* 17, #2 (1942): 57–82.

Bearss, Ed & Chris Calkins. *The Battle of Five Forks.* Lynchburg: HE Howard, 1985.

Blair, William A. *Virginia's Private War: Feeding Body and Soul in the Confederacy, 1861–1865.* NY: Oxford, 1998.

Blankenship, George E., compiler. "History of Olympia Lodge #1, 1852–1935." Olympia Historical Society and Bigelow House Museum. www.olympiahistory.org.

Bordewich, Fergus M. "Digging Into a Historic Rivalry." *Smithsonian* 34, no. 11 (2/2004): 96–107.

Browning, Peter, ed. *To the Golden Shore: America Goes to California, 1849.* Lafayette, CA: Great West Books, 1995.

Brumbaugh, Virginia. Interview by author re Fitzhugh family history, Marysville, WA. 10/2/2004.

Bryson, W. Hamilton. "The History of Legal Education in Virginia." *History of the Marshall-Wythe School of Law, 1979.* William and Mary Law School Scholarship Repository: 180–81.

Buse, Michael "Tug." "Machine of Manifest Destiny." *PNQ* 112, no. 1, Winter 2020/2021.

Buswell, Howard. Papers. CPNWS, WWU.

Butruille, Susan G. *Women's Voices from the Western Frontier.* Boise, ID: Tamarack Books, 1995.

Calkins, Chris M. *The Appomattox Campaign: 3/29–4/9/1865.* Coshocton PA: Combined Books, 1997.

Calkins, Chris M. *The Final Bivouac: The Surrender Parade at Appomattox & Disbanding of the Armies, 4/10–5/20/1865.* Lynchburg: H.E. Howard, 1998.

Camfield, Thomas. *Port Townsend: An Illustrated History of Shanghaiing, Shipwrecks, Soiled Doves & Sundry Souls.* Port Townsend: Ah Tom Pub., 2000.

___. *Port Townsend: The City that Whiskey Built.* Port Townsend: Ah Tom Pub., 2002.

Campbell, John. Diaries, 1853–1894. John Campbell papers, UW.

Carter, Elizabeth Osborne Grayson. "Journal 7/1/1860–10/31/1872." Oatlands Plantation Archives. Leesburg, VA.

Cepa, Laurie. Personal research re Mason Fitzhugh family. Courtesgy of Laurie Cepa.

Clallam County (WA). Records. WSA, NW.

Clarke, S.J. *Biographical Record of Webster County, Iowa.* Chicago: S. J. Clarke, 1902.

Clinton, Catherine. *The Plantation Mistress: Woman's World in the Old South.* NY: Pantheon, 1982.

Connery, William S. *Mosby's Raids in Civil War Virginia.* Charleston: The History Press, 2013.

Cook, Jimmie Jean. *"A Particular Friend, Penn's Cove": A History of the Settlers, Claims, and Buildings of Central Whidbey Island.* Coupeville, WA: Island County Historical Society, 1973.

Cooper, William H. Jr. *Jefferson Davis, American.* NY: Vintage Books, 2000.

Coppage, A. Maxim, and James W. Tackett, compilers. *Stafford County Virginia, 1800–1850.* Concord, CA: J. W. Tackett, 1980.

Corcoran, Neil B. *Bucoda: A Heritage of Sawdust and Leg Irons.* Bucoda Improvement Club, 1976.

Crooks, Jennifer. "Rebecca Howard: An African-American Businesswoman in Early Olympia." www.thurstontalk.com.

Cullen, William. *Narrative.* Bancroft Library, UCB.

Daily Alta. San Francisco, CA.

Delgado, James P. *To California by Sea: A Maritime History of the CA Gold Rush.* Columbia: Univ. of South Carolina Press, 1990.

Democratic Recorder. Fredericksburg, VA.

Des Moines Tribune. Des Moines, IA.

Deur, Douglas. *An Ethnohistory of Traditionally Associated Contemporary Populations, Ebey's Landing Historical Reserve.* US Dept. of the Interior, National Park Service, 2009.

Directory Publishing Company, compiler. *Langley's San Francisco Directory.* Volumes 1877, 1881–1882, and 1883. San Francisco: Francis Valentine & Co.

Divine, John B. *Eighth Virginia Infantry.* Lynchburg: H.E. Howard, 1983.

Dover, Harriett Shelton. *Tulalip From My Heart.* Seattle: Univ. of Washington Press, 2013.

Duncan, Kathy. Correspondence re Mason Fitzhugh family. Jamestown S'Klallam Tribe Enrollment Office.

Ebey, Winfield. "Diary." UW.

Eby, Jerrilynn. *They Called Stafford Home: The Development of Stafford County, VA from 1600 until 1865.* Heritage Books, 1997.

Edson, Lelah Jackson. *The Fourth Corner: Highlights from the Early Northwest.* Bellingham: Whatcom Museum, 1968.

Eldridge, Edward. "Sketch of Washington Territory." Bancroft Library, UCB.

Encyclopedia of Virginia Biography. Richmond VA, 1915. www.ancestry.com/search/collections/48228, 2000.

Encyclopedia Virginia. "George Fitzhugh." encyclopediavirginia.org/entries/fitzhugh-george-1806-1881.

Ericson, Carol. Personal research re William King Lear family. Courtesy of Carol Ericson.

Falmouth (VA) Boy Scout Troop 835. *Olde Towne Falmouth Historical Trail*. Brochure, undated.

Felder, Paula S. "The Falmouth Story." *The Tell Tale Hearth*. 1981–82 issues. Historypoint.org.

___. *Fredericksburg on the Rappahannock River*. Heathsville VA: Northumberland Historic Press, 2003.

Fendall, Doug. Correspondence re Benham-Fitzhugh family connection.

"The FFVs of Virginia." William & Mary College Quarterly Hist. Mag. 23, no. 4 (4/1915): 277.

Fischer, David Hackett. *Albion's Seed: Four British Folkways in America*. NY: Oxford Univ. Press, 1989.

Fischer, David Hackett & James C. Kelly. *Bound Away: Virginia & the Westward Movement*. Charlottesville: Univ. Press of VA, 2000.

Fitzhugh, Alexander. Service Record, War of 1812. Record Group 94. NARA online.

Fitzhugh, Edmund C. Service Record. Compiled service record of Confederate general and staff officers and non-regimental enlisted men, Reel 94. Library of Virginia, Richmond.

"The Fitzhugh Family." Virginia Magazine of History & Biography II: 838–861; VIII (6/1901): 314–317, 430–432. Reprint, Baltimore: Genealogical Pub. Co., 1981.

Fitzhugh family files. Virginiana Room, Central Rappahannock Regional Library, Fredericksburg, VA.

Fitzhugh, John. Interview by Eileen Chatters, 1986. Stafford County Oral History Project. Stafford County Museum and Cultural Center, VA.

Fitzhugh, Leta. Correspondence re Fitzhugh family history.

Fitzhugh, Patricia. Personal research files and correspondence re Fitzhugh family.

Fitzhugh, Sally. Interview by author re Fitzhugh family history, 9/24/2000. Stafford County, VA.

Fitzhugh, Sally French. Interview by Larry Evans, 1976. Unpublished. Central Rappahannock Regional Library, Fredericksburg, VA.

Fort Bellingham Post Returns, 8/1856–4/1860. Microfilm, WSA, NW.

Fox-Genovese, Elizabeth. *Within the Plantation Household: Black & White Women of the Old South*. Chapel Hill: Univ. of North Carolina Press, 1988.

Fredericksburg (VA) Star

Friday Harbor (WA) Journal

Georgetown College. Archives, Lauinger Library, Georgetown University, Washington, DC.

Gibbs, George. Papers, RG 7209. Smithsonian Institution Archives, Washington, DC.

Gordon, Lesley J. *General George E. Pickett in Life & Legend.* Chapel Hill: Univ. of North Carolina Press, 1998.

Gorsline, Jerry, ed. *Shadows of Our Ancestors: Readings in the History of Klallam-White Relations.* Port Townsend: Empty Bowl, 1992.

Grayson-Carter Family Papers. Oatland Plantation Archives, Leesburg, VA.

The Great Register 1878. California Information File, SFPL.

Grigsby, Kevin Dulany. *Howardsville: The Journey of an African-American Community in Loudoun County, Virginia.* Loudoun County, VA: Kevin Grigsby, 2008.

Haight, Mary. *The Story of Bellingham.* Bellingham: *Bellingham Reveille*, 1917, 1918.

Hatch-Evans, Gail and Michael. *Ebey's Landing National Historical Reserv: Historic Resources Study.* Washington, DC: National Park Service, 2005.

Heitman, Francis B. *Historical Register and Dictionary of the U.S. Army, 1789–1903.* Washington: Government Printing Office, 1903.

Hermanson, James. *Port Townsend Memories.* James Hermanson, 2001.

_____. *Witness to the First Century: 1889–1989.* Port Townsend: Jefferson County Historical Society, 1989.

Hewitt, Henry L. "Diary 5/8/1853–3/18/1856" and "Letters, Drafts, Receipts 1851–1862." *WHQ* 24, no. 2. 4/1933: 133–148.

Historical Illustrative Company, compiler. *Illustrated Fort Dodge (Iowa).* Des Moines, IA: Hist. Illus. Co., 1896.

Holcomb, Martha. Research files re William King Lear family. Courtesy of Martha Holcomb.

Hunton, Eppa. *Autobiography.* Richmond: William Byrd Press, 1933. Library of Virginia Rare Book Room. Richmond, VA.

Infoplease. *Biographical Directory of the U.S. Congress, 1771–present.* www.infoplease.com.

Interstate Publishing Co. *An Illustrated History of Skagit and Snohomish Counties.* Chicago: Interstate Publishing, 1906.

Island County (WA): Auditor's records. WSA, NW.

Jackson, Donald Dale. *Gold Dust.* Edison, NJ: Castle Books, 1980 (2004 edition).

Jeffcott, Percival R. *Nooksack Tales and Trails.* Bellingham: Sincyrly Ours, 1995.

_____. Papers. CPNWS, WWU.

Jefferson County Historical Society, eds. *With Pride in Heritage,* Port Townsend: Jefferson County Historical Society, 1966.

Johannsen, Robert W. *Frontier Politics on the Eve of the Civil War.* Seattle: Univ. of Washington Press, 1955.

_____. "National Issues & Local Politics in WA Territory, 1857–1861." *PNWQ* 42 (1/1951): 3–31.

Jones, Tyla. Correspondence re Julia Fitzhugh Barkhousen family.

Jordan, Phillip D. "The Close and Stinking Jail." *PNWQ* 60, no. 1 (1/1969): 1–9.

Katz, Willis A. "Bion F. Kendall, Territorial Politician." *PNWQ* 49, no. 1 (1/1958): 29–39.

Keehn, David C. *Knights of the Golden Circle: Secret Empire, Southern Secession, Civil War.* Baton Rouge: Louisiana State Univ. Press, 2013.

Keeting, Virginia. *Dungeness: The Lure of a River.* Port Angeles: Sequim Bicentennial Committee and *The Daily News*, 1976.

Kellogg, George A. *A History of Whidbey's Island.* Coupeville: Island County Hist. Society, 1934, 2002.

Kimball, Charles. "A Brief Sketch of San Francisco" from the San Francisco Directory 1852–53, copied for USGenWeb by Maggee Smith, 1997.

Kimball, Gregg D. *American City, Southern Place: A Cultural History of Antebellum Richmond.* Athens: Univ. of Georgia Press, 2000.

Kimball, Lori, editor. *The Diary of Elizabeth O. Carter: Loudoun County 1860–1872.* Leesburg, VA: Oatlands, Inc., 2021.

King, George H. Sanford. Papers. VHS, Richmond, VA.

King, George H. S. *Register of St. Paul's Parish 1715–1798.* Fredericksburg: GHS King, 1960.

King, John Nevin. Letters, 1857–1873. King Family Papers. Illinois State Historical Society.

Kleber, John E., ed. *The Kentucky Encyclopedia.* Univ. Press of Kentucky, 1992.

Kluger, Richard. *The Bitter Waters of Medicine Creek: A Tragic Clash Between White and Native America.* NY: Alfred A. Knopf, 2014.

Knight, N.R. "Early Washington Banking." *WHQ* 26, #4 (10/1935): 251–259.

Lambert, Mary Ann. *The House of the Seven Brothers of Ste-tee-thlum.* Port Orchard: Publishers Printing, 1961, 1991.

Lang, William. "'Ambition Has Always Been My God': William Winlock Miller and Opportunity in Washington Territory." *PNWQ* 83, no. 3 (1992): 101–09.

___. *Confederacy of Ambition: William Winlock Miller & the Making of WA Territory.* Seattle; Univ. of Washington Press, 1996.

Lawson, James S. *Autobiography.* www.history.noaa.gov.

Leonard, Cynthia M. *The General Assembly of Virginia: 1619–1978.* Richmond: Virginia State Library, 1978.

Levy, Jo Ann. *They Saw the Elephant: Women in the California Gold Rush.* Norman: Univ. of Oklahoma Press, 1992.

Library of Virginia. Collections. Richmond, VA.

Library of Virginia. *Dictionary of Virginia Biography.* www.lva.virginia.gov.

Longacre, Edward G. *Pickett, Leader of the Charge: A Biography of General George E. Pickett, C.S.A.* Shippensburg, PA: White Mane Pub., 1998.

Lotchin, Roger W. *San Francisco 1846–1856: From Hamlet to City.* Lincoln: Univ. of Nebraska Press, 1974.

Loudoun County (VA) Circuit Court Clerk. Records. Leesburg, VA.

Loudoun County Civil War Centennial Commission. *Loudoun County & the Civil War: A History & Guide.* Leesburg: Potomac Press, 1961.

MacEachern, John. "Elwood Evans, Lawyer-Historian." *PNWQ* 52, no. 1 (1/1961): 15–21.

McConaghy, Lorraine & Judy Bentley. *Free Boy: A True Story of Slave and Master.* Seattle: UW Press, 2013.

MacGregor, Jerrilynn Eby. Correspondence re Stafford County history.

McGhee, Barry. Interview by author, 10/2/2000 re Stafford County history. Fredericksburg (VA) Circuit Court.

McLallen, Pete. Personal research and correspondence re Cora Weems Bowie family history.

Meany, Edmond S. "Captain William Hale Fauntleroy, a Neglected Character in Northwestern History." *WHQ* 18, #4 (10/1927): 289–300.

Miles, Charles. *Michael T. Simmons*. Vivian Ellison Bower, 1980.

Miller, William Winlock. Papers. Yale Collection of Western Americana. Beinecke Library, Yale University, New Haven, CT.

Mofford, Glen A. "The Confederate Saloon, 1863–64." www.raincoasthistory.blogspot.com.

Moncure, Thomas Jr. Interview by author, 10/3/2000 re Stafford County history.

Morrison, James Jr. *The Best School: West Point 1833–1866*. Kent OH: Kent State Univ. Press, 1986.

Muscatine, Doris. *Old San Francisco: The Biography of a City from Early Days to the Earthquake*. NY: Putnam, 1975.

Musselman, Homer D. *Stafford County in the Civil War*. Lynchburg: HE Howard, Inc., 1995.

Naylor, Elaine. *Frontier Boosters: Port Townsend & the Culture of Development in the American West, 1850–1895*. Montreal: McGill-Queens Univ. Press, 2014.

Neal, Patricia. Personal research files re William King Lear. Courtesy of Patricia Neal.

Nelson, Erik F. "Tobacco to Tourism: The Varying Fortunes of Fredericksburg & Falmouth," 91–110. In Central VA Battlefields Trust, *Fredericksburg History & Biography, vol. 1*. Fredericksburg: CVBT, 2002.

Newell, Gordon. *Rogues, Buffoons & Statesmen*. Seattle: Hangman Press, 1975.

Newman, Roger. Research and correspondence re Washington Territory marriage laws.

Oliphant, E.P. Autobiographical sketch, *The Republican Standard* (Uniontown, PA) 5/22/1882. Reprint *WHQ* (1920): 254–65.

Orcas Island Museum. Collections. Eastsound, WA.

Owens, Julie Chandler. Interviews by author 9/12/2000, 10/2000, re Fitzhugh descendants.

Peters, Joan, compiler. *Stafford County Court Records, part 1: Abstracts of Free Negroes & Slaves in Stafford County Court, Minutes and Order Books*. CGRS, 2002.

Peterson, William J. *The Story of Iowa: The Progress of an American State*, vol. 3. New York: Lewis Historical Pub. Co, 1952.

Philadelphia (PA) *Public Ledger*

Phillips, Bud. "Fayette McMullen had a Fiery Nature and was Successful in Political and other Ventures." *Bristol Herald Courier* 11/17/2013. Online.

Pioneer-Democrat (Olympia, WA)

Political Arena (Richmond, VA)

Port Townsend (WA) *Leader*

Power, J. Tracy. *Lee's Miserables: Life in the Army of Northern Virginia from the Wilderness to Appomattox*. Chapel Hill: Univ. of North Carolina Press, 1998.

Puget Sound Herald (Steilacoom, WA)

Quinn, Arthur. *The Rivals: William Gwin, David Broderick & the Birth of California.* Lincoln: Univ. of Nebraska Press, 1994.

Rasmussen, William. "First Fitzhughs of Virginia." *American Art Review* 9, no. 2 (1997): 80–84.

Reid Family Papers. Courtesy of Julie Chandler Owens.

Richards, Kent D. *Isaac I. Stevens: Young Man in a Hurry.* Pullman: Washington State Univ. Press, 1993. Revised edition, 2016.

Richmond (VA) *Enquirer*

Rizzo, Joseph. Loudoun County Museum. Correspondence re Loudoun County geography.

Roblin, Charles E. "Schedule of Unenrolled Indians." U.S. Department of the Interior, Office of Indian Affairs. Microfilm, NARA, Seattle.

Roeder, Henry. Narrative. Bancroft Library, UCB.

Roth, Lottie Roeder. *History of Whatcom County,* vol. 1. Seattle: Pioneer Historical Pub. Co., 1926. 1992 reprint by Windmill Publications, Mount Vernon, WA.

Russell, Jervis. *Jimmy Come Lately: History of Clallam County, a Symposium.* Port Orchard: Clallam County Historical Society, 1971.

Sampson, Chief Martin. *Indians of Skagit County.* Des Moines WA: Lushootseed Research, 1998.

San Francisco (CA) *Call*

San Francisco County Cemetery Records, Reel 2: Masonic Cemetery Removals. SFPL.

San Francisco County Department of Health. Death Certificates 1882–1889, v. 3. SFPL.

San Francisco (CA) *Ledger*

San Juan County (WA) Records: Assessor, Auditor, Health Department, Probate Court, Superior Court.

Schools, Norman. *Virginia Shade: An African American History of Falmouth, Virginia.* Bloomington: iUniverse, 2010.

Schuyler County Jail Museum, compiler. *Schuyler County, Illinois History.* Rushville: SCJ Museum, 1983.

Selcer, Richard F. *Faithfully and Forever Your Soldier: General George E. Pickett, CSA.* Farnsworth House Military Impressions, 1995.

Seymore, W.B. "Pioneer Hotel Keepers of Puget Sound." *WHQ* 6, no. 4 (10/1915): 238–242.

Sheffer, Nicholas V. "A Story of Pioneering," parts 1, 2, 3. *Lynden Tribune,* 8/1909.

Shuck, Oscar T. *History of the Bench and Bar of California.* Los Angeles: Commercial Printing House, 1901.

Simmons, Michael T. Annual Reports. Puget Sound District Indian Agency. Photocopies, WSA, NW.

Smiley, H.D. *Abraham Lincoln and the Washington Territory.* Eureka, MT: Smiley, 1987.

Stafford County (VA) Records: Auditor, Circuit Court, Commissioner of Revenue. Stafford County Courthouse and MF, Library of Virginia.

Starr, Kevin and Richard J. Orsi, ed. *Rooted in Barbarous Soil: People, Culture and Community in Gold Rush California.* Berkeley: Univ. of California Press, 2000.

Steele, Volney. *Bleed, Blister, and Purge: A History of Medicine on the American Frontier.* Missoula: Mountain Press, 2005.

Steilacoom Historical Museum Association. *Town on the Sound, Stories of Steilacoom.* Steilacoom: SHMA, 1988.

Stowe, Steven M. *Intimacy and Power in the Old South: Ritual in the Lives of the Planters.* Baltimore: Johns Hopkins Univ. Press, 1987.

Strong, Harry M. "The Adventures of a Pioneer Judge and His Family." *Columbia* (Winter 2002–03): 18–23.

Suttles, Dr. Wayne. Research files. Courtesy of Dr. Suttles. Later at UW.

Swan, James. "Washington Sketches." Bancroft Library, UCB.

Swindle, Lewis J. *The Fraser River Gold Rush of 1858 as Reported by the California Newspapers of 1858.* Victoria: Trafford Pub., 2001.

Taylor, Jeanette. *The Quadra Story: A History of Quadra Island.* Madeira Park, BC: Harbour Publishing, 2009.

Thomas Balch Library. Files. Leesburg, VA.

Thompson, Erwin N. *Historic Resource Study of San Juan Island.* Denver: National Park Service, 1972.

Trowbridge, William Petit. "Journal of a Voyage on Puget Sound in 1853." Ed. by Lancaster Pollard. *PNWQ* 33 (1942): 391–407.

Tulalip Papers. Washington State University Libraries, Manuscripts, Archives, and Special Collections.

Tyler, Lyon Gardiner, et al. *Virginia Biographical Encyclopedia. Vol. 1–5.* Richmond, 1915. Online at many websites.

U.S. Attorney General, Department of Justice. Records relating to the appointment of federal judges and U.S. attorneys and marshals for the Territory and State of Washington. F.A. Chenoweth (1857) and E.C. Fitzhugh (1857). NARA, RG60, MF 1343, Roll 1 (1853–1861).

U.S. Census, various years: Stafford County (VA), Whatcom County (WA), Loudoun County (VA), Webster County (IA), Island County (WA), Jefferson County (WA), San Juan County (WA), San Francisco County (CA), Thurston County (WA).

U.S. Department of the Treasury. Slave Emancipation records, 1851–1863. NARA, Washington, DC.

U.S. Military Academy (West Point). Cadet Application Papers, 1805–1866. E.C. Fitzhugh #247. NARA, MF publication #688.

U.S. War Department, General Order #44. *The War of the Rebellion: A Compilation of the Official Records of the Union and Confederate Armies.* Washington, DC: Government Printing Office, 1880–1901.

Van Deen, Judy, ed. *Sails, Steamships and Sea Captains: Settlement, Trade and Transportation in Island County Between 1850 and 1900.* Coupeville: Island County Historical Society, 1993.

Van Miert, Rosamonde. *Settlers, Structures and Ships on Bellingham Bay 1852–1889.* Bellingham: E.R. Van Miert, 2004.

Victoria (BC) *Gazette*

Vigilance Committee, 1851. Papers. SFPL.

Virginia Auditor of Public Accounts. Claims for Payments of Militia Fines Collected. RG 48, Box 1354, #477. Library of Virginia.

Virginia Historical Society. Collections. Richmond, Virginia.

Vouri, Michael. Correspondence re San Juan Island history.

___. "Raiders from the North." manuscript draft, 1997. Courtesy of Michael Vouri.

___. "The San Juan Sheep War." *Columbia* 14, no. 4 (Winter, 2000–01): 22–30.

Wahl, Tim. Research and maps re 1850s Bellingham Bay land claims, Sehome Coal Mine.

Waite, Kevin. *West of Slavery: The Southern Dream of a Transcontinental Empire.* Chapel Hill: Univ. of North Carolina Press, 2021.

Walla Walla (WA) *Statesman*

Wallace, Jefferson. "The Fauntleroy Family." *VA Historical Magazine* (7/1891): 2–18.

Washington State Archives, Northwest Region. Records of Clallam, Island, Jefferson, San Juan, Skagit, Snohomish and Whatcom Counties. Bellingham, Washington.

Washington State Secretary of State. "Historic Sites of the WA State and Territorial Library: 1853 to the Present." www.sos.wa.gov.

Washington Statehood Census, 1889: Orcas Island.

Washington Territorial Court, Second Judicial District. Minute Book, 1859. WSA, SW.

Washington Territorial Court, Third Judicial District. Case files, Journals. Jefferson County Clerk. WSA, NW.

Washington Territory Superintendency of Indian Affairs. Reports and letters received, Bellingham Bay Agency. NARA. Some copies in NWEC. CPNWS, WWU.

Washington Territory Supreme Court Records. WSA, SW.

Washington Territory v Henry Barkhousen #51 (1878). Skagit County Superior Court Records, WSA, NW. Bellingham, WA.

Washington Territory v E'lick (aka Harry Peeps). No original case file, only Journal A. Jefferson County Clerk, WSA, NW. Unnumbered case file at WSA, Puget Sound (Bellevue, WA). Appeal, Washington Territory Supreme Court, WSA, SW.

Washington Territory v E.C. Fitzhugh #211 (1858). Third Judicial District (Jefferson County Clerk, WSA, NW. Bellingham WA), transferred to Second District (WSA, SW. Olympia, WA).

Washington Territory v Mary Phillips #1070/45 new series (1879). Washington Territory Third Judicial District, Jefferson County Clerk. WSA, NW. Bellingham, WA.

Washington Territory v William Strong & E.C. Fitzhugh #465 (1860). Washington Territory Second Judicial District. WSA, SW. Olympia, WA.

Washington Territory Volunteer (Militia) Records. 10/14/1855–2/11/1856. WSA, SW. Olympia, WA.

Waugh, John C. "What in the World is so Awkward as a Plebe?" *Civil War Times* (May 2002): 30–37.

Weekly Messenger (Fort Dodge, IA)

Wellman, Candace. *Interwoven Lives: Indigenous Mothers of Salish Coast Communities.* Pullman: Washington State Univ. Press, 2019.

___. *Peace Weavers: Uniting the Salish Coast through Cross-Cultural Marriages.* Pullman: Washington State Univ. Press, 2017.

Wells, C.A. Harwell. "The End of the Affair? Anti-dueling Laws & Social Norms in Antebellum America." *Vanderbilt Law Review* 54, no. 4. (5/2001): 1805–1847.

Whatcom County records: Auditor, Commissioners Proceedings v. 1. WSA, NW.

White, Richard. *Land Use, Environment & Social Change: The Shaping of Island County, WA.* Seattle: Univ. of Washington Press, 1980.

Williams, Harrison. *Legends of Loudoun: An Account of the History and Homes of a Border County of VA's Northern Neck.* Richmond: Garrett and Massie, 1938.

Williams, Major William. Edward Breen, ed. *The History of Early Fort Dodge and Webster County, Iowa.* (pre-1874) Reprint, Fort Dodge: KVFD-KFMX, 1962.

Wyatt-Brown, Bertram. *Southern Honor: Ethics and Behavior in the Old South.* NY: Oxford, 2007.

Young, William A. & Patricia C. *56th Virginia Infantry.* Lynchburg: H.E. Howard, 1990.

Index

Page numbers in italic reference illustrations.

NOTE: W.T. = Washington Territory

ECF = Edmund Clare Fitzhugh

CSA = Confederate Army

USA = U.S. Army

☙

Godfrey (Dr. Alexander Fitzhugh's slave), 29
Go-liah (Upper Skagit), 204. *See also* Penn
Cove
Grayson, Alexander (cousin of Ann Grayson),
228
Grayson, Ann Fitzhugh (wife), 222–31, 233,
237, 239, 241–43, 247–48, 262, 293n11 (death)
Grayson, Benjamin IV (brother of Ann
Grayson), 226–27, 244–46
Grayson, Elizabeth Osborne (aunt of Ann
Grayson), *See* Carter, Elizabeth Osborne
Grayson
Grayson family history, 7, 224, 226
Grayson, Fitz (cousin of Ann Grayson), 226,
244
Grayson, George (uncle of Ann Grayson) (of
Newstead Farm), 229
Grayson, Dr. John (cousin of Ann Grayson),
226, 228
Grayson, Maria Margaretta Fitzhugh (ECF
aunt, mother of Ann Grayson), 223–25
Grayson, Mary Stuart (sister of Ann
Grayson), 229, 239, 241, 247
Grayson, Richard (brother of Ann Grayson),
226
Grayson, Richard O. (father of Ann Grayson),
223, 225
Grayson, Robert (cousin of Ann Grayson),
228, 239
Grayson, Dr. Thomas (brother of Ann
Grayson), 226, 228–40, 244, 246
Grayson, William, 224
"Great Sheep Raid," 68–72
Greene, Roger (W.T. Chief Justice), 260. *See
also* Intermarriage; Tribal Custom Mar-
riage
Griffin, Charles (Hudson's Bay Company),
69–72
Gwin, William (Senator), 42–45, 119, 178–79,
192, 210, 253

Haida (Alaska, BC), 52, 88, 95, 204. *See also*
Northern Raiders
Haller, Granville (USA), 215
Hammond, Richard P., 41, 53–54, 252, 255.
See also Bellingham Bay Coal Company;
Sehome Coal Mine
Hampton, Wade III (CSA) (Hampton's
Legion), 220, 228
Hampton's Legion (CSA), 220, 228
Hancock, Winfield Scott (USA), 227
Hastie, Thomas, 205, 208–9
Hathaway, Captain Eli, 202. *See also* Penn
Cove

Hazards (game), 168–69
Helmcken, Dr. John, 207
"Heroic Medicine," 8
Herring, John v J.E. Jewett, 148
Heth, Henry, 105. *See also* Duels & dueling
Hewitt, Christopher C. (Chief Justice), 199
Hewitt, Henry, 53–54, 183
Hill, Robert, 142
Holmes Harbor (Whidbey Island, WA), 85,
88. *See also* Treaty War
Howard, Jacob & Sophy (Carter slaves), 241,
242
Howard, Rebecca, 154, 167, 264, 283n37
Howard, Captain William, 52, 56, 59. *See also*
Pattle Mine
Howardsville, 241
Howlett Line. *See* Hunton's Brigade
Hubbs, Paul, 149
Hudson's Bay Company (HBC), 51–52, 58, 65,
131, 143, 168, 260; Fraser River Gold Rush,
125, 127, 130; Puget Sound Agricultural
Company Supreme Court case, 165; Rep-
arations hearings, 160, 241–43; Sheep raid,
68–72
Hunt, Dominic (murder), 143–45
Hunter Iron Works (Falmouth VA), 4
Hunton, Eppa (CSA), 218, 220, 226, 233, 240.
See also Hunton's Brigade
Hunton's Brigade (CSA), 218–36, 239
Hyatt, John, 132

Intermarriage, 3, 60, 85, 90, 93–95, 99, 101, 124–
26, 149, 154, 163–64, 169, 203, 260 (Chief
Justice Greene opinion). *See also* Davis,
Robert Hugh; Douglas, James; Fitzhugh,
Julia Seya'hom; Fitzhugh, Mary Qui'las;
Forsyth, James W.; Intermela, Charles
& Julia; Jarman, William; Olney, Oscar;
Peabody, Russell; Pearson, Charles; Pear-
son, Sarah Seya'hom; Pickett, George E.;
Roeder, Henry; Simmons, C.C.; Tennant,
John; Wilson, Andrew; Wynn, Jenny;
Wynn, Thomas; Yesler, Henry
Intermela, Charles & Julia (Yesler), 263–64
Island County government, 58, 66, 109, *123*

Jackson, Andrew (President), 43
Jackson, Stonewall (CSA), 227
Jarman, William ("Blanket Bill"), 62–63. *See
also* Tribal custom marriage
Jefferson County, 114–15. *See also* Port
Townsend; Third District Washington
Territorial Court
Jenkins, John, 132

judicial appointment, 110–13, 117–20; Treaty War 83–87, 159–60. *See also* Breckinridge-Lane presidential campaign; Chenoweth, Francis; Lander, Edward; Northern raiders; Treaty War

Strong, William (W.T. Associate Justice), 109, 113, 119, 124, 138–39, 167–72

Stuart, Reverend David (great-great-grandfather) (father of Sarah Stuart Fitzhugh), 5

Stuart, Jeb (CSA), 227–28

Stuart, Sarah (great-grandmother) (Mrs. Capt. Thomas "Boscobel" Fitzhugh), 5–6. *See also* Boscobel

Suckley, Dr. George, 82, 85–86

Superintendent of Indian Affairs. *See* Stevens, Isaac I.

Supreme Court. *See* Washington Territory judicial system

Susan (daughter of Suquardle aka Chief Curley, wife of Henry Yesler), 263. *See also* Intermarriage; Intermela, Charles & Julia

Swan, James, 149

Taliaferro, John, 20–21

Tawes, Mary Bird, 60, 80

Tawes, McKinney (mining engineer), 59–60, 88–89, 137, 162–63

Taylor, Colonel Walter H., 216

Tennant, John (civil engineer, deputy sheriff, legislator, probate judge), 59–60, 88–89, 110, 116, 122–24, 155, 162, 190–91, 200–201, 242, 248–50. *See also* Sehome Coal Mine; Sehome (Mine) community; Washington Territory Legislature

T.G. Richards Building (Whatcom), 132, 135, 250

"The Old Settler" (poem), 56–57

Third District Washington Territorial Court (during ECF term), 109, 119, 123, 137–53, 190–92, 198–99. *See also* Brown, Sam; Chenoweth, Francis; Coveland; Hewitt, Henry; *Madison v Madison*; Port Townsend; Roeder, Henry; Washington Territory judicial system; *Washington Territory v E'lick*

Thomson, Reverend Arthur Conover (husband of ECF daughter Mary Fitzhugh), 267

Tibbals, Henry, 146, 148–49

Tilford, Frank (lawyer), 41

Tilton, James (W.T. Surveyor General), 74, 83, 126, 242–43, 251. *See also* Pickett, James Tilton; Treaty War

Tlingit (First Nations) (Kake village), 52, 95. *See also* Ebey, Isaac; Northern raiders

Tompkins, J.R., 137

Tom'whik'sen (Lummi village), 51, 57, 61, 91. *See also* Lummi (tribe)

Treaties (Coast Salish, W.T.), 82–83, 129. *See also* Davis, Robert Hugh; Shaw, Benjamin; Stevens, Isaac Ingalls; Treaty War

Treaty War (W.T., 1855–56), 83–87, 159–60. *See also* Chenoweth, Francis; Hudson's Bay Company; Lander, Edward; Stevens, Isaac Ingalls

Tribal custom marriage, 61–62, 64, 76–77, 260. *See also* Intermarriage

Trowbridge, Lieutenant William, 51–53. *See also* Pattle Mine

Tse'swots'olitsa (Emily) (Julia Seya'hom Fitzhugh's mother) (wife of Seya'hom), 61–62

Tsi'lixw (Lummi), 51, 57. *See also* Whatcom Mill

Tucker, Sarah (great-great-great-grandmother) (Mrs. William "The Immigrant" Fizhugh), 3–4. *See also* "First Families of Virginia"

Tulalip Indian School, 261

Union Church (Falmouth, VA), 11–12

"Union Resolutions" (1861), 192. *See also* Washington Territory Legislature

United States v Schooner 'Lord Raglan,' 122, 132, 143

University of Pennsylvania Medical School, 8. *See also* Fitzhugh, Dr. Alexander

Upper Skagit (tribe), 204. *See* Penn Cove; Whidbey Island

Upperville (VA), 228, 244

U.S. Coast Survey, 51–53, 55, 59, 74, 95. *See also* Fauntleroy, William

U.S. Military Academy (West Point), 20–25

U.S. Northwest Boundary Survey, 118, 131, 161–62

U.S. presidential election (1856). *See* Buchanan, James

U.S. presidential election (1860), 172–82

Vail, Charles, 84, 91, 96–97, 129, 281n47

Van Bokkelen, J.J.H., 41, 84, 118–19, 142, 147, 190. *See also* Democratic Party; Northern Battalion; Treaty War

Victoria (BC) (Fort Victoria), 52, 58, 168, 207–8, 210. *See also* Douglas, James; Fraser River Gold Rush; "Great Sheep Raid"; Hudson's Bay Company

About the Author

WHILE VOLUNTEERING AS a research assistant at the Washington State Archives, Northwest Region, Candace Wellman discovered dozens of cross-cultural marriages in her county's earliest decades, including nearly every official and military officer. Historians ignored the indigenous community mothers, as she found was the case in towns across the nation. For two decades Wellman researched and wrote, aided by hundreds of collaborators and utilizing her extensive experience in research methods, genealogy, and sociology to examine sources old and new to write biographies.

Peace Weavers: Indigenous Mothers of Salish Coast Communities (WSU Press, 2017) won the national 2018 WILLA Award for scholarly nonfiction from Women Writing the West, and *Interwoven Lives: Uniting the Salish Coast through Cross-Cultural Marriages* (WSU Press, 2019) was a finalist in 2020. *Man of Treacherous Charm* is about one of the husbands in the first book.

Along the way, Wellman discovered the only known specimen collected of the long-extinct purebred Coast Salish Wool Dog, laying without notice in a Smithsonian Institution drawer for 150 years. The pelt's hair is now used to authenticate the use of wool dog hair in Coast Salish ceremonial blankets held in museums, and Wellman's detailed examination was the basis for an updated illustration of the dog at the National Museum of the American Indian.

Wellman holds bachelor's degrees in sociology from Washington State University and history/secondary education from Western Washington University. As a WSU sociology graduate student focusing on marriage and socialization, she taught an American Courtship and Marriage course. Originally from eastern Washington, the Bellingham resident lives with her husband Mike and cat Penny, her writing supervisor. She is a local history consultant who speaks regularly about women's history and regional settlement at author events, book clubs, and classes from middle school to college level.